Germany Since 1945

D0106013

Lothar Kettenacker is Deputy Director of the German Historical Institute London and Professor of History at the University of Frankfurt am Main.

OPUS General Editors

Christopher Butler
Robert Evans
John Skorupski

OPUS books provide concise, original, and authoritative introductions to a wide range of subjects in the humanities and social sciences. They are written by experts for the general reader as well as for students.

Germany Since 1945

Lothar Kettenacker

Oxford   New York

OXFORD UNIVERSITY PRESS

1997

Oxford University Press, Great Clarendon Street, Oxford OX2 6DP

Oxford New York

Athens Auckland Bangkok Bogota Bombay Buenos Aires
Calcutta Cape Town Dar es Salaam Delhi Florence Hong Kong
Istanbul Karachi Kuala Lumpur Madras Madrid Melbourne
Mexico City Nairobi Paris Singapore Taipei Tokyo Toronto Warsaw

and associated companies in
Berlin Ibadan

Oxford is a trade mark of Oxford University Press

British Library Cataloguing in Publication Data
Data available

Library of Congress Cataloging in Publication Data
Kettenacker, Lothar.
    Germany since 1945 / Lothar Kettenacker.
    "OPUS."
    Includes bibliographical references and index.
    1. Germany—Politics and government—1945- . 2. Germany (East)—
Politics and government. 3. Germany—History—Unification, 1990.
4. Political culture—Germany. 5. Germany—Economic
conditions—1945–1990. I. Title.
    DD257.4.K45 1997   943.087'9—dc21   96–52760
ISBN 0–19–289242–8 (alk. paper)

1 3 5 7 9 10 8 6 4 2

Typeset by Graphicraft Typesetters Ltd., Hong Kong
Printed in Great Britain by
Caledonian International Book Manufacturing Ltd., Glasgow

In memory of my father
(1906–1976)

Contents

List of Maps

List of Graphs and Tables in Statistical Appendix

The legend reads:

- Germany
- Saarland, incorporated 1935
- Rhineland, remilitarized 1936
- International boundary 1937
- Province boundary 1937
- Austria, unified with Germany, March 1938
- Sudetenland, annexed by Germany, September 1938
- Czech part of Teschen annexed by Poland, October 1938
- To Hungary, November 1938
- Bohemia and Moravia, annexed to Germany, March 1939
- Memelland, annexed by Germany, March 1939
- Ruthenia, autonomous from September 1938, annexed by Hungary, March/April 1939
- Slovakia, as a client state of Nazi Germany, nominally independent from September 1938

0   50   100 miles
0   100   200 km

DENMARK

Kiel
Lübeck
Hamburg
Bremen
Hanover
Magdeburg
Münster
Dortmund
Essen
Kassel
Erfu
Aachen
Cologne
Frankfurt
Main River
Mainz
Mannheim
Nuremberg
Karlsruhe
Stuttgart
River Danube
Augsburg
Munich
Basle   River Rhine
Bern
SWITZERLAND
LIECHTENSTEIN
A
ITALY

NETHERLANDS
Amsterdam
River Rhine
Waal
Maas River
BELGIUM
Brussels
Liége
Meuse River
Luxembourg
Reims
Nancy
Strasbourg
FRANCE

Weser River
Elbe River
Rhine River

G   E

1. Territorial changes to Czechoslovakia and Germany, 1935–April 1939

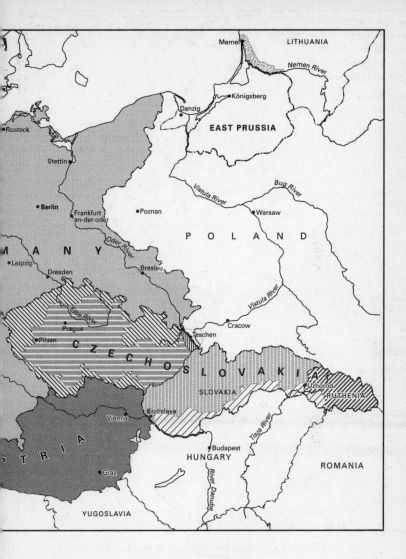

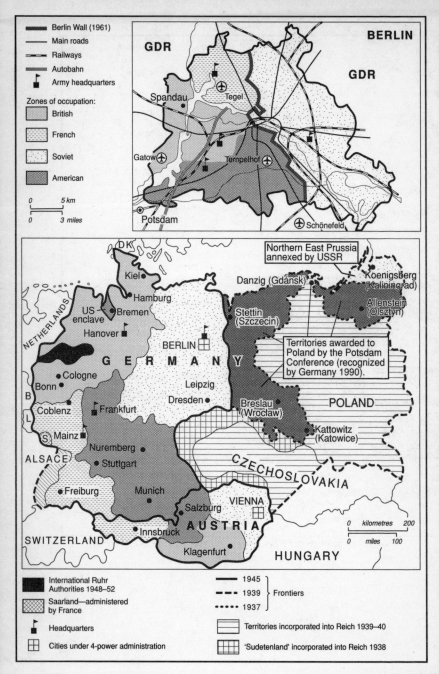

Key (Berlin inset)

- Berlin Wall (1961)
- Main roads
- Railways
- Autobahn
- Army headquarters

Zones of occupation:
- British
- French
- Soviet
- American

0 ___ 5 km
0 ___ 3 miles

BERLIN

GDR

GDR

Spandau
Tegel
Gatow
Tempelhof
Potsdam
Schönefeld

Main map

DK

Kiel
Hamburg
US enclave
Bremen
Hanover
NETHERLANDS

GERMANY

BERLIN

Cologne
Bonn
B
Coblenz
L
Mainz
S.
Frankfurt
Leipzig
Dresden

Northern East Prussia annexed by USSR

Danzig (Gdańsk)
Koenigsberg (Kaliningrad)
Stettin (Szczecin)
Allenstein (Olsztyn)

Territories awarded to Poland by the Potsdam Conference (recognized by Germany 1990).

Breslau (Wrocław)
POLAND
Kattowitz (Katowice)

Nuremberg
Stuttgart
ALSACE
Freiburg
Munich
Salzburg
VIENNA

CZECHOSLOVAKIA

SWITZERLAND
Innsbruck
AUSTRIA
Klagenfurt
HUNGARY

0 ___ kilometres ___ 200
0 ___ miles ___ 100

Legend

- International Ruhr Authorities 1948–52
- Saarland—administered by France
- Headquarters
- Cities under 4-power administration

- —— 1945
- – – – 1939 } Frontiers
- ····· 1937

- Territories incorporated into Reich 1939–40
- 'Sudetenland' incorporated into Reich 1938

2. Post-War Germany, after 1945

3. Germany after reunification was achieved on October 3, 1990

Introduction

May 1945 marked the most important caesura in German history since the initial formation of a nation state. A generation later historians were to debate its true significance. Was it zero hour[1] (*die Stunde Null*) or did more remain than met the eye? On the face of it only a political regime had collapsed, not the crucial fabric of society: the industrial base, an entrepreneurial middle class, a skilled and well-organized work-force, a competent civil service in control of regional and local government, an efficient banking system (though no currency worth mentioning), to name but the most important elements. It is true to say that all these forces had fuelled the Nazi war machine and had largely remained in place when it was finally crushed. No far-reaching reforms were undertaken as part of an overall cleansing process. Only the chief perpetrators and their henchmen were purged and punished. The occupation powers, at least the Western Allies, did not see fit to instigate a complete overhaul of the institutional framework. Nor were they sufficiently in agreement as to what was to be done. The obvious need for physical reconstruction did not allow for additional upheavals. Everybody seemed to cling to what he had saved, be it possessions, skills, or entitlements. This was particularly true of the civil service, which fought tooth and nail for the retention of its status. There did not seem to be any real alternative, at least not in the Western zones, to getting on with the immediate task of making homes and towns habitable again.

Moreover, the break with the immediate past was convincingly stark: the Wehrmacht and Nazi Party, the day before in total control, had now been disbanded, arrested, and hunted down; the whole of the country was occupied by foreign troops; chaos and paralysis everywhere; *finis Germaniae* in the sense that the Reich had gone under like a huge battleship, in an atmosphere of *sauve qui peut*. Of *Führer, Volk und Reich* only the people had survived, though in a state of shock and disarray.

Nor had German society and its value system remained intact. After all, the revolution of 1918 was a job half finished in that the

semi-feudal Hohenzollern monarchy had collapsed, not the whole
social pyramid on which it had rested. There is probably enough
evidence to argue that the twelve years of Nazi rule amounted,
in their accumulated effects including the catastrophe of 1945, to
the German revolution if ever there was one. The Nazi movement
has been described as both reactionary and revolutionary. Hitler
for one regarded himself as a revolutionary and was certainly full
of contempt for the bourgeois world of class, money, and status.
Dahrendorf quite rightly interprets this short and intense period
as the brutal breakthrough to modernity with nearly all the hallmarks of a social revolution.[2] Otherwise National Socialism would
not have released this deadly energy. By May 1945 the old ruling
elite, in particular the landed gentry, had vanished, just like the
society of the old South at the end of the American Civil War. Less
than two years later Prussia, its economic base and spiritual home,
now only a shadow of the past, officially ceased to exist.[3] Not only
the Third Reich, but also the Second had drawn its last breath.
The idea of the Reich had been destroyed beyond repair. The German dream of the Reich reborn, a Reich half feudal, half modern,
both mystical and real, domineering and protecting, had turned
into a nightmare. The war, terrible and devastating as it was, had
the liberating effects of a catharsis: it brought about, over a period
of time, a total change of heart and soul and a radical break with
the past, in as much as it was identified with extreme nationalism,
militarism, power politics, and racism. This was exactly what the
Allies had in mind when they insisted on unconditional surrender
and total occupation, without quite believing that they would succeed. Through their imposition of new facts of life they substantially contributed to the revolutionary change. For the Germans
the experience of defeat and dependence was more important than
later policies of re-education. As so often, defeat proved to be more
salutary and sobering than victory.

The morale of the people, and the industrial capacity of the economy, which surprisingly had not been seriously impaired by the
incessant bombing raids, helped to accelerate the reconstruction process after 1945. When the shelling suddenly stopped the Germans
were in no mood to look back and wonder what had gone wrong.
That had to come later. To expect otherwise is naive. The dictates
of the hour were to find food and shelter and stay alive. Millions

of bombed-out city dwellers and refugees had to be fed and housed, roads, tracks, and bridges repaired. The overall impact then was not apathy but a mentality which was down to earth, pragmatic, and forward-looking. However, it was also on the whole devoid of feelings of grief and compassion, let alone collective guilt, as though the war had only generated victims. For nearly two hundred years Germans had always been looking ahead and hoping for a better future: longing for a united nation state, a powerful empire, a master role in Europe or, as after 1945, just the re-creation of a decent home. It was a weakness and a strength—certainly the latter after the war because the past was so awful and the goal more modest and private than ever before.

The question arises as to whether the experience of the ensuing fifty years, the longest period of peace and prosperity in German history, has eventually transformed Germany into as normal a European state as any other of its neighbours. Only a closer look at this period can furnish an answer. It is a period which has been strangely underexposed compared to the disastrously eventful first half of the century. The fact that war has left a deeper imprint than peace has led some to the distorted view that the 'real Germany' ceased to exist in 1945 only to be reawoken in 1990. One might as well contend that a Germany that had been decentralized, peaceful, and inward-looking until 1870 had come into its own. The truth lies somewhere in between these two clichés, and this book seeks to establish where that might be.

Acknowledgements
I wish to express my thanks to Jane Rafferty for her extraordinary help in preparing and revising the manuscript, and to Josefine Noll for compiling the tables.

1 Germany under Allied Occupation

In a British Cabinet paper of 10 January 1945 about Germany's likely reactions to defeat, the author suggests that the country should be dissuaded from resuming the path of power politics: 'Germany must be encouraged to aim at being a super-Sweden, better planned and healthier than any State ever was before, with better social, medical and educational services and a higher standard of living than any State ever had.'[1] This was no mean programme for a people who were on the brink of the most catastrophic defeat of their history. Half a century later the great majority would probably say with some pride that this incredible forecast was not a bad guess, adding that they too had been liberated by the defeat of Nazi Germany in 1945. The Germany of 7–9 May 1945, when the High Command of the Wehrmacht surrendered unconditionally to General Eisenhower in Reims and later to Marshal Zhukov in Berlin-Karlshorst, looked very different indeed. Harry Hopkins, a friend of Roosevelt, was reminded of Carthage when he first caught sight of Berlin. The city was, as Averell Harriman remembered, 'a wasteland of crumbled brick and stone, whole blocks of apartment houses and factories having been toppled into the streets as if a sulky child had smashed a sandcastle in blind rage'.[2] The Ruhr area, the industrial arsenal for the Nazi war machine, was described by one British observer as 'the greatest heap of rubble the world has ever seen'.[3] Up to 50 per cent of the fabric of most of the larger cities had been destroyed. As a result of Allied carpet-bombing some of the 131 towns and cities targeted were virtually obliterated (more than 75 per cent destroyed), cities such as Düren, Kleve, Emden, Koblenz, Pforzheim, Kassel, Hanau, architectural gems like the Baroque cities of Würzburg and, with more devastating effect, Dresden. Several cities suffered more than a dozen raids (Kiel 90). Strategically unimportant towns of character like Donauwörth, Bayreuth, and Freudenstadt in the Black Forest were hit as late as April 1945. Of the 770,000 inhabitants of Cologne (72 per cent destroyed) only around 40,000 stayed behind in cellars and ruins. Altogether half a million people perished in the inferno of the burning cities. To this figure one has to add two million soldiers, dead and missing, and approximately two million people who died during the great exodus from the Eastern territories.[4] In the British Zone alone, 1,500 road and 1,300 railway bridges were completely destroyed, often by old men or youngsters in uniform, in their futile attempts to slow down the Allied armies.

Field Marshal Montgomery told the Germans on public posters that the Allies had come as conquerors to teach them the lesson that war does not pay and that after all they were responsible for the leadership, whom they had cheered on in earlier days. The directive for Eisenhower as military governor of the United States zone (JCS 1067) carried more or less the same message.

The British were indeed most concerned about the salutary effects of defeat, as the most crucial decisions about the future were dictated by the desire for a change of heart by the German 'master race'. They were the first to work out a framework for the end of hostilities and the ensuing period of occupation based on the principle of indirect rule: no bargaining over terms, joint Allied occupation of the whole country, one and the same instrument of surrender, a separate zone of occupation for Berlin as the home of the Allied Control machinery, all these were originally British ideas to which the other Allies consented.[5] The demarcation of the three major zones which were to mark the division of Germany had already been mapped out and submitted for Allied agreement on 15 January 1944, one year before Yalta. The British put all their trust in Allied co-operation. Churchill's answer to peace feelers, even those from German opponents of Hitler, was 'absolute silence'.[6] For more than a year the three major Allies, through their ambassadors in the European Advisory Commission, discussed the British proposals for joint control. By inviting the Soviets to join the club the Anglo-Americans were pursuing a dual strategy: holding down Germany and persuading the Soviet Union to co-operate with the West after the war. Sensible as this policy might have been in a different context, it did not work out with Stalin. Common sense is no recipe for dealing with ideologically motivated dictators.

Stalin's approach was a clever one because ideology, i.e. distrust in his capitalist partners, and *Realpolitik* complemented each other. During the war he could not afford to antagonize the West, which, he assumed, was tempted to strike a last-minute deal with the German army to keep the Soviet Union at bay. He was therefore eager to accept the offer of a separate zone reaching up to the River Elbe and a seat on the Control Council in Berlin without committing himself any further. Negotiations on these primarily technical matters dragged on, so that there was no time to discuss various policy directives for the whole of Germany to be issued by the Control Council and then supervised by the Allied Control Commission. Towards the end of the war Western negotiators waited in vain for an authorized delegation from Moscow to discuss policy matters. These draft directives for the occupation period did not touch upon such sensitive issues as frontiers and reparations, which were left to the Big Three Conferences. But they were sufficiently revealing to convince the Soviets that the Germany the Western Allies had in mind did not square with their notion of a 'people's democracy' based on one-party rule. In fact Stalin had much more confidence in what the German Communists in Moscow—Ulbricht, Ackermann, *et al.*—worked out behind closed doors than in anything he might have to agree to in negotiations with equal partners on the other side of the ideological divide.[7] The gulf which separated East and West could never be closed and looking back it was naïve to think that there was a real chance of continuing the wartime alliance. The Germans knew this all along, but were suspected of fostering a clash between the Allies. Antagonism was bound to intensify once the war drew to a close. Under the impact of the climatic change the provisional and primarily technical arrangements for joint occupation froze into solid structures which eventually led to the division of Germany along zonal boundaries. There was no way of avoiding the Cold War by a policy of systematic appeasement. It was only a matter of being more or less prepared for an eventual showdown. The West certainly was not, and, having been duped, tried to make up for it by taking a stand against their former ally. In a democratic society this was not possible without overstating the dangers.

The first conflict between the former allies came at the Conference of Yalta (4–11 February 1945). As far as Germany was concerned, no real progress was made. Stalin, conscious of his hold over Eastern Europe, was in no mood to make substantial concessions. Agreements were only possible on procedural questions and vague promises for the future such as the Declaration on Liberated

Europe, which was in its ineffectualness reminiscent of the Atlantic Charter. Reluctantly Stalin accepted France as a fourth occupying power on the understanding that the French Zone had to be carved out of the British and American areas. All the other decisions for joint occupation had already been settled and simply received the final blessing of the Big Three. No agreement could be reached about Poland's western border. Churchill and Roosevelt resisted the inclusion of Lower Silesia, the region between the Glatzer and the Lausitzer Neiße, into Poland. Churchill in particular objected to the expulsion of further millions of Germans who would have to be housed and fed in the already devastated rump of Germany. Stalin replied that they had already left in a hurry. In theory the thorny question was to be finally settled by a later peace treaty, a position later strongly defended by the refugees in the Federal Republic. In reality the area was handed over unilaterally to the Poles and did not form part of the Soviet zone of occupation. The West could do nothing about this or any other Russian move within the latter's sphere of influence.

The burning question was who would control the whole of Germany now that it looked like the largest power vacuum in Europe. At Tehran the Big Three seemed resolved to dismember Germany in one way or another.[8] Experts at the State Department and the Foreign Office, however, did not approve and did not brief their leaders accordingly. So no definite decision was taken. By the time of Yalta, when the power game became more serious, both sides had second thoughts. Through his stake in Germany Stalin could hope to exert influence over the whole of the country whereas the Western Allies wished for joint control to be a *raison d'être* for continued co-operation. Both proved to be wrong. Germany was to become the battleground of the Cold War and to remain divided for the duration. Why then did Stalin, at Yalta, insist on a reference to the Allied right to dismemberment in the joint Allied instrument of surrender, which had already been passed by the European Advisory Council? This puzzle has never been solved, because the Soviets soon lost interest in the dismemberment issue and on 9 May, one day after surrender, Stalin let it be known that he had no intention of dismembering or destroying Germany. The most likely explanation is that he was afraid of a last-minute deal by his partners with the Wehrmacht behind his back. His fury over the secret negotiations in Berne regarding the surrender of the German army in Italy is most telling in this context.[9] In the end Eisenhower drafted a short military document of surrender without any of the ominous references to dismemberment, because, apparently, no version certified by the European Advisory Council was ready in time.

Planning and reality clashed in other respects too. When British officials produced the first drafts about the three occupation zones a few months after Stalingrad, 'it could not be foreseen how deeply the Western allied forces would penetrate into Germany.'[10] The British Chiefs of Staff were never very optimistic about their own military achievements. The invasion of the Continent was still a long way off. Surprise and relief were registered when Moscow accepted the zonal demarcation lines soon after they were submitted in January 1944. It was not until May 1945 that the Foreign Office realized 'we gave them more than they ever expected to get.'[11] By that time Anglo-Saxon troops had advanced deep into Mecklenburg and Thuringia. The remainder of the Soviet Zone would hardly have been a viable entity as a separate state. Final appeals by Churchill to the new American President Harry Truman to stand firm were to no avail. Truman was not prepared to renege on the zonal agreement with Stalin and thus precipitate the Cold War. After all, the British approach so far had been specifically designed to forestall power politics. The Soviet government's reaction was predictable: no sector of Berlin or seat on the Control Council unless the Western Allies withdrew westwards into their respective zones of occupation. This they duly did in early July 1945 in exchange for their part of a capital which was no longer functioning as an administrative centre and a unifying force. Would the city change back into the seat of a central government or would it just be a liability to the West? The career of Berlin as the symbol of the West's determination not to yield one inch began the moment the city lost its traditional role as the capital.

Though Berlin was a wasteland in May 1945, its prospects of once again becoming the true capital did not look too bad at the beginning. All three major Allies had abandoned their plans for dismemberment, though not France, the latecomer. The Germans too, of course, were trying to hold the country together; in particular, the administrative elite, appointed by Military Government, and the

Social Democrats, returning from exile and re-establishing their party organization. For a while Churchill had tried to hold on to the last German government under Admiral Dönitz, which was leading a somewhat farcical existence in Flensburg, a small enclave left unoccupied by the British near the Danish border. The remnants of the German High Command exercised little or no effective authority. Much as the British would have liked to rule in an indirect manner via a German government, it was soon all too obvious that it would not serve any useful purpose and had to be removed to spare London any further embarrassment *vis-à-vis* its allies.

On 5 June 1945 the four Allies signed a declaration regarding the defeat and unconditional surrender of Germany and the assumption of supreme authority in view of there being no central German government or administration. In theory the Control Council was henceforth in charge. This is what the Germans learned in their authorized newspapers the following day. On that occasion Marshal Zhukov made it quite plain to his Western colleagues that 'retirement to the zones and establishment of the control apparatus were inextricably linked.'[12] Eisenhower had three million men under his command. Had there been no such clear-cut zonal agreement he might well have been prompted to conquer the whole of Germany up to the Oder. Naturally he was unhappy to relinquish his command and had previously recommended that 'the Western Allies occupy their portion of Germany on a unified basis'.[13] This would have been a sensible answer to the controversial question of who should get the North-Western Zone and it would also have anticipated the bizone of 1947. Eisenhower's plan, however, was considered politically inexpedient because of alleged Russian anxieties. As a matter of fact, it also hurt British pride to share a zone with the Americans, under American command. Eden had cabled to Churchill in September 1944: 'It is essential that the Americans, Russians and ourselves appear before the Germans and the world as equals.'[14] On 14 July 1945 Supreme Headquarters Allied Expeditionary Force (SHAEF) went 'out of existence'.[15] Eisenhower changed from Allied Commander into an American Commander. No doubt it would have been a clear signal to the Russians had he been allowed to carry on. Since the Cold War was unavoidable, a united military command of the Western powers would have improved the setting considerably. The Western powers did not gain any advantage by avoiding the appearance of ganging up against Stalin. He knew that one day they would do so anyway.

The next signpost was Potsdam, the first post-war conference (17 July–2 August 1945). Its declared purpose was to implement the decisions taken at Yalta. However, now that the technical and procedural arrangements for the conclusion of hostilities and the occupation period had been put in place, it became clear that the scope for further agreement between the Allies had been exhausted. Historians, Germans in particular, tend to complain that the Allies had not made up their minds as to what to do about Germany. This is unfair: they could not possibly have gone any further together than they actually did. The wartime Alliance between the Western democracies and the Socialist dictatorship was only united in its negative war aims. As Churchill put it: 'Here are the two obvious and practical targets to fire at—Nazi tyranny and Prussian militarism' (21 September 1943).[16] They were the only targets about which there was no disagreement. Significantly, security came first. The specific purposes of the occupation according to Potsdam were predominantly negative: 'the complete disarmament and demilitarisation of Germany', including German industry; the dissolution of the Nazi Party; the punishment of war criminals; and the purging of Nazi personnel from public office. The political principles in the Potsdam Declaration were sufficiently ambivalent to allow for a different course of action. No central government was to be established for the time being and the administration was to be directed 'towards the decentralisation of political structure and the development of local responsibility'.[17]

Apart from the overall impact of an alliance falling apart, with its members securing their spoils, the division of Germany was facilitated by three crucial decisions:

1. Supreme authority for Germany did not rest with the Control Council, but, on the insistence of a Moscow facing a permanent majority of Western powers, with the zone commanders 'each in his own zone of occupation and also jointly in matters affecting Germany as a whole'.[18] What was, in fact, a flawed construction was later praised by the British negotiator as a 'judicious compromise',[19] because every commander was master in his own house.

2. The failure to set up, as also stipulated in Potsdam, 'certain

essential central German administrative departments, headed by
State Secretaries, particularly in the fields of finance, transport, communications, foreign trade and industry'.[20] In October 1945 the idea
was vetoed by France, which had not been invited to Potsdam, and
whose government was determined to prevent the emergence of a
unified German state. Henceforth the Soviet Union could conveniently take cover behind the French position. After Potsdam the
United States government was more anxious than its allies to replace
Military Government by democratically elected German authorities and to get the economy going. An initiative by General Lucius
D. Clay to press ahead with three of the four zones, excluding France,
met with no response. By that time Britain and the Soviet Union
were fearful of each other's influence over the rest of Germany.

3. It is generally accepted that the unity of Germany was most
crucially compromised by the allocation of reparations. This issue
was hotly debated at Yalta and then referred to a Reparations Commission in Moscow. There was agreement only on the point that
this time reparations should be exacted in kind, i.e. in goods and
services, not in money. Britain had objected to the first figure mentioned by the United States as a basis for negotiations: 20 billion
(pre-war) dollars, to be split between the Soviet Union (50 per cent)
and all the other claimants. The Americans insisted on the 'first
charge principle': if the bill for food and raw materials (for export)
was not met first, Washington, as in the past, would have to put
up the money for German reparations. The American negotiator,
Edwin Pauley, explained the matter to his Soviet counterpart as
follows: 'All we are saying is that you must feed the cow to get
the milk . . . We want to be sure that the small amount of fodder
required will be paid for with some of the milk.'[21] Contrary to the
Russians, the Americans had no intention of letting the cow lose
weight. The transfer of large tracts of Germany to Poland, predominantly in the agrarian, food-producing East, exposed Britain and
the United States to the serious danger of widespread famine and
chaos in their zones. The Americans had worked out that 50 per
cent of German resources lay in the Soviet Zone and therefore proposed that each of the powers look to its own zone for reparations.
If the Russians wished to obtain additional equipment or materials from the Western zones, they could do so in exchange for food

or coal needed to feed and warm the German population in the West. Eventually this compromise was adopted, even though it could not be squared with the stated principle that 'Germany shall be treated as a single economic unit' (Potsdam).[22] Additionally, the Soviet Union was to receive from the Western zones 10 per cent of industrial equipment allocated as reparations without payment and 15 per cent against deliveries from the Eastern areas.

What prompted the Americans to suggest this rather radical solution was the realization of what had been going on in the Soviet Zone while the Reparations Commission in Moscow had been talking endlessly about figures and percentages. Averell Harriman remembered: 'When I saw how completely the Russians had stripped every factory they could get their hands on I realised that their conception of surplus tools and machinery which could be taken from Germany was far tougher than we could ever agree to.'[23] One thousand two hundred enterprises were hastily dismantled in a fortnight, possibly out of fear that the Allies would call a halt in favour of a systematic policy. Electricity cables and toilets were ripped out of private homes on 'orders' from Moscow. For the United States, it was clear that the Russians had no intention of feeding the cow they wished to milk. This was not only morally indefensible, it was bad economics too.

There are many twists and turns on the road leading to West Germany's prosperity. The initial settlement of the reparations issue was the first and perhaps the most important change of direction. One cannot escape the conclusion that the two developments, partition and prosperity, were closely linked: no prosperity without partition, or to put it another way, a united post-war alliance would have 'milked' the whole of the country for much longer and much more effectively than was the case. A British expert, Alan Cairncross, who weighed all available statistics, estimates that by 1953 East Germany had paid at least 7 billion pre-war dollars, which comes very close to the reduced Russian demand of 8–8.5 billion dollars made in Potsdam.[24] The amount of reparations in terms of plant and current production exacted from the Soviet Zone was at least comparable with the aid received by Western Europe under the Marshall Plan. Whereas the latter turned out to be a valuable investment for the future, dismantling German industry, whether in East or West Germany, proved to be an utter failure. Reparations from the Western zones, including German external assets, were negligible by comparison. However, the potential of reparations and current production in the long run was much greater than anyone in 1945 would have thought feasible.

During the crucial years between 1945 and 1949 British and American taxpayers forked out a great deal more than they received just to keep the German population alive. The ensuing negotiations about the permitted level of German industry were fraught with difficulties about statistics; there was not even a consensus about the size of the German population. The negotiations centred upon a definition of the acceptable standard of living and on steel production. The Level of Industry Plan soon became obsolete due to the relaxation of restrictions and the expansion of production. The failure of the Russians and French to agree to a common import/ export scheme for Germany prompted General Clay, on 4 May 1946, to suspend deliveries of reparations from the American Zone. The British and French had no option but to follow suit. The end of the whole story was the whittling down of the list of plants earmarked for dismantling. The problems this caused during the take-off phase of German recovery were no longer acceptable. The reconstruction of Germany was judged to be more in the interests of long-term security than the dismantling of a few more German plants capable of producing armaments. The reparations issue, which had overshadowed the whole of the Weimar Republic and contributed to the breakdown of the first German democracy, dissipated within a few years of the end of the Second World War. In this, as in most other matters, the Americans, commanded by General Clay, were the driving force.

Even though Potsdam failed to hold the Alliance and Germany together, it did provide the agenda for Allied negotiations about the future of Germany for the next three years. As has been argued above, the Allies were only united in their negative approach. Allied priorities, as designated at Potsdam, all happened to start with 'de-': demilitarization, denazification, and decentralization. The positive aims, generally prefixed with 're-' (re-education, reconstruction, and to some extent reform) were determined by superpower rivalry, in particular, the desire to consolidate the zones of occupation and

win the favour of the German people. The Russians tried to present
themselves as the champions of German unity, while the Western
powers offered political freedom coupled with a better standard of
living. While both powers pursued a containment policy *vis-à-vis*
their zones of occupation, they felt the need to justify their measures in terms of maintaining or at least not jeopardizing the German nation state.

Once the Wehrmacht was disbanded and the Nazi Party dissolved, the chief political aims on which the Allies agreed had been
reached. What divided them henceforth was their attitude to the
Germans, which in many ways reflected the difference between
the more conventional fighting on the Western front and the geno-
cidal war in the East (*Vernichtungskrieg*), as well as their different
concepts of Germany's future. Demilitarization was a matter of economic security closely linked with reparations, as mentioned above.
The treatment of prisoners of war served as a pointer to the future.
The Western powers, especially Britain, refused to declare all cap-
tives prisoners of war and sent quite a few home to help with the
harvest and coal production. Most German soldiers who had half
a chance tried desperately to fall into British or American hands.
A great many German prisoners captured by the Red Army served
and died as forced labour even after 31 December 1948, when
all prisoners were supposed to be repatriated. The treatment of
prisoners of war,[25] on top of the horror stories of refugees from
the East, did incalculable damage to the Soviet Union's standing
in Germany. Communist propaganda could not make up for it.

The dissolution of the Nazi Party did not close the chapter on
denazification. The horrific pictures of the concentration camps
made a deep impression in the West. Punishment, purging, and
re-education were asked for by public opinion. In Potsdam final
agreement was reached on the method of trial of those major war
criminals 'whose crimes had no geographical localisation'. In dis-
cussions on the matter during the war Churchill made it clear that
he would have preferred Hitler and his henchmen to be declared
outlaws and executed on the spot.[26] However, when, at Tehran,
Stalin seemed to favour the liquidation of the whole German General Staff, the British Prime Minister was shocked and rejected the
'cold-blooded murder of soldiers who have fought for their country'.[27] In the end, Stalin took an 'unexpectedly ultra-respectable

line' and proposed a military tribunal, an idea which was eventually adopted despite British misgivings.[28] The charter specified three offences: 'Crimes against Peace, War Crimes and Crimes against Humanity'.

Most controversial were two charges introduced by the Americans: the intrinsically criminal nature of certain organizations like the SS and the 'common plan or conspiracy' to commit any of the above crimes.[29] The main culprits, Hitler, Goebbels, and Himmler, had escaped justice by committing suicide. Eventually a list of twenty-four defendants was drawn up, amongst them Göring, von Ribbentrop, Keitel, and others. The Allies wanted to make sure that the trial, to be held in Nuremberg, the alleged capital of the Nazi Party, would not drag on for too long and that its impact would not be lost on the German people. However the legal grounds may be judged, the documentary evidence against the defendants was overwhelming. The trial was fair in the sense that the outcome was no foregone conclusion: twelve were sentenced to death by hanging, including Generals Keitel and Jodl, both of whom had pleaded to be shot; three received life sentences, amongst them Rudolf Hess, Hitler's deputy; others had to serve between ten and twenty years, amongst them Dönitz, the last head of government, and Albert Speer; three were acquitted. Nor would the court of eight judges consider individuals liable because of adherence to certain organizations. Only three out of the six organizations put forward by the prosecution were declared criminal: the leadership corps of the Nazi Party, the SS, and the Gestapo-SD. The impact of the trial on the German people—it was widely reported—is difficult to gauge. Some surely dismissed it as victors' justice, a mere ritual; others were relieved that only a few culprits stood accused, not the whole people. Others again were appalled by the details which came to light, such as the Hoßbach protocol outlining Hitler's intention to launch a war of aggression or the Wannsee minutes detailing the plans for the Final Solution. The forty volumes of documents were certainly a great boost to historical research and the sustained effort to come to terms with the past in the long run.

Further trials were to follow, conducted by the Americans, mainly against German Foreign Office diplomats, generals, and industrialists. In the three Western zones more than 5,000 defendants were sentenced, with 806 death sentences, of which 486 were actually carried out. Evidence about what happened in the Soviet Zone is only just coming to light, with no reliable statistics at present concerning former Nazi leaders being secretly executed or deported.

In view of later U-turns it is important to emphasize that initially denazification was taken very seriously, above all by the Americans, who had fought a 'crusade' against Nazi Germany. According to JCS directive 1067, issued to Eisenhower by the American Joint Chiefs of Staff, all Party members of any influence were to be dismissed, many of them being subject to 'automatic arrest'; by the end of 1945 no fewer than 117,512 were interned in the US Zone, almost twice the number of internees in the British and Soviet zones of occupation. It is alleged that Military Government officials questioned the soundness of JCS directive 1067, once they saw what Germany was like. But, argues John Gimble, an American historian of this period, in order tacitly to revise its economic stipulation US officials pressed ahead with the denazification process in accordance with public opinion at home, which needed to be appeased, especially after the exposure of the concentration camp horrors.[30] Working under the eyes of a critical press corps, no American official, least of all General Clay, could afford to favour a soft option. The whole German population was faced with *the* notorious questionnaire (*Fragebogen*—also the title of a famous novel by Ernst von Salomon) and its 132 enquiries about every person's past.

Soon it was realized that the Germans themselves had to be involved in this cleansing operation if the tender plant of democracy was to take root. The law for the 'Liberation from National Socialism and Militarism' of 5 March 1946 requested German denazification panels to process the population according to five categories, from chief culprits to fellow travellers to exonerated persons. Altogether German panels vetted 3.6 million Party members in all three Western zones. Was it all a farce and a whitewash because the great majority were exonerated or got away on the basis of flimsy affidavits by friends and clergymen? Only 1,654 were found to be really guilty (*Hauptschuldige*; there are no figures for the British Zone). People were resentful of the whole procedure, knowing well how difficult it was to separate the sheep from the goats when everybody followed the same leader. In his massive study of denazification in Bavaria Lutz Niethammer has shown that in the end purging and rehabilitation were fused into one and the same process.[31] Those who were cleared, whatever their true record, now had a perfect alibi and a case for re-employment. More serious still is Niethammer's contention that denazification as a bureaucratic procedure produced a psychological defence mechanism against any real attempts at collective soul-searching about the past. Persuading others that one was not guilty of any wrongdoing meant that one half-believed it oneself. Forgetting, conforming, and achieving seemed to be what was called for. However, it has been pointed out that denazification did have its merits: it for ever banned Nazi ideology from political discourse. Any public figure who espoused such ideas forfeited his position and his career. Nor was this a tacit understanding. Most journalists and commentators saw it as their duty to expose the inhuman character of National Socialism and to prepare the ground for a democratic revival. The claim that the past was constantly repressed does not stand up to scrutiny. However, there was enormous pressure on the main parties to pardon war criminals and 'put an end to the matter'. Empathy with former Nazi officials was often more widespread than with victims or resistance-members. Somehow all Germans came to see themselves as 'victims' of the previous regime. The Stuttgart Declaration of Guilt pronounced by the Protestant Church in October 1945 perhaps reveals the chasm between public and populist opinion: the bishops' admission ('We accuse ourselves . . .') of German guilt, and more importantly of the failure of the Churches to protest more courageously, met with a great deal of grassroots opposition.[32] Most German citizens had no idea what havoc and misery their support for Hitler and his armies had brought to other people. Self-pity as a result of post-war deprivation was much more pronounced than pity for sufferers of German aggression. The percentage of those who felt that National Socialism was a good idea badly carried out actually rose, rather than declined, to 55 per cent in 1947.[33] Alexander Mitscherlich later referred to the Germans' 'inability to mourn', which he explained by their disaffection with the once-adored Führer, who had to shoulder all the blame now that he was dead.[34]

The Soviet military administration (SMAD) chose a different path to what they perceived to be 'democracy': a thoroughgoing transformation of the social and economic order, coupled with the dismissal of all former Nazis from positions of authority (520,000 up to 1948), either in government or in industry. The approach was well planned and assiduously carried out: land reform, i.e. the splitting up of estates of over 245 acres (7,000 estate owners were dispossessed without compensation), popular with the peasantry and refugees from the East, preceded collectivization in the 1950s; the purging of Nazis also served to weaken the middle-class element of society; nationalization was at first confined to large industrial plants, as envisaged in the West. Old popular-front tactics of the 1930s were revived under the banner of anti-fascism. The recruitment of the non-Nazi bourgeois elite was meant to win sympathy and to conceal the long-term seizure of power by the Communist Party, which already occupied crucial positions. Young Communist agents like Wolfgang Leonhard were briefed by their leader, Walter Ulbricht: 'It's got to look democratic, but we must have everything in our control.'[35]

Soviet priorities were different from the outset. Reforms were to be pushed through for ideological ends, regardless of administrative or economic efficiency, which had a high premium in the West. Nor were matters agreed upon in the Control Council, as had been envisaged during the planning phase. The Americans and British were not prepared to follow suit where they saw no benefits for themselves. Nevertheless, developments in the East could not be ignored lest the Communists gain undue advantage in the power game for the whole of Germany. This applied in particular to the early admission of political parties and their activities in the Eastern Zone. Small commandos of Communist emigrants were flown in from Moscow and set to work for an all-powerful left-wing alliance; Ulbricht and his group arrived as early as 2 May, the day Berlin surrendered. The Western powers, notably Britain, preferred instead to work with a hand-picked administrative elite until the time for parties and free elections had come, that is, until the Germans, politically manipulated for twelve years, could be trusted to make the right decisions. However, the Americans, eager to relinquish military government anyway, realized that there was no time to waste if they did not want to leave the political arena to the East German parties. From their point of view building up democracy from the grassroots was both a safeguard against unwelcome developments and the best method of conditioning, not to say re-educating, people to their new way of life. Working and waiting for a change of heart was not to their liking nor was it in the interest

of the Weimar politicians in the Western zones, who were eager
to show their mettle.

In the hope that they had a winning horse in the Communist
Party, the Russians were the first to open the race by permitting
political parties to organize as early as 10 June 1945. Within a
few weeks those parties which could hope for recognition had
established themselves in the Soviet Zone: the Communist Party
(KPD), the Social Democrats (SPD), the Conservatives or Christian
Democrats (CDU), and the Liberals (LDPD). Significantly, all parties
had 'D' for Deutschland as part of their names, to emphasize their
claim to represent the whole of Germany. All the former right-wing
parties were regarded as too compromised. The Christian Democrats
grew out of the old Catholic Centre Party and now encompassed
both Christian denominations, Catholics and Protestants, as well
as a new kind of Christian, i.e. non-Marxist, Socialism. As early as
20 June the new leaders called for the nationalization of all mineral
resources and key industries. At Potsdam the Western Allies had
been upstaged and they agreed that 'all democratic political parties with rights of assembly and public discussion shall be allowed
and encouraged throughout Germany'.[36]

Soviet schemes proved to be counter-productive in that they were
all too transparent. Political parties, notably the KPD, were to be
set up in Berlin before the Western powers took over their sectors
of the city. Everywhere the latter faced district councils more or less
openly controlled by Communists. The Russians also hoped for
the various Party organizations firmly entrenched in Berlin to be
accorded the leading role in the Western zones. The pattern of Soviet penetration became clearer by the day: manipulation from the
centre and from above, faith in agents and skeleton forces rather
than administrative structures, and above all the perception of national unity as the overriding German interest. The Soviet authorities based their assumptions on a misguided assessment of the past,
combined with their own preferences. The Western Allies made
the same mistake when planning for the future. Neither allowed
for the shattered state of mind of the German people in the wake
of total war and unconditional surrender. People never seemed to
count, despite all the pro-democracy rhetoric.

What has been said about Weimar politicians emerging from exile
or 'inner emigration' and their political ambitions did not apply

to the majority of the German people. After the experience of the previous twelve years most Germans retreated into themselves and were not at all keen to get involved in party politics again. If parties were already held in low esteem by the end of the Weimar Republic, they were more than discredited in 1945. On the whole the Germans went along, grumbling and moaning, with what their new masters told them to do. The Americans pressed ahead under the energetic leadership of General Clay, who did not wish to be outflanked by the Russians. He realized that in no time the latter had set up a political and administrative pattern in Berlin which, though confined to their zone, could easily be used for the control of Germany as a whole. A counterweight had to be put in place in the Western zones.

The political reorganization of Germany began with two developments which were bound to clash: the establishment of military government in the shape of Civil Affairs detachments which purged and rebuilt local and regional government, and the spontaneous emergence of so-called 'Anti-Fascist Action Committees' (Antifas), which sprang up as Workers' and Soldiers' Councils had done during the 1918 revolution. All the Allies were agreed that revolutionary chaos was to be avoided. After all, Germany had been conquered, not liberated. Sooner or later all local Antifas were dissolved, even in the Soviet Zone. The Russians only trusted German Communists who were trained and briefed in Moscow. The first and most urgent task of US, British, and French Civil Affairs Officers was to find suitable personnel to staff town halls and district councils, i.e. experts with a clean record. This was not an easy task since US detachments were not willing to tolerate any former Nazi Party members. The British tended to be more pragmatic, in that competence and administrative convenience seemed to matter more than political affiliation and the past. When the outspoken US General Patton expressed the very same view, he was soon dismissed by Eisenhower due to enraged public opinion at home. British officers appreciated without saying in so many words that former small-fry Nazis—others were arrested anyway—were more amenable to their instructions than approved anti-Nazis like, for instance, the SPD leader Kurt Schumacher. As a consequence replacements in both zones were inevitable, though for different reasons.

The pattern of reconstruction on the local level was much the same everywhere. The existing structures had to be revitalized quickly in view of large-scale devastation and the many urgent tasks which lay ahead. On the regional or zonal level there was scope for change. Since the Anglo-American armies covered the most ground in the West, they were also the first to think in terms of reorganizing regional administration. By the end of the war the American (17.2 million inhabitants, 30 per cent of German territory), the British (22.3 million inhabitants, 27 per cent territory), and the French (5.9 million inhabitants, 12 per cent territory) zones amounted to nearly two-thirds of the whole of post-war Germany. What was to be done with the political landscape? The answer to this question was much more important to the Anglo-Americans than the admission of political parties. Here, then, was the creative contribution the Western powers could make to the future well-being of a new Germany. In this they no doubt succeeded: the Americans by their policy of early investiture of 'administrative barons' and early local elections, and the British by their imaginative draftsmanship, which led to the creation of new and viable regional units.

Looking back, it can be seen that foreign interference in reorganizing Germany has always proved beneficial. All German attempts in the 1920s at redrawing the map of the Reich ended in failure. Vested interests were too strong and always had been in territorial matters. Both the State Department and the Foreign Office had come to the conclusion that it was much better to dismember Prussia than the Reich. This idea helped to appease those in Washington and London who were clamouring for the most radical carve-up. 'The federal states', wrote Sir Orme Sargent on 9 September 1944, 'should be more or less equal in strength so that no single state should be able to dominate the Central Government.'[37] The Americans were even more anxious to decentralize Germany and lost no time in reorganizing their zone. By May 1945 they had already established regional Military Government headquarters in Bavaria (without Palatinate), Greater Hesse, the northern parts of Baden and Württemberg, and the enclave of Bremen. By 19 September of the same year these areas had become federal states, invested with all legislative and executive powers. Without the backing of any parliaments the newly appointed Minister-Presidents were only accountable to and dependent on the Office of Military Government of the United States (OMGUS). A clean record and administrative competence were what mattered, not party affiliation. When the law-and-order conservative Fritz Schäffer (Bavarian People's Party), Minister-President in Munich, went soft on denazification he was sacked and replaced by the Social Democrat Wilhelm Hoegner. In Württemberg-Baden, Reinhold Maier, a liberal lawyer, was appointed. His deputy was Heinrich Köhler, a former deputy and minister of the Catholic Centre Party. Hesse was represented by Karl Geiler, a distinguished academic without party affiliation. Bremen would never have made it as an independent city-state in the later Federal Republic if it had not been an indispensable American supply base. The Governing Mayor, Wilhelm Kaisen, a Social Democrat of long standing, was elected by the Senate, which was appointed by OMGUS and of mixed political persuasion. In the American and British zones territorial administration solidified long before political parties entered the arena. The impact of this development on the federal structure of Germany was considerable: it reinforced the traditional position of the civil service and made thoroughgoing reforms more difficult, but it also provided stability at a time when insecurity was widespread. When *Länder* parliaments came into being and began to debate the Constitution, the administrative framework was already in place and the country was on the road to recovery. Ever since, it has been said, not without justification, that Germany is ruled by its civil service, which is also most strongly represented in all political parties and parliaments. All later attempts by the British and the Americans to break up the professional civil service and replace it with a less privileged public service came to nothing. As soon as Clay realized that the Control Council was not succeeding in overcoming French obstruction and in setting up central government departments for the whole of Germany, he went ahead in his zone and created the *Länderrat* as a co-ordinating committee. This was a much more powerful instrument than the British *Zonenbeirat*, which emerged later and only had an advisory capacity.

Britain faced more serious problems in its zone, first of all a more diverse spectrum of territories: four small states, like Schaumburg-Lippe, four powerful Prussian provinces, and the proud Hansa city of Hamburg, which would not be submerged into a new north-western state also including Schleswig-Holstein and Lower Saxony. More importantly, Britain, financially exhausted by the war, had to look after the largest population in the smallest area of arable land. However, London had fought tenaciously with Washington over the North-Western Zone because of the industrial heartland and the German ports, both of which turned out to be empty treasure boxes. Now the British were forced to export considerable amounts of foodstuffs from their own depleted stores in order to prevent large-scale starvation in Germany. As a result, bread had to be rationed in Britain. To get the economy going, the Control Commission for Germany/British Element (CCG/BE), the official title of Military Government, chose to establish central zonal departments, similar to the Russian approach.

However, the future of the Ruhr constituted the greatest challenge, not least because of the intense interest shown by the Soviet Union and France. Economic security, the level-of-industry debates, reparations: all these questions centred on the Ruhr. British diplomacy made the most of it by keeping all the other powers in the game without giving away anything. Various plans were put forward: a separate state, completely severed from Germany (the French proposal), international ownership and control of the whole of the industrial complex (20 per cent for each of the four powers), and finally a newly founded state consisting of the Ruhr as a trustee of the German people. British Military Government, notably the Deputy Governor Sir Brian Robertson, favoured the formation of a new state based on the Prussian provinces of North Rhine and Westphalia. On 23 August 1946 these two provinces were dissolved and 'Operation Marriage', the creation of a new federal state, took place.[38] The *raison d'être* of this development, the transfer of coal and steel into public ownership, though never renounced by the Labour government, was postponed indefinitely. The Americans, who had the upper hand in what became the Anglo-American Bizone, made no secret of their disapproval of rapid nationalization. Election results in the Western zones raised further doubts as to whether a majority of the population would back public ownership. It was pointed out, moreover, that a decision of such magnitude could not be taken by just one of the *Länder* single-handed.

It was not until 1946 that the Germans could show their hand, first in the local elections in the US Zone, later in regional elections for the *Länder* parliaments everywhere else. OMGUS had opted for proportional representation in a revised form which was then adopted elsewhere. Up to the elections the Social Democrats were reckoned to be the strongest political force in Germany: an impressive political record unscathed by the Nazi past, strong working-class backing, an all-German identity, and an emphasis on social justice and a planned economy, which was representative of a widespread mood. In the end political sympathies were fairly evenly divided between the SPD and the Christian Democrats and their Bavarian sister party (the CSU), with 36.8 per cent for the former and 35.5 per cent for the latter in all the *Länder* elections between 1946 and 1948. Roughly speaking the dividing line was formed by two rivers, the Rhine and the Main: south of the Main and west of the Rhine the Christian Democrats did better; in the north and east the Social Democrats were the leading government party, usually nominating the Minister-President. Elections reinforced the tendency towards coalition or even all-party government, the model generally favoured by the occupying powers. The Communists were still a force to be reckoned with (9.6 per cent in all Western zones) and scored slightly better than the Liberals (FDP, 9.5 per cent). However, in view of what had happened in the Soviet Zone, the Social Democrats were in no mood to enter into coalition governments with the KPD; only in a wider coalition were Communists occasionally tolerated.

Even though SMAD was the first authority to legalize political parties it was a latecomer as far as elections were concerned, and this for good reason. All major political initiatives which were to transform the social order of the Soviet Zone were carried through without a parliamentary mandate. Yet the first appeal of the newly licensed Communist Party did not contain any reference to 'socialism'. The imposition of the Soviet system was rejected as untimely. The development of free trade and entrepreneurial initiative was to be completely unimpeded 'on the basis of private property'.[39] Political pronouncements by the SPD in the Western zones at the same time were more radical and explicitly socialist. However, the three non-Communist parties of the East were straightaway forced into an 'anti-fascist bloc', a precondition of their public appearance. The Communists realized that they could not hope for a mass following unless it was 'organized'. For most people it was all too obvious that the KPD were the stooges of the Soviet government. The aim was to create an 'anti-fascist democratic order to save the nation'. This was carried through by a series of 'reforms' such as the dispossession of banks, including savings banks, as early as July 1945, followed by land reform in September, as mentioned above, and by the confiscation of all industrial enterprises (October 1945–May 1946). All these measures were imposed by decree of SMAD, without prior consultation with the Western powers. A plebiscite in Saxony *post festum*, claiming that the property in question belonged to 'war and Nazi criminals', served as the only democratic fig-leaf. Resolutions by the 'anti-fascist bloc', dominated by the Communists with Soviet backing, could not but be unanimous and therefore approving. All that the bloc system and Western coalition government had in common was their appearance.

Worse was to come. If the free elections in Austria, as well as the local elections in the American Zone, were anything to go by, the KPD was to suffer a devastating defeat. Apparently the Austrian Communists had reckoned that they would gain as many votes and seats as the Social Democrats. When the idea of a union was first floated towards the end of the war, the KPD refused, fearing for its identity. All of a sudden they started to campaign for the very same idea. In the meantime leading Social Democrats, disillusioned by six months of Soviet patronage of the KPD, said No to forced fusion, most vigorously Kurt Schumacher, the undisputed leader in the Western zones. A party ballot in the Western sectors of Berlin was revealing: 82 per cent against fusion, with 62 per cent in favour of a genuine coalition with the Communists. Nevertheless, on 22 April 1946 the Socialist Unity Party (SED) came into being, claiming to be the most progressive national force, which would fight with all its energy for 'economic, cultural, and political unity'. Up to the present day it is not quite clear how many SPD delegates were taken in by this and how many yielded because of harassment and intimidation. The West looked on but was powerless.

The unscrupulous exercise of power by the Soviets in their sphere of influence convinced the Western Allies that the time had come to reconsider their policy in Germany. George Kennan's famous long telegram from Moscow in February 1946, exposing long-term Soviet intentions, and Churchill's Iron Curtain speech in Fulton, Missouri, a month later are among the best-known indications of a fundamental shift in public opinion in the West. Germany, however, was the terrain where intelligence about Soviet intentions could be gauged and gathered more consistently than elsewhere. The British were most desperate for a common economic approach as promised in Potsdam. They could no longer afford to shoulder the burden of their zone without receiving food deliveries in return for reparations to Russia. When the Paris Conference of Foreign Ministers became deadlocked, US Secretary of State James Byrnes declared that the United States was well prepared to join forces and zones with any other occupying power. On 25 July 1946 the British Cabinet accepted the American offer, which was, so Bevin learned, not open to the Soviet Union. A month later Byrnes went public. His Stuttgart speech of 6 September 1946 has been hailed as a dramatic fanfare of change in Germany.[40] The message was that Germany's political freedom and economic well-being were also America's concerns. If full unity could not be achieved, the United States would support the greatest possible degree of unification, including a provisional German government. The road to the later Federal Republic was signposted. 'Bizonia', the economic merger of the American and British zones on 1 January 1947, marked the first stage. The new area included 50 per cent of German territory and 64 per cent of the population. The economies of the two parts were compatible; not so, however, the political structures, with the more federalist and self-governing system in the South and the more centralized bureaucracy in the North. Clay and Robertson, the two Allied supervisors, made it plain that political fusion was not yet on the cards. A parliamentary assembly, as proposed by the Minister-Presidents, was refused. Control was to be exercised by Military Government. The common administrative departments were spread over both zones without any co-ordinating agency.

Politics and economics could not be neatly divided. After all, the future social and economic order was the bone of contention in post-war Germany. Kurt Schumacher complained bitterly that the new bizonal departments were in the hands of 'capitalists'. The pre-Godesberg Social Democracy was still bent on a policy of rigorous nationalization based on a unitary state. In the freezing winter of 1947, with its concomitant breakdown of transport and dwindling of coal and food supplies, a planned economy for decades to come seemed to be a foregone conclusion. In all eight *Länder* governments of the Bizone, the Social Democrats were in charge of the economic departments. The head of the new bizonal office for economic affairs in Minden, Westphalia, was Victor Agartz, a determined devotee of a nationalized and highly centralized economy. Yet his backing by the British government was highly unpopular with the Christian Democrats and Liberals, who accused him of establishing a centralized economy 'on the Soviet model'.

The administrative set-up of the Bizone underwent several changes which enhanced the development towards a separate West German state in all but name. The first revision provided for an Economic Council consisting of fifty-two deputies and the concentration of all departments in Frankfurt am Main. The second strengthened the executive and added a second chamber (*Länderrat*) which represented the individual states. These alterations, which served to improve efficiency, were imposed by the occupying powers without much consultation with German politicians. General Clay's personal involvement was decisive at important junctures. He made sure, for instance, by insisting on a more democratic system of representation, that the Christian Democrats and other opponents of a planned economy gained the upper hand in the Economic Council. That the new right-wing majority should use its power to push through their candidates for the various departments, however, was certainly not what the military authorities had intended. They would have preferred a consensual, all-party approach of the kind which had hitherto been the Allied policy in executive appointments. To give but one example: when the Americans swapped the Conservative Fritz Schäffer for Hoegner as Minister-President of Bavaria, they installed Ludwig Erhard at the same time as Minister of Economics. Without much of a fight, the Social Democrats, in spite of their strength in regional parliaments, went into opposition where, unknown to them at the time, they were to remain for the next twenty years.

The SPD has always been blamed in German politics for withdrawing from power too readily in any crisis it faced. Votes and decisions in the *Wirtschaftsrat* (Economic Council) were directed by two men who were not members, but kept all the reins in their hands: Konrad Adenauer, chairman of the CDU in the British Zone and the most cunning of foxes, who turned down the chairmanship of the Executive Committee, the nearest thing to a German cabinet,

'because of my age'[41] (seventy-two years), and Kurt Schumacher, a
Social Democrat of great integrity and courage, who would never
collaborate with the Communists or compromise on principle. For
Adenauer politics was about power rather than principle and he
sensed that the tide was turning against a controlled economy, of
which the Germans had had too much. The third man of destiny
who now emerged from the shadows was Ludwig Erhard, who
replaced Johannes Semler as director of the economic department
of the Bizone; Semler had been sacked for making derogatory re-
marks about American deliveries of foodstuffs ('chicken fodder').
Whereas so far politicians had not been moved by visions of the
future, but the needs of the present day, Erhard had a positive message: a liberal, though not unrestrained, market economy would
sort out the muddle. Deregulation was the answer; nationalization
in his view was 'hocus-pocus'.[42] Some people in the CDU, notably
its left wing, had serious reservations about Erhard, an academic
expert on public finance with no party affiliation. Erhard would
never have made it without the strong backing of the Liberals. He
was to be their most valuable asset in the years to come, even
though he never joined the FDP. With a staunch Liberal at the economic helm a coalition between the two big parties, the CDU/CSU
and SPD, could be ruled out for the foreseeable future.

The main purpose of zonal merger was to accelerate Germany's
economic recovery. However, everyone realized that no real progress could be made without currency reform. Because of the political implications, this was just as much of a hot potato as European
monetary union today. The Germans made no fewer that 250
plans, but were told that a matter of such importance fell within
the realm of Allied control: a separate currency for the Western
zones meant final partition and none of the occupation powers
wished to force this issue. The Reichsmark was totally useless: the
amount of money in circulation had increased by 1,000 per cent
since 1935, public debts twenty-seven fold. The black market was
rampant and the barter system threatened to paralyse the whole
economy. Shopkeepers tried to withhold goods rather than sell
them for 'bad money'. Cigarettes became the accepted means of
payment on the black market. Nor were work ethics helped by
the fact that one single cigarette was worth as much as a worker's
daily wage. Not surprisingly there was a shortage of labour. Clay's

financial adviser, Joseph Dodge, was convinced that currency reform was unavoidable. Why did it take more than two years to implement it? For a long time the Western Allies hoped against hope that a common solution to this problem might still be feasible. Furthermore, it was thought that the German bizonal administrative machine could cope with inflation, or else shoulder the burden of an eventual currency reform.

An important stage in this development was the Marshall Plan, first outlined in the Secretary of State's Harvard speech of 5 June 1947, which complemented Truman's containment policy. Freedom and political stability depended on economic recovery and a revival of international trade. The recipient countries had to agree to a programme for reconstruction. After all, Europe used to be one of the most important markets for the United States. Marshall aid, as a gigantic export subsidy for US industry, was meant to benefit both the USA and Europe, which was supposed to use the dollar aid to purchase American goods. The offer, also open to Eastern Europe, was rejected by Moscow for the whole of its sphere of influence. This clearly marked the two camps which were now jockeying for position in the Cold War. The London Conference of Foreign Ministers in December 1947 was the last, totally unsuccessful, attempt at bridging the gulf. Molotov, referring to news about plans for a West German government, demanded an Allied resolution that these would not materialize. Marshall told him that they had decided to initiate practical steps towards unification rather than to indulge in rhetoric. The die was cast. On 20 March 1948 the Soviet government withdrew from the Control Council in protest against further moves to form a separate West German state. The Western powers and the Benelux countries had met in London to discuss the structure of a future West German state, mainly how to overcome French resistance, and procedural steps to this end.

A showdown was inevitable, but it was not to be outright war, as both General Clay and Sir Brian Robertson, the British Military Governor, feared. The United States pressed ahead with currency reform, which was long overdue, and Russia responded in kind by cutting off Berlin. The impact of Marshall aid and the currency reform on the German economy will be discussed elsewhere. The new money, the Deutschmark, was printed in the United States in great secrecy. The Germans were only involved with the very last stage, when a group of experts was driven to a remote place near Kassel in order to translate an American concept, worked out by one of Clay's advisers, Edward Tenenbaum, into German legislation. Erhard was upset that he had only been initiated shortly before the public announcement and offered to resign. Clay refused, and Erhard jumped the gun by announcing the news on the radio before the Military Governor had had a chance to do so, thus giving the impression that it was his decision. More importantly, Erhard went on to lift price controls on 90 per cent of all goods and services, though not basic commodities, without prior consultation with Military Government—and this at a time when the economy was still tightly controlled in the United Kingdom. When taken to task by Clay for altering the price regulations, Erhard's famous reply was: 'I have not altered them, I have abolished them.'[43] In other circumstances Erhard would have been dismissed forthwith. But the gamble worked. The Allies had no other option but to approve of the new legislation. The immediate and apparent success of the currency reform was overwhelming. All of a sudden, shop windows were full of desirable consumer goods which had not been on display for years. Obviously manufacturers and stores had been hoarding goods in anticipation of the reform. Even though the transitional period was not without problems—rising prices and unemployment in particular—the upsurge of the economy generated the necessary impetus for the state-building process. Marshall aid, currency reform, and the Berlin airlift have to be seen as one big boost to German morale.

The first Berlin crisis no doubt produced the decisive psychological breakthrough. The term 'Allies' took on a new meaning. At the outset the Western Allies had regarded the joint administration of Berlin as a symbol of the common victory over Germany and a means of holding the Alliance and Germany together. Within three years the city had been transformed into the battleground of the Cold War, the exact opposite of its original purpose.

Russian expectations did not come to fruition either. The former capital did not function as a lever to exert influence over the Western zones. After the forced fusion of the SPD and KPD it was not even possible to 'democratically control' the city government. In the last free elections of 1948 the SED gained only twelve out of 104 seats in the city chamber. Soviet support for the SED proved

to be counter-productive with respect to the Berlin population, who
could not be cowed by threats and chicanery. Pressure on Berlin
increased following the London Conference and the partial transfer of governmental power to the bizonal administration. On 21
January 1948 the Western governors on the Control Council were
told by their Soviet colleague in no uncertain terms that Berlin
was part of the Soviet Zone, a claim which was to be repeated over
and over again in the following years. From then on, the thumb-
screws were turned by systematically impeding the free movement
of people and goods to and from Berlin. The last excuse for the full-
blown blockade was the extension of the new currency to Greater
Berlin. It was not until after the Russians had issued their own new
currency and simultaneously imposed the blockade that the Western powers began distributing the Deutschmark. The new money
had already been flown to Berlin under the guise of military supplies, while the Russians were assured that the new measure would
not cover Berlin. Ernst Reuter, soon to be Governing Mayor of West
Berlin, the most courageous campaigner for the city's freedom, was
right when he said: 'Whoever controls the currency wields the
power.'[44] In a way this dictum held true for the whole of Germany
up to and beyond the currency union of 1990. In the long run political and economic freedom could not be totally divorced. When,
in November 1948, even the exchange of goods between the two
halves of the city was stopped, the Soviet government justified this
order by reference to 'self-defence against the aggressive currency
reform of the Western Powers'.[45]

There is now agreement among scholars that both East and West
pursued a containment policy and that Stalin never seriously contemplated outright war. The Berlin blockade is perhaps the most
convincing example in favour of this thesis. Strategically the city
was undefendable and many military advisers in the West were
inclined to abandon it. Not so General Clay, who first thought of
forcing his way back into the city by armed convoy. He declared that
only war could drive the United States out of Berlin. SPD leaders
implored the world to come to the rescue of Berlin after the city
fathers, gathered in the old town hall in the Eastern Sector, were
intimidated by an organized rabble. Clay told his government: 'If we
are determined to defend Europe against Communism then we must
not budge one yard. We can suffer humiliation and political pressure

without losing face as long as it doesn't come to war. If we retreat our position in Europe is threatened.'[46] His attitude was shared by President Truman, who dispatched two squadrons of B-29 bombers, capable of carrying atomic weapons, to Europe. To provide for a population of 2.5 million by air alone was without precedent and few thought it was feasible. But it was possible, due to Clay's determination, American and British logistics, and the morale of the Berlin population under siege. In 262 days American and British planes, the so-called *Rosinenbomber*, flew 270,000 flights carrying food, fuel, and raw materials for industry undisturbed by the intimidation of Soviet MiGs. In no time the French built a new airport in Tegel with the help of 19,000 German workers. Negotiations with a view to ending the blockade revealed that the Soviets were pursuing a dual policy: delaying the formation of a separate West German state or, alternatively, if that failed, a withdrawal of the Western powers from Berlin. Moscow failed on both counts.

When the blockade was eventually lifted on 12 May 1949, the West German state was a virtual reality. Moreover, the Germans in the Western zones, not only the Berlin population, were now won over to the idea of a separate state, securely anchored in the Western Alliance. The successful way in which the Berlin crisis was handled played a crucial role. In the summer of 1948 Clay had had the impression that quite a few German politicians doubted American resolve to break Soviet resistance. Apparently they were worried lest another Foreign Ministers Conference might achieve a breakthrough to German unification which would expose them as 'separatists'. If Berlin appeared to be the all-important trump card, its meaning changed from being the linchpin of a united, more or less centralized German state to being the symbol of freedom and prosperity and the pledge of eventual reunification. The divided city, an outpost of the West, represented the German problem in a nutshell. By paying tribute to Berlin as the capital of the once-united and eventually to be reunited nation state the West Germans appeased their national conscience.

In June 1947 an all-German conference of Minister-Presidents in Munich, the first and last meeting of its kind, had failed to work out an agenda for joint action. The Minister-Presidents from the Western zones were neither permitted nor prepared to subscribe to a central German administration as demanded by their Eastern

colleagues. After that most West German politicians, notably Adenauer and Schumacher, were resigned to the evolution of a West
German state as an interim solution. But they did not wish to be
publicly identified with this aim and went on pretending to work
for German unity. They, as well as the Allies, were uncertain about
the strength of national feeling amongst ordinary Germans. All sides
in this poker game posed as the true champions of national unity
and denounced their opponents as 'separatists'.

The division of Germany was both a contributing factor to and
a result of the Cold War, which was, in many respects, less avoidable than the preceding 'hot war'. The Germans, with their deep
fear of Bolshevism and the Red Army bent on revenge, sensed this
much earlier than their new masters. They were also the real bene-
ficiaries of this climatic change, for which they had actually hoped
while still under the spell of Goebbels' propaganda. The price they
had to pay for this bonus, this kick-start into accelerated recovery,
was the partition of their country. The burden was not too heavy
on the West Germans since it was mainly the unlucky East Germans who were to finance the mortgage for the next forty years.
There was no serious disagreement between the two main parties
about which course to take. Even though they had very little in common otherwise, Adenauer and Schumacher responded to this central question in a very similar way. Adenauer foresaw and favoured
a West German state as early as October 1945. Schumacher, who
was more nationally-minded, reconciled himself and his party to
the inevitable by arguing, in May 1947, that there was no other way
to eventual unification than 'economic magnetization of the West'.
He added: 'It is surely a hard and probably a long road.'[47] Basically
there is no difference between Schumacher's 'magnet theory' and
Adenauer's 'policy of strength' (*Politik der Stärke*) as expounded in
the 1950s.

A political history of the post-war years would be incomplete without drawing attention to the fact that most Germans were in no
mood to get involved in politics. On the whole they did not mind
leaving this business to their new masters and the professionals the
latter chose to employ. Allied commanders were surprised that after
all the futile last-ditch attempts to hold up the invading armies,
they did not meet with the slightest resistance after surrender. The
material and psychological conditions were such that for most

people survival, how to find food and shelter, was everything. Very popular and to the point was Bertolt Brecht's saying: '*Erst kommt das Fressen, dann kommt die Moral*' (First comes food, then morals). Basic instincts took over and guided people from one day to the next. After visiting Germany former US President Herbert Hoover reported that the mass of German people had, as regarded food, heating, and housing, reached the lowest point known in Western civilization for a hundred years.[48] In his remarkable account *In Darkest Germany* the British publisher Victor Gollancz describes in detail, with numerous photographic illustrations, the appalling housing situation in cities like Hamburg (77,000 people in cellars etc.) and the 'slow starvation' food rations of 1,550 calories.[49]

Nevertheless, post-war society was not in a state of total chaos and disintegration. In the countryside life went on, it appeared to Allied observers, as though nothing had happened, while nearby cities offered a picture of total devastation and misery. With the breakdown of public transport and communications social cohesion was confined to the extended family, the neighbourhood, and the local community, and also to gangs of youths roaming the streets. The distribution network became regionalized, often to the detriment of the larger cities, which had to fend for themselves. As a result of the dismissal of so many officials, party bosses, and managers, society was in a state of flux. Rank and status lost much of their previous meaning. Smallholders in the West counted for more than famous landed families who had lost all their estates in the East. One such family started a dry-cleaning business,[50] others took up small-scale farming because it was the only trade they knew.

Providing food, shelter, and employment for the 10 million refugees (as of 1 April 1947) posed one of the greatest problems. Most of the 'expellees' from the Eastern territories settled in the Soviet (3.9 million) and the British (3.19 million) zones, whereas the American Zone (2.9 million) was the first port of call for the refugees from the Sudetenland. Nearly one million people moved from the Soviet Zone to the West in due course, without any such migration eastwards. These refugees had stories to tell which seemed to confirm anti-Russian fears and helped to persuade the population in the West that they were better off without the Soviet Zone. In spite of the war losses, by October 1946 the population of the Bizone had increased by 25 per cent in relation to 1936. There was also a surplus of 7 million women altogether in all four zones. The Germans were in deadly fear of the displaced persons (DPs) who had been exploited as forced labour and now roamed the countryside. By the end of the war there were over 8 million DPs in Germany, mainly from Eastern Europe, most of whom were soon to be repatriated.[51] In the spring of 1948, 850,000 had to be cared for in the Bizone. Most reports about acts of violence committed by DPs were vastly exaggerated and statistics show that crimes, both of capital and property, were roughly on the same level as those committed by Germans. Nevertheless, German anxieties were not altogether unfounded and the Military Government tried, on the whole successfully, to maintain law and order, sometimes resorting to drastic steps to protect the population. It is important to realize that during the occupation period the Germans relied for their protection, from external as well as internal threats, on the security provided by the Allies. There can be no doubt that this had long-term psychological repercussions: since power had been abused by Germany's leaders, it was now seen to be more secure and effective in the hands of others. The experience of having the Reich's fate determined by its neighbours had been greatly resented in the past. Now, all of a sudden, such interference was perceived by the vast majority of West Germans as wholesome and salutary. Resentment, where it surfaced, was directed against certain measures by the Allied authorities, not against foreign occupation. Occasional appeals to national sentiments by party politicians, both on the right and on the left, did not have much impact on the elections up to August 1949, which in any case were local or regional. Thanks to total occupation, post-war Germany was free from the upheavals and revolutionary turmoil which characterized the early years of the Weimar Republic.

2 Drifting Apart: The Two Republics

The response of the West to the worsening of the Cold War in 1948 was to set up the West European Union, to this day the only purely European defence alliance, and to press ahead with the foundation of a West German state. After the demise of the Control Council it was France that stood in the way of further progress, fearing that her neighbour might again become too powerful. However, West Germany without the French Zone would make no sense. Britain and the Social Democrats favoured a decentralized state with a federal government firmly in control. France would have preferred a loose confederation of fairly independent states, not unlike the German Bund. A compromise between these two positions had to be found.

Again the chief impetus came from General Clay, who visualized something like the United States of Germany, both as strong and decentralized as the States. The compromise worked out at the Six Power Conference in London in the spring of 1948 centred on some kind of international control of the Ruhr, Germany's industrial heartland. This did not augur well for the future, because German politicians were now facing separation in the East and West, as well as a weak government in between. The recommendations for the formation of a West German state under Allied supervision, which were agreed upon in London, are generally referred to as the 'birth certificate' of the Federal Republic. These documents were handed over to the Minister-Presidents on 1 July 1948 as the only political representatives of Germany at the time. The party leaders had no comparable standing and were not much liked by the Military Governors. The Minister-Presidents were summoned to Frankfurt, seat of the Economic Council, and instructed—not invited—to convene a National Assembly in order to work out a proper constitution, democratic and federalist in character. Furthermore they were to make recommendations for a realignment of the *Länder* with a view to producing a lasting equilibrium. Last but not least, they were told to accept an Occupation Statute which was to circumscribe Allied prerogatives in the fields of foreign policy, foreign trade and reparations, and related matters. In other words, West Germany was to become a self-governing dominion under Allied supervision.

The chiefs of the *Länder* met a week later near Koblenz to discuss the position. None of the German politicians wished to be identified with the formal division of his country. Would they not appear to be mere puppets of or collaborators with foreign powers who planned to create a separate German state? Carlo Schmid, a close adviser and confidant of Schumacher, warned that any initiative towards a separate state would be reciprocated in the East.[1] The Germans could not be expected to build a proper house, but only an emergency shelter which would provide protection for the time being. The Minister-Presidents agreed that no constitution for a permanent state should be drafted or any elected assembly convened. Instead, an organizational framework called the 'Basic Law' (*Grundgesetz*) was to be worked out by a Parliamentary Council of *Länder* delegates. The real constitution, it was argued, was the Occupation Statute, which made clear who really was in charge, and which therefore ought to precede the promulgation of the Basic Law. For the first time, but not the last, German politicians disliked the responsibilities forced upon them. The inclusion of the French Zone and more self-government was all they aspired to achieve. That Germans wished for fewer powers than the Allies were prepared to concede struck Clay as 'odd in the light of history'.[2] The term 'Basic Law' was quite an understatement for what was to become the most successful and enduring constitution Germany has ever enjoyed. The German reservations did not please General Clay, who had set his mind on creating a proper German state, as though it were a new army he had been ordered to build up in no time. Later on, Foreign Secretary Dean Acheson wondered whether the idea of a West German state was 'the brainchild of General Clay', rather than the outcome of a government decision.[3]

While General König, the French Governor, was quietly satisfied with this state of affairs, Clay and Robertson lobbied the German leaders to be more forthcoming and accept the inevitable. The mayors of Hamburg and Bremen, Max Brauer and Wilhelm Kaisen, and the heads of the smallest states, as well as Hans Ehard, Minister-President of Bavaria, were among the first to realize that the road to state-building was the right one under the prevailing conditions. The most influential supporter of Clay was the newly elected Governing Mayor of Berlin, Ernst Reuter, who, facing the blockade, knew what was at stake. He persuaded his colleagues to drop their reservations by arguing that 'the division of Germany is not being created; it is a fact.'[4] He was not fighting for the restoration of the *status quo ante*, but for recognition of the fact that politically and economically Berlin was part of the free West. In this he proved to be right against all the odds. Eventually, a compromise was reached in that the Allies accepted the German proposals for terminology and procedure.

The Minister-Presidents, now the only collegium speaking for Germany as a whole, convened a meeting of experts, mostly constitutional lawyers, to the tranquil island of Herrenchiemsee in order to prepare a draft constitution. To the party bosses, this looked like a devious scheme of the regional chieftains trying to safeguard their rights at the expense of central government. It was nothing like that. In the history of constitutional assemblies the work of Herrenchiemsee—the draft constitution and a report completed within a fortnight—was an outstanding achievement, just because the experts shunned party politics. Their ideas and problems inspired the debates in the Parliamentary Council. It was due to the convention of Herrenchiemsee that crucial elements were enshrined in the Basic Law—unalterable human rights, the two-chamber system, a strong executive, the Constitutional Court, to name but a few—which were to determine the political culture of the Federal Republic. One of the most hotly debated issues was whether the German state had actually ceased to exist in 1945 or its main functions had only been suspended for the time being. In the latter case, supported by the majority of experts, the German nation was called upon to exercise its democratic right of self-government. Otherwise it would be up to the individual states to form a new federation. Today the whole issue might appear to be irrelevant. However, the theory of continuity implied acceptance of full responsibility for Germany's past, especially *vis-à-vis* Israel. The SED regime in the East, allegedly born without the 'original sin of fascism', was never prepared to share this burden.

The Parliamentary Council did have all the hallmarks of a constitutional assembly, except for the lack of popular assent. The 65 Deputies were chosen by the *Länder* in accordance with the last elections and on the basis of one seat per 750,000 inhabitants. Although the two main parties, the CDU/CSU and SPD, could muster the same number of Deputies, 27 each, the splinter parties (Liberals: 8; Deutsche Partei: 2; old Centre Party: 2) contributed to a safe conservative, or rather anti-Socialist, majority. The average age of 56 years, as well as the fact that 61 per cent were public servants, contributed to the conservative outlook of this assembly. This was a blessing in disguise because most Deputies had vivid memories of the Weimar Republic and how it came to grief; eleven Deputies had been members of the Reichstag. Never before could lessons learned from a disaster be applied so quickly and thoroughly as in this case. In the Parliamentary Council party politics played a more important role than at Herrenchiemsee. It turned out to be a shrewd move by Konrad Adenauer to accept the chair, which under normal circumstances would not carry much clout. However, as the first and only leader of the West German population after the war, its incumbent rose to prominence. Soon Adenauer was a national figure: his features, strongly resembling those of a Red Indian chief, his age and experience as Governing Mayor of Cologne, his Rhenish dialect and sense of humour, coupled with a paternalistic demeanour, made a deep and lasting impression on the traumatized minds of post-war Germans.[5] Of course, nobody at the time anticipated that this hearty old man of 72 would dominate German politics in a benevolent but autocratic manner for the next fifteen years, until his country was securely anchored in the Western world. Adenauer was an old cynic. He had no faith in the common man, he once admitted to Carlo Schmid.[6] He certainly looked upon his fellow countrymen as unruly children who needed a strong hand, while everyone else felt that the Germans were too disciplined to be good democrats.

The Parliamentary Council met in Bonn and Adenauer was at pains to ensure that the city also became the capital of the new state, even though he too originally favoured Frankfurt as a city more steeped in history. The decisive vote on 10 May 1949 was no foregone conclusion, but the result of Adenauer's successful scheming and lobbying. A popular legend has it that the proximity of Adenauer's home in Rhöndorf was crucial. According to another theory, Bonn was more appropriate as the capital of a provisional and fragmentary state than the old imperial city of Frankfurt. The truth is probably more banal: the passionate support for Frankfurt by the Social Democrats who controlled the city council tipped the scales in favour of Bonn. The CDU/CSU was more sympathetic towards the Catholic Rhineland and its westward orientation. Moreover, Bonn would not outshine the *Länder* capitals or undermine the federal structure of the new state. In the end Bonn came to symbolize the peaceful and somewhat provincial character of the Federal Republic.

The shadow of Weimar hovered over the proceedings of the Parliamentary Council. The Allies had already removed one of the main faultlines by dismembering Prussia and providing for a more balanced union of member states. They insisted on power-sharing between the centre and the constituent parts. This was their main concern. Among the Deputies of the Parliamentary Council mistrust of the electorate was widespread. The President was not to be elected by popular vote or endowed with special executive powers. All plebiscitary elements of the Weimar constitution were expunged. Faced with the choice between a Senate as the second chamber or an assembly of delegates from the *Länder*, the Deputies opted for the latter. The position of the Parliament was strengthened in as much as it had the right to elect and dismiss the Federal Chancellor. The most far-reaching device was the so-called 'constructive vote of no confidence': a new Chancellor could only be elected in mid-term if a majority of Deputies voted his successor into office, so that the country would never be without a government. The stability of government was much enhanced compared to Weimar. The electoral law also helped in this respect: parties had to muster at least 5 per cent of the vote to get into the Bundestag. The result was fewer parties and less haggling over coalition policies. As compensation, proportional representation gave the smaller parties such as the Liberals a better chance than elsewhere. As a matter of fact, the FDP participated in most governments from 1949 onwards.

The most contentious issue was the relationship between the central government and the individual member states which had already been established and which enjoyed the support of the occupying powers. While the Bundestag was legislating for the whole of the country, it was the *Länder* which would be in charge of administration. Now that the Military Governors had insisted that the *Länder* should also hold the purse strings, they would raise most of the taxes. For Schumacher and the SPD this was totally unacceptable. A future government could not be at the mercy of the *Länder*. The conservatives, including Adenauer, were prepared to throw in the towel when the crisis deepened and it became clear that the Germans faced the unusual alliance of the American and French Military Governors. Clay, a Southerner and as such no friend of power concentrated in the capital, objected to the legislative prerogative of the central government, especially in financial matters. He suspected that the SPD feared for their nationalization programme, more reason for him not to yield. Schumacher's motives were probably more honourable than that. Although he accepted the Western state, he did not wish the SPD to be used as a tool of foreign and particularist interests. Only a strong central government could hope to overcome the division of the country. Schumacher's intransigence paid off and helped to create a viable central government, even though it was not to be controlled by his own party for some time to come. With the foundation of NATO on 4 April 1949, which assuaged French security anxieties, the overall political climate changed in favour of a more generous attitude towards the Germans. Technical difficulties could not be allowed to hold up the formation of a German state and a bulwark against Soviet aggression. Due also to British mediation, Clay was forced by his own government to give in. Subsequently a sensible compromise was worked out.

The name of the new state was less controversial, but nevertheless significant for its identity. Here a suggestion by the federalist lobby of the CDU/CSU (Ellwanger Kreis) met with general approval: *Bundesrepublik Deutschland*. Quite a few conservative Deputies were clinging to the ominous 'Reich'. Carlo Schmid, chairman of the SPD in the Parliamentary Council, dismissed this idea out of hand by pointing out that for Germany's neighbours 'Reich' implied a claim to supremacy and domination.[7] A clear majority of Deputies wished to see the new Germany completely divorced from this tradition, even if it meant that the 'Reich' founded by Bismarck would vanish for ever. In the end the 'Reich' only survived as an oddity because the East German Railway stuck to its old name of 'Reichsbahn'. The fact that there was so little argument over the national symbols needs some explanation. For the founding fathers of the Federal Republic nationalism and all its paraphernalia were thoroughly discredited. The colours of the new state were to be those of the liberal and democratic movement which led to the Frankfurt Parliament of 1848: *Schwarz-Rot-Gold*. Of the old national anthem, only the third verse was considered appropriate, referring as it did to *Einigkeit und Recht und Freiheit* (Unity, Right, and Liberty). Of paramount importance was that Germany should not, as the first verse of the anthem seems to suggest, stand *über alles* (i.e. above all else). When the Basic Law was finally promulgated on 23 May 1949 the members of the Parliamentary Council stood up and sang a sentimental German *Lied* of the early nineteenth century which expressed a longing for the German fatherland of the future. In his final address Adenauer maintained that they all believed they had made an essential contribution to the reunification of the whole of the German people.[8] No doubt, many Deputies had great reservations about their role in creating a liberal and democratic state which left their East German countrymen in the cold. But they did not see any viable alternative. The Basic Law had been approved by all the *Länder* Diets a week earlier, except for Bavaria, which rejected it but then agreed to succumb if two-thirds of the other states passed it. Bavaria, which called itself a *Freistaat*, was most anxious to emphasize its supposedly special status within the new union.

Even with its own constitution, the new German republic remained under Allied occupation. On 12 May 1949 the Military Governors had handed the Basic Law with their consent to a delegation of the Parliamentary Council, thus demonstrating their overall supremacy. They might as well have passed over the details of the Occupation Statute which they had announced earlier. The Germans would have preferred this procedure so as to absolve themselves from bringing about the division of their country. However, this had to wait until the election and until a new government was firmly in place. Nevertheless, the occupation regime changed its character. Military Government and zonal division were suspended. Henceforth control was exercised by a High Commission composed of the representatives of the three powers: John McCloy, who took over from General Clay; Sir Brian Robertson, who changed into civilian clothes; and André François-Poncet, the French Ambassador to Berlin before the war. German laws could only come into force if no objections were raised by the High Commission within twenty-one days. The principle of Allied unanimity, as in the former Control Council, strengthened the German position. West Germany was to become a self-governing Allied Protectorate.

The smooth passage of the Basic Law was made possible because the most contentious element, the social and economic order of the Federal Republic, was left to the free interplay of political forces. Both the CDU/CSU and the SPD had hopes of becoming the leading party which would be able to determine this issue in future.

While the Economic Council in Frankfurt handled everyday business up to the last minute, West Germany experienced its first, shortest, and most crucial election campaign. The political landscape was so diverse that there were no clear pointers to the future. Altogether sixteen parties campaigned for seats, and seventy independent candidates, but only four were represented in all *Länder*: apart from the big two, the Liberals and Communists. The CDU/CSU, on the advice of Adenauer, simply dropped its legendary 'Ahlener Programme', which had rejected capitalism in favour of Christian Socialism, and now opted for Erhard's social market economy. Round-faced Erhard, not yet a member of the CDU, exuded confidence and optimism. However, the economic miracle had not yet materialized and unemployment was still at 10 per cent, a level quite staggering at that time. Nevertheless, the Social Democrats lost the battle for nationalization and for the soul of the country because they misjudged the public mood. Adenauer could afford to sit back and simply watch them ruin their chances. Schumacher reintroduced the language of class struggle and appealed to national sentiments by attacking the victorious powers and their grip on German industry in the Ruhr. He also made a grave mistake by referring to the churches as the 'fifth occupation power'.[9] Nor did his venomous attacks on Adenauer endear him to the German public, who were no longer used to the occasionally outrageous rhetoric of a democratic election campaign. Adenauer, though more restrained and statesmanlike, not only exploited the blunders of his opponent but also claimed that the Social Democrats had joined forces with the Communists in the East and that a socialist Germany would be 'no dam against Communism'.[10] This was blatantly unfair, but probably quite effective. The Liberals steered a clever course between the two main antagonists as they had already done in the Parliamentary Council. They wooed the voters who rejected the

CDU's dependence on the churches in educational matters and opposed the economic programme of the SPD. Moreover, they made sure that they would be an indispensable partner in government. In a way, the German Liberals now made up for their missed opportunities in the past. With 11.2 per cent of the votes and 52 seats they achieved one of their best electoral results in the history of the Republic. Their influence was decisive in tipping the balance against the grand coalition much favoured in nationally minded quarters of both big parties. A grand coalition might have set the pattern for the following decades, with potentially disastrous effects for the fledgling democracy.

In the election of 14 October 1949 the CDU/CSU gained 31 per cent of the votes as against 29.2 per cent for the Social Democrats. Together with the FDP and the Conservative splinter parties (*Bayern-Partei* (BP), *Deutsche Partei* (DP), and the Zentrum) Adenauer could muster 235 votes for a right-wing coalition. He was indeed voted into power on 15 December with the smallest of margins (his own vote: 202 out of 404). Against the advocates of a grand coalition within his own party he argued that an overall majority of the electorate had had enough of controls and shortages and had opted for a free market economy. The first cabinet, still small in comparison with later governments, consisted of a coalition of the CDU/CSU, the FDP, and the DP, who supplied the Minister of Transport, Hans-Christoph Seebohm (1949–66). Part of the deal was that Theodor Heuss, chairman of the Liberals, would become the first President of the Republic. The genial Swabian professor, who exuded a *tranquilitas animi* and a rare sense of humour, proved to be Germany's most popular politician.[11] Of the two grandfathers who ruled the country, he was the more liberal and good-natured. Heuss was elected on 12 September, not by the people as under the Weimar constitution, but by the Bundesversammlung, consisting of the Bundestag and an equal number of Deputies to be elected by *Länder* Diets.

What was to be the official birthday of the Federal Republic? It is highly significant that the date chosen was not the first meeting of the Bundestag (7 September), or the formation of the first government under Adenauer (15 September), but 23 May 1949, when the Basic Law was officially and ceremonially promulgated. The Basic Law was to be the Magna Carta of modern Germany, which would help to overcome the feeling of insecurity and helplessness of its citizens. In 1949 democracy had not yet taken root and the economic miracle was still a long way off. The *Rechtsstaat*, however, was home-grown and something to be proud of. To live again under the rule of law, extended by a catalogue of human rights and supervised by an independent constitutional court, was for most Germans a great achievement, which reconciled them to the division of their country.

The development of the Soviet Zone into a separate state has been depicted as a reluctant response to the state-building process in the West. However, this in itself was the outcome of failed ambitions. After the war the hard-core emigré Communists had great hopes of turning the whole of Germany into a 'people's democracy', i.e. pursuing an independent path to socialism, another kind of National Socialism, as it were (though this term was, of course, taboo). It was the first of many illusions. Neither their master in Moscow nor the German electorate were inclined to go along with this venture. Stalin did not want a self-possessed German Communist state on his doorstep. For him East Germany was a means to an end, possibly a neutralized Germany, not an end in itself.[12] Nor did the Germans feel like swapping one kind of pseudo-socialism for another, which would again serve as the ideological platform for a one-party state. The German Communists arriving from Moscow misjudged the mood of the people at home. Realizing that they had no popular following they turned to manipulation from above and a constant appeal for national unity, first under the guise of a 'popular front' approach, then in the name of 'democratic centralism'.

As early as November 1946 the steering committee of the SED submitted a draft constitution for a 'German Democratic Republic' which, of course, was meant to cover the whole of Germany. In the end it was only adopted by the *Länder* parliaments of the Soviet Zone. Regional parliaments in the Western zones passed constitutions for their own territorial jurisdiction. The ever-widening gulf between pretensions and realities was the significant feature of the East German state right from the beginning. It is difficult to ascertain at which point the SED abandoned plans for control of the whole country and chose to obstruct the emergence of a West German state. As in Nazi Germany, propaganda and policy were all too often inseparable. Perhaps more can be learned about this from the SED archives which are now accessible. By the time the SED launched the movement towards a People's Congress, in November 1947, it was clearly in support of Soviet intentions to abort the West German state. The invitation to the First Congress suggested as an agenda the formation of a delegation to the London Conference of Foreign Ministers. This group of supposed representatives of the German people, amongst them Walter Ulbricht and Wilhelm Pieck, was meant to back up Molotov's position. When Pieck submitted that the delegation should get a fair hearing by the Foreign Ministers of the West, the conference was adjourned without any agreement on reconvening it. Later, the Second and Third Congresses served as a camouflage for the establishment of a separate East German state. The manipulative character of the procedure was revealing: large numbers (2,000 and more) of political appointees, who were prepared to follow the party line, rather than democratically elected delegates. They were hand-picked from political parties and mass organizations like the Free German Youth (FDJ) and the Free German Trade Unions (FDGB), with only a comparatively small number of delegates from the Western zones (20 per cent or fewer). The potential for corruption inherent in any language was fully exploited: the use of 'democratic', 'free', 'German', etc. was as common as it was fraudulent. When the chairmen of the Eastern CDU, Jakob Kaiser and Ernst Lemmer, refused to countenance the People's Congress they were, under pressure from SMAD, replaced by the more co-operative Otto Luschke and Georg Dertinger.

In spite of the SED's poor showing in the West a Second Congress for 'unity and a just peace' was convened, which claimed to be representative of the German people and was again carefully orchestrated by the SED. A 'People's Soviet' (*Volksrat*) consisting of 400 members was constituted, which was to be in session between Congress meetings. Evidently the Volksrat was the counterpart of the much smaller but more competent and democratically elected Parliamentary Council in the West. As a constitutional assembly it was large enough to be turned into the first East German parliament without the inconvenience of free elections. On 11 May 1949 the Volksrat approved the draft constitution for the German Democratic Republic, worked out by a committee under the chairmanship of Otto Grotewohl, the leader of the emasculated Eastern

SPD. According to its phraseology, the constitution appeared to be as democratic as any in the West, including a catalogue of basic and human rights, except for the fact that there was no provision for a legitimate opposition or an independent judiciary. One omnibus article against slander (*Boykotthetze*) gave the government the power to harass and persecute all those who opposed what amounted to one-party rule in the guise of permanent coalition government.

The Third People's Congress in May 1949 coincided with the promulgation of the Basic Law in the West. The points were now set for the two lines to separate altogether. The election was a farce because there was no chance to vote for individual parties and candidates. The only option was a block vote for pre-selected candidates from various parties and mass organizations such as the 'Democratic Women's Federation' and the 'Cultural Federation for the Democratic Reconstruction of Germany', all creatures of the SED. The voter had to agree or disagree with the statement: 'I am in favour of German unity and a just peace. Therefore I vote for the following candidates'.[13] Altogether 66 per cent of the voters made their mark as expected. This was a more credible result, especially in view of the many abstentions, than later elections, where the supposed proportion was 99 per cent. A quarter of the Deputies (528 out of 1,969) were recruited from the Western zones with the help of the KPD. The Congress confirmed the new constitution—confirmation and acclamation were the standard procedures—and elected the 'Second German Soviet', which had no delegates from the Western zones. On 7 October its 400 Deputies were transformed into the 'Provisional People's Chamber of the German Democratic Republic'. Wilhelm Pieck became the first President of the new German state and Otto Grotewohl, the convert from the SPD, the first Prime Minister. Congratulations from Comrade Stalin, referring several times to the unitary, democratic, independent, peace-loving Germany which had been created, put the final seal on the birth of yet another German state.[14]

The whole procedure for setting up a puppet regime in the East was so farcical and phoney that today it is hard to believe that political leaders in the West were in such deadly fear of a Communist takeover of the whole of Germany. Maybe too many were reminded of the Nazi seizure of power and believed that Germany had paid too dearly for underestimating the dangers ahead. Others no doubt were afraid of the intimidating practices of SMAD backed by the Red Army. Others again, like Adenauer, did not have much confidence in the political wisdom of the German people, whom they felt might fall for empty promises of national reconciliation and reunification.

In the following years, while the Federal Republic increased its scope for action by a process of incremental improvement, the GDR was subjected to a Stalinist regime imposed by the SED. The SED revealed its true nature in the same measure as all attempts to block the West German state had proved futile. First the popular-front approach was abandoned; then the claim to a specifically German road to socialism was dismissed as 'social democratic aberration'. No doubt Tito's independent stand *vis-à-vis* Moscow played an important role. In August 1949 Yugoslavia was officially branded as an 'enemy of the Soviet Union', just because Tito pursued an independent foreign policy, seeking a *rapprochement* with the West. Everywhere Titoism was to be exterminated, by way of highly publicized show trials against its real or alleged adherents, in Poland (Gomulka), Czechoslovakia (Slansky), and Hungary (Rajk). The pattern was too clear to be lost on the SED, the assiduous follower of the satellite parties. In 1951–2 more than 150,000 Party members were dismissed as agents of the 'Schumacher circles', i.e. closet Social Democrats. State, society, and the economy were remodelled under the direction of the SED, who now openly took on the mantle of Marxism-Leninism and pretended to be the avant-garde of the working class, 'the highest form of class organization of the proletariat'. The rituals of the Party bordered on the ridiculous. Was the membership card, 'the most precious thing a man can own in his life', to be carried in a satchel around the neck or fastened to the underwear?[15] These and other such topics were debated in earnest.

At the First Party Conference of 28 January 1949 the principle of 'democratic centralism' was officially adopted and meant that every twist and turn of official policy, all measures of any significance, had to be approved by the Politbüro, the highest organ of the Party machine. Naturally, the Party had an interest in extending its hold on the economy by nationalizing more and more assets. Thus a vicious circle was set in motion: the forced pace to 'socialism' depressed the economy, which resulted in a massive exodus of the population to the West (447,000 from January 1951 to April 1953).

This in turn persuaded the Party to tighten its grip on the population for fear of losing control, which then made things worse. All means of coercion were systematically expanded and strengthened: the political bias of the judiciary; the extension of the 'Kasernierte Volkspolizei' (standing police force, i.e. in barracks) to 50,000 in 1951; the setting up of a Ministry of State Security (8 February 1950) with a countrywide surveillance system, which was to become the most distinctive feature of the German Democratic Republic in the decades to come. In 1952 the five *Länder* were replaced by fourteen new districts, and thus the last vestiges of federalism were removed. The idea was to fuse Party and state into one and the same control machinery. The Party boss of the district (*Sekretär des Rates*) was the most powerful local chief in all Party as well as administrative matters.

This process went on beyond Stalin's death (March 1953) until the fuse finally blew and the people rose up against their oppressors on 17 June 1953. After that the Party relented somewhat and switched back to the familiar propaganda tune of national unity and the need for a peace treaty.

The uprising of 17 June 1953 was the most traumatic event in the history of the GDR. Like the Wall erected in 1961, it came to symbolize the division of Germany: the West Germans enjoyed a public holiday, while the East Germans were reminded that their first attempt at self-determination was brutally suppressed by Russian tanks. The historiography is also revealing. According to the SED version, the uprising was a counter-revolution instigated by Western agents; its treatment by West German historians reflects the transition from Cold War to détente.[16] Thus the *Volksaufstand* (people's uprising) of the mid-1950s was relegated to a mere *Arbeiteraufstand* (workers' uprising) and the intervention of the Red Army was interpreted as responsible and restrained, given that 'only twenty-one' people were killed. Up to the present day there is no consensus among West German historians as to how many people actually were killed and whether the appearance of Russian tanks was the decisive turning-point.

The immediate causes are well known: in order to cope with an economy fast deteriorating as a result of enforced collectivization of farms and nationalization of private enterprises, the SED raised productivity targets by 10 per cent: in other words, demanded more work for the same pay. However, following Stalin's death, the new Soviet leadership favoured a more lenient approach in the East German buffer state, popular with the peasants, small businessmen, and artisans. The SED bosses dutifully adopted the new course, which was in flagrant contradiction of their previous policies and thus exposed the Party as the puppet of a foreign power. However, when it transpired that this more relaxed attitude did not apply to the new production targets and that they were not, after all, to be lifted, the workers rose up in protest, led by the builders constructing the Stalin Allee, the would-be showpiece of East Berlin. On 16 and 17 June strikes and unrest spread throughout East Germany and soon developed their own momentum. When, by 2 p.m. on 17 June, the cabinet relented and reduced the production targets the masses in Berlin and elsewhere raised the stakes and demanded free and secret elections, price reductions, free trade unions, and no persecution of the strike leaders. Some of their slogans were too much for the Party leaders, who took refuge in the Red Army headquarters: '*Wir wollen Freiheit, Recht und Brot, sonst schlagen wir die Bonzen tot*' ('We want freedom, rights, and bread, or else we'll strike the bosses dead').[17]

Two young East German historians, Armin Mitter and Stefan Wolle,[18] who have been thoroughly researching this sorry chapter of their history since the archives were opened, come to the conclusion that the events leading up to 17 June amounted, to all intents and purposes, to a 'people's uprising', even though workers were in the forefront of events. They think it is misleading to focus attention on the events of 16 and 17 June while ignoring the overall picture: the desertion of collectivized farms and the mass exodus of professionals and skilled workers, the general unrest since the regime had closed the border with the West by installing a five-kilometre-wide exclusion zone from which all unreliable people were deported in the most brutal fashion. In May 1952 the border was sealed off so that Berlin remained the only escape route until this gap was also closed in August 1961. In 1957 westward migration was denounced as *Republikflucht,* a crime punishable by up to three years in prison. In a letter to Otto Grotewohl, the Prime Minister, the German Protestant Church took up these grievances: 'Things must be in a really bad way if the peasant is prepared to leave his home and land and the tradesman his workshop to face an uncertain future.' According to Mitter and Wolle, the general situation in February 1953, brought about by enforced nationalization, resembled an 'overheated, uncontrollable steam engine smashing everything in its way and ready to explode at any time'. Their casualty figures for 17 June are also remarkably different from those in previous West German accounts: fifty killed in clashes with the Soviet occupation and German police forces; twenty demonstrators summarily executed by the Russians, along with at least forty Russian soldiers who refused to raise their arms against the demonstrating masses; three SED functionaries killed. All in all, more than 500,000 people demonstrated in over 350 places in an attempt to bring the Communist regime down. 'Without the intervention of Soviet troops', they conclude, 'the GDR would have collapsed in June 1953 within a few days.' This is the reason for the widespread purges afterwards, the eagerness of the SED to extinguish all memories, and the embarrassment of West Germans who looked on helplessly, agonized, and then resorted to the politics of symbolism, of official rather than personal remembrance. Among those purged were two prominent SED functionaries—Rudolf Herrnstadt, the editor of the Party paper *Neues Deutschland*, and Wilhelm Zaisser, head of the Ministry of State Security—for conspiring to get rid of Ulbricht with the help of Moscow, not because they sided with the demonstrators. After the rising, the Soviet leadership saw no alternative but to back Ulbricht.

3 From Cold War to Détente

Looking back, it seems that German post-war foreign policy has been straightforward, predictable, and on the whole remarkably successful, in sharp contrast to the path chosen in the first half of the century. Reunification in 1990 was the reward for forty years of patient efforts, for never forcing the issue as in the 1930s. The secret is encapsulated in the phrase *Politik der kleinen Schritte*, i.e. being content with small steps in the right direction, never going it alone or resorting to power politics. Right from the start the signposts were there for all to see: sovereignty for the Federal Republic, German unification, and European integration. The only controversy was over the ways and means of achieving these goals, and in what order. For the first decade the SPD opposed Western integration because it appeared to reduce the chances of German reunification. In retrospect, the inherent logic of Adenauer's priorities seems undeniable. First independence and room for manœuvre had to be achieved, by anchoring Germany safely in the Western community. Only then could the country be opened up to the East and progress be made towards détente and unification.

While the first stage towards independence in 1955 was fairly swift, the second stretch of the road was long and winding. The final destination was only reached after an unexpected final twist. The whole experience was that of a long, exhausting, and apparently never-ending journey, which imprinted itself on the collective consciousness. The lesson is unlikely ever to be lost on the Germans: they learned that war does not pay—one of the Allies' main war aims—and that success comes through patience and steadfastness. The lessons learned after 1871 about the decisiveness of military power were totally different and are now in disrepute.

For Europe the founding of the Federal Republic was a low-key event which did not attract much publicity. It also suited the mood of the German politicians, for whom the emergence of a separate state was no great cause for celebration. On the face of it, all that had occurred was a transfer from Military Government to a limited form of self-government. All laws and major decisions, both at federal

and regional level, still required the assent of the High Commissioners, who, moreover, represented Germany abroad. Nor was
Germany in control of her own economy. Despite growing unemployment, industrial plants continued to be dismantled, particularly in the former British Zone, and the future of the Ruhr area
looked uncertain. Yet it was this very situation which enabled
Adenauer to consolidate his position, to the extent that the regime
he was to establish become known as the *Kanzlerdemokratie* (Chancellor's democracy). Adenauer was the only legitimate spokesman
for Germany in dealing with the Western Allies and he used this
monopoly to dominate foreign policy throughout his period in
office. Out of weakness grew strength. The old Chancellor laid the
foundations of a state that was as solid and bland as most of the
public and private buildings constructed during his time. His mentality and political outlook were to shape the new republic: West
European, conservative, Catholic, anti-Prussian, and anti-Socialist.
As early as 1945 he clearly foresaw the division of Germany as a
result of the Cold War. He therefore pleaded for a separate West
German state closely integrated into Western Europe, not least to
satisfy French security interests. At the time, such thoughts could
only be revealed in a private letter.[1] Some years later they were to
become his party-political programme.

It has been said that the spire of Cologne Cathedral was the focal
point of Adenauer's political horizon. The Rhineland was part of
Western Europe, Paris closer than Berlin. What is more, he exuded
the autocratic self-assurance of a Roman cardinal. According to one
German author, who learned his trade as an emigré journalist in
Britain, Adenauer got the Germans used to the idea that authority
and democracy were not incompatible and thus reconciled them
to the latter.[2] There can be no doubt that he provided the kind
of safe leadership the Germans badly needed if they were to climb
out of the abyss into which Hitler had led them. Above all, he felt
it his mission to protect the Germans from themselves, from their
penchant for political follies, by tying them as closely as possible
into the West European community of nations. And this he had
to do during his lifetime; otherwise it might be too late. The fundamental agreement between Adenauer and the Allied High Commissioners on security, both as regards the real threat posed by the

Soviet Union and the potential danger within Germany, created the confidence necessary for Germany's position to be improved slowly, step by step. Even though the Germans as a whole could not yet be trusted, Adenauer could because he had no delusions of grandeur. As he explained in his first statement to the Bundestag, the only way to regain freedom was to expand Germany's sphere of authority little by little, in concert with the High Commissioners.[3] The Germans were, he said, by descent and disposition, undoubtedly part of the West European world. The wisdom of Adenauer's policy was founded on its simplicity and his sense of proportion: no risk-taking, no deviation from the straight and narrow. It was exactly the right recipe at a time when there were very few options left.

Adenauer did not hesitate to put his ideas into action. The new government was prepared to sign the Petersberg Agreement with the High Commissioners on 22 November 1949 and thus to accede to the international Ruhr authority which controlled the production and distribution of coal and steel. In return for this concession the Allies cut down and promised soon to suspend the dismantling of industrial plant, which was still going on and, in view of 9 per cent unemployment, was causing increasing resentment among both employers and trade unions. In one of the most heated parliamentary debates that followed, Schumacher denounced Adenauer as a *Kanzler der Allierten*[4] (Chancellor of the Allies), a remark for which he was banned for twenty sessions. The irony is that Schumacher was not so far from the mark. A year later the Foreign Office concluded: 'Adenauer is probably the best Chancellor we can get.'[5] The Petersberg debate was the first of many confrontations between the two main parties on the question of how to regain political equality. The SPD misjudged Germany's position as well as public opinion by insisting on a policy of national intransigence towards the occupying powers. Adenauer instead preferred a conciliatory approach, being content with small but steady improvements. In retrospect, the opposition's attitude proved to be a bonus for the government in as much as it helped Adenauer to extract more concessions from the High Commissioners and to discredit the opposition as the party of permanent negation (*ewige Neinsager*).

Two further developments enhanced Bonn's standing in international affairs: a change of heart in France and the outbreak of

the Korean War. On 9 May the French Foreign Minister Robert
Schuman proposed a joint European management of coal and steel
production, consisting of France, Germany, Italy, and the Benelux
countries, which became known as 'The Six'. This initiative resulted
from a reassessment of French security interests. Since all attempts
at substantially weakening Germany had failed, the second-best
option was control through institutional integration. The danger
of surplus production and cutthroat competition was an additional
factor. Adenauer welcomed Schuman's plan at once and appreciated that it was based on the principle of equality. The proposal
corresponded entirely, as he recalled in his memoirs, with the ideas
he had been advocating for a long time.[6] The political dimension
of this new departure was not lost on the German Chancellor. It
was the first step towards economic integration. For this reason
Schumacher fought the idea with all his waning strength. In one
of his last interviews he stressed the SPD's priorities: the unification
of Germany, as well as the establishment of a new peaceful order,
was more important than any form of integration with other countries.[7] After Schumacher's death the Social Democrats did not cease
to employ this argument, though to no avail and with decreasing
conviction.

On 25 June 1950 North Korean troops crossed the demarcation
line along the 38th parallel. Korea was the only other country
divided into a Communist and a Western democratic half. The ana-
logy with Germany was all too apparent. The situation worsened
considerably with the intervention of Chinese troops. The Truman
Administration, convinced that the Soviet Union was determined
to dominate the whole of Eurasia, quadrupled its defence budget
and began to rearm feverishly. West Germany could be expected
to make a substantial contribution to her own defence. The US
Chiefs of Staff were most outspoken in their demand for German
troops and least bothered about the qualms of Germany's neighbours. France, however, continued to feel threatened more by German rearmament than by what was happening in East Asia. On
26 October, the French Prime Minister René Pleven followed up
an idea first expressed by Churchill in the Council of Europe and
suggested the formation of a European defence force. Again Adenauer went along with the proposal, fully aware that this might even
be a faster lane towards full equality. An independent German army

was never his aim, but here was the chance to change Germany's status from occupation to partnership. Unexpected opposition to rearmament from within the country enhanced his negotiating position *vis-à-vis* the High Commissioners. If he was to persuade the Bundestag to give its blessing to a German army, he had better have something to show for it: a complete revision of the occupation status was called for.

On 26 May 1952 the Foreign Ministers of the three powers met for the first time in Bonn to sign the treaty which replaced the occupation regime. However, the *Deutschlandvertrag* (Germany Treaty), as Adenauer was quick to call it, was only to come into force in conjunction with the treaty regarding the European Defence Community (EDC), signed in Paris a month later. The Allies granted West Germany the powers of a sovereign state, but reserved their rights as regards Germany as a whole, i.e. in the event of reunification, which was laid down as a common goal. To the surprise of the High Commissioners, Adenauer had insisted that a reunited Germany should be 'integrated into the European community', which could then only refer to the European Defence Community.[8] No wonder this turned out to be the most controversial clause in the treaty, because obviously it did not facilitate the unification process. How could the Soviet government's consent be expected if they were to face the whole of Germany in the opposing camp? It was not until March 1953, after passionate debates, that the Federal Parliament ratified both treaties.

The last obstacle to Germany's new status as an accepted partner in the Western Alliance was the diplomatic offensive launched by Stalin on 10 March 1952. Was it Germany's last chance for unification? The consensus among historians, with a few dissenting voices,[9] is that it was but a last attempt at luring West Germany into neutrality and splitting it from the West. The Soviet government's agenda was unacceptable to the Western powers: first a peace treaty, then the creation of a government for the whole of Germany, and finally, free elections. The three Western powers and Adenauer were in total agreement that free elections had to come first. Schumacher implored the Chancellor at least to consider Stalin's advances. Adenauer would have none of it and pressed ahead with concluding negotiations about West Germany's integration into the Western community. From then on suspicions lingered that at heart

Adenauer was not really interested in reunification. All that can be safely said is that he was more anxious to safeguard West Germany's freedom and security as a member of the Western Alliance than to achieve national unity, if both could not be had at the same time and at the same price. Planting Germany firmly in the Western camp was a worthwhile goal in itself, even though for tactical reasons he emphasized its importance as a means towards unification. There can be no doubt that a Germany unified under the conditions prevailing in 1952 would have been a very different proposition from that of 1990. For one thing, the reparations issue to be settled in a peace treaty might well have hampered economic recovery, which more than anything helped to lay the foundations for democracy. The following decades were a crucial period for 'Westernizing' the greater part of Germany for good.

The exchange of notes between the Soviet and the Western governments petered out once the signatures under the treaties incorporating the Federal Republic into the Western Alliance had created a new situation. The thread was then taken up by the Conference of Foreign Ministers suggested by Churchill in early 1954, in Berlin, with inconclusive results.

With the sudden death of Stalin in March 1953 and the end of the Korean War in June, the international climate improved considerably. The uprising in East Germany (17 June 1953), moreover, exposed the weakness of Soviet domination in Eastern Europe. And the Federal Republic had not, in the meantime, built up a huge army which posed a threat unless tied down in a European framework. Indeed, conscription was not sanctioned by the constitution until March 1954. The need for an integrated European defence force at the expense of national sovereignty seemed to be less urgent now than in 1950. Apart from Britain, which remained outside the new pact anyway, France was most anxious to maintain a high degree of national independence once the threat from the East had dissipated. On 30 August, the Assemblée Nationale rejected the idea of an integrated European army. After all, with NATO joint defence was already in place. The lesson to be learned here is all too obvious: the ratification process of a treaty requiring parliamentary assent must not be allowed to drag on for too long. In August 1954 the first attempt to weld together Western Europe failed. The second run, though, taken within the next twelve months, proved much more successful. On 2 June 1955, the same Six agreed in Messina to expand the coal and steel arrangement (Montan-Union) into a veritable European economic community. At the time, this initiative appeared to be such a poor substitute for the EDC that Whitehall almost completely ignored it.

For Britain, the damage caused by the French refusal seemed to be the more pressing issue. What was to be done with Germany, still waiting patiently for the implementation of her part of the treaty bringing the occupation period to an end? In a sense the Federal Republic was now worse off than the GDR, which had been recognized as a sovereign state by Moscow on 25 March 1954 following the stalemate produced by the Berlin Conference. Adenauer was shattered by the French veto. Since May 1952 West Germany had been in a 'kind of suspended animation'.[10] It was now the British Foreign Secretary Anthony Eden who picked up the pieces and worked out a sensible alternative plan. Adenauer could not have hoped for a better outcome. With Churchill's blessing, Eden invited Germany and Italy to sign the Brussels Treaty of 1948, which would be transformed into a mutual defence pact. Increased British military commitment in Europe was a decisive inducement for France. Since the new pact lacked the supranational features of the EDC, no problems about British military commitment arose. In a series of conferences in London and Paris the details were hammered out. On 29 December 1954 the Assemblée Nationale ratified the Paris Agreements after Washington and London had made it clear that their patience with France was running out fast.

By now the crucial question was not whether Germany would join the defence of the West, but whether her army would unsettle the balance of power. Public opinion in Germany was greatly alarmed at the prospect of rearmament so soon after the war. The Bonn government therefore did not hesitate to agree to restrictions on her new military strength: no ABC (atomic, bacteriological, and chemical) weapons, no large warships, rockets, or bombers. More importantly, the government also promised not to engineer reunification or alteration of borders by force. These premisses of German foreign policy were never questioned by any of the major parties during the following decades. The future of the Saar was another price which Adenauer was prepared to pay in order to appease Paris: a new European state which tied its economy to France provided the population assented in a referendum. However, on 23 October 1955 the voters of the Saar area rejected the agreements, so that there was no alternative but a return to Germany on 1 January 1957.[11] The constitutional process of reintegrating the Saar was later to serve as a precedent for the incorporation of East Germany's new *Länder*.

On 5 May 1955 the Federal Republic entered the stage of European and international politics as a sovereign state. To mark the event a fairly low-key ceremony was held in which the new flag was hoisted in the Chancellery garden. There was no reason to feel triumphant. Germany was divided as never before and its capital remained under the control of the victorious powers, who had also reserved their rights over Germany as a whole in the event that such an entity ever re-emerged in the future.

Only four days later, ten years after unconditional surrender, the Federal Republic joined NATO as its fifteenth member. The SPD had opposed this development right from the beginning, arguing that the policies of rearmament and reunification were mutually incompatible. Its leader, Erich Ollenhauer, implored the Chancellor in January 1955 to give unification a last chance and to test the final Soviet offer of 'free elections'. Adenauer's reply shows that he was, unlike the opposition, fully aware of Germany's precarious international position and very limited scope for independent action as a result of losing the war. Only with the backing of all four powers, not just the Soviet Union, and only as part of the Western Alliance could Germany hope both to achieve unification and preserve its freedom. This is what he meant by *Politik der Stärke* (policy of strength): not power politics of the old kind, as has been insinuated by his opponents, but diplomacy carried out on the basis of safety first. Everything the Soviet government had suggested in recent days and weeks, he explained to Ollenhauer, could be negotiated as well, once the Paris Treaties were ratified.[12] The absolute majority which he achieved in the 1957 election was ample proof that the West Germans went along with his cautious approach and approved of the slogan *Keine Experimente* (no experiments). Another read *Einheit in Freiheit*, which really meant 'No unity if freedom and prosperity were at risk.' This may not have been a very generous attitude towards the East Germans, who were left to fend for themselves, but it is hard to imagine any other realistic option open to the fledgling Federal Republic at the time.

Once West Germany was secured within the Western Alliance, the first tentative steps towards the Soviet Union were undertaken. In the summer of 1955 Adenauer accepted an invitation to visit Moscow, much to the surprise and indignation of the United States. The German Chancellor was certainly not a puppet in the hands of the Western Allies. He also wished to convince both the German public and the Soviet leadership that he had not abandoned the quest for unity. However, the Soviet government was only interested in international recognition of the new state of affairs. Adenauer was unable to extract any concession except the Soviet pledge to release the last prisoners of war in return for his consent to establishing diplomatic relations. In the eyes of the public this was one of his greatest triumphs, but the experts were less optimistic and one commentator wrote that the freedom of the 10,000 had been bought with the continued servitude of 17 million. The policy of short-term gains paid handsomely in the election and was in tune with the feelings of the West German population. Yet it is important to note that in those years between Stalin's diplomatic initiative of 1952 and Adenauer's visit to Moscow, one idea took root. The 'key to the German question', as it was then put, lay in Moscow.

Right from the point of departure in 1955, German foreign policy got stuck. Its main goal, German unification as enshrined in the preamble of the Basic Law, appeared to be unattainable. Although the Western powers pledged support for these aspirations they had their own reasons for coming to terms with the Soviet Union under Khrushchev. With the Geneva summit in June 1955 hopes for a new era of détente were raised. In the following years various plans for disengagement were discussed, such as the Rapacky Plan to create a nuclear-free zone at the time when the German forces on both sides of the Iron Curtain were being built up. Adenauer became increasingly paranoid about the possibility of an understanding between the superpowers over Germany's head. He was not so far off the mark. Recent research still to be published shows that Macmillan was ready to defuse the second Berlin crisis by strategic withdrawal. Adenauer insisted that the Federal Republic was the only true representative of the German people and that a solution to the German problem was a necessary precondition of détente and not vice versa. The GDR was illegitimate and to be shunned by the international community. The first test of the so-called Hallstein Doctrine—West Germany's right to sole representation[13]—came when Tito recognized the East German regime in 1957. Bonn severed diplomatic relations with Belgrade and let it be known that it would not entertain diplomatic relations with any government which exchanged ambassadors with Pankow, the domicile of the East German leadership. The Soviet government was the only exception, as one of the four powers responsible for Germany as a whole. At the same time Bonn demanded atomic weapons for German NATO forces under US control. Adenauer did not wish to be left in no man's land when the Alliance switched its strategy to nuclear deterrents. All this was bound to entrench the division of Germany, especially when the East German regime began to fortify its border against the West along the zonal demarcation line. In March 1958, unknown to the public, Adenauer tried to break the stalemate by proposing an 'Austrian solution' for the GDR: neutrality for the Eastern, though not the Western, part of Germany. It seems that Adenauer was thinking of a contractual renunciation of national unification in exchange for civil rights and political freedoms for the East German population, which in his view was more important. He added that if this proposal were to leak out, he would be stoned by his fellow countrymen.[14] However, Adenauer met with no response from the Kremlin. In 1958 Khrushchev, intent on consolidating the Soviet position in post-war Europe, issued an ultimatum regarding the future status of Berlin. Berlin was the most potent symbol of a united Germany. While the Western powers were determined not to be kicked out of the former German capital, they too had no interest in changing the *status quo* since it could only be to their disadvantage in view of the strategic situation. In de Gaulle, the new French President, Adenauer found an ally for a policy of standing firm, especially after the death of John Foster Dulles, the United States Foreign Secretary and friend of the Chancellor.

With the arrival of the new US President John F. Kennedy the German question was finally pushed off the international agenda. The main aim now was to save West Berlin, not to reunite Germany, which seemed to be completely out of reach. When Khrushchev met the new President in Vienna in early June 1961 he renewed his threat to Berlin, announcing his intention to conclude a separate peace treaty with the GDR and suspending unilaterally Soviet rights in Berlin. Kennedy responded with a tough speech leaving no doubt that any infringement of Western rights in West Berlin amounted to a *casus belli*. Soon the NATO Council defined the three 'essentials' which the West was determined to defend: the presence of Western troops in West Berlin; unimpeded access; and the economic lifeline connecting West Berlin with the Federal Republic. This was a clear signal that the future of East Berlin was a different matter. In the meantime the number of refugees fleeing from the East through Berlin, the only gate left open, had swollen to such an extent (16,000 in early August; 160,000 since 1 January 1961) that the very existence of the GDR was threatened.

On 30 July 1961 Senator William Fulbright, a close confidant of the President, wondered publicly why the East Germans were not sealing their border in Berlin, because he thought 'they have a right to close it.'[15] The time-bomb which had been ticking for four years, the Berlin Crisis, exploded, though in a controlled fashion, when, in the early hours of 13 August, the East German regime hastily erected a wall round West Berlin, actually intended to imprison its own population.[16] Since it was a desperate measure, the West condoned the violation of the Four Power status of Berlin. At least West Berlin was now safe for the time being. The Wall became the most conspicuous monument of the Cold War and of the failure of socialism. However, it gave a new lease of life to the GDR, which otherwise might have collapsed 28 years earlier than it did. Bonn's road to unification had reached a dead end too. From now on the GDR could no longer be ignored. The Wall also marked the end of Adenauer's career: he did not rush to Berlin as was expected of him, but continued the election campaign as though nothing had happened. He lost his majority that day and was soon on his way out. Only three days later, on 16 August, he assured the Soviet Ambassador that the government had no interest in worsening relations with Moscow.

It was Willy Brandt, the Governing Mayor of West Berlin, who rose to the occasion and began to practise his concept of *Ostpolitik* by improving relations between the two halves of the city in a pragmatic way. The division of the city caused personal hardship on a hitherto unprecedented scale. A protocol of 17 September 1963 governing the issue of passes for West Berliners was the first small step in the right direction. Détente in Germany started in the citadel of the Cold War. In no small measure the credibility of this new approach was due to the previous conversion of the SPD to the social market policy (the abandonment of Marxism at the Party Congress in Bad Godesberg in 1959) and to the late acceptance of the Western Alliance. Through a long learning process the SPD had made its peace with post-war realities. In this respect the party was about to outdo the Conservatives, who clung to the doctrines of the Cold War.

During the last years of his tenure, Adenauer turned more and more to de Gaulle for comfort and support, after the latter had emerged as President of France in 1958.[17] He did not necessarily share de Gaulle's vision of a *Europe des patries*, nor did he wish to build up Europe as a third world power and counterweight against the United States. But he firmly believed in reconciliation and close co-operation with France as the nucleus of the European Economic Community, which had come into being with the Treaty of Rome (1957). Relations with France grew more intimate while the demands by Britain and the United States for a more flexible approach threatened to isolate West Germany as the last pocket of the Cold War. De Gaulle's visit to Germany in 1962 and his proposal for a Franco-German union coincided with low tide in German relations with Washington. Adenauer regarded the Franco-German Treaty of 22 January 1963 as the crowning glory of his political career. *Rapprochement* between the two countries was transformed into a special Franco-German relationship covering foreign policy, security, and culture. Regular consultations between the two governments were firmly agreed upon. However, when the treaty was up for ratification, the Bundestag insisted on the inclusion of a preamble which stressed the continued importance of the Western Alliance and thus undermined any designs de Gaulle might have had to disengage Germany from the Atlantic community. At no time was there any doubt amongst the German political class that American protection was absolutely essential for the security of the Federal Republic. De Gaulle's *force de frappe* was never considered to be a viable alternative to the nuclear umbrella provided by NATO.

Since the SPD had joined the ranks of the 'Atlantic lobby' around Foreign Minister Gerhard Schröder and Ludwig Erhard, the economic miracle-worker, ultimate reliance on the United States took on the character of a new orthodoxy. Two motives were now prevalent: (1) anxiety about the new American strategy of flexible response, advocated by Kennedy and his Secretary of Defence Robert McNamara, who demanded more German troops but refused to supply them with nuclear weapons, and (2) the realization, especially on the part of the SPD, that progress towards peaceful change was only feasible on the basis of détente, and that the latter would only work if closely co-ordinated with Washington. Worries about military strategy were not to trouble relations for very long. The plan for a 'Multilateral Force' (MLF) within NATO remained an episode. In the end the United States government was not prepared to share its nuclear responsibility with its allies.

The stage was already set before Adenauer's resignation on 15 October 1963. Foreign Minister Schröder was given more latitude by the new Chancellor, Ludwig Erhard. His main contribution was to open up West Germany towards Eastern Europe by establishing trade, though not yet diplomatic relations, with all of Moscow's major satellite states. He supported Britain's entry into the EEC and was careful not to antagonize the United States. 'In the last resort our whole foreign policy', he said, 'is aiming at reunification.'[18] On this front he did not achieve any significant breakthrough. However, public opinion did become more flexible, thus preparing the ground for Bonn's new departure. For instance, both churches advocated recognition of the Oder–Neiße border and reconciliation with Poland.

The transition to a new *Ostpolitik* was a slow one and required a softening of attitudes on both sides. Adenauer had not been as intransigent as his public utterances suggest. Behind the scenes he was prepared to recognize the GDR and to put Berlin under UN protection as Khrushchev had demanded, provided free elections were granted after five years (Globke Plan).[19] He also proposed putting a stop to the propaganda war between Moscow and Bonn. However, his initiative met with no response from the Soviet leadership. When Brandt became Foreign Minister in the grand coalition of autumn 1966, there was no sudden change of gear. The new government under Kurt-Georg Kiesinger tried to catch up with the policy of détente as advocated by the Western capitals. The maintenance of peace under difficult circumstances was now understood to be the first priority. What certainly changed above all was the rhetoric. One of the favourite slogans of the time was 'peaceful co-existence'. The previous position of the Bonn government had been: détente, yes, but not until the cause of tension, i.e. the division of Germany, had been removed. This egocentric view was now dropped in favour of the assumption that recognizing the *status quo* was the best way to overcome it. Brandt was more modest still: the goal of overcoming the division ought to be replaced by a policy of reducing the burden.

However, reality still differed markedly from rhetoric. When Czechoslovakia dared to liberalize its system unilaterally, the country faced a brutal reminder of the fact that it lay within the Soviet orbit. After the Wall, this was another dead end. There was no way around Moscow. Nor was it possible to circumvent the GDR. The occupation of Prague by Warsaw Pact troops, including East German troops, amounted to a ghastly set-back, but remarkably not to a reversal of détente.

The new and eventually successful *Ostpolitik* was due to a breakthrough on two political fronts in the West: the recognition of the post-war state of affairs, i.e. states and frontiers, by the new Lib-Lab government of Willy Brandt and Walter Scheel formed after the election of 28 September 1969 and, at about the same time, the acceptance of the *status quo* in Asia by the new US President Richard Nixon, who sought a *rapprochement* with China. On the face of it these were, in both instances, concessions by the West which, in their cumulative effect, led to a globalization of détente. The new understanding between Washington and Peking forced the Soviet Union to come to terms with the Western powers in Europe and to be reassured of peaceful co-existence on its Western flank. In the long run, the new sense of overall security had a much greater impact on the closed societies behind the Iron Curtain than on the open ones in the West, who felt nothing but insecurity at the buildup of armaments and the ensuing risk of nuclear war.

The Germans were generally aware of their contribution to this process, but not sufficiently of the part played by the United States, who under the guidance of Henry Kissinger skilfully co-ordinated its *Ost-* and *Westpolitik*. For the 'progressive' supporters of the Brandt–

Scheel government the image of the United States was too tarnished
because of Vietnam, racial unrest, and Watergate for them to
appreciate the benefits accruing from Washington's *Realpolitik*.
However, the inner core of Brandt's advisers, notably Egon Bahr,
were aware that the responsibilities of the Four Powers, above all
of the United States, for Berlin and for Germany constituted the
crucial cornerstone of their endeavours to achieve détente. This was
not at all obvious from the beginning to Kissinger, the President's
Security Adviser, who feared that the German Left might be wooed
into neutralism in order to further the chances of unification.
While foreign journalists were worried about the New Right emerging in Germany, government officials were more disturbed about
the pacifist and neutralist ideas of respectable politicians on the
Left, such as Gustav Heinemann, the new President of the Federal
Republic. Some American officials with close ties to the CDU, such
as Clay, Acheson, and McCloy, continued to be on their guard.[20]
Nixon and his new administration, after thorough briefing from
Bonn, were assured that the new German government was on the
right track. The background to the new departure was the old position of the Grand Coalition: co-operation in Berlin between the
two German states, in order to improve human relations and maintain the substance of the nation, but no *de jure* recognition of the
GDR as a separate state; no violation of existing borders in the
East, but no formal recognition either.

As always, the test case turned out to be Berlin, where, under
Willy Brandt and his press spokesman Bahr, the *Politik der kleinen
Schritte* (policy of small steps) and *Wandel durch Annäherung* (change
through *rapprochement*) had first been put into practice. A mini-
crisis about West Berlin had broken out in February 1969 because
of Bonn's determination to hold Presidential elections in the old
capital. Ulbricht threatened to withhold passes for Berliners to visit
relations in the East of the city. Nixon suspended the SALT talks,
flew to West Berlin, and fully supported Bonn's stand. William E.
Griffiths, the most renowned expert on *Ostpolitik*, stresses the interdependence of what occurred on both fronts of the Soviet empire.
On 2 March 1969 the Soviets threatened the flights to West Berlin
carrying the West German electors for the Presidency, while, on
the same day, news of a serious clash of troops along the Sino–
Soviet Ussuri border reached Moscow. 'On the following day the

flights occurred without incident, as did the Presidential elections, a fact hardly unrelated to the Ussuri incident.'[21] Future harassment of West Berlin, however, could not be ruled out. No wonder that when Willy Brandt, Governing Mayor of West Berlin, became the Federal Republic's first Social Democratic Chancellor in the same year, the security of West Berlin moved to the top of the agenda. Nor is it surprising that he addressed himself to Brezhnev, the Soviet leader, not to Ulbricht, his East German vassal. The overall climate was important too. Of course Moscow was pleased that Gustav Heinemann, the candidate of the left for President, triumphed over the National-Conservative Gerhard Schröder; that Brandt, the former emigré and approved anti-Nazi, succeeded Kiesinger, who had once worked for Goebbels' world radio service, as Chancellor; and above all, that the new government lost no time in signing the Non-Proliferation Treaty, thus confirming previous pledges to stay away from the nuclear club. This time it really looked as though the Germans were finally prepared to accept the post-war world as it was and had no further plans to redraw the map of Europe. This change of heart would allow the Russians to lift their guard and pay more attention to their Eastern front. Another, more openly admitted, interest of Moscow was increased economic co-operation with Germany. Without Western technology and credit the Soviet Union could not hope to exploit her natural resources and raise the living standard of her deprived population. A third motive might have been the hope, raised by the left-wing clientele of the new governing party, of weakening German ties with the United States and moving the Federal Republic into a more neutralist position.

The United States was chiefly interested in a new Berlin agreement—after all, this was the Achilles heel of the West—and mutual force reductions. Washington hoped to silence the voices of those, like Senator Mansfield, who favoured a unilateral withdrawal from Europe. These apparently isolationist tendencies alarmed the Germans and this is one explanation for their desire to negotiate non-aggression treaties with the East.

The motives of Brandt and Bahr for embarking on *Ostpolitik* were politically more controversial and more in evidence: (1) *de facto* recognition of the GDR's existence, but with the proviso that it was not a foreign country and that relations were of a special nature; (2) recognition of the Oder–Neiße border, with the reservation of a

final peace settlement concluded with a united Germany; (3) confirmation that the Munich Agreement of 1938 was invalid, though
Bonn did not accept that this had been the case all along. The
price the Soviet Union had to pay for German acceptance of post-
war realities was the treaty safeguarding Western rights in Berlin,
i.e. free access to West Berlin, and a strengthening of ties between
the Federal Republic and West Berlin. After all, the second Berlin
Crisis of 1958 came about because Khrushchev threatened to hand
over transit controls to the GDR. Now that the latter would be
officially recognized, harassment had to stop for good.

The series of treaties and agreements which were to follow was
closely connected by various linkages (*Junktims*). All in all it was
one of the great diplomatic achievements of this century, which
will be studied by diplomats for some time to come. The centre-
piece was the treaty between Bonn and Moscow, primarily negotiated by Bahr on the German side, and signed on 12 August 1970.
In Article 3, the contracting parties undertook 'to respect without
restriction the territorial integrity of all States in Europe within
their present frontiers'.[22] And this is then specified to include 'the
Oder–Neiße line, which forms the Western border of the People's
Republic of Poland, the frontier between the Federal Republic and
the German Democratic Republic'. Two aspects were important.
The Soviet Union was made to understand that the rights of the
Four Powers were not to be affected by this treaty. Moreover, Foreign Minister Scheel handed over a letter on the occasion of signing the treaty stating that the latter 'does not conflict with the
political objective of the Federal Republic of Germany to work for
a state of peace in Europe in which the German nation will recover
its unity in free self-determination'.[23] The ultimate motive for German *Ostpolitik* could not be put more succinctly. The letter was
crucial if the treaty was to be ratified by the Federal Parliament some
time in the future. Ratification was the only leverage for a quadripartite agreement on Berlin, which Moscow was most reluctant to
grant in view of fierce opposition from Ulbricht. The demonstrably
free and enticing city of West Berlin was the thorn in the flesh of
the first German socialist state. Ulbricht insisted on *de jure* recognition of the GDR and a Berlin Agreement to be negotiated between East Berlin and Bonn on his terms. With the arrival of Brandt,
Soviet and East German interests began to diverge. For the Soviet

Union overall stability on the Western front was of overriding importance, whereas the SED regime was in constant fear of destabilization through increased contacts with its prosperous neighbour. In the end the East German leader proved to be too inflexible and was replaced by Erich Honecker.[24] At the same time relations between the three Western powers and the Federal Republic grew more intimate over the Berlin question since it was their ambassadors who negotiated on Bonn's behalf, in one of the few remaining Four Power venues, the Allied air-control centre in West Berlin. The common goal was a Soviet guarantee of Western, notably West German, access to the city that would make it impossible in the future for the SED regime to precipitate another Berlin crisis. Negotiations amongst the Four only began in earnest after the Soviet government realized that the Moscow Treaty would not be ratified by the Bundestag without a solution for West Berlin. The Brandt government's majority was a slim one. This time the Soviet and the GDR governments were expected to recognize the existing realities in West Berlin, i.e. the *de facto* incorporation of the city into the Federal Republic.

The real bone of contention was the legal position: insistence on the Four Power status of the whole of the city versus the Soviet claim that they were only talking about West Berlin and that it was up to the GDR to control access. The way out of this dilemma was twofold: the formula finally adopted referred to the 'relevant area', neither to 'West Berlin' (the Soviet view) nor to 'Berlin' (the Western view). The Agreement[25] contained four annexes referring (A) to transit traffic by road, rail, and waterways (but not by air), (B) to 'the ties between Western Sectors of Berlin and the Federal Republic of Germany' to be 'maintained and developed', (C) to 'communication between the Western Sectors of Berlin and areas bordering on these Sectors' (i.e. East Berlin and the GDR), and (D) to 'representation abroad of the interests of the Western Sectors of Berlin' by Bonn. Both to appease the East German regime and to tie its hands, details were worked out between the respective East and West German and West Berlin authorities, between September and December 1971, before the final quadripartite protocol was signed on 3 June 1972. The delay was due to the problems which all the *Ostverträge* encountered in Bonn. The Bundestag would not ratify them unless West Berlin was safe and Moscow would not give its final stamp of approval to the Berlin Agreement until Bonn had renounced all previous claims in Eastern Europe. The crucial concessions *vis-à-vis* Poland and Czechoslovakia had already been made in the Moscow Treaty before they were elaborated on in the treaties between Bonn and Warsaw, signed on 7 December 1970, and between Bonn and Prague, signed on 11 December 1973. In these treaties reference was made to 'the principles embodied in the United Nations Charter' and the inviolability of existing frontiers, more specifically the Oder–Neiße border, as agreed in Potsdam on 2 August 1945 and the Munich Agreement of 29 September 1939, which was declared to be 'void' (Article 1).[26] What was important in the case of the former Sudetenland was that the treaty should not affect the situation of any natural or legal person between 30 September 1938 and 9 May 1945.

The passage of the treaties with Moscow and Warsaw through the Bundestag was not an easy one since the Lib-Lab coalition had in the meantime lost its majority, particularly in the second chamber. The opposition rejected the treaties in their existing form on the basis that they gave too much away. Nevertheless, the majority of the CDU/CSU abstained in both chambers in the decisive vote of 17 May 1972, thus making ratification possible. The tangible benefits of the Berlin Agreement, which otherwise would not have come about, as well as a common declaration by the Bundestag, were the two inducements which appeased the Conservatives, led by Rainer Barzel. The ten reservations made by Parliament served as a kind of preamble to the treaties: for example, Germany as a whole was not committed; the German right to self-determination, as well as the rights and responsibilities of the Four Powers relating to Germany as a whole, and to Berlin, were not affected; German membership of NATO and the policy of European integration would not be compromised. In other words, the German question was not yet solved, but any future solution could only be a peaceful one. This was the crucial pledge. Altogether, the *Ostverträge* amounted to what Theo Sommer referred to as a 'quasi peace treaty'[27]—not in any legal sense, but as regards their practical political effects.

On the historic occasion of Brandt's visit to Erfurt, the Chancellor had already relinquished the Hallstein Doctrine: 'Neither of us can act for the other, neither can represent the other part of

Germany abroad.'[28] During the follow-up visit of Stoph, the GDR head of state, to Kassel, Brandt proposed twenty points which proved to be the outline of the later agreements and Basic Treaty. The aim was clear: recognition of two German states as the price for maintaining the substance of the nation by fostering exchange on all levels. The idea that there was an all-embracing German *Kulturnation*, as distinct from the mere *Staatsnation*, the current mould of the German *Volk*, was first developed by Friedrich Meinecke,[29] and gained wide acceptance after the First World War, when many Germans found themselves outside the borders of the Reich. This concept would then also cover Austria, much reduced since the collapse of the Habsburg Empire, which had been prevented from joining the Reich by the victorious powers in 1918. The East German leaders, having eagerly appealed to German national feeling in the 1940s and 1950s, when it suited them, now tried to expunge the notion of a common heritage from the new constitution of 1968 and from official rhetoric. The utter confusion about its identity, whether Socialist, German, both, or neither, greatly contributed to the eventual demise of the GDR. Brandt's unscheduled welcome by the population of Erfurt, much to the embarrassment of the leadership, proved, however, that the Germans locked up behind the Wall had not given up hope of one day being united and free. To most of them freedom meant freedom to travel west and, in the end, to be reunited with West Germany. Brandt urged restraint because he was 'afraid of kindling hope that could not be fulfilled'.[30] This cautious attitude, sensible though it was on this occasion, was to colour all West German dealings with the East in the years to come. The fear of another uprising which would quash all hope for peaceful change, as occurred on 17 June 1953, was uppermost in the minds of the West German political elite. East Berlin's only desire was to be recognized without reservation by both the Federal Republic and the Western world. As a result of Bonn's disregard, the East German leadership had developed over the years an acute sense of inferiority, which, as emerged after unification, had engulfed the whole population.

Walter Scheel, the West German Foreign Minister, persuaded Western countries to defer recognition until after the successful conclusion of inter-German negotiations (Scheel Doctrine). Negotiations began in earnest in August 1972, after the transit arrangements as part of the Four Power Agreement on Berlin had removed the last obstacle. The Treaty was initialled on 8 November, eight days before the West German elections, by Egon Bahr for the Federal Republic and Michael Kohl, the chief negotiator for the GDR. Signed on 21 December, it was ratified by the Bundestag on 11 May 1973. The CDU/CSU, apart from a few independent Deputies like Walter Leisler Kiep who defied the whip, opposed the treaty, claiming that more could have been achieved. This is extremely doubtful since the Soviet leaders clearly had every reason to support the SPD in the forthcoming elections. A sticking point in the negotiations had been Bonn's insistence on the special nature of relations between the two German states, which could only be fully separated in law by the four powers responsible for all of Germany. The Four Powers were given, as one expert (Zündorf) explained, the role of judges, to whom it fell to divorce a couple who had already been living separate lives.[31] After pressure from Moscow, East Berlin dropped its demand for *de jure* recognition and no longer insisted on the exchange of ambassadors.

Another issue which was to prove crucial at the time of reunification concerned the question of nationality. The contracting parties agreed to disagree. West German citizenship was defined by the law of 1913 and included all ethnic Germans, whereas the GDR had created its own citizenship in 1968. Up to the very end of the East German state, the Federal Republic's Basic Law automatically granted citizenship to any German from the other half. Bonn never yielded to demands to redefine its citizenship and thereby keep East Germans at bay. Nor would the necessary revision of the constitution have been a feasible proposition. The Four Power framework and the Federal constitution remained a constant reminder that there was a Germany beyond the present state of German affairs.

Apart from the usual references to the principle of the United Nations Charter, the preservation of human rights, peace and international security, etc., the *Grundlagenvertrag*[32] contained two articles which specified the normalization of relations. In Article 4 the Federal Republic finally abandoned its claim to the right of sole representation (*Alleinvertretungsrecht*). It was agreed that 'neither of the Two States can represent the other internationally or act in its name.' The breakthrough to international recognition long coveted

by the East German leadership turned out to be a fatal gift because
it also opened the door the other way, i.e. to what could be dubbed
infiltration by the West, notably West Germany. The two contracting parties stated their 'readiness to regulate practical and humanit-
arian questions in the process of the normalization of their relations'.
A host of notes, protocols, and arrangements followed, covering
'co-operation in the fields of economics, science, and technology,
traffic, judicial relations, post and telecommunications, health, culture, sport, environmental protection, and in other fields'. No doubt
these arrangements had potential benefits for East Germany at a
time when terms of trade within the Comecon had begun to deteri-
orate. For instance, the GDR was the only East European country
with access to the EEC (as a silent partner). The windfall from visiting visas for millions of West Germans, i.e. the minimum amount
of currency to be exchanged, and the ransom for the release of
political prisoners, amounting in total to 3 billion DM, were welcome sources of income. But these and other measures, such as
the fact that goods in the so-called Inter-Shops were only available for Deutschmarks and that only old-age pensioners received
permission to visit the West in large numbers, also had a deeply
demoralizing effect on the population. Not that Western influence
corrupted the East Germans, as many officials and churchmen might
have believed. It was exposure to the West which revealed the corrupt nature of the regime.

The most difficult of these arrangements concerned the Protocol on the Establishment of Permanent Representation (*ständige
Vertretungen*), which took another two years of hard bargaining
(concluded on 14 March 1974). Bonn categorically ruled out an
exchange of ambassadors. Though each Representative, as they were
now called, would be accredited to the other's head of state, Bonn's
envoy, Günter Gaus, would deal with the GDR's Ministry of Foreign Affairs, whereas the East German Michael Kohl was referred
to the Federal Chancellery.

Both German governments were encouraged, if not pressurized
as in the case of the GDR, by their respective superpowers to speed
up negotiations so that they could both take part in the Conference on Security and Cooperation in Europe (CSCE) which, after
preparatory talks, was held in Helsinki between 1973 and 1975. The
aim was a comprehensive security pact which could be interpreted

as an extension of German *Ostpolitik* to the whole of Europe. The GDR's eagerness to join the United Nations and Moscow's intense interest in an overall settlement were used as diplomatic ammunition by the United States to back up the Federal Republic's *Ostpolitik*. If the CSCE process was designed to extract Western recognition of Soviet domination in Eastern Europe and possibly to disengage the United States from Europe, the end result was exactly the opposite. Here, as with German *Ostpolitik*, the cunning of history had its way. The Helsinki Final Act of 1975 was regarded by all of the 35 participating European states as a triumph of détente. What mattered for the Soviet Union was the general agreement that the political and territorial *status quo* of 1945 was inviolable and no obstacle to permanent peace. However, the signatories promised *inter alia* that they would 'also respect each other's rights freely to choose and develop its political, social, economic and cultural systems'.[33] Furthermore they pledged to 'refrain from any form of armed intervention or threat of such intervention against another participating State'. The expectations in the East were completely different from those of the West. For the West intervention, such as the invasion of Czechoslovakia in 1968, was incompatible with the Helsinki Agreement. The Soviet Union wanted to be assured that no intervention from the West would be forthcoming in the event of internal upheavals in the Eastern Bloc. The Soviet Union, as a concession to the West, also agreed to the so-called Basket III, which guaranteed the human rights of citizens throughout Europe. At the time this might have appeared to Soviet leaders to be as meaningless as the Declaration on Liberated Europe signed by Stalin at Yalta. However, times had changed and the democratic movement in Eastern Europe, not least in East Germany, could, and would, refer to a document signed by the Soviet government in the full glare of history. At the very moment when the Soviet empire was recognized by the whole world the seeds for its final destruction were planted.

It had taken West German politicians a long time to realize that détente was bound to work in their favour. But once they had grasped this simple truth they stuck to it with a kind of obstinacy which occasionally irritated their allies. Of those determined to hold on to détente despite all the temporary set-backs, the most active protagonist was the German Foreign Minister, Hans-Dietrich

Genscher, born in Halle, East Germany.[34] He made sure that no change of government, as in 1982, would impede the constant improvement of relations with the East, particularly East Germany. It was a final vindication of *Ostpolitik* that the CDU/CSU, which had rejected the treaties in 1972–3, was as eager to subscribe to the same approach ten years later.

However, the benefits of *Ostpolitik* for the West were not as obvious at the time. On the one hand, inter-German trade doubled and the number of visitors from West Germany and West Berlin to the East of the country rose from 1.1 million in 1969 to 6.3 million in 1976. On the other hand, the SED regime, worried about subversion, intensified its ideological offensive against West Germany. Dissidents were still persecuted and punished and anti-imperialist propaganda remained in full swing. The expulsion of the popular *Liedermacher* (singer and songwriter) Wolf Biermann caused an uproar among East German artists and intellectuals.

More serious, however, were the set-backs to détente on the global level, which persuaded many establishment figures in the West that *Ostpolitik* had foundered altogether. In 1974 the Soviet Union began deploying a new intermediate range of nuclear missiles, code-named SS-20 by NATO and targeted on Western Europe. In December 1979, the Red Army invaded Afghanistan. The Western powers, notably the United States, felt cheated by the Soviet government. While diplomats were negotiating in Helsinki about confidence-building measures, Moscow secretly stepped up the armaments race, hoping to decouple Europe from the United States. NATO accepted the challenge and recommended the installation of Cruise and Pershing II missiles as part of a programme of nuclear-force modernization in Europe. However, that decision could not easily be imposed on a country like West Germany, where public opinion had fully embraced the ethos of *Ostpolitik*. Before Afghanistan the Soviet threat could not be easily demonstrated to ordinary citizens. The logic of deterrence somehow seemed to belong to the Cold War past, which had, so it appeared, been overcome for good. In a way, East Berlin and Bonn found themselves in similar situations *vis-à-vis* their populations: their warnings fell increasingly on deaf ears, especially among the younger generation. The left wing of the ruling Social Democrats were in fundamental disagreement with US security policies. Some of their leaders even justified the Soviet invasion of Afghanistan as a defensive move. In this situation Chancellor Helmut Schmidt persuaded NATO to go along with the so-called 'dual-track' decision: the deployment of the new missiles in Europe soil should be linked to negotiations about the dismantling of the SS-20 missiles.

For many Germans détente took on the character of a gospel truth. However, to remain effective it had to be backed up by vigilance and a readiness to resort to deterrents. Schmidt himself, a former defence minister, was 'a firm believer in military balance', preferably 'at the lowest level possible' and supplemented by 'economic, political and cultural co-operation between East and West' wherever possible.[35] However, the Chancellor was deserted by his own party, which questioned the government's security policy and also voted for an equally radical economic programme, which could not be supported by the Liberal coalition partner. When their ministers were forced out of the Cabinet, the FDP switched allegiance and helped Helmut Kohl to become Chancellor on 1 October 1982. With the solid backing of the electorate he resumed his predecessor's foreign policy, undeterred by the growing peace movement. While encouraging the peace movement in the West, the SED tried to suppress the emerging campaign against militarism at home (*Schwerter zu Pflugscharren*—'swords into ploughshare') and thereby exposed its double standards.[36] In the West the political system was never seriously under threat. The SPD, now in opposition, firmly rejected the 'dual-track' decision of their former Chancellor. The Bundestag nevertheless voted on 22 November 1983 in favour of accepting the new missiles. However, many young people and intellectuals protested against the installation of the new deadly weapons, the population at large put their trust in the protection provided by the United States. As in the 1950s, the Social Democrats lapsed into a policy of wishful thinking and were regarded as unfit to manage the economy and the security of the country. The right beliefs took precedence over the power to change things in small ways.

Nevertheless, the overall climate had changed and the new government had no mandate to abandon *Ostpolitik*. Nor did it have any designs of doing so. The deployment of the new missiles should not hamper intra-German relations, which developed a momentum of their own. The new Chancellor, though, was more outspoken

about the ultimate goals: 'self-determination, human rights, the unity of our divided nation.'[37] This clear message was his way of being
predictable. The German nation which preceded the nation state was
not at the disposal of the two governments. This language appeared
more and more embarrassing to many leaders of the SPD, who
went out of their way to accommodate the SED regime. As in the
1950s they were led to believe that there was a stark choice between firm adherence to NATO and overtures towards the East.

Final recognition by the West had fateful consequences for the
East Berlin leadership. It bolstered their self-confidence regarding
their protecting power, the Soviet Union. The Politbüro of the SED
believed that the developments further east, generally associated
with Gorbachev and his support for *glasnost* and *perestroika*, could
be safely ignored at home. Even though the Soviet leader did not
see fit to impose his ideas on East Berlin, they too fed into the
process of fermentation and eventual disintegration.

Relations between Bonn and Moscow improved almost in the
same measure as Soviet relations with East Berlin deteriorated.[38]
The gaspipe deal against American wishes was a great boost, whereas Bonn's subsequent acceptance of the new United States missiles
had the opposite effect. As from 1986, economic co-operation and
mutual interests and security took precedence over everything else.
The revolutionary breakthrough in the long-standing disarmament
talks, worked out between US President Reagan and Gorbachev at
Reykjavik, signalled the definite end of the Cold War between the
two superpowers. It may well have been that the Strategic Defense
Initiative (popularly known as 'Star Wars'), strongly supported by
Reagan, convinced Gorbachev that the arms race would impover-
ish the Soviet Union more than America and should be called off.
Reagan had startled the world when he declared that he and the
Soviet leader were determined to abolish all nuclear weapons by
the year 2000, starting with a drastic reduction of the numbers of
intercontinental missiles. The two leaders also agreed to remove all
intermediate-range nuclear forces (INF) from Europe, including those
which had just been installed in the face of strong opposition.

Instead of rejoicing, the German government and right-wing
Social Democrats were alarmed at the prospect of facing superior
land forces in the East without a nuclear deterrent. All of a sudden
the military balance seemed to be seriously tilted. However, the way

out of this dilemma made things worse, at least from a German perspective. Following the US–Soviet treaty on INF, NATO tackled the question of modernizing its short-range nuclear forces in Europe, in order to maintain a flexible response and to make up for the Warsaw Pact's superior numbers of conventional forces. It did not require Soviet propaganda for most Germans, including members of the government, to realize 'the shorter the range, the deader the Germans.'[39] Most Germans now also began to set more store by Gorbachev's new approach than by the kind of security provided by theatre nuclear weapons, whether old (Lance missiles) or new, which would, in any case, explode on German soil. In early 1989 public opinion polls in Germany showed that more than two-thirds of West Germans no longer believed in a military threat from the East, as they had done in the early 1980s.[40] The stage was set for a cataclysm of events which profoundly changed the face of Germany and Europe.

4 Market versus Socialist Economy

Restoring lasting peace and democracy were the twin goals of Anglo-Saxon post-war planning for Germany. No one in an official position was unaware that Hitler and the Nazi Party owed their electoral success and eventual rise to power primarily to the Great Depression. Democracy, only fully introduced in 1918, went under because its linchpin, the liberal economy, had given way under stress. Economic misery would breed radicalism, be it Fascism or Bolshevism. When Churchill returned from his Atlantic meeting with Roosevelt in August 1941 he explained to the Cabinet: 'We now take the view that impoverished neighbours are bound to be bad neighbours, and we wish to see everyone prosperous, including the Germans. In short, our aim is to make Germany "fat but impotent".'[1] Fifty years on this sounds like an enlightened prophecy come true. The Germans are, on the whole, prosperous and peaceful to the point of being embarrassingly well fed and clad, and most reluctant to put their former military prowess to the test. It is as well to be reminded that this is what two of the three major victors in the Second World War, conscious of the lesson of history, were clearly aiming at.

British wartime thinking was focused on the apparent dilemma of how to reconcile economic disarmament with reparations and a decent standard of living for Germany. John Maynard Keynes even foresaw that as a result of total occupation Germany would gain an undue economic advantage by not having to provide for her own security.[2] The State Department took an even more far-sighted view. World peace did not, in the last resort, depend on the import quotas for magnesium or molybdenum, but on the successful re-integration of Germany into the world economy. Post-war policy recommendations made by the State Department in April 1944 include: 'Full employment of manpower and resources in the production of commodities of a non-military character, for which the German economy is well adapted'.[3] The German economy was to be more dependent than ever on imports of raw materials and exports of finished goods so that it had no chance to go astray. It was exactly the recipe which the Federal Republic was to adopt in the years to come, being a good customer who would supply the world market with capital and consumer goods. Economic disarmament proved to be a blessing in disguise. The last stocks of aluminium hoarded by the aircraft industry were turned into light but sturdy suitcases which proved invaluable in the overcrowded trains after the war. These were the pointers to the future: manufacturing for the everyday needs of the people, not the exceptional demands of the state.

Henry Morgenthau's intervention in September 1944 was totally out of character with previous United States policy planning. The notorious memorandum allegedly pertaining to the destruction of industry and the pastoralization of Germany, signed by Churchill against his better judgement, has been given more attention by historians than it really deserves. Churchill only referred to the 'war-making industries in the Ruhr and in the Saar',[4] which would have been put out of action anyway. What is more, at the very same conference (Quebec) the United States eventually yielded to British pressure for the North-Western Zone. The implementation of Morgenthau's ideas was now Britain's responsibility and, as far as the Saar was concerned, probably France's. Churchill got more than he gave: the desired North-Western Zone and a continuation of Lend-Lease on generous terms. He probably realized that the plan would never be executed in full by the British Cabinet, which had already condemned it in the strongest terms: 'Our name would be associated with avoidable and purposeless suffering, not with just retribution.'[5] Britain would be pressed, the Cabinet concluded, to send relief goods into Germany rather than exacting reparations for the reconstruction of Europe. This is indeed what happened, and after the war Britain did all it could in the inter-Allied negotiations to raise the permitted level of German industry, until the whole issue vanished from the agenda.[6] The final irony, for all the outraged pub-talk Morgenthau had engendered in post-war Germany, is that some of the heavy industries, mainly those in the Ruhr, which he had in mind above all, proved to be a liability rather than an asset to the German economy in later years. Even though the first US directive on Germany (JCS 1067) shows certain traces of Morgenthau's influence, it is hard to establish whether it actually did delay economic reconstruction in Germany.

What can be established with certainty, however, is that the governments in both Washington and London never contemplated an immediate return to a market economy following surrender. With the end of Nazi exploitation practices, so the argument ran, and the burden of reparations, the German economy was bound to collapse, and indeed it might have. To avoid total devaluation of the Reichsmark it was necessary, at least for a transitional period, to maintain the Nazi system of controls, above all price and credit controls and the rationing of private and industrial consumption. In spring 1944 Washington was prepared to send 5,000 to 6,000 civil affairs officers to run the German economy in the hoped-for industrialized North-Western Zone. Later changes to this plan arising from Morgenthau's intervention were more cosmetic than real. Roosevelt felt that Germany should 'stew in her own juice'[7] for a while. The system of controls, however, remained, particularly the *Reichsnährstand* in charge of food production and distribution. The agrarian Southern Zone, which nobody wanted, turned out to be less of a burden than the industrial north. Apart from providing food and fuel for a starving and freezing population, the main concern of the British, indeed all four Allies, was what to do with Germany's industrial heartland, the Ruhr area. Democratic supervision as in Britain seemed to be the answer.

North Rhine-Westphalia was, to some extent, founded for the purpose of providing common ownership of the coal and steel industries.[8] Several of the German *Länder*, notably Hesse and Schleswig-Holstein, adopted a constitutional clause which could open the door to nationalization. However, the Americans made sure that this door remained firmly shut. They argued that socialization could not be introduced piecemeal and must wait for a West German government to make up its mind. Of course, the American Military Governor, Lucius D. Clay, was dead against it and knew that time —and Ludwig Erhard—would work in his favour.

By December 1947, as mentioned above, hopes for a common Allied approach to the German economy had definitely collapsed at the London Conference. A currency reform in the Western zones was now unavoidable. This would set the final seal on the division of Germany and therefore had to be pushed through by the Western Allies, notably the Americans. To sum up: after the war the stage was not set for a competitive market economy, but rather the opposite. The small Liberal Party was the only one with no qualms about capitalism. However, the dialectics of history sometimes work wonders. The very experience of rationing, i.e. the administration of shortage, on the one hand, and a booming black market on the other, turned the tide towards conventional acceptance of the unacceptable.

Moral support from Clay for Erhard was more than matched by American material help. Even though experts now argue that according to all indicators the economic recovery had been sustained by the end of 1947,[9] there is no doubt that the promise of Marshall Aid was a great psychological stimulus for the German economy. The European Recovery Program (ERP), as Marshall Aid was called, was not the dispensing of charity, but help in order to promote self-help. The Marshall Plan provided aid to pay for commodities and services that Europe needed and at the same time, and this was the ingenious idea, it required recipients to pay for what they received in their own currency and then to use the accumulated funds to promote recovery. West Germany was by no means the greatest beneficiary (it was fourth in line, with 1,412.8 million dollars; Britain and France received twice this amount)—but it made the best use of the counterpart funds, which flowed into industrial investment, rather than, as in the case of Britain, being squandered in redemption of the national debt. During the first two years of ERP West Germany was the only country whose industrial production doubled. Of course, the country also started from a much lower level. The counterpart funds were 'the starters that "fired the engine" of the German economy', as was stated in the original report of the President's Committee.[10]

The market economy was not a ready-made model imposed on Germany as a result of a few snap decisions within a couple of months in 1948. What Erhard pushed through was something new, which was by no means welcomed by all German industrialists, who were used to protectionism and price-fixing,[11] and fought a protracted battle against decartelization. Nor were the trade unions happy about the sudden rationalization of manpower in the name of competition. However, Erhard had the support of a small but vocal group of academic experts, who had been advocating a new economic order for some time: a third way between a planned economy and a return to *laissez-faire*. Neo-liberals like Friedrich von Hayek, Wilhelm Röpke, and Alexander Rüstow, who had fled Nazi

Germany, joined forces with representatives of the ordo-liberal Frei-burg School around Franz Böhm and Walter Eucken. It was a home-spun economic philosophy in the sense that it attributed to the state an important supervisory task. The market economy would only prosper within a legal framework which guaranteed fair competi-tion and at the same time took account of all the needs of society. The neo-liberals were no admirers of big business, which tended to conglomerate and extinguish competition. Anti-trust laws, as de-manded by the United States, were just the kind of legislation the neo-liberals had in mind. Wherever he could Erhard tried to sup-port the *Mittelstand* (entrepreneurial middle class) and the spread of a medium-sized industrial structure in West Germany. Much as they were against state control, men like Röpke also warned against privatization for its own sake. Essential utilities such as energy, water, railways, and the like should not be private enterprises, since as such they would become uncontrollable monopolies. Anthony Nicholls summarizes the principle of neo-liberalism as follows: 'State intervention to create proper conditions for free competition was to be encouraged: state intervention in the economic process, let alone supranational direction, was to be avoided.'[12]

The academic advocates of neo-liberalism had no idea of how to regenerate the prostrate economy of post-war Germany. It was important that the Americans should prevent the early imple-mentation of a definite economic order based on the temporary exi-gencies of the post-war era. Also crucial was their backing of Erhard and his academic advisers. The director of the Frankfurt Economic Council was both the preacher of the new gospel of prosperity through growth and the man who made it possible. His chief lieu-tenant at the Federal Ministry of Economics and the most *dirigiste* of the ordo-liberals was Alfred Müller-Armack, who coined the phrase *soziale Marktwirtschaft* (social market economy) and favoured coun-tercyclical management of the economy. It was he who worked out the concept, translated it into legislation, and put the latter into effect. Erhard himself was no great administrator and failed as the second Federal Chancellor, as predicted by Adenauer. A whole string of measures was introduced: in November 1948 wages were set free; income tax was reduced; iron, steel, and chemical industries, as well as banking, were decentralized; credit schemes for small enterprises were made available; and so forth.

The actual stupendous growth of the West German economy was of course due to a complex set of factors, not only to Allied plans or the splendid ideas of German professors. There is consensus amongst experts that the industrial capacity of Germany was not as much affected by Allied bombing as first appearances would suggest. Capital stock was in remarkably good condition, extensive and fairly modern. In May 1945 gross fixed capital was 20 per cent above the figure for 1936. It was not until 1944 that damage by aerial bombardment surpassed current industrial production. According to an American estimate, Germany's machine-tool holdings had increased by 75 per cent since 1938.[13]

The second most important production factor, manpower, was also in ample supply. War losses and the withdrawal of forced labour were more than made good by millions of refugees, both from the territories east of the Oder–Neiße line, now administered by Poland, and from the Soviet Zone, which offered an even bleaker future than the Western zones. According to the census of 1939, the population in the British Zone had, by 1946, increased by 11.3 per cent and in the American Zone, with the influx of the Sudeten Germans, by 17.1 per cent. It should be noted, however, that agricultural areas in the north and south received a larger share than the industrial heartland, where manpower was required in the long run. It would also be more appropriate to speak of womanpower rather than manpower since millions of men had perished in the war or were still being held in Soviet prison camps. Still, all in all the resources for a new start were in place. If industrial recovery was still rather slow at first, it was for other reasons: a shortage of raw materials, Allied restrictions, dismantling of armament factories, and not least a badly damaged transport system, which was, however, swiftly repaired on the insistence and with the help of the occupation authorities. The Allies were mainly interested in the production of coal and foodstuffs to keep the population alive and warm. Though coal was sold abroad below the world market price ($10.50 instead of $25–30 per ton) it was a valuable commodity for financing crucial imports of raw materials and agricultural products.[14] The iron and steel industry was another matter and subject to inter-Allied negotiations about acceptable levels. However, the various and steadily rising production limits were never effective restrictions on steel output. The shortage of everything and a worthless currency in ample supply were bound to lead to a black market and a barter economy. As Alan Kramer put it: 'In the cities the black market soon came to dominate everyday life, turning social norms upside-down, rewarding dishonesty and penalising those who worked hard.'[15]

The new currency, coupled with deregulation, gave the kick-start which set the economy going at an ever faster pace for the next ten years. However, it was not quite the smooth sailing that the term *Wirtschaftswunder* implies. For British officials Erhard had gone too far too fast in abandoning controls without proper consultation. Con O'Neill, for instance, felt that apart from economic theory he was 'a fundamentally foolish man, rather aggressively nationalist in outlook, and no friend to us or our ideals.'[16] If the Americans were somewhat more sanguine, many German politicians, especially at *Länder* level, were predicting disaster. It was, as Nicholls put it, 'a leap into the chilly waters of the market'.[17] Prices rose slightly in the autumn of 1948, though not markedly over the next two years. More importantly, unemployment went up by 500,000 within the first six months of 1948. The SPD and the trade unions were up in arms and on 12 November 1948 called a 24-hour general strike. As Minister of Economics in Bonn, Erhard came under strong pressure from his colleagues and the occupation authorities to go back on his policies, i.e. retain controls, raise taxes, and loosen the purse-strings. Eventually Erhard and Wilhelm Vocke, President of the newly established Central Bank (*Bank Deutscher Länder*) agreed, as a gesture of social appeasement, to finance work creation schemes to the tune of 2 billion DM.

There is agreement among historians that the boom caused by the Korean War, and the consequent need to rearrange economic priorities, had a major impact on the German economy. But disagreement prevails about how to interpret the shift. Was the same ship being relaunched or were the economic mechanisms essentially altered or changed as a result? The Americans were ready to put their economy on a war footing, reminiscent of measures taken during the war, and expected their Allies to do the same. With memories of the war still fresh, Germans tended to hoard, not least industrial bosses. Raw materials became scarce, prices rose, and in no time Germany had run up a trade deficit with its European neighbours. Erhard was forced to reintroduce coal rationing. Worse was to come in the shape of a letter of 6 March 1951 by John McCloy, the US High Commissioner and Marshall Plan administrator, telling Adenauer in no uncertain terms that 'a significant modification of the free market economy' was required.[18] How could Germany, the latecomer to free trade, refuse to make a contribution to the 'defense of the free world' by not diverting resources from the production of 'non-essential goods or luxuries'? Soon enough the production quotas for steel were raised again and the manufacture of small arms permitted within new limits. After all, Germany was the only country with spare manufacturing capacity. As a result the output of the mechanical engineering industry almost doubled between 1950 and 1952.

The ambivalence caused by the Korean War was all too obvious: on the one hand, a boost for production and exports, especially the highly valued German machine tools, and on the other, a serious challenge to the new market economy through the threatened reintroduction of controls. Were the advocates of economic planning on the Left right after all? The Federal Republic, still an occupied country and dependent on Marshall Aid, could not afford to antagonize the United States. The Federation of German Industry came to Erhard's rescue by introducing a system of self-regulation as an emergency solution, i.e. allocating the supply of raw materials, guiding exports, and so forth. Erhard withstood Allied and to some extent Cabinet pressure to abandon his liberal economic policies. 'By standing firm,' Nicholls writes, 'even at the cost of a few largely meaningless concessions, Erhard prevented a relapse into planning which might have had ruinous consequences, not only for West Germany, but also for Western Europe.'[19] For some authors this marked the 'revival of societal corporatism' (Abelshauser); others like Berghahn and Kramer refer to a new bilateralism between state and industry, to the exclusion of the trade unions. In fact, the ordo-liberal school had never given its blessing to a totally free-for-all economy anyway. Erhard was a great believer in the beneficial nature of economic growth, which was bound to generate prosperity, but he never liked state-directed investment in violation of market forces, as was now called for. The Investment Aid Law of December 1951 was meant to clear the bottle-necks in the transport system, the energy sector, and the iron and steel industry, and thus to meet Allied expectations. A special levy on the flourishing consumer goods industries yielded a subsidy of 1 billion DM for those industries that had fared less well. State help was now needed for pressing political reasons. This lesson was not forgotten when, in the future, some of these industries, like coal and steel, now propped up, proved not to be viable and had to be scaled down.

After the Korean boom, the German economy really took off. It was, and has remained ever since, export-led. The first trade agreements were made with Switzerland and the Netherlands. Trade expanded most rapidly with OEEC countries, those which also benefited from Marshall Aid. Overcoming the dollar gap proved to be the greatest obstacle, which Marshall Aid was designed to remove. Recent research shows that the Deutschmark was not undervalued.[20] Germany was not establishing its role as a leading European trading nation through dumping. The growing volume of exports was staggering, and, no doubt, greatly helped by the liberating of trade through the European Payment Union (1950). At least one-half of the overall growth in production between 1950 and 1954 was generated by demand from abroad. By 1950 the percentage of exports (9.3 per cent) had surpassed the level of the 1930s for the whole Reich. By 1960, with 17.2 per cent, it reached the top level of the pre-1914 period, and was then to climb to 26.7 per cent in 1980. The total value of imports and exports of the old Federal Republic increased from 19.7 billion DM in 1950 to over 1,311 billion DM in 1990. Almost one in three employed persons produces goods and services destined for abroad. One of the three leading world exporters in 1991, Germany sends more than half of her exports to EU countries, mainly France, Italy, the Netherlands, and the United Kingdom. More or less the same countries, again with France in the lead, are also the main suppliers. If all other European states to the north and east, especially Poland, the Czech Republic, and Hungary, are included, the most recent figures show that more than 70 per cent of German trade is conducted within Europe. Not surprisingly, Germany has the greatest interest in expanding and synchronizing the European Union.

In spite of the traumatic effects of the war, West Germany had managed to re-establish the pre-war pattern of trade. By 1952–3 80 per cent of goods were known to their consumers by their old brand names. Well over half the exports in the 1950s came from the traditional three sectors in which pre-war Germany had excelled: mechanical engineering, motor cars, and electrical and chemical products. The motor car manufacturers were soon to outpace all others. Alan Kramer has pointed out that the most important exporting industries happened to be those with the fastest expansion during the war.[21] Allied policies of economic demilitarization and dismantling could not have had much of a retarding effect. Still, in the 1950s, Germany was not yet permitted to build and export tanks, aeroplanes, or submarines. But it was supplying mechanical equipment such as machine tools to the armaments industries of the victorious powers.

It is doubtful whether the West Germans of the 1950s knew much about the workings of the social market economy. But wages and salaries went up, inflation and unemployment figures dropped, and much was done to improve living standards, especially housing conditions. For most, the *Wirtschaftswunder* had a real meaning and probably did more than any other experience to restore self-respect to the Germans. They knew it was not a miracle, but something they had made possible by their own hard work. Pride rested on 'Made in Germany' as a mark of quality. In this sense, most West Germans who built up their country in the 1950s could be described as self-made men and women. This mentality did not always endear them to the outside world. But it is true to say that the export boom was never, as perhaps in Japan, conceived as a subtle revenge for the lost war. Characteristically, there was virtually no resentment against foreign troops or foreign investment (for example Ford or General Motors). On the contrary, both were welcomed, because they helped to enhance the military and economic security of the divided country. To an old trading nation like Britain it was all too obvious that export industries depended on the maintenance of peace and international co-operation. For the Germans this was a new lesson, which grew on them in proportion to their growing trade.

The impact of this *Händlergesinnung* (mercantile ethos) is still incalculable. Some commentators like Hans-Peter Schwarz think it has gone too far: from an obsession with power to a neglect of power.[22] Since in the past power had been identified with military power and had, as such, been delegitimized, quite a few Germans would dispute the concept of economic power as applied to the Federal

Republic or, for that matter, the Bundesbank. In the 1950s the Federal Republic joined every international, preferably European, organization going, to prove that she was just as worthy and reliable a business partner as anyone else: the Organisation for European and Economic Cooperation (OEEC): 1950; the European Payment Union (EPU): 1950; General Agreement on Tariffs and Trade (GATT): 1951; European Coal and Steel Community (ECSC/Montan-Union): 1951; International Monetary Fund (IMF): 1952; European Economic Community (EEC): 1957.

The Federal Republic regarded itself as the only legitimate successor state to the Third Reich and felt that the claim to unification could be upheld in international law. This meant that the German state had not ceased to exist in 1945. As a consequence, Bonn accepted its liability to pay the Reich's debts to foreign countries, which the London Debt Conference of 1951 estimated at about 13 billion DM. The chief German negotiator was the influential banker Hermann Abs, who succeeded in reducing the overall amount to 7.5 billion DM, to be paid in annual instalments—567 million DM per annum for the first five years and then 765 million DM per annum. Initially, this appeared to be a tall order, but with the growing surplus in foreign currency, the burden lost much of its weight. Equally important, though politically more difficult, was the question of restitution and compensation to victims of Nazi persecution, notably those of the Holocaust. The avowedly anti-fascist GDR saw no moral obligation to provide compensation. The driving force for restitution to Israel and the Jews was Adenauer, rather than the CDU. Adenauer had not forgotten that the only friends who came to his aid after his dismissal in 1933 were Jews. In June 1952 Bonn agreed to deliver capital goods to Israel amounting to 3 billion DM over twelve years.[23] Individual claims by victims of oppression, not only Jews, were settled by two laws in 1953 and 1956 (Federal Indemnification Laws), which foresaw payments of about 2 billion DM per annum up to and beyond the end of the century. Recognition of this international obligation, so much in contrast to the Reich's position in the inter-war years, did much to enhance Bonn's reputation abroad.

From early on, Bonn was aware that the large export surpluses aroused mixed feelings abroad. Officials point out somewhat apologetically that the Federal Republic is one of the largest contributors to the European Union and international organizations.[24] Surpluses are also said to be justified to offset deficits in other fields, particularly the large sums of money spent by German holiday-makers and the money sent home by foreign workers in Germany to their relations.

How was it that the West German economy grew to such an extent during the first thirty-five years, that the country's reputation was re-established as one of the leading industrial nations? Though GNP more than quadrupled in that period, economic growth was by no means steady.[25] During the reconstruction phase of the 1950s, the annual growth rate of GDP (not to be confused with GNP) rose by 8.2 per cent per annum, only to slow down to 4.6 per cent during the boom years of the 1960s, and to drop further at the time of the energy crisis of the 1970s (2.8 per cent), slumping to 0.7 per cent in the early 1980s, before again reaching 2.6 per cent in 1984. The spectacular performance in the 1950s was due, as already mentioned, to a low level of production, untapped manpower resources, and an underutilized capital stock, which was soon to be modernized on a large scale. Demand, both at home— Germany was starved of consumer goods—and abroad accelerated growth and used up all available labour. In the 1960s the economy worked at full capacity and manpower became a problem. As a result, foreign workers were hired in large numbers. They, too, contributed substantially to West Germany's GNP: unemployment was less than 1 per cent and inflation no more than 2.5 per cent, a combination never to be matched in later years. However, the 1960s also experienced a sudden unexpected economic slump. After a phase of consolidation (1952–8) and European integration (1959–66), the steam ran out and West Germany went through its first depression, with GDP down to 2.9 per cent and industrial growth to 1.2 per cent. This crisis turned out to be short-lived, but this was no miracle either. It was the result of a new departure in economic policy which was quite at odds with Erhard's prescription. The Germans learned in no time how to handle an economic downswing, and this lesson was probably more important than all the positive indicators of the preceding boom years.

A Grand Coalition under Kurt-Georg Kiesinger broadened the scope for the government to play a more active role, by granting special funds for improving the infrastructure (rail, road, and telecommunications).[26] In 1967 the Bundestag passed a law to promote the stability and growth of the economy (*Stabilitätsgesetz*) which has been described as the Magna Carta of modern German economic management. The active promotion of economic growth, full employment, price stability, and a sound trade balance was now regarded as a legitimate task of government. The new Minister of Economics, Karl Schiller (SPD), a disciple of Keynes, also introduced what he called *konzertierte Aktion* (a constant exchange of views with all partners of industry), mainly in order to urge wage restraint and secure peace on the labour front. Schiller co-operated closely with the notorious right-wing Bavarian politician Franz-Josef Strauss, who was head of the Treasury. Together they initiated the *mittelfristige Finanzplanung*, i.e. medium-term financial planning encompassing the budgets at all levels of government, federal, state, and local.

Global direction of the economy to such an extent was hardly compatible with Erhard's original concept of the social market economy. The term 'social' had, by now, taken on a different connotation: the maintenance of prosperity and full employment, coupled with high salaries and wages, based on a well-managed economy. It also meant that agriculture remained heavily subsidized, now under the cloak of EEC regulations. Moreover, heavy industry in the Ruhr needed help, not so much to expand as to be scaled down with the minimum hardship for the redundant work-force. Whatever government was now in power, there was no going back on the new approach to global and advanced economic planning. This approach also had the backing of the German public, which for generations had expected the government to look after the individual citizen. Nevertheless, the West German system was not, as many intellectuals speculated at the time, converging with the GDR command economy.

The growth pattern of the West German economy underwent structural changes as well. As a proportion of the whole economy, agriculture went down from 10.7 per cent to 2.1 per cent during the first thirty-five years, even though its productive value almost doubled due to rationalization, mainly a reduction in labour (25 per cent to 5.5 per cent of the whole work-force), and through capitalization. Service industries rose from 39.6 per cent to 55.3 per cent during the same period and are showing signs of further growth in accordance with the general trend. In the first instance, the German economy's tremendous boom was, of course, due to the spectacular and unprecedented development of manufacturing industries. In the 1950s the annual growth rate was 10 per cent and was fuelled in later years by a steady increase in the export market. Productivity almost quadrupled in the period from 1950 to 1984. However, in relation to the economy as a whole, the share of manufacturing began to decline in the 1970s and 1980s, in terms of both GDP and manpower. Not surprisingly, the high rate of domestic investment, which was significantly higher than in the United States or the EC, though lower than in Japan, is the chief explanation for the expansion of Germany's economic capacity. Even today, investment decisions on German boards are made with astonishing ease and generally with the full backing of the 'house bank'.

Nearly all German citizens prospered as a result of the unprecedented economic boom: the income of private householders increased sixteenfold up to 1985, the rate of saving by an average of 12.8 per cent per annum. However, the state (*die öffentliche Hand*— literally, the public hand) was the main beneficiary: growth in revenue and expenses was substantially higher than growth in GDP (9.9 as against 8.6 per cent per annum). Yet for a long time only a small number of economic experts expressed concern about the steep rise in public expenses. The rest of society seemed to be content, because old-age pensions went up, the promotion prospects for civil servants and public employees increased, and the infrastructure in general improved visibly. It was only when the national debt experienced another steep rise after German unification that people in general became alarmed about the state of affairs. It was shortly after the method of influencing the business cycle by the injection of public funds had been sanctioned in the late 1960s that the national debt began to double every couple of years, thus, in the long run, blunting this very instrument.

More and more Germans depend on regular wages and salaries. The size and structure of the labour market has changed substantially over the last forty years: it rose from 20.4 million in 1950 to over 28.6 million in 1994 (plus 6.3 million in the new Federal States), with 2.6 million guest workers. However, the number of self-employed went down considerably from 15 per cent (1950) to 11 per cent within about twenty years (1973). Industry is still by far the biggest breadwinner, in spite of the inevitable shift towards the service sector, with nearly one million employed in mechanical engineering (1994) and 655,000 in the automobile industry. Even though half of the total work-force is still employed by the big, well-known companies, small firms clearly predominate: only 2.6 per cent of companies employ more than 1,000 people.[27] These small and medium-sized firms, spread all over the country and often family-owned—90 per cent with fewer than 300 employees—tend to be more flexible and innovative than bigger companies and offer a wide range of high-quality products, of which 43 per cent are sold abroad (motor vehicles: 55 per cent). This is surprising in view of the fact that the Anti-Trust Law of 1957 has not proved all that effective and did not stop the trend towards further concentration.

Any foreigner is keen to know the 'secret' of Germany's economic performance, which has been outpacing that of her European competitors for some time. There is no magic about a smoothly running engine, which can be described as a combination and precise interaction of various parts. The usual references to the German penchant for hard work, efficiency, and perfection are not very helpful. Nor is the explanatory power of the Protestant work ethic all that great: after all, the predominantly Catholic south and southwest did much better after the war than the north and north-east. Perhaps it makes sense to single out a few key elements which account for a great deal of the success: vocational training, industrial relations, management skill, and not least the banking system.

Vocational education in Germany has been the envy of other industrial nations such as Britain, even though it is in many ways a relic of the old guild system (*Zunftwesen*). The latter, with its strict rules and regulations, has probably shaped the German mentality more than anything else. Vocational training is a sort of 'dual system', with on-the-job training backed up by theoretical instruction at vocational schools (*Berufsschulen*). Trainees only receive a small remuneration during their apprenticeship (usually lasting three years). Employers are only allowed to train apprentices if they have a 'master's certificate' or employ masters. In some trades, such as hairdressing, butcher's shops, and bookselling, for example, they provide a source of cheap labour. The pride of the skilled worker is still on a level with that of an artisan of former times. So far the only acceptable apprenticeship for the sons of the middle classes is a traineeship in banking. This may, and should, change in the future because in the long run German society will not be able to absorb the number of would-be professionals graduating from the polytechnics and universities. Authorities are worried that in the 1990s, for the first time, more students are enrolled in universities than there are apprentices in vocational training (1.8 million students as against 1.6 million apprentices in 1994). More than half the apprentices acquire their know-how in small firms. However, it is recognized that the big companies, with their own specialized workshops, provide the best training. This means that they are prepared to invest in their future manpower. Very often the next step up the social ladder is a professional education in one of the polytechnics (*Fachhochschulen*), which for a long time specialized in producing graduate engineers with high qualifications. These were much sought after by industry: they were younger than university graduates (*Diplomingenieure*), more pragmatic in their approach, and better suited, because of their social backgrounds, to liaise between management and the shop floor. A high level of social mobility has greatly invigorated industrial management, where accent, old school tie, etc. are no guarantee of a career.

Since the system of modern industry-related unions emerged in the British Zone and proved to be so successful, the myth spread in later years that this was primarily due to British efforts.[28] As a matter of fact, of the crucial elements, only one, and the least important, was introduced at the insistence of Military Government (for security reasons): a decentralized structure which the German union leaders disliked at first because of its potential to weaken their position in the fight for public ownership. The idea of modern industrial unions was undisputed and co-determination was pushed through against strong British reservations. Co-determination, the British felt and still feel, blunts the negotiating mechanisms, and is therefore readily denounced as 'corporatism'. However, it gave German unions a stake in industry and turned out to be much more beneficial for the unions as a whole, thus greatly improving industrial relations.

After the war German trade unionists, as elsewhere, were hoping for a new post-capitalist system with truly shared responsibilities for unions and employers. Co-determination started in the Klöckner steelworks as early as 1946. A year later nearly all plants and coal-mines in the British Zone had adopted the same rules. But with the Cold War accelerating, the odds were against a 'democratization of the economy' as practised in the Soviet Zone. The new social order that emerged was recognized as a defeat for the trade union movement. However, Hans Böckler, their charismatic leader, made his peace with Adenauer and concentrated on building up a powerful organization, the German Trade Union Federation (*Deutscher Gewerkschaftsbund*: DGB), which was set up on 13 October 1949. In the following four decades the DGB pursued three practical goals: a new Works Constitution Law (*Betriebsverfassungsgesetz*: BFG); co-determination; and better working conditions, such as the forty-hour and later thirty-five-hour week, equal pay for men and women, the same sick-pay for blue- and white-collar workers, additional holiday entitlement, Christmas bonuses, and so forth. In other words, the unions were not intent on changing the system as a whole, nor were they only concerned with pay. In their way, they made the best of the social market economy, which in itself was a sort of hybrid. The unions were never satisfied, however, with what they actually achieved, which is probably the attitude to be expected of any pressure group.

The first BFG of 1952 was described as the 'dark moment for democratic development', because the unions were banned as the official shop-floor representatives and the works councils were confined to matters of social policy. The improved BFG of 1972 under Brandt's chancellorship also fell short of union expectations, even though they were now entitled to represent the workers collectively. Furthermore, the rights of the works councillors were substantially increased: they now had a clear say in issues such as hiring and firing, vocational education, etc. Nor were the unions pleased with the laws concerning co-determination, first for heavy industry (*Montanmitbestimmungsgesetz*, 1951), and then the extension to other large-scale companies (*Mitbestimmungsgesetz*, 1976). The unions objected to the voting system for the supervisory boards of firms employing more than 2,000 workers because it favoured the employers.

Co-determination extends to all activities of a company affecting the work-force, not just to social issues. The unions are not involved in everyday management, but are represented on the supervisory board (*Aufsichtsrat*) on an equal basis with the shareholders. The supervisory board may appoint or dismiss the management and demand proper information on all company matters. Each board of

directors must have at least one labour director, who is chiefly concerned with matters of personnel and working conditions. Clearly
the smaller a firm, the less the trade union influence. The DGB has
10.7 million members, out of an overall German work-force of 35
to 36 million. The German Union of Salaried Employees (*Deutsche
Angestelltengewerkschaft*: DAG) has only 575,000 members, which,
to no one's surprise, shows that white-collar workers are less likely
to join a union than blue-collar workers and tend to identify more
closely with management. Of course, there are many other professional associations, such as the powerful German Civil Service
Federation (*Deutscher Beamtenbund*), which will be discussed in
the next chapter. No one is forced to join a union by a 'closed-
shop system'. The degree of unionization varies greatly, but is, on
average, less than 50 per cent. German trade unionists have been
accused by their international colleagues of being too accommod-
ating *vis-à-vis* employers. This is grossly unfair, if only because over
the last forty years they have clearly negotiated the best working
conditions for their members of any industrial society, so much
so that they are now criticized for having done their job too well,
thereby tempting German employers to look for cheaper labour
abroad. There can be no doubt that it is only with the full participation of unions that the process can be reversed, that perks and
privileges can be dismantled, in order to safeguard employment
(*Bündnis für Arbeit*).

The history of capital owners and industrial management is beyond the brief of this study. In view of their involvement in the
preparation of Germany for war, and the subsequent exploitation
of Europe, it is indeed astonishing that German entrepreneurs
recovered their property rights after 1945. The Cold War seems to
have made them as indispensable as the preceding world war. Since
they owed their reinstatement in no small measure to the market
economy, one would have thought that they must all have been
ardent supporters of Ludwig Erhard. Volker Berghahn has revealed,
however, that this was by no means the case.[29] Still shaped by an
authoritarian and paternalistic outlook, German entrepreneurs rejected the new regime of decartelization, competition, and workers'
participation. Lobby organizations were set up to fight all these
measures tooth and nail. Employers and unions appear to have one
belief in common: whoever is more highly organized will make the

running. Compared with the Confederation of German Employers'
Associations (*Bund der Arbeitergeberverbände*: BdA) and the Federation of German Industry (*Bund der Deutschen Industrie*: BDI)
the American and British counterparts could only be described,
so Berghahn argues, as 'weak'. The third most important lobby is
the German Chamber of Industry and Commerce (*Deutscher In-
dustrie- und Handelstag*: DIHT). By 1961 there were more than 6,000
employers' associations with 53,000 full-time staff. Adenauer's autocratic style of leadership was very much to their liking and the
head of the BDI, Fritz Berg, often bypassed Erhard by appealing
directly to the Chancellor. The pressure of these associations is such
that it has sparked off a long-standing public discussion about how
to curtail their influence, for instance that of the car and road
lobby. It is significant that the associations tend to lobby the ministerial bureaucracy rather than parties or parliaments. The legislation
to which employers objected most vigorously was the Anti-Trust
Law (*Kartellgesetz*) of 1957. Erhard regarded this as the cornerstone
of his whole economic edifice, or, as he put it, 'the economic equivalent of the Basic Law'.[30] The law, despite its many exceptions
and loopholes, broke with an unholy German tradition and paved
the way for American-style management in Germany.

Nevertheless, certain positive elements of German industrial culture survived into the next generation, above all the highly professional and not purely commercial attitudes of management and,
closely connected, concern for the long-term future of companies.
Chairmen are usually selected for their professional expertise, say
in engineering or chemistry, not purely for their financial know-
how.[31] Investment decisions are not made for short-term financial
gain, or to satisfy shareholders. Here the traditionally close connections between industry and banking play a crucial part. The
main credit banks are strongly represented on supervisory boards
and it is they who, by controlling most of the shares, also exercise the greatest influence on the board of directors. There are not
that many medium-sized companies represented on the stock market. Generally the public is not greatly interested in stocks and
shares. Though private deposits increased considerably from 1980
(491 billion DM) to 1990 (678 billion DM), the preferred holdings
are savings accounts or government bonds.

By now the proverbial pride of every German is supposed to be the Deutschmark, so much so that critics have referred to a Deutschmark nationalism. The guardian of the currency is the Bundesbank in Frankfurt am Main, which regulates the amount of money in circulation as well as the credit supply to industry. The Bundesbank is constantly called upon to perform a balancing act: it is greatly respected for its constitutionally guaranteed independence from government interference, and yet it must support the latter's general economic policy. Clashes between Bonn and Frankfurt are numerous and legendary, especially while the SPD nominee, Karl-Otto Pöhl, was in charge. The most publicized conflict arose over the currency union between East and West Germany in June 1990, on the basis of one Deutschmark for one Ostmark, which proved politically expedient and economically disastrous. Since the Deutschmark is the leading currency within the European Monetary System, decisions by the Bundesbank, even minute changes in the Lombard rate, are registered everywhere, more often than not with intense frustration.

Resentment of the Bundesbank's influence is most acute in London, which once exercised great financial power via sterling and still feels that the City of London ought to remain the financial powerhouse of Europe. The subtitle of David Marsh's account— *The Bank that Rules Europe*—says it all.[32] The unspoken reasoning is: Why would Germany, which now exercises financial power as Britain once did, want to give it up voluntarily? Germany cannot be expected to sink its most cherished icon, the Deutschmark, in the morass of a European monetary union. Therefore we will be saved from a European currency. This is common sense and wishful thinking at the same time, because the German clock ticks differently. Most Germans do not wish to be identified abroad as financial power-brokers. They are, incidentally, less concerned about the Bundesbank than about the influence of the Deutsche Bank, by far the biggest of the three major German banks, which controls a large chunk of German industry.[33]

How do the Germans as individuals benefit from their successful economy? Many take pride in being members of an allegedly classless society. This is far from the statistical truth, but the perception is nevertheless important. Perhaps it is true to say that the Germans identify more with their social environment than do some of their neighbours, and not only since the emergence of an ecology movement. Generally speaking, they are more in favour of public than of private wealth, and certainly offended by public squalor. The tremendous increase in public revenues over the last forty years and the corresponding improvements to the infrastructure have benefited everyone. The appearance of schools, hospitals, stations, post offices, and the like made a deep impression on the East Germans when they came over after the fall of the Wall, sometimes only for a day, to see what it was really like.

Private wealth, however, is most unevenly spread. The idea that everyone started off with 40 DM after the currency reform in 1948 was, of course, a myth, which served to legitimize the fact that ten years later society appeared to be much more stratified. By 1950 employees owned 35 per cent of the real wealth (*Realvermögen*), fifteen years later less than half of this amount (17 per cent).[34] In 1960 and 1973 less than 2 per cent of households were in possession of more than 50 per cent of productive capital. The famous title of Erhard's book *Wohlstand für Alle* (Prosperity for All) did not mean that prosperity in terms of wealth and property was equally distributed. In the mid-1960s 15,000 DM millionaires, and 3 per cent of all persons subject to capital gains tax, controlled 41 per cent of all taxable wealth. Germans tend to save, but not necessarily with the intention of acquiring a stake in industry. Home ownership (currently about 40 per cent) is generally their most ambitious aim. It might be less widespread than in Britain or Italy, but in Germany rented accommodation offers a reasonable alternative. However, comparing the built-up landscape in West and East Germany, one is struck by the vast expanse of residential areas in the West, both in suburbs and small towns, which simply do not exist beyond the River Elbe. Here, only top party officials or the few self-employed craftsmen could afford houses. The rest of society had to put up with old dilapidated blocks of flats, or ugly pre-fabricated concrete slabs.

Early on, the West German government became concerned about the disparity of wealth and attempted to expand the class of property owners, in three main ways: first, by incentives for future homeowners; secondly by tax allowances for annual savings (936 DM per annum by 1983) and for all those who built rent-controlled blocks of flats (*Sozialwohnungen*); thirdly, by privatization. The housing programme proved to be the most successful scheme, whereas privatization of government property (Volkswagen, Preussag, VEBA) and the distribution of so-called 'people's shares' (*Volksaktien*) did not contribute much to the effective redistribution of private wealth. The most efficacious social palliative was, without doubt, the Pension Insurance Law of 1957, which made pensions subsidized, unitary, and index-linked to the cost of living.[35] It was introduced just in time for the CDU/CSU to achieve an absolute majority in the 1957 elections. It was this law, more than any other, which heralded the arrival of the welfare state in West Germany. The underlying idea was that one generation in work would pay for the previous one. The demographic changes since the mid-1970s, with an ageing population and a decreasing birth rate, do not augur well for the future in this respect.

The history of the East German economy will, in years to come, always be interpreted as an integral part of the demise of the state, and less as a viable alternative to the social market economy. The SED leadership was never in a position to determine the course of its economy without reference to the interests first of the Soviet Union and then of Comecon. The clearly divergent developments of the two German economies after the war was one of the prime causes of the division of the country, as has already been mentioned in a different context. Reconstruction had been severely hampered because the Soviet government pursued a policy of rigorous exploitation, based on the inter-Allied reparations agreement reached at Potsdam. Reparations were exacted by way of goods and current production, dismantling of capital stock (probably more than 1,000 plants), and forced labour in the Soviet Union. In addition, 213 of the most important factories in the chemical, mechanical engineering, electronics, precision tool manufacture, and optical industries were transformed into 'Soviet joint stock companies' (*Sowjetische Aktiengesellschaften*: SAG). All other plants were turned into *Volkseigene Betriebe* (VEB), 'people's own enterprises', later developed into large *Kombinate*. During the first few post-war years industrial production grew faster than in the Western zones because SMAD would impose no restrictions. Land reform for the benefit of smallholders in 1945–6 was followed by collectivization in the 1950s, in other words renewed expropriation, in successive stages (*Landwirtschaftliche Produktionsgenossenschaften*: LPG, types 1–3). Commerce and trade were nationalized as of 1948 (*Handelsorganisationen*: HO and *Produk-tionsgenossenschaften Handwerk*: PGH).

The GDR was obliged to follow the Soviet model of investing primarily in heavy industry at the expense of consumer goods production. The lack of incentives was bound to reduce productivity in the long run. Attempts to raise the level of productivity by Stalinist methods led to the uprising of 17 June 1953.[36] After Stalin's death more attention was given to the growth of the consumer goods industry. When Walter Ulbricht announced a new Seven-Year Plan (the last Five-Year Plan was quietly abandoned) he set a tall order for the GDR: production was to be increased to the extent that by the end of 1961 the socialist Germany would catch up and overtake the per capita consumption of most consumer goods and foodstuffs in West Germany, thereby proving the superiority of the socialist economy over the capitalist one. By 1961 Ulbricht had been forced to build a wall around his socialist Eden to prevent his citizens from seeking a better future in the West. Most East Germans who migrated to the West between 1949 and 1961 did so for economic rather than purely political reasons, i.e. opposition to the regime. According to the most recent statistics, presented in a book by Helga Heidemeyer on flight and migration from the GDR, altogether 2.75 million East Germans migrated to the West and stayed there.[37] This figure does not include the nearly 500,000 people who returned to the GDR, having become disillusioned with life in the West (a surprisingly high figure). More than 50 per cent of migrants to the West were in the 18–44 age group and the largest categories were children (20.6 per cent) and those with a background in industry and trade (20.7 per cent).

In the boom years of the 1950s refugees from the GDR were quickly absorbed into the West German work-force and substantially contributed to the rapid expansion of the economy. The balance was redressed to some extent, however, by the numerous old-age pensioners who were to follow in the 1980s, having been allowed to leave the GDR once they had ceased to be productive. Socialist planning over several years was, of course, severely hampered by a constantly diminishing work-force, which could not be replenished from abroad as in the West. The wall, officially referred to as an 'anti-fascist bulwark', made it possible for the East German regime to settle down. Dietrich Staritz suggests that the SED leadership went on to celebrate 13 August 1961 as the 'secret birthday of the GDR'.[38]

In June 1963 the government decided to launch the 'new economic system' (*Neues Ökonomisches System*: NÖS) with the intention of decentralizing control and encouraging more responsible management. Instead of concentrating on quantitative output, profitability was now recognized as legitimate. The system nevertheless failed because it was incompatible with fixed prices. By transforming the remainder of private enterprise into VEBs in the 1970s, it was hoped to refine the methods of planning and control.

Living standards in East and West Germany were to have a determining impact on whether the SED regime had a chance of survival at the end of the Cold War. Essentially, commodities like basic foodstuffs and rents were heavily subsidized in the East, and substantially cheaper than in the West. The consumption of coffee and fresh fruit was, not surprisingly, twice as high in the Federal Republic. The West Germans were well ahead in all expensive consumer items, such as fridges, washing machines, and motor cars, but not, however, when it came to television sets, cameras, and the like.[39] East Germans had to work much longer hours to afford such items as shoes and clothes. Working hours needed for specific purchases went down in the West much faster than in the East between 1950 and 1990: for a kilo of meat, from 2 hours 40 minutes to 54 minutes; for a kilo of coffee, from 22 hours 19 minutes to 48 minutes; for shoes, from 18 hours 53 minutes to 7 hours 25 minutes; for bread, however, from 20 minutes to 10 minutes. The latter is an indication of those commodities that remained relatively cheap in East Germany, i.e. those such as bread, sugar, and rents, which did not have to be imported and paid for in hard currency.

Those who were in possession of hard currency from relatives in the Federal Republic were asked to exchange it for so-called forum cheques which would entitle them to buy Western goods in the notorious Inter-Shops. Another outlet were the Exquisit-Shops, which catered for the better off, mainly the *nomenklatura* and the few self-employed professionals, for example chemists or plumbers, decorators, etc. These shops, designed to tap unused purchasing power, usually sold goods at real prices, produced for export only.

In retrospect, the state of the East German economy, especially the condition of capital stock, was much worse than Western experts had allowed for. To a large extent this was due to the fact that economists in the West were duped by East Berlin's output of statistics and propaganda. Inter-German trade and the annual display of products at the Leipzig Fair also conveyed a distorted picture, because they revealed nothing about the amount of subsidies the government was prepared to pay in order to stimulate exports and acquire Western currency. East Germany was at the top of the Comecon league. However, while the regime compared its performance with Poland and the Soviet Union, its citizens always looked to the West. These different perceptions could never be reconciled. According to the memoirs of the erstwhile Minister of Economics, Günther Mittag, the GDR was virtually bankrupt by 1984 and only survived on foreign, increasingly West German, credit.[40] One of the chief reasons for this sorry state of affairs was that the Soviet Union, from 1975 onwards, raised the price of raw materials to the world market level. Socialist solidarity was obviously starting to crumble.

Today we have a much clearer picture than before about the true state of the economy because the books have been made available and potential purchasers of East German plants have been able to take a close look. Nor do political inhibitions or editorial safeguards any longer prevent the facts from being described in plain words. Nowhere has the failure of the socialist command economy been more glaringly exposed than in East Germany: the ludicrous process of making Five- and Seven-Year Plans which were either totally without consequence or became excuses for wasting manpower in all kinds of unproductive jobs (such as academic sinecures for Party stalwarts). An already inflated public service was controlled by a huge Party bureaucracy. Almost incalculable are the costs incurred by the obsession with external and internal security. Huge amounts of money were spent purely for the sake of international prestige, for example on the promotion of sport or computer-chip production. What is surprising is that the East German economy survived as long as it did. There is no doubt that the unscrupulous exploitation of inter-German relations with a view to acquiring hard currency played a crucial role here: from the ingenious dealings of Alexander Schalk-Golodkowski's *Kommerzielle Koordinierung* (Koko), which is alleged to have netted 20 billion DM between 1966 and 1989, to the human trade in buying out over 33,000 political prisoners (3.3 billion DM), to the officially licensed theft of petty cash from letters (3.2 million DM between 1984 and 1989).[41] Bonn initially paid 40,000 DM for each captive, and this later rose to 95,000 DM. When the need for foreign currency increased public prosecutors were briefed to sentence people to at least a year's imprisonment so that they would be eligible for a lucrative deal. At the same time Bonn raised the credit limit (swing) to boost inter-German trade and facilitate family reunions. All these were dubious and ultimately futile measures to hide the real state of public finance and to postpone the day of reckoning.

5 The Constitutional Framework

'Political culture' is a somewhat vague but politically correct version of the more ambiguous term 'national character', which was banned after the war in view of its racist misrepresentations. It is now widely used by German academics in search of the magic concept which would fuse history, the political system, and national mentality into one amalgam. There will never be complete agreement as to what the precise ingredients of political culture are. But no one will deny that the federal constitution is one of the most distinct and distinguishing features of German political culture, and one which pertains to the past, the present, and the future. German federalism is by no means confined to the constitutional debate, as might appear from a glance at the literature, preoccupied as it is with the relationship between the federation (*Bund*) and its member states (*Länder*). The public does not take much interest in the legislative functions of the Federal Council (*Bundesrat*). Nor do people follow the deliberations of the *Länder* parliaments with any great interest. Yet it would be wrong to conclude that Germans are not attached to their *Land* because they do not bother much about, say, the state of relations between Munich and Bonn at any given moment.

For a long time Germany was more a geographical than a political notion, similar to Europe today. A loose confederation of tribes evolved, over the centuries, into a variety of fairly independent states, under the embrace of the Holy Roman Empire—to be precise, more than 350 principalities before Napoleon cut them down to roughly one-tenth of that. Germany could easily have developed into four or five independent and homogeneous states, just like Switzerland and the Netherlands, who defied the old Empire. Ethnically, the Swiss, the Austrians in the Vorarlberg, the Alsatians, and the Swabians, now part of four different nation states, certainly have more in common than the citizens of Hamburg and Garmisch-Partenkirchen. The tribal as much as feudal character of the medieval empire and the proliferation of those ancient lands into small states with large courts as the chief entrepreneurs have left a deep mark on present-day Germany. Today's dialects are merely the out-ward manifestation of distinctly different mentalities and one can only hope that they will not be suppressed by overambitious school-teachers. Adenauer's strong Rhenish dialect and Heuss's Swabian tongue did not have any adverse effect on the prestige and author-ity of these father figures—on the contrary. With good reason, Germans abroad are usually asked, more easily than Frenchmen or Swedes, from which part of Germany they come. 'I am a German' has never been a satisfactory answer, though for the last forty years it has always implied West Germany. Not surprisingly the tribal identity is most marked in those *Länder* which survived intact, as in the case of the city of Hamburg, or Bavaria and Saxony. The latter, too, are the only *Länder* which call themselves free states (*Freistaaten*), which does not mean anything in constitutional terms, but apparently a great deal psychologically. Saxony only adopted this imaginary title in 1990, in order to strengthen its identity within the larger fatherland. The Bavarian government did the same be-tween 1848 and 1871, fostering a separate identity by invigorat-ing Bavarian folklore.[1]

The most convincing evidence for the tribal and federalist nature of modern Germany is the process of incorporating the former GDR in 1990: not so much the constitutional aspect (Article 23 of the Basic Law) as the genuine democratic pressure of the popula-tion for the speedy re-establishment of the five *Länder* which had been abolished in 1952. Experts, including the highly respected historian Karlheinz Blaschke, argued convincingly in favour of two or three economically viable states.[2] However, this was to no avail. There was precious little time and the pressure from below could not be overcome. In no time, the old flags were fetched up from the cellars. The people of Saxony, who are reputed to have objected to their king's departure in the revolutionary turmoil of 1918, are now said to have adopted their chief minister Kurt Biedenkopf as 'King Kurt'. Tribal and dynastic feelings clearly cannot be disen-tangled; over time they have become fused. Bismarck was certain that for the Germans dynastic loyalties mattered most.[3] By now this attachment has been transferred to the administrative and cul-tural centres of the *Länder*, which once accommodated the courts of kings, dukes, princes, and prince-bishops. The latter competed with each other in their architectural ambitions and as patrons of the arts and sciences. It is the federal structure of Germany which ensures that this cultural diversity is preserved, even if it means the maintenance of opera houses and theatres in close proximity to one another.

Much has been written about the Prussian ethos of state and state service, elevated to a quasi-religious status by the philosopher Friedrich Wilhelm Hegel. However, the ruler, as the principal employer and commissioner of the region, affected people's lives much more immediately and had more meaning for them than any sermon from the pulpit. The state, in the shape of court and office buildings, dignitaries, and officials, was almost as close at hand as a lord of the manor in England. Now, in the age of democratic self-government, people are, at least in theory, even more involved in local and regional affairs. However, in reality it is still often a matter of securing comfortable positions, or so it appears to outsiders.[4]

The present relationship between *Bund* and *Länder* is by far the most balanced and harmonious in German history, the First Reich being a loose confederation with not much unifying or protecting power at the centre (Vienna), the Second Empire dominated by Prussia in every respect, and the Weimar Republic described as a decentralized unitary state, which was then hijacked by the Nazis. The success of the present federal structure is due, first, to the input of the victorious powers who created the framework, and secondly to the lessons of history, as applied by the founding fathers of the Parliamentary Council. Both elements are indispensable.

As mentioned above, by the end of the war the Anglo-Saxon powers had reached the conclusion that it was better, and certainly more feasible, to dismember Prussia rather than the Reich. The overall intention was to diffuse power by decentralization in an acceptable way: first, no system could be maintained unless it had the support of the population, and secondly, federalism was the structure which best corresponded to Germany's historical development and would be suitable for the re-education of the German people. Both Prussia and the smaller states had to give way to more viable entities. The creative work fell to Britain, which had acquired the North-Western Zone with most of the new Prussian provinces. The American enclave of Bremen and Bremerhaven was the *quid pro quo* for settling the dispute over the allocation of zones. Whether Bremen would otherwise have regained its status as the 'Freie Hansestadt

Bremen' (on 23 January 1947) is questionable. During the Third Reich it had been lumped together with Oldenburg. Only two historic states survived fully intact: Hamburg and Bavaria. After 1945 most of the new *Länder* were reconstructed from Prussian provinces or old historical territories, as in the case of Niedersachsen (Kingdom of Hanover, Oldenburg, Braunschweig, Schaumburg-Lippe), Baden (Grand Dukedom), and Württemberg (Kingdom), or the consolidation of the various parts of Hesse (Kassel, Nassau, and Darmstadt), together with the free city of Frankfurt. In other words, to all intents and purposes Germany was already decentralized when the war ended. Berlin, which had figured prominently in Allied planning, lay in ruins and the victorious powers had to rely on regional authorities. Plans to re-establish central administrations in Berlin came to nothing, not only, as Elisabeth Kraus has discovered, as a result of French objections, but also because of Soviet and British reservations.[5] As far as Prussia was concerned, it was already quartered by the zonal division of Germany: each of the four Allied zones contained bits of it. When it was officially dissolved by the Control Council resolution of 25 February 1947, the once proud and powerful state had long since ceased to exist.

The Americans were the first to realize that this state of affairs was a blessing in disguise and soon grasped the opportunity to establish regional power structures. There was always a chance that sooner or later Berlin might fall into Communist hands. Decentralizing Germany was a means of immunizing the country against both the nationalist and Bolshevik virus. The Americans forged ahead with setting up *Länder* administrations in their zone, which, except for Bremen, were already fully functioning by the end of 1945. It took the British some time to catch up. The longer timespan of relative autonomy might be one reason, though not the only one, why the *Länder* of the US Zone were the most determined federalists, i.e. advocates of *Länder* rights, in the ensuing constitutional debate. All experts are agreed on one point: it was important that the individual *Länder* were there long before the federation, the Federal Republic of Germany, came into being. Between 1945 and 1949 the *Länder*, all fully equipped with their own constitutions,[6] were in fact the only legitimate and effective instruments of government in Germany. It was an open question how much power they would be prepared to devolve to the new centre. The political parties which hoped to form the central government soon developed into a counterweight against the interests of the *Länder* Minister-Presidents, or *Landesfürsten* as they were soon dubbed. The power balance between *Länder* and *Bund* was the most hotly discussed issue in the constitutional debate, not, as might be assumed, the question of socialism versus capitalism.

The Basic Law was a compromise and it was entirely the work of the Germans, not the occupation powers, who had prepared the ground. There was general consensus between victors and vanquished that the new West German state was to be federalist in the sense of being truly decentralized. In the case of Germany, decentralization and democratization were seen to be indispensable and complementary. The main issues during the constitutional debate were the powers of the *Bundesrat* and the financial system. Strictly speaking, the *Bundesrat*, which represents *Länder* interests, is not a second chamber as part of the national parliament. There are no deputies elected by popular ballot, only a certain number of delegates who are instructed by their respective cabinets to cast their votes *en bloc* (three to five votes per *Land* according to size). The proportion of legislation requiring consent by the Bundesrat has increased to over 50 per cent, despite, or perhaps because of, the general trend towards greater centralization.

While the Bundestag is the main legislator, the administrative tasks are almost entirely in the hands of the *Länder*, with the exception of the foreign service and the federal forces and postal services. In certain areas the *Länder* administer the law on behalf of the *Bund*; in others, like culture and education, they are autonomous. Revenues are split between *Bund* and *Länder* according to a fixed scale, especially as far as the most productive taxes are concerned (income, corporation, turnover, mineral, oil, and trade taxes), which account for more than four-fifths of total revenue. Other taxes are exclusively federal revenues, like customs and excise and certain consumer taxes; some are only raised by the *Länder* (vehicle, property, inheritance, etc.). In 1969 a system of horizontal financial compensation was introduced to even out the disparities between the richer *Länder*, such as Baden-Württemberg, and the poorer, like Schleswig-Holstein and the Saarland. Since then, common tasks have been tackled by a growing number of inter-governmental *Bund–Länder* commissions. This development is referred to by political scientists as 'co-operative federalism'.

On the whole, federalism has worked reasonably well for Germany. According to an official publication of 1995 its main purpose is 'to safeguard the nation's freedom' as 'an essential element of the power-sharing arrangement'.[7] In many parliamentary democracies the mechanisms of checks and balances are in danger of breaking down. Federalism has proved to be an additional safety precaution. It has also helped to integrate political parties, notably those in opposition, into the system. After all, the polarization of political parties was one of the reasons for the collapse of the Weimar democracy. Long before the SPD took over power in Bonn, it was already in control of an increasing number of *Länder* governments. Competition between the states, for instance in education, has been of benefit to the whole country: experiments in one *Land* can be examined for their usefulness in others.

For the general public federalism means, first and foremost, greater participation in the political process and more diversity, above all in cultural affairs. Few Germans feel deprived because they do not live in Berlin. Most are quite content to live near one of the eighty-five cities (over 100,000 inhabitants), which accommodate no more than one-third of the population. Improving the public transport system (*Nahschnellverkehr*) around these cities is judged to be more important than their actual expansion. The great majority (46 million) live in towns with between 2,000 and 100,000 inhabitants. To make a point: the provinces are nowhere and everywhere. Provinciality in this sense is part of the German identity. When Berlin was a cultural metropolis on a par with Paris and London for a few years in the 1920s, it was, significantly, rejected by most Germans and denounced as the modern Babel.[8] To the surprise of foreigners, Berlin was only chosen as the new capital of the united Germany by a small margin of votes, mainly from the parties on the fringe. A majority of Bundestag deputies of the two established parties (CDU/CSU and SPD) favoured Bonn, fearing that Berlin, quite apart from its unfortunate Prussian tradition, would downgrade the rest of the country and undermine the idea of federalism (CDU/CSU: 164 for Bonn, 154 for Berlin; SPD: 126 for Bonn, 110 for Berlin).[9]

There are two areas of political responsibility which are exclusively a matter for the *Länder*: local government and education. No doubt their impact on the political culture of Germany is considerable. While the first exercise of national autonomy by the Frankfurt

Parliament of 1848 (Paulskirche) was rather short-lived, local self-government as initiated by the reformer Karl Freiherr vom und zum Stein (1775–1871) was older and more durable. Apart from the twelve years of Nazi rule, German cities and towns always enjoyed a high degree of autonomy. At Potsdam the Allies agreed to decentralize the political structure and to revive local self-government on the basis of democratic principles. Democracy was to be rebuilt from the lowest level upwards. The Americans insisted on denazifying the local government law (*Deutsche Gemeindeordnung*: DGO) of 1936, but would otherwise not interfere with the existing structure. There were three types of local government in Germany, which to varying degrees favoured a strong executive around the Mayor (*Bürgermeister*) and/or the municipal authorities (*Magistrat, Stadtrat*). The British, used to gentlemen-citizens dabbling in politics, disliked the politicized official and felt, as one of the advisers later wrote, that 'the true division should be between those who made policy and those who carried it out.'[10] Most German experts regarded this distinction as wholly artificial and bound to create confusion. With so much work to do in Germany's devastated cities, clear-cut political responsibility and efficiency were more important than a dual procedure which was legitimized by its avoidance of the *Führerprinzip*. Nevertheless the British succeeded in implementing their system, which is only now in the process of being dismantled.

Local government reform was meant to be the first step on the road to an overhaul of the whole German bureaucracy, which was regarded as one of the major culprits in the recent disaster. However, no further progress was made and the council system remained the only institutional change implemented by the British occupation authorities. The irony is that today many British experts, worried about inner-city decay, wonder whether they should not adopt the French or German model of responsible local government. How, then, to account for the impression that cities in the north and south of Germany do not show any marked difference? The most likely explanation is that the German input prevailed in the end: first, the professional civil service, especially the competent middle ranks, which dominate local government; second, the pattern of co-operation between councillors and administrators, who often have the same background; third, the overall range of responsibilities (mainly education and culture, housing, health, general welfare and recreation, local transport, and policing) and above all the means to finance them.

Obviously the way towns and cities are run depends in no small measure on the funds available to them. Apart from capital assets, taxes constitute the main revenue, with the land rate (*Grundsteuer*) and trade tax (*Gewerbesteuer*) as the most profitable local taxes. Consequently, one of the chief priorities of local government in Germany is to attract businesses and industries. Boroughs are also entitled to a certain percentage of what the *Länder* receive from taxes levied nationally (income, turnover, and company taxes). These contributions are often for specifically defined purposes like school buildings or the maintenance of hospitals, local roads, etc. Since local governments are also permitted to take up credit, a great many of them are heavily in debt.[11] Difficult as it is to match *Länder*, like for instance Berlin and Brandenburg, or the Saarland and the Rhineland Palatinate, reforms to rationalize local government have been implemented everywhere. Small villages are the easiest targets: their independent government and schools have been disappearing at a rapid rate since the mid-1960s. The intention is to create municipalities of 5,000 to 8,000 inhabitants, often one town surrounded by a cluster of villages. Within the last twenty-five years 24,000 boroughs have been cut by more than half. In 1972, to give another example, the 143 local districts (*Kreise*) in Bavaria were reduced to 71. The same has happened in East Germany, notably Saxony, since reunification. The depletion in the countryside of all kinds of services would have met with more opposition than it actually did had it not been for the private motor car, which has now been accepted as one of life's necessities. On the other hand mayors and town clerks have now assumed the role of the princes of old in competing with one another to set up grammar schools, universities, and theatres.

Culture and education are the most distinctive, and certainly the most expensive, features of German federalism. Since 1973 more than a third of *Länder* budgets in the old Federal Republic has been spent on education, from primary schools to universities. After the war, the Allies were determined to decentralize responsibility for schools and make sure that central government would never again be in a position to indoctrinate the whole nation. However, it was felt that apart from a purge of personnel and a denazification of teaching, 're-education' or 'reorientation' was best left to the Germans themselves. The British in particular preferred to make suggestions rather than impose reforms. Their recommendations, which were by no means radical, were all taken up by the *Länder* at a later stage: abolition of school fees, extension of the school-leaving age from fourteen to fifteen, transfer of teacher-training colleges to universities, launching of comprehensive schools, and greater emphasis on adult education.

What were not fulfilled, however, were British hopes for university reform. The proposals of a Commission on University Reform, initiated by Military Government, were largely rejected by German vice-chancellors in 1949. An increase in staff was welcomed, but not the introduction of 'tutor lecturers', because the emphasis on teaching divorced from scholarship was deemed to be incompatible with German traditions. Up to the present day higher education suffers from its elitist and overambitious approach and its relative indifference towards society's practical needs. The German university system as conceived by Wilhelm von Humboldt, one of the great reformers of the post-Napoleonic era, was not designed to cater for nearly two million students. Nevertheless, its main principles are still faithfully adhered to: autonomy from the state, freedom of teaching and learning, and the intrinsic unity of research and tutoring (*Einheit von Forschung und Lehre*). In theory students are to be initiated into the methods of research rather than trained for a professional career. Repeated attempts at making higher education more accountable to society, including framework legislation by Bonn (*Hochschulrahmengesetz*, 1976), met with stiff resistance from both conservative academics and left-wing students. Professors are in fear of losing their privileges and students do not wish to be subjected to the rigours of professional training as practised by German technical colleges (*Fachhochschulen*).

Governments have therefore concentrated their efforts on the expansion of existing capacity and building new universities, in order to cope with the growing number of students. The rise in student numbers is staggering: from 172,000 in 1950 to 836,000 in 1975 and twice as many since then.[12] In 1960 only 8 per cent of youngsters had the qualifications necessary to go to university, whereas today more than one-third apply for a place. Fortunately the number of students enrolled in technical colleges has also experienced a steep rise, though a growing number of these students tend to change over to the university system after graduation (three years). The expansion of higher education did not happen by chance, but was actively fostered in the 1960s by all concerned, who were roused to action by Georg Picht's prognosis in 1964 of a *Bildungskatastrophe* (educational catastrophe) in Germany and Ralf Dahrendorf's claim that education was a civil right. The demand for more social justice and equality was fused with the general anxiety that the Federal Republic was losing out to its competitors because of a shortage of graduates. Even a doubling of grammar school leavers, so Picht argued, would not meet the needs of the economy for qualified professionals.[13] The number of grammar school pupils in the 1960s did indeed more than double. Society was called upon to exploit its potential of human intelligence to maintain the present level of prosperity. By that time the labour market for graduates was still confined to a small elite, which contributed to the unequal distribution of wealth.

Only ten years later did it become clear that society could not possibly absorb the rapidly growing number of graduates who were aspiring to a profession as well as a highly paid career. It seemed at the time that there were just not enough openings for doctors, lawyers, bankers, and company directors. Nor were *Länder* governments, as the biggest employers, prepared to take on as many teachers as were ready to join the staffs of grammar schools. Under the shadow of terrorism, the fear of a potential academic proletariat haunted the public. Fortunately, so far, these fears have proved to be unfounded. The reasons are manifold: expansion of the service sector, shifting expectations, increasing awareness of education for its own sake. With the expansion of higher education the prestigious and influential position of the *Akademiker*, notably the *Herr Professor*, is gradually declining. As a consequence, though not as a necessary result, caste feeling amongst the educated classes is also less pronounced than in the past. Graduates, called *junge Akademiker* in German, no longer assume that, due to their education, the state owes them a kind of grace-and-favour living, and that something is fundamentally wrong with society if these expectations are not fulfilled. Without this almost imperceptible change of consciousness, the expansion of higher education and the resulting unemployment among young graduates could have caused serious social tensions. After all, students were among the first to fall for the Nazis, in spite of the latter's poor intellectual credentials.

The problems of today are different: students tend to spend on average seven years at university, almost three years longer than officially recommended. If one includes national service, whether in the forces or in hospitals, and professional training (e.g. the *Referendariat* for the civil service), then young educated Germans usually enter professional life much older (normally aged between 28 and 30) than their counterparts elsewhere. Not much progress has been made in slimming down courses (*Studienreform*). For most students the free-wheeling life at university, interspersed with occasional employment, is much more attractive than regular office hours in a humdrum junior position. As one critical observer describes Germany's dilemma, its higher education system generates the oldest university students and its retirement system the youngest old-age pensioners.[14] There is an increasing awareness among the decision-making elite that in view of the enormous increase in the national debt after reunification the country cannot afford this kind of generosity much longer. A growing number of students, desperate not to waste too much time, now tend to opt for a three- or four-year course at a British or American university. Altogether there are approximately 10,000 German students enrolled at British institutions of higher education; only half of them are grant-supported.

Primary and secondary education is, on the whole, well structured. The three-tier system which evolved after the war has been constantly improved upon, with a view to making it more flexible. All children enter primary schools at the age of 6. After four years (in Berlin, six) pupils are channelled into three different types of secondary school, according to their abilities, which are assessed during an 'orientation phase': (1) the principal secondary school (*Hauptschule*) until the age of fifteen, followed by vocational training; (2) the intermediate school (*Realschule*) for six years, which, after further training in technical schools (*Fachschule/Fachoberschule*), qualifies one for a three-year course at one of the polytechnics (*Fachhochschule*); (3) the traditional nine-year grammar school (*Gymnasium*), which provides the entrance ticket for university, the only restrictions being in certain popular subjects with limited places (*numerus clausus*), like medicine, pharmacy, etc. For such courses the last school report may be taken into account.

Similar to the approach in higher education, reform efforts have been focused on three areas: (1) an expansion of the existing system to allow for the rise in numbers and for extension into rural areas and into hitherto untapped social milieux; (2) the introduction, in line with the European trend, of comprehensive schools, though not in all *Länder*, to facilitate transition from one type of school to another; (3) reform of the upper phase of the grammar/comprehensive school. A course system has replaced conventional classes, with a view to cutting down on content in favour of special subjects and greater emphasis on methods of learning, thus preparing pupils better for universities. However, in view of falling standards in general knowledge, these reforms are being scaled down again in favour of more traditional teaching methods. The comprehensive school system has proved to be politically most controversial, with SPD governments in favour and conservative governments against. Regrettably, though not untypically, the public debate has been distorted by a disposition towards antagonistic positions: what one side sees as equality of opportunity and democratization is criticized by the other as uniformity and levelling.

It so happens that some middle-class parents in Hesse, for instance, go out of their way to send their sons and daughters on long train journeys into conservative Bavaria for the sake of a more traditional education. In the past, the German grammar schools prided themselves on imparting a high level of general knowledge (*Allgemeinbildung*) in an age of increasing specialization. They are still dominated by the middle class, but have attracted, over the years, a growing number of pupils from other social milieux. There is no denying, however, that middle-class pupils still have a head start over others, because of the supportive attitude of their parents, especially as regards extra coaching. Since the curricula are worked out by the *Länder* ministries for education, there is no difference in standard between a city or a small town *Gymnasium*. Nor is the small town (approximately 10,000 inhabitants) necessarily a bad placement for a *Studienrat* (teacher with a permanent position), since accommodation may be cheaper and his status in the local society more elevated. On the whole the state-controlled, non-paying *Gymnasium* is nowadays less elitist and more democratic than it used to be. The introduction of *Gemeinschafts-* or *Sozialkunde* in 1950 (a sort of course in civil rights), in conjunction with a critical reassessment of German history, did much to enhance these democratic values. No doubt this development was further assisted by the teaching of English as the first foreign language, with all its concomitant aspects, in all schools as of 1955, when the Federal Republic gained independence.

While outstanding, internationally acclaimed achievements are generally associated with research arising from university education, it is the intermediate level, leading to the *Fachhochschule* degree, which has done most to foster social mobility, underpin the economy, and stabilize the whole fabric of society. One-third of all pupils opt for this course. They may not be the future leaders, though some of the best undoubtedly will rise to the top. But then it is not leadership or individual distinction that has marked out post-war Germany among its neighbours, but rather stability and prosperity through dogged perseverance.

The balance sheet of federalism would be incomplete without drawing attention to its negative effects, which are no less an element of the political culture of Germany: devolution of power has led to a proliferation of bureacracy. All the sixteen *Länder* governments have their string of ministries, which employ a growing number of ministerial officials. The latter have to justify their existence by issuing innumerable regulations and guidelines. Not without reason are they still referred to as *Staatsdiener*, i.e. state servants, even though they are supposed to serve society. Former East Germans often complain that they have to fill in more forms than ever before and that nothing can be done, especially in the vital building sector, without planning permission from countless officials. It is not quite true to say that it is the bureaucracy which rules the country. But it is fair to suggest that civil servants initiate most of the laws, both on the federal and the *Länder* level, and that they never lose sight of their own interests. Their pressure group, the civil service union (*Deutscher Beamtenbund*: DBB), has proved to be by far the most effective lobby, because public employees constitute the strongest 'party' in all parliaments.

As a rule, the higher-grade civil servants join the DBB, not the trade union of public employees, the *Deutsche Angestelltengewerkschaft*, which tends to attract the lower grades. Altogether the civil service and the body of public employees have expanded enormously since 1949.[15] Promotion to well-paid positions is now much faster than it used to be. In the 1970s the Bundestag consisted of no less than 42 per cent public employees, approximately ten times their proportion of the population. Overrepresentation is even more marked in the *Länder* parliaments (e.g. Hesse, with 61 per cent in 1975) with teachers as the strongest single group. However, it has been pointed out that public servants do not form a homogeneous body with a clear-cut voting pattern and that they are subject to the party whip.[16]

The story of how the German civil service regained its predominant position after the war is most significant. Both British and American military governments were intent on creating a comprehensive public service, which had completely severed its ties with the previous mandarin caste, and also sought to prohibit civil servants from running for political office. They failed in the face of delaying tactics and staunch resistance.[17] The Civil Service Law of 14 July 1953, based on the blueprint of 1937 in its denazified version, re-established the traditional German civil service (*Berufsbeamtentum*) with only minor concessions to the Allied reform programme. The reinstatement of all civil servants dismissed in 1945, and in particular the recognition of their pension rights, had already been achieved two years earlier.

These officials, reinstated in accordance with Article 131 of the Basic Law, preferred to join the ranks of the federal administration established from 1949 onwards. Once again, all the old privileges were guaranteed by law, in return for the pledge of the civil service not to go on strike: tenure for life, automatic salary increases, additional health insurance met by the government, and pensions of up to 75 per cent of take-home pay at retirement. Since the *Länder* are in charge of administering the country, they are the ones that have to finance all this. At the present time approximately 40 per cent of their budgets are allocated for personnel costs. According to recent forecasts there will soon be more officials in retirement than in active service. The *Länder* will be suffocated by spiralling costs unless they are prepared to set up separate pension funds to which civil servants have to contribute.

The Germans are conscious and proud of living under the rule of law (*Rechtsstaat*), which is, in Germany, founded on a much older tradition than parliamentary democracy. 'Law and order' is left untranslated in English if reservations are expressed, because the German translation *Recht und Ordnung* is perceived as intrinsically positive. From the point of view of social psychology, respect for the law is one thing, belief in it is another. In the case of Germany, this can be interpreted as an expression of insecurity. Belief in the constitution has developed into a kind of secular faith. It unites the political left and right and has produced the idea of *Verfassungspatriotismus*,[18] i.e. patriotism based not on 'king and country' but on the constitution. There are good and plausible historical reasons for this: the Weimar Republic went under because its avowed enemies undermined the very constitution which protected them. Hitler kept referring to the 'Weimar system', which he was determined to abolish. The leaders of the student movement of 1968 also rejected the 'system' and while the Führer prepared himself for the march to Berlin the radicals of West Germany, followers of Mao Tse-Tung, put fear into law-abiding citizens by their 'long march through the institutions'. Perhaps students are taken too seriously in Germany.

The result of all this was that on 28 January 1972 Willy Brandt, the darling of the left, and the Minister-Presidents of the *Länder* jointly issued the notorious 'extremist directive' (*Radikalenerlaß*), which reminded all concerned that according to existing laws no person could enter public service without subscribing to the democratic order as laid down in the constitution. This measure was soon denounced as tantamount to a *Berufsverbot* (ban on practising a certain profession), directed against people who were suspected of belonging to the German Communist Party. The damage to Germany's reputation abroad was considerable, even though it can be assumed that other governments had their own more discreet ways of keeping radicals at bay. The difference in Germany was that left-wing teachers as well as ordinary postmen or railway conductors feared for their jobs. Some regional administrations simply ignored the directive, unless someone had exposed himself as an active agitator. Government and the CDU opposition clashed over the question of whether defiant acts or mere membership of certain organizations was sufficient evidence of unconstitutional behaviour to justify a bar to public employment. In 1975 the Constitutional Court (*Bundesverfassungsgericht*) ruled that rejection was admissible on the basis of 'membership of a political party that pursues aims hostile to the constitution, regardless of whether that party has been found unconstitutional by decision of this court'. The effect of this ruling was the exact opposite of what it set out to achieve. The *Länder*, led by Lib-Lab governments, issued new guidelines which stated that membership of any organization not specifically banned could not be held against any applicant for the civil service. Some more conservative authorities continued with their security checks on job-seekers; others abandoned this procedure altogether. These checks were a matter for either the federal or the *Länder* Offices for the Protection of the Constitution (*Verfassungsschutzämter*), which were set up for the specific purpose of gathering intelligence on extremist organizations on the far left and the far right.

Both the *Bundesverfassungsgericht* and the *Verfassungsschutzämter* are institutions unique to Germany. They certainly are in reality, and not only in theory, guardians of the democratic order. Nowadays they are more concerned with the rise of the extreme right and xenophobic activities than with left-wing terrorism. But there can be no doubt that they are always in danger of overreacting and that they are proof of a deep-seated feeling of insecurity.

The ruling with regard to the required loyalties of the civil service shows that the Constitutional Court occupies a very special position in Germany. As the guardian of the constitution, it has no equivalent in other European countries. Even though English case law, i.e. rule of precedent, has no place in German legal thinking, the decisions of the Constitutional Court are exceptional in that they are binding on all courts and public authorities.[19] The background for its inception is the Nazi dictatorship, which represented a total perversion of the Weimar constitution without actually abolishing it. The political importance of Karlsruhe, the seat of the court, for the consolidation of democracy in Germany cannot be exaggerated, especially during the initial post-1949 period. The court is not supposed to determine political action but to rule on disputes if called upon by certain authorities. These mainly tend to be disputes between central government and the *Länder* or between individual federal institutions. Moreover, individual citizens are also able to file complaints, if they feel their basic rights have been infringed by the authorities. Altogether Karlsruhe has passed judgment on some 80,000 cases, mainly with regard to constitutional complaints, of which 2,000 have been successful. Even though the federal judges are not supposed to be active politicians, they are, in view of the nature of their decision-making, selected by parliament. For each of the two senates, four of the judges are chosen by the Bundestag and four by the Bundesrat, where a different party might prevail. After their tenure of twelve years they may not be re-elected. Of the issues on which the Constitutional Court has made up its collective mind, some have been dictated by a more conservative interpretation of the constitution, some by a more liberal one, more often than not by the objective of finding a judicious compromise. Apart from the ruling on civil servants' loyalty, other famous rulings, to name but a few, concerned the prohibition of the German Communist Party in 1956, by then a small splinter party which was forced underground; a defence of the freedom of the press in connection with the *Spiegel* affair in 1965; the rejection of the Bavarian government's claim that the Basic Treaty between the two Germanies violated the constitutional commitment to seek unification (1973). The Constitutional Court is also called upon to see to it that statutory law is brought into line with the demands of the Basic Law, for instance the equality of men and women, or that children born both in and out of wedlock should be treated as equals. Only after repeated admonitions by Karlsruhe did parliament sanction this right by law in 1969.

Though it has become somewhat easier for those other than law graduates to enter the civil service, the predominance of lawyers (*Juristenmonopol*) still remains a bone of contention in Germany, the more so since it not only applies to government administration but also to other administrative positions in society. A great many pressure groups are run by lawyers. Ralf Dahrendorf compared the German law departments with the English public schools and the French Grandes Écoles as training grounds for social elites.[20] He points out that those German grammar school pupils who had no specific interest would study law as a general leadership qualification, partly because that left them with so many options at a later stage. Almost half of all law students used to come from civil service families and about 40 per cent would again flock to the public service, including of course the judiciary. Since both lawyers and administrators are moulded by the codified *status quo*, their close interrelation is bound to enhance conservative attitudes in Germany. The common denominator is the law and how it is to be applied.

In fact the general belief in the righteousness of the written law borders on the religious. Whatever is legal appears to be justified *per se*. Germans have not always been sufficiently aware of the fundamental difference between legality and justice. The Constitutional Court was set up for the specific purpose of making sure that the two do not differ too much in the real world. It is important to notice that as a rule all law is statutory (*geschriebenes Gesetz*), be it in the form of the civil law as codified in 1900 (*bürgerliches Gesetzbuch*: BGB), i.e. the bible of the German lawyer, or the Basic Law, the German constitution, to name only the two most important pieces of legislation. There is no such person, for instance, as a 'common-law wife' in Germany, despite the three million unmarried people living together. Germany is one of the countries that adopted the continental civil law, strongly influenced by Roman law, as opposed to common-law societies. Nearly all areas and aspects of society are covered by legislation; precious little is left to negotiation. In any crisis situation the government feels called upon to pass a new law which, though initiated to cope with a certain emergency, is conceived in general terms and is likely to remain on the statute book for a long time.

When terrorism hit Germany in the 1970s, the Bundestag, then controlled by a Lib-Lab government, saw no alternative but to pass amendments to the criminal law and other laws which would, and did, make it easier to prosecute people who incited others to break the law or to undermine the security of the Republic. With no national police force to deal with a crisis situation and law enforcement a matter for the *Länder* all the government could do was pass a new law. Chancellor Helmut Schmidt was right to make the point: 'We cannot get rid of terrorism by legislation alone; we must destroy the spiritual soil that nourished it.'[21] He questioned the German preference for solving problems by enforcing the law and leaving it at that. No doubt some radical students of the 1968 movement and later terrorists broke the law and had to be dealt with accordingly. The question is whether applying the law was the only answer, as many Germans believed at the time.

For foreigners it is not easy to grasp that a body like the Constitutional Court which is not accountable to the electorate should be able to wield so much political power in a democracy. All restrictions on the popular vote devised by the founding fathers of the Republic served to uphold the rule of law against the potential onslaught of a misguided majority. The courts can be trusted to uphold human and civil rights, especially those of minorities, and nowadays citizens are treated as such, not as subjects. However, every detail is now regulated by law, subject to jurisdiction, and is no longer at the discretion of administrators or politicians. No wonder that some observers are worried about the general trend towards a *Justizstaat*, where the 'lawlords' are the real rulers of the country. The danger of a reincarnation of the *Obrigkeitsstaat* (authoritarian state) in the shape of supreme courts should not be dismissed out of hand. Is it up to a court of eminent judges to decide whether the German forces should be allowed to operate out of area (i.e. NATO territory) for peacekeeping purposes? Elsewhere this would be decided by a cabinet meeting or parliamentary vote.

6 Party Politics and Public Opinion

The Federal Republic claims not only to be a *Bundesstaat*, with a decentralized power base, a *Rechtsstaat*, which sanctions the rule of law, and a *Sozialstaat*, concerned about the welfare of its citizens, but also a *Parteienstaat*, a parliamentary democracy run by political parties. Of these four functions of state, the last is undoubtedly the most problematic from a German point of view. Does this mean that democracy has not taken root after all?

Historically, political parties did not enjoy as much prestige as state authorities. They were either too weak to determine government policy, as under the Kaiser, too numerous and divisive to form a stable government, as in Weimar Germany, or too repressive and corrupt, as during the Nazi and SED dictatorships. In some respects the political party was perceived to be the very antithesis of the state, which took care of all the people. Parties represented modern society, or rather the plurality of social interests, whereas the state was supposed to stand for the community (*Volksgemeinschaft*). It was mainly parties, and their special-interest pleading, which gave democracy such a bad name in Germany. In one of his most successful speeches, the first to be recorded on gramophone, Hitler made a mockery of the Weimar parties (31 July 1932): 'The attempt, however,' he said, 'to divide the nation into classes, estates, professions, and denominations, and to lead it piecemeal to the economic happiness of the future, has today met with total failure.'[1] After the unprecedented disaster of Hitler's one-party rule, young Germans returning from the miseries of war and captivity were not much inclined to trust another party.

The political parties which sprang up in 1945 were mostly founded by Weimar politicians of the older generation, who had emigrated or, like Adenauer, totally withdrawn from public life. The ease with which Hitler had ousted all parties in the summer of 1933 made them realize that the Weimar constitution had been flawed in this respect. Only in passing, and not in a complimentary context, did the constitution refer to political parties: 'Officials are servants of the whole of society (*Gesamtheit*), not of a party' (Article 130). Most constitutional lawyers at the time looked down on parties as 'an extra-constitutional phenomenon'.[2] There was, then, a glaring gap between the Weimar constitution and the reality of politics. The members of the Parliamentary Council made sure that the Basic Law would eventually legitimize political parties. In Article 21 the new constitution recognized their crucial role in the 'formation of the political will of the people'.[3] There was no restriction on the founding of parties, as long as their statutes were based on democratic principles and provided the funding they received was publicly accounted for. Sponsorship of parties was to become contentious. If financial contributions were deducted from tax, would special-interest groups gain undue advantages?

In 1965 the SPD-led government of Hesse requested the Constitutional Court at Karlsruhe to examine whether Bonn was entitled to provide 38 million DM for party campaigns in the budget. Karlsruhe was no longer willing to tolerate public funding of parties, which had secretly crept in since 1959 without legal basis. It was only now that the Bundestag passed a law (*Parteiengesetz*) on 24 July 1967, in accordance with Article 21 of the Basic Law, which defined the nature of political parties and the rights of their members. It was no accident that Germany was governed for the first and last time by a grand coalition. Whereas before then parties had hardly existed in a legal sense, every aspect of their statutes was now scrutinized and regulated. Above all, and this is probably unique in Europe, parliament went out of its way to recompense parties for their 'necessary expenses in connection with an appropriate election campaign'.[4] This would only apply to federal elections, to the amount of 2.15 DM per elector. A few years later this largesse was extended to *Land* elections as well, and the amount was raised in line with inflation. However, this is not all: the business of parliamentary parties is subsidized, and so are the party foundations (Konrad Adenauer-, Friedrich Ebert-, Friedrich Naumann-, and Hanns Seidel-Stiftung).

Most observers of the German party system are agreed that there are certain characteristic features which distinguish the Federal Republic from Weimar Germany:

1. All political parties now depend upon permament membership and an organizational machinery with full-time officials.
2. There is a strong trend towards the professionalization of politics. No doubt the overrepresentation of officials with a university degree plays an important part: they just switch track from one public career to another with no risk to their pension rights or their chances of promotion. The number of self-employed Deputies has steadily declined. This career pattern of professional politicians, with its concomitant lack of achievement outside politics, is increasingly resented by the public at large. The CDU/CSU has been least affected by the rise of intellectuals in politics.[5]
3. The three-party system has evolved, which encompasses between 75 per cent and nearly 90 per cent of the electorate, and which represents the chief strands of German political history: the conservative, socialist, and liberal tendencies, with the Greens now threatening to eclipse the Liberals.
4. The political culture of the parties is centrist, which reflects an electorate gravitating towards the middle ground.[6] This development has been enhanced by the pivotal role of the Liberal Party (FDP) and the federal structure. The latter excludes the politics of confrontation and tends to institutionalize co-operation between the parties, which are never fully out of government.
5. There has been an erosion of traditional political milieux, such as the working class, the Catholic, and the national Protestant milieux, and the modern *Volkspartei*, i.e. catch-all party, has emerged.
6. Closely connected with this phenomenon is the unimpeded process of secularization, which has been accelerated by the anti-religious stance of the two German dictatorships.

What about the three main parties, which have dominated all federal governments since 1949 in various combinations?[7] The only major innovation after the war was the creation of the Christlich-Demokratische Union (CDU) and its Bavarian sister party, the Christlich-Soziale Union (CSU). The idea of a popular Christian party consisting of both Catholics and Protestants is older than the CDU. However, all attempts by the old Catholic Centre Party during the Weimar period to appeal to Protestants were doomed to failure.

It was the repression of Christianity and the persecution of both churches by the Nazi regime which called for a fresh and successful start. The movement towards a new all-embracing Christian *Volkspartei* was not orchestrated from the top but emerged simultaneously in Berlin and in the Catholic Rhineland, which used to be the power base of the old Centre Party. The formative years were to become crucial for the CDU, first as a gathering of personalities with a similar outlook and then as a union of political groups surfacing in various parts of Germany.[8] Earlier than elsewhere the CDU established itself on 25 February 1946 in the British Zone and elected Dr Konrad Adenauer as its chairman.

In his first pronouncements Adenauer distanced the party from earlier socialist ideas, though he would have preferred the name 'Christlich-Soziale Partei'. For all its Christian rhetoric, the CDU remained anchored in the predominantly Catholic political and cultural milieu of West Germany. In those *Länder* like Lower Saxony with a clear Protestant majority, the new party fared best in Catholic enclaves which had voted for the Centre Party in the past. While today the CDU is clearly identified with German conservatism, this was by no means the party's image at the beginning. Nor could the party be easily equated with other conservative parties abroad, such as the Tories in Britain or the Republicans in the United States. To many Protestants the new party was not sufficiently national-minded, or rather it was too anti-Prussian. Members of former right-wing parties had no say in the early days. In many ways the CDU was a federation of regional parties around local dignitaries, first under the banner of Christian democracy and then increasingly as the followers of Konrad Adenauer, whose name served as a political programme.

The CSU was not just the Bavarian offshoot of the CDU, though it emerged at the same time and in similar circumstances. The political profile was even more regional and anti-Prussian, more distinctly Catholic (over 90 per cent), and more property-minded, and it was a more dominant political force in Bavaria, with 52.3 per cent of the votes cast in the first elections in 1946. Its social base was the class of modest property: farmers, tradesmen and retailers, small-town entrepreneurs.[9]

In contrast to the centrist trend of German politics outlined above, the CSU's position was challenged by right-wing Bavarian traditionalists who had once separated from the Catholic Centre Party to form their own Bavarian People's Party. The last chairman of this party, Fritz Schäffer, had been installed by the Americans as the first post-war Minister-President of Bavaria. It was not until November 1946 that the traditionalists founded the *Bayernpartei*, a motley collection of old-fashioned monarchists and fiercely independent Bavarian autonomists, who united under the banner 'Bavaria for the Bavarians', determined to resist the 'Prussian invasion', i.e. migrants from any other part of Germany. They had their stronghold in Lower Bavaria, the most industrially backward region of Germany. However, they were neither religious fundamentalists—the CSU was dismissed as ultramontane (i.e. under the influence of the Vatican)—nor German nationalists. Their support peaked in the first federal elections, when they sent 17 Deputies to the Bundestag in 1949, forcing the rival CSU down from over 50 per cent to under 30 per cent. After that, the CSU recovered its lost ground and the *Bayernpartei* vanished into obscurity. The same fate was in store for a few other parties on the right, in particular the *Deutsche Partei*, with its stronghold in Lower Saxony, and the Union of Expellees (*Bund der Heimatvertriebenen*: BHV), which won most of its votes in the first federal elections in those *Länder* with a high percentage of refugees from the East (Schleswig-Holstein, Lower Saxony, Bavaria).

The CSU had learnt its lesson in that it now strove to cultivate its separate Bavarian identity. With the ascendance of the populist Franz-Josef Strauß the threat from the right seemed to be banished for good. Except for a short period in the 1950s, the CSU never lost its overall majority in the *Landtag*. To many Bavarians the CSU appears to be the *Staatspartei*, the governmental party in perpetuity. The party succeeded in harmonizing two very different strategies without endangering its social stability: preserving the agrarian structure and thereby the loyalty of the peasantry, combined with rapid but carefully managed industrialization, especially in the field of the new high-tech industries. Thus in Bavaria industrial modernization and political conservatism are not at odds with each other. The CDU followed the same road quite successfully in Baden-Württemberg, which experienced a staggering growth rate. In the west and north of Germany the party had a harder task because it had to cope with an increasingly outdated industrial infrastructure (coal, steel, and shipyards, etc.), and an electorate which was more attuned to the Social Democrats.

The Social Democrats were the only post-war party with an unblemished record reaching back to the eve of German unification.[10] If there was a truly national party which could do without lessons in democracy, it was the SPD. Only the Social Democrats had the guts, in an atmosphere of outright intimidation, to vote against Hitler's Empowering Act (*Ermächtigungsgesetz*, 23 March 1933). A great many Social Democrats perished as a consequence in prisons and concentration camps. The Social Democrats in the Western zones rallied around Kurt Schumacher,[11] their charismatic but difficult leader who had spent many years in concentration camps. There were reasonable grounds to assume that the Social Democrats would be the governing party in Germany for decades to come. Why were these expectations not fulfilled? Ironically, the party with the best credentials of opposition to National Socialism was hampered by the legacy of the past and its image of being too national-minded and too socialist. The Western Allies and many German politicians, notably Adenauer, were soon to realize that German unity could only be secured on Soviet terms. This was clearly too high a price to pay. Schumacher's chief rival was Otto Grotewohl, head of the SPD's Berlin Central Committee, who claimed the leadership of the whole party and who embraced the concept of a united labour front with the Communists. Reuniting the two working-class parties appeared to many to be as much the dictate of the hour as the joint action of Catholics and Protestants in creating the CDU. However, Schumacher and the leaders returning from exile, amongst them Willy Brandt, had enough evidence for their belief that democratic socialism and the Stalinist perversion of Communism were fundamentally incompatible. They had no illusions about the role of German Communists as Moscow's agents, acting in the interests of Soviet foreign policy and long-term plans. The forced merger of Social Democrats and Communists in the Soviet Zone was no boost for the electoral chances of either party in the Western zones.

Another more serious handicap for the SPD was its failure to follow Schumacher's advice and to extend its influence beyond the traditional working-class milieu. The great majority of its members were workers born before 1910 and active before 1933. No serious attempt was made to appeal to the younger generation, whose formative years had been spent under Nazi rule. The SPD was, as it were, content with regaining access to its old home, instead of venturing out into the new post-war world. Furthermore, economic expertise was sadly lacking amongst its leaders. Was the policy of strict nationalization according to Marxist doctrine the only answer (Victor Agartz) or could socialism be compatible with comprehensive planning (Erik Nölting, and later Karl Schiller)? It was another fifteen years and the famous party conference in Bad Godesberg in 1959 before the party finally came to the conclusion that a modern economy cannot be run according to the insights of a nineteenth-century social philosopher. In the meantime the SPD was resigned to holding on to the true faith and opposing the conservative German government in Bonn as a matter of principle. Even after Godesberg the party had problems with the necessities of political power, of striving for it and holding on to it. There can be no doubt that the SPD was devoutly attached to the constitution. But throughout the 1950s it was perceived as continually questioning the very premisses of German economic and foreign policy successes: the free market and integration with the West. The idea that the Bonn republic was but a provisional state and a transitional phenomenon fitted perfectly into the collective mentality of a party which lived in hope of the final advent of socialism. Not surprisingly, for a long time the majority of Germans had no confidence in the SPD's political wisdom and management skills on the federal stage.

The German Communist Party (KPD) in the Western zones never posed a threat to the Social Democrats as a serious rival on the left. However, it did, to some extent, deter the middle class from voting SPD during the Cold War period. At first the KPD was more restrained in its radical demands than its big brother in the Soviet Zone. Its campaign for national unity did not meet with much response. Nor did the thesis of the special German road to socialism go down very well with Social Democrats, who saw for themselves what was happening in Eastern Germany. Shadowing the SED, the KPD obediently abandoned this idea when it became an official heresy following Tito's break with Moscow. After that the KPD reverted to the obsolete rhetoric of the class struggle, with the predictably low result of 5.7 per cent of the vote (15 seats) in the first federal election. Four years later the party did not manage to surmount the 5 per cent hurdle or gain a single seat (its share of the vote was 2.3 per cent). Why the Constitutional Court should then have felt obliged in 1958 to ban the party has never been understood. General unease about this decision led to a readmittance of the party ten years later, though not, for legal reasons, under the old name. It was now known as the *Deutsche Kommunistische Partei* (DKP). Soon afterwards Germany witnessed the proliferation of a whole string of rival Communist parties, mostly of Maoist persuasion, as a result of the student revolution.

The Liberals had a head start in Berlin as early as 16 June 1945 under the leadership of two former ministers of the Reich (Eugen Schiffer and Wilhelm Kölz). As the only undisputedly bourgeois grouping they were well suited to camouflage Soviet intentions. However, when the *Liberal-Demokratische Partei Deutschlands* (LDPD) complied with Soviet wishes and formed part of the popular front in February 1946, the party forsook all influence in the Western zones. In Württemberg and Baden the Liberals, never a powerful force in German politics, had struck their deepest roots. It is therefore no surprise that Swabian Liberals of the old school, Reinhold Maier and Theodor Heuss, the first President of the Republic, should emerge as the leading lights. The Liberal Party surfaced everywhere under various names and guises: the *Deutsche Volkspartei* in Württemberg, the *Liberal-Demokratische Partei* in Hesse, the *Freie Demokratische Partei* in Bavaria. The *Freie Demokratische Partei* (FDP) of the British Zone was constituted on 7–8 January 1946, even before the party had established itself in all new *Länder*.

The self-perception of the Liberals as the party of the entrepreneurial middle class has always carried more electoral weight than its political programme. In 1949 the parliamentary party, which gained only one-third of the votes of the two big parties, contained more self-employed Deputies than any other party. It was not for purely opportunistic reasons, then, that the Free Democrats kept their options open for coalitions with both the CDU/CSU and the Social Democrats, and have thus participated in government throughout the history of the Federal Republic, except for two short periods, when the conservatives won an overall majority in 1957 and during the Grand Coalition (1966–9). In economic matters the Liberals were firm advocates of Erhard's free market economy and remained close allies of the CDU/CSU. On the other hand, in foreign affairs, education, and legal reform there was, from time to time, a strong inclination towards the left. This dual perspective, already evident in the Parliamentary Council of 1948, is founded in the two strands of German liberalism. From 1961 onwards, under the leadership of Erich Mende, the FDP consolidated its position and presented itself as the 'party of the second vote'.[12] All those middle-class Germans who resented the influence of the Church on politics and who felt that the predominantly Catholic CDU/CSU had abandoned the Protestant half of Germany tended to vote for the Free Democrats. In the 1970s, under the Lib-Lab government, the Liberals were seen as a necessary counterbalance to the SPD's preference for more economic planning and higher social security contributions. The FDP presented itself as the junior partner in government, which kept a check on the majority party to make sure that it did not veer too far from the middle course. In many ways the FDP likes to play the same role in German politics which Britain hopes to play in Europe, in matters of both policy and politics, i.e. securing independence and a maximum of influence with a minimum of power.

The three government parties which moulded the Federal Republic gave expression to the changing climate at the time, both in domestic politics and international affairs. Whether they were leading public opinion or simply responding to it is difficult to assess. No doubt Adenauer, with his strong opinions and determination to act on them, belonged to the first category. His no-nonsense attitude towards all dissenting voices and policy suggestions put the Republic firmly on track towards economic consolidation and integration with the West. On the whole the CDU/CSU Deputies served as his loyal retainers, benefiting from his growing prestige. Adenauer's face on election posters bordered on a personality cult. This towering father figure provoked adverse reactions among journalists and left-wing intellectuals, who stressed that his autocratic approach to politics corresponded to the authoritarian character of many Germans whose formative years had been before 1945. There is some truth in this. Emissaries of the national conservative opposition to Hitler told the Pope in 1940 that military dictatorship might be a necessary stepping-stone for the return of democracy.[13] What has been termed *Kanzlerdemokratie* was, of course, a far better option.

Adenauer's slow and forced withdrawal from power between 1961 and 15 October 1963 had all the hallmarks of a rebellion by the younger generation, who had come of age and would not be bossed around any longer. Apart from the fact that he was growing too old and stubborn, there were several incidents which contributed to his downfall. In 1959, he started toying with the idea of becoming President, before realizing how curtailed his constitutional powers would be. When the Berlin Wall went up in August 1961 Adenauer was in no hurry to see it for himself and express dissatisfaction. The same year the CDU/CSU lost its overall majority in the federal elections, its share of the vote falling from 52.2 per cent to 45.3 per cent, and had to take the FDP back into the government, even though its leaders had directed their campaign against Adenauer. The Chancellor was also implicated in the so-called *Spiegel-Affäre* of 1962, when the influential Hamburg newsmagazine was subjected to unwarranted police action because of a critical article regarding the capability of the federal forces.[14] The impression prevailed that the government wished to silence the only magazine with an impressive record of investigative journalism. *Der Spiegel* came to symbolize the freedom of the press. It was one of the most serious and damaging domestic crises in the history of the Federal Republic, which forced the Minister of Defence, Franz-Josef Strauß, out of office. The public had already been alerted to a further onslaught against the media by Adenauer's failed attempt earlier on to create a government-controlled television channel. In February 1961 the Constitutional Court had ruled that this idea was not compatible with Article 5 of the Basic Law. Eventually the second German television channel (ZDF) was organized as a public corporation, along the lines of the first channel (ARD).

The 1950s had been a decade often unfairly described as a period of restoration.[15] It was in these years that the foundations of institutional democracy, economic recovery, social security, and integration with the West were laid, even though many Germans were not yet as liberal and open-minded as one might have wished. The 1960s are usually, and aptly, referred to as a transitional phase, the second half also being a time of fermentation. Due to a whole variety of influences working on society, such as increasing prosperity, the media (notably television), and the expansion of education, social mores went through a process of rapid transformation

(*Wertewandel*), with the level of expectations rising constantly. Some observers summarized developments in the late 1960s as a cultural revolution.[16] No doubt the generational conflict grew more intense than ever before or after. The younger generation questioned their parents' failures during the 1930s, without proper regard for their sufferings in the 1940s and their achievements in the 1950s. Human rights, especially that of self-fulfilment, replaced the work ethic and the emphasis on what were now dismissed as *Sekundärtugenden* (secondary virtues like industriousness, punctuality, cleanliness, etc.)

Marriage as an institution underwent rapid change in those years.[17] In 1967 43 per cent of young men and 65 per cent of young women still objected to cohabitation by unmarried couples. Only six years later 87 per cent of men and 92 per cent of women no longer had any qualms about living together. It took a few more years for divorce to become equally acceptable. By the early 1980s no more than 15 per cent of the population (4 per cent of the young generation) rejected divorce on principle. In this respect, as in most other questions pertaining to public norms and values, the West Germans had caught up, for better or for worse, with the West European trend, leaning more towards Britain, the Netherlands, and the Scandinavian countries than to the purely Catholic countries of the west and south.[18]

In the second half of the 1960s, German democracy had to face its first acid test: a potentially explosive combination of circumstances arose with an unexpected deceleration of the economy, a change of government after seventeen years of conservative rule, and the eruption of extremism at both ends of the political spectrum. The political class was acutely aware that German democracy was on probation and that the Western world was looking over their shoulder. Events were triggered by the sudden economic depression: unemployment rose steeply, revenues sank, and a budget deficit loomed. Chancellor Erhard, the father of the *Wirtschaftswunder*, now seemed to be out of his depth. When the government decided to raise taxes, the FDP recalled its ministers and precipitated a political crisis.[19] The outcome was an exercise in power-sharing, the first and only grand coalition of the two big parties under the chancellorship of Kurt-Georg Kiesinger, the Minister-President of Baden-Württemberg, and a suave and conciliatory Swabian gentleman. The left and the Western press were quick to point out that

Kiesinger had been a member of the Nazi Party, employed by the Foreign Office broadcasting service. It soon turned out that he had made a living by coaching law students, staying away from government service, until he was drafted into it when the war broke out. Later he was denounced to the Gestapo because he had foiled anti-Jewish broadcasts. Willy Brandt, the emigré opponent of Nazism, took over the foreign affairs portfolio and began to push for a new departure towards the East, without being able to go as far as officially recognizing the GDR.

The Grand Coalition managed to set Germany back on track in the most difficult circumstances.[20] However, the government has not been given the credit it deserves, because the spotlight was focused on the change-over to Brandt and the radicalization of fringe movements to right and left. It is the duty of historians not to be blinded when certain events are overexposed by the media.

Karl Schiller, the unemotional Hanseatic academic in charge of the economy, and the notoriously temperamental Franz-Josef Strauß, Minister of Finance, formed a team to sort out Germany's economic and financial problems. The general public loved this spectacle and called the unlikely duo, after two characters created by the popular nineteenth-century cartoonist Wilhelm Busch, 'Plisch' and 'Plum'. In their way, as the exponents of the Grand Coalition, these two greatly contributed to the centrist culture of German politics. They demonstrated that two very different personalities of previously antagonistic parties could work closely together for the good of their country. Few had qualms about expanding the management powers of government to keep the economy on course. The so-called stabilization law (*Stabilitätsgesetz*) of June 1967, referred to above, was perhaps the most important achievement of this government. It enabled Bonn to guide the economy by a cyclical policy: to raise credit up to 5 billion DM, to alter income and company taxes within certain bands, and to build up financial reserves for public investment if called for to stimulate the economy. To orthodox free-marketeers this looked like another 'empowering law'. However, handy analogies with the past are mostly misleading.

The instruments for guiding the business cycle proved very successful in years to come and the results were striking.[21] By 1969 the economy had reached new spectacular growth levels (7 to 8 per cent), inflation was down to 1.5 per cent, and the number of unemployed dropped from 600,000 to 200,000. Another major change, medium-term fiscal planning (*mittelfristige Finanzplanung: Mifrifi*) was introduced by Strauß to balance future budgets by making cuts at the right time. Of course, this was no guarantee that the books would be balanced for ever. In fact, the national debt rose steeply in the next twenty-five years, but *Mifrifi* did do the trick in that business confidence returned.

In May 1969 the federal–state relationship was put on a new footing. The federal government was authorized, as outlined above, to redistribute revenues in the interests of burden-sharing (*Länderfinanzausgleich*). Bonn was now responsible for establishing an economic balance between the *Länder* in one way or another (co-operative federalism). One could argue that under Kiesinger the domestic system of government was overhauled in the same way as foreign policy under Willy Brandt, with his determined approach towards a new *Ostpolitik*.

Many leading commentators at the time did not see things like this at all. The two big parties now joined forces; the opposition was virtually non-existent and democracy appeared to be in danger. Even though the student unrest clearly preceded the formation of the Grand Coalition, its momentum gathered pace because the politically active and generally left-wing student unions could draw support from those who had lost faith in the SPD. For the hard core of the student movement,[22] the Socialist German Student Federation (*Sozialistischer Deutscher Studentenbund*: SDS), the party had been on a slippery slope ever since it had abandoned Marxism for the sake of gaining power at its Godesberg rally in 1959. The SDS, which would not toe the party line, was expelled in 1961 and, left to roam in the wilderness, became obsessed with *Herrschaftsstrukturen* (patterns of repression) and *Konsumterror* (terror of the consumer society), which were discovered everywhere and discussed at length.

Whereas many students had certain reservations about 'the establishment', the hard-core activists rejected the 'system' as such, just as Nazis and Communists had done in Weimar Germany. The German university, once the model institution for higher education elsewhere, had not been conceived to cope with the mass of students now flooding seminars and lecture halls. Grievances about teaching and supervision were justified and institutional reform was overdue. But student leaders were not in the least interested in making higher education more efficient. Instead they pressed for more participation in university matters. Universities became more and more politicized and union activists were on the lookout for issues, generally far from home, to mobilize the student body. They adopted new methods from the American campuses like go-ins and sit-ins to vent their frustrations.

The Free University of Berlin, founded after the war as a democratic alternative to the East Berlin Humboldt University, was the hotbed of student unrest, not least because it attracted students who wished to avoid the draft. Frankfurt am Main, with its famous school of neo-Marxist philosophers and sociologists (Adorno, Horkheimer, and Habermas), was another centre of the student 'revolution'. Students of the social sciences, whose career prospects were none too rosy, were clearly in the forefront of the movement. The free-wheeling life at university campuses was emotionally and intellectually so much more satisfying than 'selling themselves to the capitalist system' in a subordinate position. It was not until students demonstrated in force against the Vietnam War (February 1966) that they became a real public nuisance. To the people of West Berlin the Americans were their main protecting power (*Schutzmacht*), which should not be antagonized on the most sensitive spot in the Western world.

Public reaction to the student uprising was far from reassuring: the establishment—professors, officials, and politicians—appeared to be confused, the police tended to overreact, as though dealing with a civil war, and the Springer press (*Bildzeitung*) fanned student anger by articulating the feelings of the 'silent majority'. Panic and hysteria fed on one another and at a demonstration against the Shah of Iran's visit to Berlin Benno Ohnesorg, a bystander, was shot by a policeman. Demonstrations now flared up in all German university cities and thousands of students who had been keeping their distance joined in. Support for the movement peaked at Easter 1968 when Rudi Dutschke, the charismatic leader of the Berlin SDS, was gunned down and severely wounded by a right-wing fanatic. A few days later in Munich, a photographer and an uninvolved student were the first fatalities, killed by flying paving stones.

From now on many student sympathizers withdrew their support and the level of violence dropped.

Unrest escalated once more in the summer when the Bundestag debated the Emergency Laws (*Notstandsgesetze*), which had been on the political agenda for some time.[23] Up to that moment, the Allied powers had reserved their right to intervene in German affairs if the authorities could not cope with the situation. The Grand Coalition offered the chance to pass a law which would end this infringement of German sovereignty. For the left this was yet another indication that West Germany was about to embrace 'fascism' and become a police state. Undeterred by the demonstrations, the overwhelming majority of Deputies voted for the emergency legislation on 24 June 1968. The people's uprising did not materialize as some leaders of the APO (*Außerparlamentarische Opposition*), as they now called themselves, had hoped. At most one-third of all students were involved in mass demonstrations at any one time, and what is more, the working class remained totally unsympathetic, unlike in France. Ordinary citizens, conscious of their hard-won living standards, found it absurd to think that Mao Tse-Tung—he had just failed with his 'Great Leap Forward'—should be held up as a model for West Germany's industrial society.

An interpretation of the student revolution has to take into account the fact that the phenomenon was an international one and not confined to Germany. Actually, one student leader, Daniel Cohn-Bendit, who was to become a member of the Green Party, was active in both Germany and France before he was expelled from Paris. However, in the case of Germany the terms of reference were slightly different. After the First World War young men were sorry to have missed the war and tried to make good by joining paramilitary organizations engaged in political warfare. After the Second World War the students once again felt deprived, this time of their chance to oppose Hitler, and to do better than their parents. The German student rebellion was a kind of *Ersatzwiderstand* (substitute resistance) since in their eyes fascism was only an extreme manifestation of capitalism. The students might as well oppose the capitalist Federal Republic, which would soon show its fascist face when under pressure. While the students were preoccupied with the alleged shortcomings of democracy at home, the rest of the population was only too aware of what had happened in

Czechoslovakia in August 1968. The fact that the students did not feel obliged to stage demonstrations against Soviet tanks in Prague discredited the whole movement in the eyes of ordinary citizens. After Prague, which had a sobering effect, the student movement lost its momentum.

When the Social Democrats ousted the conservatives in the 1969 elections many on the left returned to the fold and the movement petered out. A few faithful APO members joined various Communist splinter parties and a very small core of fanatics around Andreas Baader and Ulrike Meinhoff drifted into terrorism. An astonishingly large number of the 'group of 1968' (*Achtundsechzige*) later became part of the establishment, from academia to big business. However, it would be unfair to end on a cynical note. Even if the student movement achieved little in concrete terms, except for half-hearted university reform, it came to symbolize a fundamental shift in public and private values, away from the authoritarian mentality of the past to a more open and tolerant social climate. The 'system' did not crumble, but authority in whatever shape or form, not least the student body as the 'elite of the nation in the making', was lowered to a more approachable level.

While most West Germans felt that democracy and the *Rechtsstaat* were under siege from the APO, the foreign press—in both West and East, incidentally—gave the impression that the electoral successes of the NPD (*National-Demokratische Partei Deutschlands*) were much more alarming. Innumerable headlines referred to a renaissance of Nazism or *Refaschisierung der Bundesrepublik* (as in the Soviet and GDR propaganda versions). What had happened?

It would have been most surprising if there had been no Nazi sympathizers left in Germany. The NPD was founded in 1964 by representatives of right-wing splinter parties, like the Sozialistische Reichspartei (SRP), the Gesamtdeutsche Partei (GP), and the Deutsche Reichspartei, which were either banned or unable to gain more than 3 per cent of the votes in any election. Nor did the NPD itself manage to get more than 2 per cent in the 1965 federal elections.[24] However, in the autumn of 1966 the party all of a sudden climbed over the 5 per cent hurdle and sent eight deputies to the Hessian Diet (*Landtag*). The trend continued in further state elections (9.8 per cent in the Baden-Württemberg election of 1968). At the time it was difficult to know what to make of this worrying phenomenon. After all, the Nazi Party's vote rose from only 2.8 per cent in 1928 to 37.4 per cent within four years. According to official estimates, 10 per cent of ordinary NPD members (approximately 30,000 in all) and about 15 per cent of its staff had belonged to the Nazi Party. Propaganda slogans were certainly reminiscent of the past: resentment of foreign influences, particularly Western pop culture (*Verfremdung deutscher Werte und Lebensformen*), and opposition to the divisive nature of party democracy. *Volk*, *Volkstum*, and *Volksgemeinschaft* were values *per se*, regardless of the wishes of the individual or of the majority of voters. The term *Volk* was much more akin to this thinking than *Nation* or *national* as in the party name. NPD party rallies too, with their marching columns ending up in beer-halls, conjured up disturbing images of the past. Germany's political class was visibly relieved when the NPD, scoring no more than 4.2 per cent, failed to send any of their candidates to the Bundestag after the election of 28 September 1969. The spectre had vanished. Four years later the vote dropped to 0.6 per cent. By now it was clear that NPD voters did not identify with any programme or ideology—the NPD had none—but were all affected by a certain malaise which the party skilfully fuelled.

Election analysts discovered that NPD voters had come from all of the three established parties, including the SPD, to which they were then to drift back. Of the many reasons for this unexpected protest movement, three are more obvious than others: the recession, which hit farmers, retailers, and tradesmen, previously the clientele of the Nazi Party, harder than others; the anti-authoritarian, not to say 'un-German' behaviour of left-wing students, who shouted 'Ho, Ho, Ho Chi Minh', and engaged in pitched battles with the police; and last but not least, the sudden collusion (*Kumpanei*) of the two big parties, coupled with the eclipse of the FDP, the refuge of national conservatives.

The year 1969 marked the great watershed in German politics.[25] For many observers the final change of power after twenty years without any turmoil seemed to lay to rest any remaining doubts about Germany's democratic credentials. In fact no German Chancellor since Hitler had been greeted with more euphoria than Willy Brandt. The emigré journalist and opponent of Nazism seemed to personify the 'other', i.e. better Germany, and it was as though he were somehow able to absolve his countrymen from the sins of the past. Moreover, he was perceived to be the intellectual in politics *par excellence*, who would bridge the gap between *Geist* (intellect) and *Macht* (power), always notoriously wide in Germany. Advocates of social progress and leaders of liberal public opinion, including the editors of the most influential weekly magazines, *Der Spiegel*, *Die Zeit*, and *Der Stern*, believed that a new Periclean age of German democracy had dawned.

In reality Brandt's accession to power was no foregone conclusion. After all, the CDU/CSU had emerged as the strongest party, with a loss of less than 2 per cent (from 47.6 per cent to 46.1 per cent), whereas the FDP had lost almost 40 per cent of its voters. Erich Mende, one-time vice-chancellor and exponent of the conservative wing, had been replaced in September 1967 by the more left-wing liberal Walter Scheel. In 1969 the party had revealed its new political outlook by voting for the SPD Chancellor Gustav Heinemann as federal President. The party was not in a strong bargaining position after the outcome of the elections, nor was the gain of 3 per cent for the SPD that impressive. If the Grand Coalition had introduced majority voting, as had been seriously discussed, the liberals would have been wiped out for good and the SPD might not have gained power for the rest of the century, considering that the CDU/CSU had always conquered a clear majority of constituency seats (as opposed to candidates elected by the second, i.e. 'party' vote). This, no doubt, would not have augured well for democracy in Germany.

While Brandt saw himself as the future Chancellor as soon as the results were in on election night, the more formidable lieutenants of the SPD, notably Herbert Wehner, the party stategist, and Helmut Schmidt, leader of the parliamentary party, had grave doubts about Brandt's stature and the FDP's reliability. Wehner had second thoughts about Brandt's character traits and Schmidt about his formative years as popular head of the spendthrift Berlin city government, which was wholly subsidized from Bonn. However, Brandt had the backing of Walter Scheel, the leader of the FDP, and more importantly, of public opinion. Among his supporters he raised expectations and hopes of more democracy, more social justice, and more equality of opportunity which he could not possibly fulfil. But he was not a cynical politician who did not believe in what he offered. It was just that he was not sufficiently aware of the political restrictions on 'doing good'. He was more of a visionary than a power-broker, more interested in effecting a change of perspective than in the feasibility of short-term goals. Nor did he make many specific promises which he could not keep. Unlike foreign policy, domestic initiatives had to be paid for in hard currency. One of Brandt's early supporters, Ralf Dahrendorf, later observed that the 'great slogans' of his government remained 'paper promises and never became serious social objectives'.[26]

Brandt was not one of Germany's strong Chancellors, who knew how to impose his will on Cabinet colleagues. He rarely made use of his constitutional powers to direct them, preferring persuasion and consensus to hard decisions. Two years into his term of office, these leadership deficiencies began to show. Many reform projects collided with the economic facts of the early 1970s. First Alex Möller, the Minister of Finance, resigned, then Karl Schiller, who as 'super minister' in charge of both finance and economic departments had given the impression of being in control of the economy. Deficit spending, though first favoured by Schiller, got out of hand and the projected rise in the public debt was alarming. Nevertheless, due to Brandt's immense popularity, the SPD overtook the CDU/CSU for the first time in the 1972 elections (45.8 per cent to 44.9 per cent). The election campaign was the most emotional and rousing in the history of the Federal Republic, with the highest turnout of voters (91.1 per cent). Not only did the media support the coalition, but so too did a string of writers and artists, for the first and last time. Brandt was also the idol of the young generation, having lowered the voting age to eighteen. Almost 75 per cent of eighteen- to twenty-one-year-olds voted for him. They resented the dubious and abortive attempt by the conservatives to depose their 'Willy' in mid-term.

After the election Brandt's second government was soon on rocky ground once again. The erosion of his authority, always more charismatic than real, was now debated in public. The economic situation, which required a firm restraining hand, grew worse. The rise in oil prices affected Germany more than other countries because it cast a shadow on the motor car industry, the main breadwinner. Moreover, with the temporary banning of the use of cars on Sundays, Germans felt deprived of their chief status symbol. At the same time the Chancellor was depicted as not in control of his 'children', the academic youth who appeared to be intoxicated by social pipe-dreams. The leftward trend, the drift of the SPD encouraged by the election results, seemed to be unstoppable. Former student leaders, who hoped to be able to transform society from the top, soon came to replace the more moderate elements in the party's chief steering committee (at the Hanover Congress, April 1973). The gulf between what was desirable and what was feasible grew throughout the 1970s and detracted not only from Brandt's standing, but also from that of his successor, Helmut Schmidt, who was waiting in the wings. The reform legislation of Brandt's administrations which did pass the Bundestag covered a wide range of areas but tended to be incremental, more in the nature of extending the benefits of the existing welfare state: increases in pensions and the extension of pension rights regardless of contributions, increases in benefits in the fields of health insurance, unemployment, children, student grants, and the like.[27]

A new co-determination law strengthened the position of trade unions and works councils. The educational reform launched in 1971 dragged on because the CDU/CSU-controlled *Länder* could not be overruled. The framework law on higher education that was finally passed in 1975 was 'no longer a breathtaking agenda but merely a codification of existing pluralisms'.[28] The German penal code was brought in line with modern thinking. The most contentious issue was abortion on request within the first four months as demanded by the feminist lobby (Clause 218 of the Criminal Code). The act enraged the opposition, which appealed to the Constitutional Court. The latter forced the government to reintroduce medical criteria, including that of social emergency (*Indikationslösung*). Of course, all these laws helped to enhance the quality of life for the individual. However, two serious qualifications have to be made in the light of subsequent developments. Social legislation, impressive though it was, could not halt the decline of the birth rate in absolute terms: between 1970 and 1975, for the first time, more people died than were born. In statistical terms, the German family has 1.5 children, at least one-third under the reproduction level (230 children per 100 marriages). Of every hundred marriages entered into in 1970, only four produced four or more children.[29] The birth rate did not decline in the GDR at that time, but it did so after unification in an even more dramatic downturn. The debate of the 1990s about *Standort Deutschland,* Germany's viability as a production site, points to another weakness of Brandt's government. The Brandt era marked a steep rise in labour costs, which are now regarded as a serious impediment to the competitiveness of German industry and further investment at home.

Brandt's downfall was inevitable, as it is with any idol who cannot satisfy the expectations of his fans. His resignation was precipitated by the Guillaume Affair,[30] which exposed his lack of political instinct and ruthlessness. He had been warned by the internal security agency (*Bundesamt für Verfassungsschutz*) in May 1973 that one of his personal aides, Günter Guillaume, was an agent of the East German secret police. Brandt refused to believe it and went on trusting Guillaume, whose access to classified material was not restricted for almost another year. On 24 April 1974 Guillaume was finally arrested. Brandt could have got away with it if the whole affair had not drawn attention to his weaknesses, which came under scrutiny. Many friends rallied round Brandt and implored him to stay on. However, Wehner and Schmidt, who mattered most in the party, gave him no encouragement. On 6 May 1974 Brandt resigned and soon afterwards was succeeded by Helmut Schmidt, who had been waiting for the hour when he could display his very different talent for leadership.

Brandt was not one to cling to office, and in this respect he represented the SPD's uneasy attitude towards power. The breakthrough in *Ostpolitik* had been achieved, for which he had been awarded the Nobel Peace Prize in December 1971. By 1974 his international reputation was not in dispute. The 'kneeling at Warsaw' was significant for the ambivalence of his image abroad and at home. On the occasion of his visit to Warsaw to sign the German–Polish Treaty on 7 September 1970, he fell to his knees after placing a wreath in memory of the Jews murdered during the ghetto uprising. This picture went around the world and did more than any public relations exercise to impress on international opinion the new moral dimension of German politics. However, a survey revealed that a majority of Germans did not think that this gesture was called for.[31] The very same people were likely to have taken exception to what they now learned about the Chancellor's personal habits, such as drinking and philandering during election campaigns. More than elsewhere, tolerance in Germany is a matter of published rather than public opinion. The good news is that the former works on the latter and not vice versa.

Brandt's career was not over: he remained chairman of the ruling party, which, as it turned out, was to become a liability to the government. Not surprisingly, Brandt felt more welcome on the international than on the domestic stage. In 1976 he was elected president of the Socialist International, and he was to involve the organization more than before in world, rather than just European, affairs. Less than six months later, Brandt was offered the chairmanship of the North-South Commission, which was set up with a view to bridging the gap between the First and the Third World. The Brandt Report, 'North-South, a Programme for Survival', which was addressed to governments and demanded fundamental reform, did not have much of an impact on those concerned. However, it did enhance Brandt's appeal to the younger left-wing generation, who were pressing for change. Brandt remained a popular father figure among the new educated under-30 party members of the SPD, who by 1973 outnumbered the old working-class clientele (now under 30 per cent).

The changing social composition pushed the party to the left, away from the middle ground and more importantly away from its own government. In spite of the SPD's poor showing in the 1976 elections compared to the CDU/CSU (42.9 per cent to 48.6 per cent), the Lib-Lab coalition remained in control. As mentioned before, the Liberals, whether leaning to the right or left, saw themselves as the guardians of a prosperous, well-managed economy. This was also Schmidt's priority. He had first risen to prominence when, as a young senator in Hamburg, he had proved his outstanding management skills in a flooding catastrophe. Ever since, he had had the reputation of being an efficient organizer with a no-nonsense approach to politics.[32] After the early death of Fritz Erler, one of the most capable politicans in the SPD, Schmidt's rise to the top in a party not blessed with go-getters and aggressive debaters was almost inevitable. The very leadership qualities which endeared him to the German public at large alienated many of the younger and left-wing members of his own party who advocated further improvements to the welfare state, regardless of the resources available. Both the world economy and East–West relations were deteriorating fast and nobody seemed better equipped to deal with these crises than Schmidt, whom most Germans, including the traditional CDU/CSU voters, saw as the experienced helmsman navigating the ship of state through treacherous waters.

This was also the period when the freak wave of terrorism[33] by the Red Army Faction (RAF) hit Germany with full force, reaching its peak in 1977 with the cold-blooded murder of the Federal Prosecutor Siegfried Buback. German terrorism, always identified with the names of Ulrike Meinhof and Andreas Baader, an unlikely couple of highly strung middle-class offspring, was the extreme manifestation of misguided idealism. The student movement had generated a climate of ideological hysteria, which a few frustrated fanatics took to extremes. It had begun with the justification of violence against property (for instance, department stores) and ended with a succession of politically motivated murders. When the chief gang was eventually arrested and tried in 1977 the government was not prepared to surrender to blackmail and murder, the killing of Jürgen Phonto, chairman of the Dresdener Bank, and of Hanns-Martin Schleyer, president of the Federation of German Industry. The most spectacular incident was the skyjacking of a Lufthansa jet on 13 October 1977, which after a twenty-four-hour odyssey landed in Mogadishu, Somalia. There the terrorists were overwhelmed by a new special anti-terrorist squad flown in from Germany. Schmidt got full marks for handling the affair in such a decisive manner. After this turning-point terrorism subsided, flaring up again only occasionally in the 1980s. Later, when the Stasi archives divulged their ugly secrets, it emerged that the East German secret police had supplied the terrorists with logistic support, training, weapons, and false passports.[34] Some of the most notorious terrorists, among them a surprising number of females, eventually went into hiding in East Germany, by adopting new identities.

Six months later the Chancellor hosted one of the first economic summits in Bonn, in July 1978. Under Schmidt West Germany was no longer the proverbial political dwarf and economic giant, but a fully accepted player on the global field.[35] This was a new experience for most Germans, who by now believed, as did the rest of the world, that they had no talent for choosing the right kind of political leaders.

It was a personal triumph for Schmidt that the SPD was able to achieve a slightly better result in the 1980 elections (42.9 per cent to 44.5 per cent for the opposition) than previously. The Liberals had successfully campaigned against Franz-Josef Strauß, the controversial CDU/CSU candidate, who polarized West German society as no one before had done. A clear majority, though admiring his energy and intelligence, deeply mistrusted his political instincts. The FPD's strategy of targeting Strauß paid off handsomely in the election (10.6 per cent). Only once, in 1961 (12.8 per cent), did the Liberals gain more support from the electorate. With the position of the Liberals strengthened and the SPD drifting further and further to the left, Schmidt's third coalition government was, from the start, on perilous ground. Schmidt was one of the chief architects of NATO's 'dual-track policy', i.e. modernizing the missile system while pushing for negotiations with Moscow. Since the Soviet Union was not impressed, the installation of a new generation of nuclear weapons seemed to be unavoidable. Brandt, conscious of the growing peace movement against this scenario, wished to save détente, while Schmidt felt obliged to honour NATO's decision. At the same time, the effects of the second oil crisis of 1979 began to spread gloom. The economic indicators such as unemployment (1.8 million) and inflation (5 per cent) were alarming, in view of previous records, and not conducive to a balanced budget, which the Liberals demanded.

The 1980s were a period when class distinctions were replaced by a new social division into those in and out of employment. This is not, however, a development unique to Germany. Sociologists referred to the *Zweidrittelgesellschaft* (two-thirds society), implying that the government was only concerned about the vote of the relatively prosperous majority at the expense of the minority, which was just maintained by social security but otherwise not taken seriously. The Liberals, led by Hans-Dietrich Genscher and Count Otto Lambsdorff, objected to the rising costs of social services, which, they argued, had a dampening effect on the economy. On the other hand, the new generation of SPD activists, mostly educated and in public employment, felt protective towards the underprivileged minority. There were also tensions within the SPD between the newcomers and its old working-class supporters, who were at loggerheads with the trendy left. Whereas Brandt tried to hold the party together by his display of empathy with the younger generation of activists, the Chancellor was striving to save the coalition.

The two strategies, pursued by two very different personalities, could not succeed simultaneously. The resolutions passed at the party congress in Munich (April 1982) read like a declaration of war on the government: workers' participation at all levels of industrial decision-making, intensified economic planning, a special 'wealth tax' to finance job-creation schemes, shorter working hours, lowering of the retirement age, and so forth. This was grist to the mill of the realists among the Liberal leaders, who expressed their doubts more openly than before as to whether the SPD was still fit to govern the country. In the end it was only a matter of how the coalition would break up.

Rather than waiting anxiously for the inevitable to happen, Schmidt seized the initiative and, on 17 September 1982, confronted the FDP ministers with the option of resigning or being dismissed.[36] Their resignation, clearly the wrong move, created the opportunity for the SPD to denounce them as traitors. Whether justified or not, the charge stuck. Within thirteen years the Liberals had twice changed sides. They never fully recovered from the stigma of being untrustworthy. However, if Schmidt had hoped for a new mandate through elections, his gamble failed. By electing a new Chancellor within twenty-one days, the Bundestag could avoid dissolution. On 1 October 1982 Helmut Kohl, federal chairman of the CDU since 1973, was elected Chancellor as a result of a 'constructive vote of no confidence'. Many Germans at the time agreed with Hildegard Hamm-Brücher, the leading lady of the liberal left, that a change-over without elections, though within the constitution, had damaged democracy.

Kohl employed another procedural device, a motion of confidence which he wanted to lose, to force early elections on 6 March 1983. The election campaign, dominated by the missile crisis and the highest unemployment rate ever (2.5 million), led to an overwhelming victory for the CDU/CSU, which achieved its best result since 1957 (48.8 per cent). The two partners of the previous coalition, the SPD (38.2 per cent) and FDP (6.9 per cent), suffered substantial losses. Obviously the voters had more confidence in the conservatives' ability to handle the economy and to deal with the critical issue of national security. Kohl gained grudging respect, not least among West Germany's allies, because he would not refrain from implementing NATO's missile decisions in the face of a growing peace movement. The new Chancellor's political role model was Konrad Adenauer. This meant never losing one's composure in adversity and never taking undue political risks. Ensuring the loyalty of party activists throughout the country was more important than media attention and popularity. He once confided to the American ambassador Vernon Walters that he was generally underrated and that this had served him well.[37] Just as under Adenauer, the CDU was meant to win elections and secure power for the Chancellor, who strove to occupy the largest possible section of the political middle ground. The political priorities were those of the majority, which tended to be silent between polls: foreign policy, i.e. the maintenance of détente, a *modus vivendi* with East Germany, a return to economic growth, and an emphasis on law and order at home. Kohl will for ever be identified with German reunification. The road to 1990 will be traced in the next chapter.

In terms of domestic policy, the 1980s were characterized by what might be called fringe politics, in other words, the re-emergence of new parties at each end of the political spectrum: the New Left or Green Party and the New Right, the Republican (*Republikaner*) Party. The two major catch-all parties clearly failed to catch all votes and to address certain issues, for fear of antagonizing the majority of voters. Dissatisfaction at the fringes must be seen as a reaction to the display of party politics at the expense of conviction politics on the centre court. The two major parties had become highly institutionalized and centralized organizations, and though they were expected, in the German tradition, to represent the whole of society, they were now accused of having turned into self-serving 'busybodies'. Foreign observers rightly point out that German parties see themselves as 'bearers of the state (*Staatsträger*) by virtue of their mission to express the will of the people'.[38] Naturally, the 'people' constituted at most the 'silent majority' which, at certain times, is bound to produce vociferous fringes. None the less, this was different from the previous outburst of political fundamentalism in the 1960s: extremism was shunned. The 1970s, after all, had had a sobering effect on the political culture of the country. Yet at the same time Schmidt's indifference towards environmental issues was also instrumental in forging the Green Party. In spite of ideological links with the APO, the Greens were more than a mere protest movement against the 'system', since they wished to bring about change, if only a reformed consciousness *vis-à-vis* the environment, in a constitutional manner. The *Republikaner* party too, though containing many individual Nazi sympathizers, stressed its constitutional credentials. Why then should these parties warrant as much attention as they did, both in West Germany and abroad?

The Green Party grew out of a motley collection of citizens' initiatives (*Bürgerinitiativen*) on the local and regional level concerned with ecological issues, above all the spread of nuclear power plants.[39] The party activists were often reformed APO members, who had realized that opposition within parliament, inside the 'system', was more effective than outside it. On 12–13 January 1980 delegates from the existing green groups met in Karlsruhe to set up the Federal Green Party. It went from strength to strength in regional elections, scoring between 7 and 8 per cent in West Berlin, Hamburg, and Hesse, before a breakthrough in the 1983 federal elections (5.6 per cent, 27 seats; they had received 1.5 per cent in 1980). From now on the Greens were a force to be reckoned with. The new party posed a threat to the Social Democrats and the Liberals, who suffered substantial losses because the Greens combined socialist and liberal ideas, some would say social libertarian ideals, with an ecological message. The latter read: the protection of the environment was more pressing than economic growth. To this was added a whole string of further claims: more grassroots democracy (*Basisdemokratie*), human (e.g. women's) rights, pacifism in the face of a threatened nuclear holocaust. A romantic, utopian streak was clearly discernible. Not surprisingly, the Greens' appeal in the 1980s was strongest among the younger and more educated voters. Between two-thirds and three-quarters were under thirty-five, the proportion of those with advanced higher education was more than twice the national average, roughly one-third being engaged in study. Young professionals employed in the public rather than private sector made up the rest of the voters. It was in generating public concern for the environment that the Greens are credited with their greatest achievement. 'The Greens have raised the right questions,' one of the CDU leaders said, 'but they give the wrong answers.'[40] One of the answers which the major parties gave was to set up new ministries for the protection of the environment, both on the *Länder* and federal level. In many ways the influence of the Greens can be compared to that of the Social Democrats of earlier decades, who, by their electoral successes, prompted governments to tackle social questions. To some extent the very success of the Greens was to limit their electoral appeal. Another serious handicap was that for a long time they did not get their act together as a party. One of the most contentious issues was the mid-term rotation of parliamentary seats to avoid professionalization and alienation from the grassroots. By the mid-1980s, the split between the pragmatist *Realos* (realists) and the purist *Fundis* (fundamentalists) nearly tore the party asunder: the *Realos* favoured co-operation, including formal coalition, while the *Fundis* were not prepared to compromise on principle in any way. Open factionalism and obvious immaturity were bound to damage the party's electoral chances in 1990. The defeat of the chaotic *Fundis*, who dominated the federal executive, in December 1988 paved the way for a professional parliamentary party which appealed to a sizeable section of the electorate.

National unity had never been a priority for the Greens. When their East German cousins, the dissidents of 1989, were overtaken by events and faced the demand for a 'united fatherland', the Greens found themselves out of their depth. They may have dreamed of the revolution, but when it actually came they were taken aback by the force and direction of its impetus. Like the SPD leaders, they missed the train which crashed through the Wall in November 1989. For the 1990 election they offered the usual agenda: a non-capitalist society, when most East Germans opted for the capitalist Federal Republic, and withdrawal from NATO, when even Gorbachev recognized the merits of a united Germany within that organization. The Greens' insistence on a separate 5 per cent threshold in both East and West, a demand sanctioned by the Constitutional Court, turned out to be counter-productive. The 'Alliance 90', consisting of a number of groups emanating from the citizens' movement (*Neues Forum*, *Demokratie Jetzt*, and others) scored 6 per cent in the East, while the Western Greens narrowly missed the 5 per cent target in the elections of 2 December 1990. The formal merger of the Greens and the 'Alliance 90' one day after the elections was the beginning of a tense relationship, in view of the very different concerns of the two partners. However, the movement as such benefited from this marriage because structural reforms, such as the abolition of rotation, strengthened the pragmatists (*Realos*) and revived electoral chances. After the 1994 elections the Greens were back in force in the Bundestag. On the whole they are more disposed to share power with the Social Democrats, their 'natural partner', notably in Lower Saxony, Hesse, and Sachsen-Anhalt. In the long run the Greens may well replace the Liberals as the party with the more convincing and up-to-date agenda, stressing human rights rather than those of the captains of industry and the wealthy. The Greens were never happy with *Promis* (i.e. prominent leaders such as Petra Kelly), but there can be no doubt that Joschka Fischer has done more than his share in instilling common sense and political realism. His recent interpretation of German history could have been written by any liberal historian who was not averse to learning lessons for the future.[41] He pleads, strangely enough, for a 'conservative' policy, which aims at developing the positive traditions of the old Federal Republic and the East German civil rights movement. Germany is first and foremost a European power, not a global player, he argues; therefore the logical priority of German foreign policy must be to foster European integration on a democratic rather than bureaucratic basis. No mainstream German politician, least of all Helmut Kohl, would object.

If the New Left has moved so far to the centre, the real battle-ground for votes and power, what about the New Right? The media attention which the *Republikaner* party[42] received from abroad no less than at home by no means reflects its electoral strength. Nor is the extreme right more strongly represented in Germany than in Italy, France, or Belgium. On the contrary, with 2.1 per cent of the vote in 1990, the *Republikaner* were certainly bringing up the rear. It would be best to ignore their political antics. However, no foreign journalist, apparently, can resist the temptation to point to yet another offshoot of neo-Nazism. Apart from the ever-present German past, it was the uncertainty about a united Germany and the eruption of xenophobic violence which worried political commentators. Two previous attempts by the German right to gain respectability had failed. The election results of 1994 suggest that the third attempt had suffered a similar fate. Their record in ballots since 1984 is so poor that one wonders whether all the fuss about the *Republikaner* is really justified. At no time did the party manage to clear the 5 per cent hurdle in national elections, except for the European elections in 1989 (7.1 per cent). Only twice did the *Republikaner* win seats in regional elections: in Berlin in 1989 (7.1 per cent), and in Baden-Württemberg in 1992 (10.9 per cent), in both cases with an above-average percentage in working-class areas. However, in Bremen in 1991, and in Schleswig-Holstein in 1992, another right-wing group, the *Deutsche Volksunion* (DVU), hardly known elsewhere, won just enough votes (6.2 per cent and 6.3 per cent) to enter parliament. The founder of the so-called REPs, Franz Schönhuber, was a member of the Waffen-SS and a journalist with Bavarian Broadcasting. The stronghold of the party is the south of Germany and its membership fluctuates between 15,000 and 25,000. Like the Greens, the REPs are rife with factionalism. Schönhuber has been deposed and re-elected several times. The ideological platform of the party is German nationalism pure and simple: 'Our programme is Germany,' i.e. the 'non-aligned and well-armed nation state'[43] within the borders of 1937 with no regard for the security interests of Germany's neighbours. With their anti-European and anti-American propaganda, the *Republikaner* are undermining the very foundations of the Federal Republic's foreign policy since 1949. Like the NPD, the *Republikaner* attach particular importance to the purity of the *Volk*: 'Safeguarding the German *Volk* means protecting future generations against foreignization.' There is no doubt that the influx of foreigners, namely asylum seekers and economic migrants, has been their chief weapon in elections. Freedom of movement within Europe is perceived as a serious threat to the German nation. As soon as the government decided to tighten the liberal asylum clause in the Basic Law, the REPs lost political ground. One of Schönhuber's particular concerns is to play down the horrors of the Nazi era and to undo the results of post-war re-education: 'The reorientation of the German people is over; the ticket counter for Canossa is closed once and for all!' The rhetorical reference to Canossa (the scene of Emperor Henry IV's humiliating penance in 1077 in order to get his ban lifted by Pope Gregory VII) is actually borrowed from Bismarck (14 May 1872, against the Catholic Church), who had then inspired Hitler (8 November 1938, against England). This is exactly the language which Hitler employed, pandering to wounded German pride.

Many of those who listened to Schönhuber had no clue what was meant by Canossa. The average REP sympathizer is likely to be less educated than the rest of society. Jürgen W. Falter, one of Germany's foremost experts on voting patterns, describes the typical West German REP voter as follows: he is a married man above the age of forty-five who lives in a small or medium-sized town, belongs to a church, which he rarely attends, has no further education beyond the minimum required schooling, is a worker or simple employee not yet worried about unemployment, and has no trade union connections whatsoever.[44] Berlin is an exception in so far as the REPs are also attractive to young voters. Predictably, an REP sympathizer is proud to be German—a rare attitude among present-day Germans—and feels strongly that Germans ought to exhibit more pride in their country. But Falter argues that two ingredients have to come together for someone to vote for the REPs: a nationalist frame of mind *and* general dissatisfaction with democracy and the major parties. As a matter of fact, dissatisfaction with other parties (82 per cent) ranks above the 'foreigner problem', i.e. xenophobic attitudes (72 per cent). Unlike the Greens, the REPs have not succeeded in forming a stable social constituency from which to operate and to mobilize political discontent. The party depends too much on floating voters from the major parties: mainly, but by no means exclusively, from the CDU/CSU. Is an all-clear signal, judged to be premature in 1993, now justified since their crushing defeat in the 1994 elections? It all depends on whether the general dissatisfaction with the major parties is a passing phenomenon or not. No doubt *Politikverdrossenheit*, as it is termed, is more widespread, especially among new and young voters, than a nationalist or xenophobic mentality.

Political indifference has manifested itself in mounting abstentions rather than in a specific voting pattern. Compared to the United States and Britain, turnout as it now stands is not yet alarming. Some analysts even think that it is a sign of maturity. However, perception in Germany is bound to be influenced by the fear that, as in the past, decreasing respect for parties and politicians might delegitimize democracy. It is not easy to decide whether the Germans are again, as they have so often been, victims of their own high standards and a misreading of history. There is general agreement that public confidence in parties and politicians has suffered considerably over the last twenty years. Various opinion polls confirm this trend. For instance, the percentage of West Germans who applauded political activity fell from 66 per cent (1971) to 36 per cent (1992) and the percentage of those who trust politicians not to consciously manipulate the truth sank from 57 per cent (1977) to 27 per cent (1992).[45] To some extent the professionalization of politics in a parliamentary democracy is inevitable. However, the general feeling in Germany is that this process has gone too far. Party politicians are increasingly perceived as an interest group unto themselves, rather than as representing the interests of others. The emergence of the term *politische Klasse*, originally coined by Italian sociologists, is symptomatic in that it denotes a growing alienation from the grassroots. The malaise about the *Parteienstaat* gathered momentum during the 1980s and reached a climax after unification, when it became obvious that the East Germans were not all that happy with the blessings of party democracy Western style. The fundamental problem, however, was that the powerbrokers of the major parties have, like polyps, penetrated every opening of society and at the same time have lost much of their distinguishing political profile. The recipe for success seems to be to seek power for its own sake, not least for its financial remuneration. In other societies this might not be a sensational discovery. However, in comparatively young democracies citizens are not yet as cynical and as far as the Germans are concerned they still expect the state to be above parties. Schmidt and Kohl, the 'two Helmuts', contributed substantially to the blurring of party images, Schmidt being immensely popular among conservative Germans and Kohl successfully pursuing exactly the same policies as his predecessor. Opposition, so it appeared to many young voters, was only possible outside the mainstream parties. The growth of the fringe parties was an inevitable outcome.

Educated Germans still see a difference, if only in theory, between society and state, with the parties as go-betweens. The alleged ethos of the Prussian state, based on the incorruptible civil servant, still lingers on in the subconscious. Therefore the prestige of politicians received a further blow when two West German political scientists had the guts to draw public attention to their painstaking research on certain remuneration practices which were evidence of 'legalized corruption'. Hans Herbert von Arnim, an expert on local government administration, disclosed the self-serving nature of German politics: 'The problem of the exploitation of the state by the parties', he writes, 'is also one of depriving the citizens of their rights and powers, which really is an incredible thing to happen in a democracy.'[46] He could show that office-holders abused their political power to grant themselves unjustifiably high allowances, salaries, and, above all, sometimes after the shortest of tenures, fat pensions. Some of von Arnim's colleagues were shocked to read about these findings not in learned journals but in popular newspapers. This, they felt, did German democracy no service. Their response is highly indicative of a certain patronizing attitude of academic guardians of German democracy, as though the latter were still in a kindergarten phase where infants should not be upset too much by the unholy behaviour of adults.

The conservative Cologne sociologist Erwin K. Scheuch was asked by the CDU *Wirtschaftsvereinigung* (Economic Association) of North Rhine-Westphalia to analyse the party system and the qualifications of politicians. The result, based on detailed examination of patronage exercised by small party cliques in and around Cologne, was so devastating that the CDU tried to suppress it. Only then did Scheuch go public, while his co-author, Ute Scheuch, left the CDU in disgust.[47] Scheuch focused on the professional politician, with no qualifications other than those which would get him an influential, well-paid position, be it a secure parliamentary seat, an office, or most likely both. The seizure of power by small cliques and clans reminds him of the feudal system of earlier times: political loyalty matters much more than expert knowledge. Scheuch, too, makes the point that the state, which is meant to serve society at large, is in danger of becoming a fief of parties and their retainers. To the historian it makes sense to see old structures reasserting themselves in modern guises.

The public debate about *Politikverdrossenheit* reached its peak when Richard von Weizsäcker, the federal President, went out of his way to speak out against the 'utopia of the *status quo*', i.e. the illusion of holding on to undiminished enjoyment of privileges.[48] Some commentators praised the President for his moral courage in exposing the defects of institutionalized democracy; others accused him of 'populism from above', i.e. feeding popular resentment of the *Parteienstaat* and thus undermining rather than strengthening the foundations of democracy. The President had been greatly impressed by the East German experience of grassroots democracy in

1989 and the earnest, party-transcending debates in the first democratic parliament after 18 March 1990. The East German approach was less professional than in the West, but considerably more open and genuine. It was, sadly, completely crushed by West German party machines moving east like gigantic combine harvesters. Von Weizsäcker felt strongly about his role as President of all Germans, East and West, party members or not, and he hoped to revitalize Germany's civic society (*Bürgergesellschaft*) by taking on board some of the features of the East German citizens' movement. No doubt the future of German democracy depends to some extent on whether the political class is prepared to curtail its own suffocating influence and allow for more grassroots democracy, especially on the level of local government.

The declining respect for Germany's political class is not necessarily a bad thing if it can be contained within a new *modus vivendi* and does not lead to a general crisis of confidence in democracy as such. It is a result of a society sobering up over a period of decades rather than of the shockwave caused by the student movement of 1968 that today's Germans tend to be more suspicious about authority than other nations. According to opinion polls in the early 1980s, 84 per cent of Americans, 61 per cent of Europeans, and only 44 per cent of Germans were in favour of strengthening authority.[49] Only 15 per cent of the German population, compared to a quarter of the American and European sample, regarded obedience as an important goal of education. Only the Scandinavian countries were more distrustful of authority in all walks of life than the Germans. However, several qualifications have to be made: opinion polls, especially in the German case, are not necessarily a reliable indication of behavioural patterns. The 're-educated' Germans in the West are only too aware that they have a reputation for an authoritarian disposition. The gap between the generations is more marked than elsewhere (two-thirds of those older than 55 would welcome a strengthening of authority). Moreover, the addition of 16 million East Germans in 1990 may have somewhat changed the picture. The impact of the last fifty years could then be interpreted as a process of disillusionment: first, the deep disappointment about the Führer and his false promises; then, after 1968, the realization that democracy was no panacea either; and finally, the collapse of the socialist utopia.

7 Culture: The Mirror Image of Society

The cultural achievements of the Federal Republic will always be compared to those of Weimar Germany and found wanting. However, this picture is one-sided in as much as it tends to focus on a small elite of avant-garde artists in a few places. It fails to encompass the background of political and social crisis. By the end of the Second World War the environment had changed beyond recognition, regardless of the dispositions of individual artists. After 1945 a state of utter exhaustion and emptiness prevailed. Cultural nationalism was completely discredited and the void was filled by new ideas from abroad, notably an influx from Britain and America. Post-war Germany proved to be a much better terrain for social and cultural reconstruction than the tensions and conflicts unleashed by the unexpected defeat of 1918. The attitudes and habits of the German people were the same, however, and would change only slowly. More often than not they had lost everything: their home, their loved ones, their possessions, their previous rank in society. But nobody could deprive them of their cultural identity. As soon as the war was over, people flocked to makeshift theatres and concert halls, and this for a variety of reasons: to forget the miseries of everyday life, to see and hear what had been proscribed by the Nazis, and last but not least to prove to themselves that they were not barbarians. In Berlin alone no fewer than 121 new plays, operas, and musicals (operettas) were staged in the second half of 1945.[1] The choice of light music and comedy on offer was quite astonishing. Most pieces came from the stock repertoire of German classics, with a few Anglo-Saxon additions (from Shakespeare to Wilde). In Berlin the four occupation powers were in competition with each other to present themselves as the guardians of German culture. There was consensus among all four Allies that exposing the Germans to the high points of their own culture was the best palliative for a defeated nation. Robert Birley, headmaster of Charterhouse, reminded his countrymen, in a letter to the *Times* on 8 May, that

Germany had admirable humanist traditions of her own which could guide her into the future.[2] Of necessity the performing arts prevailed, based, as it were, on an approved repertoire, and this set the pattern for the years to come. The professionalization of the arts, in both West and East Germany, above all the demanding quality of performances, funded from the public purse, has been one of the pre-eminent features of German culture ever since. Whether this has had a stifling impact on true creativity is difficult to say. As far as the Western zones were concerned, the development was shaped by two strong, closely related impulses: on the level of serious culture, a return to old values, as well as the slow rehabilitation of émigré artists and intellectuals, and on the level of entertainment, a certain sort of escape into what is called *die heile Welt* (the wholesome world) untouched by present-day problems or Nazi atrocities. The post-war climate was not, then, propitious for the creation of an avant-garde culture, as it was after the revolutionary turmoil of the early Weimar period.

However, it is more in reference to the reconstitution of German society than because of the concomitant cultural trends that the decade between 1945 and 1955 has been described as the period of restoration. This notion is perfectly legitimate if taken to relate to an understandable reaction to the Nazi revolution and not, as suggested by its first usage in the early 1970s, to a purely reactionary development. Culture is not timeless, does not germinate in a political and social void, even though this idea is what quite a few German writers at the time desperately tried to hold on to. Popular writers and poets, on the whole untarnished by the Nazi regime, like Werner Bergengrün, Ernst Wiechert, Franz Werfel, Thomas Mann, Gertrud von le Fort, Rudolf Alexander Schröder, Ina Seidel, Hermann Hesse, the first to receive a Nobel Prize (in 1947), and many others had already been established or had returned from exile and continued more or less the same as before in praising eternal, often mystical and religious subjects or glorifying nature.[3] The image of the writer as a genius and recluse 'far from the madding crowd' still had great appeal in Germany. At that time it seemed somehow to suggest that the true writer and artist had not succumbed to the ideological temptations of the previous regime. Of course there were others, like Hans-Werner Richter, trying to cope with the gruesome past and with present-day life, but they were only appreciated by the general public at a later stage. What Heinrich Böll has labelled *Trümmerliteratur* (rubble literature) did not much appeal to those who still lived amongst the rubble, except perhaps for Wolfgang Borchert's play *Draußen vor der Tür*, in which a prisoner of war returning from captivity finds his wife in the arms of another man and his old boss doing fine without him. The antagonistic nature of contemporary German art in the sense of *Geist* versus *Macht* did not really come to the fore until German society had reasserted itself. It therefore makes sense to look at certain aspects of society, especially those which caused concern, before returning to the cultural scene.

To what extent, then, was German society restored, to what extent had it changed? It is now generally accepted that there was no 'zero hour' in 1945. People picked up the pieces to repair and restore their lives, just as the famous *Trümmerfrauen* picked up the bricks to rebuild their homes. Nor were the Western Allies in any mood to impose a social revolution that went beyond the political margins of their own societies, quite apart from deliberately dissociating themselves from any such moves in the Soviet Zone. The result was a new state in the West, essentially different in its political and economic order from the former Reich, but not a new society. It could not have been otherwise without applying undue force and thereby violating the principles of democracy. The existing social elements served to construct a new polity. The latter proved to be, as Rainer Lepsius stresses, much more homogeneous than the Reich ever was: the individual states, the two main churches, the political and economic power structures, to name but a few elements previously so out of proportion, were now finely balanced.[4] The division of the Reich benefited the West more than the hitherto underdeveloped East. The influx of millions of penniless but highly motivated refugees brought about a social mix and a boost in economic energy as never before. By 1950 the population of the Federal Republic (excluding West Berlin and the Saarland) had, in spite of overall war losses of approximately 5 million, increased by 8.3 million, compared to the last census of 1939 for the same area. In view of its continued demand for labour and a falling birth rate, West Germany remained a country of immigrants rather than emigrants. Of course, social inequalities remained or reappeared, but they did not have the same polarizing effect as in Weimar Germany.

This was due in no small measure to the unprecedented GNP growth rate between 1950 and 1975. Within a fairly short period of time it was possible to absorb a large number of refugees, as well as those still occupied in agriculture (34 per cent in 1950), into the economy. More importantly, society at large, including the working class, gained from the economic boom: real income, which had stagnated in the inter-war period, more than tripled during the first twenty-five years and working hours were cut by half between 1870 and 1970. Right from the start the Federal Republic pledged to develop the welfare state, if only to prove its superior system *vis-à-vis* the command economy of the GDR. By 1970 housing, health, education, unemployment benefits, and old age pensions were more or less on a par with Britain, France, and Sweden. Progress in general welfare and mass consumption was so staggering up to 1975 that people began to wonder whether it could last. Almost as if to appease the public conscience, a great deal of revenue was spent on culture, since the country defined itself as both a *Wohlfahrtsstaat* and a *Kulturstaat*. There are comparatively few private sponsors. Almost all theatres and concert halls are funded by local and *Länder* governments. With subsidies making up about 80 per cent of their budgets, they are totally dependent on the public purse. On average, theatre tickets are subsidized up to 160 DM.[5]

Creative artists, like playwrights, composers, or painters, benefit from this system only when they have made it. It is true to say that there are scholarships for young artists, for example through the German Academic Exchange Service. However, the career of an artist is determined by a small band of professional critics, rather than by the market as such. The idea of a bestseller has been imported from abroad; there is no German equivalent or word for it. Consequently, trying to be popular is supposed to be unprofessional and is bound to be exposed by the critics. No federal or local politician dares to speak his mind on matters of art, like, for example, the Prince-Bishops of former times. They only feel competent to allocate the means—a certain percentage of building costs has to be spent on the arts (*Kunst am Bau*)—and then they convene a committee of experts to make up their minds. Thus Helmut Schmidt, generally known for his frankness and decisiveness, felt obliged to accept the architectural plans for his new chancellery, which he was said to have heartily disliked. One should not forget that King Ludwig II of Bavaria, most popular of all the Wittelsbacher (*the* Bavarian dynasty), was deposed and sent to a lunatic asylum by his own government because of his expensive architectural extravanganzas. Professional critics still despise his fairy-tale castles, but ordinary people, foreigners included, love them.

On the whole, people do not much care for the architecture imposed upon them after the war by the architectural fraternity. Post-war architecture furnishes a good example of the dialectics of artistic progress at the expense of popular, and one might say democratic, consent. The now much-acclaimed Bauhaus architecture of the 1920s was a sensible reaction to the pretentious style of the Wilhelmine period and also to some extent the overdecorative art nouveau (*Jugendstil*). During the Nazi period the famous Bauhaus architects like Walter Gropius and Mies van der Rohe had to emigrate, albeit reluctantly, only to be welcomed back afterwards as true modernists and to be imitated all over Germany with devastating results. Many half-damaged buildings of outstanding decorative appeal were pulled down to make way for boring high-rise flats. In an iconoclastic craze some homeowners went out of their way to 'sanitize' their art-nouveau façades, to bring them into line with modern buildings. The insensitive preference for everything modern is so entrenched in Germany that meddling with old buildings cannot even be prevented by heritage offices imposing heavy fines. In Franconia beautiful old farms are still whitewashed so as not to be outshone by the modern villas in the neighbourhood. Most of these detached villas are functional and solidly built, with proper foundations, cellars, and attics, but are, whether architect-designed or not, generally devoid of all character. Since the CDU governments of the 1950s encouraged private home ownership through tax incentives, the whole of West Germany has become littered with white boxes of undistinguished design, thus enhancing the impression of cleanliness and boredom. Today no self-respecting architect or planning officer would agree to build a mock-Tudor residence.

The urban landscape in East Germany has also been ruined, though in different ways: by neglect, by the infamous pre-fab concrete monsters and by deliberate vandalism, i.e. clearance of what would have been worth preserving, like the Schloß in Berlin and

the university church in Leipzig. Many old town centres not devastated by the war were simply left to rot. In Berlin-Marzahn, for
example, there are 59,000 flats, in Leipzig-Grünau 35,000, many in
blocks over ten storeys high. In fact, 40 per cent of all East Germans live in such flats, of which there are 2.3 million. Rents have
increased at least fivefold since unification, which has also contributed to the general malaise in East Germany. Initially, like abstract
art, architectural modernism, as represented by the Bauhaus tradition, was discredited as 'formalism'. The model to follow was neo-
classicism, in the shape of Soviet buildings. Berlin's Stalinallee was
only the most conspicuous monument to what might be called
'wedding-cake architecture' (*Zuckerbäckerstil*). Stalin liked it, and so
everybody else had to as well. Some adherents of modernism like
Hermann Henselmann changed sides for opportunistic reasons and
defended the new style. However, many young architects were to
leave their profession in disgust.[6] Large plants for the manufacture
of pre-fab slabs were purchased in the Soviet Union. It might well
be that the spread of these ugly blocks all over Eastern Europe was
due to Moscow's commercial interests. The last and possibly lasting monument of the GDR is the colossal Palast der Republik, the
alleged pride of the people and last seat of the Volkskammer, now
shut down because of its contamination with asbestos—a striking
symbol of the Socialist experiment.

So far three observations about the interdependence of culture and
society in Germany have been made: first, an inherent antagonism
between intellect and power; second, the dominance of the cyclical
pattern, more often than not dialectical in nature, at the expense
of a more pluralist approach (pluralism is preached rather than
practised); third, a pervasive professionalization which has wholly
engulfed aesthetic criticism. What these phenomena, which affect
different arts in different ways, have in common is a strong di-
dactic impetus: writers tell us, as did Lord Acton (half German),
that power corrupts, painters that realism is kitsch, and critics that
every artist should first learn his or her trade. Immanuel Kant's
categorical imperative, i.e. the normative character of the individual's
ethical striving (which leaves no room for eccentric behaviour), has
never been seriously questioned in Germany.[7] Equally, Schiller's
concept of the *Nationaltheater* as a moral institution (*moralische Anstalt*)

or Goethe's idea of the educational novel (*Bildungsroman*), have survived to the present day. All this makes high culture a serious and cumbersome business. It is hardly surprising that it has not made much of an impact abroad, except, of course, in the case of music, to which such criteria do not apply. A friend has observed —and I agree—that in German bookshops the percentage of translated literature (mainly from English) in the popular domain is quite staggering.

While in political terms high culture served as a unifying force holding the two Germanies together (*Kulturnation*), it has had quite the opposite effect as far as West German society is concerned. It is so divorced from popular culture that it tends to separate the educated from the less-educated classes, with the *Abitur* as the dividing line. Franz-Josef Strauß,[8] son of a butcher and educated as a classicist with a large stock of Latin proverbs at his disposal, is said to have once asked a person he disagreed with, 'Have you actually got your *Abitur*?' Strauß, not known for his tact, was spelling out what others would merely have thought. Is Germany, then, a class society or not? In the 1960s it became fashionable among German sociologists to refer to *nivellierte Mittelstandsgesellschaft*, a society settling down to an unspecified middle-class level. More recent research has shown this to be wishful thinking.[9] Germany is socially stratified in more or less the same way as other industrial societies in the West, and of course the growth in white-collar workers was much more marked than that of the old working class (100 per cent as against 25 per cent between 1950 and 1970). But on the whole people are no longer affected by class consciousness. The latter has always been an alien concept, superimposed by Marxist ideology. To some extent, Hitler's success can be explained by his rhetoric against the idea of a permanent class struggle, setting one part of the *Volk* against the other. In terms of social psychology, the early modern notion of *Stand* (professional estate) has, despite changes with the passage of time, never completely lost its meaning. Thus Germany can be described as a *berufsständische* society, though not a corporative state in any political sense. Most Germans feel that they belong to one or the other professional group, rather than to a class. For instance, the Federal Republic still has more than half a million farms whose owners are neither professionals nor a class of their own, but what used to be called a *Stand*. So are self-employed craftsmen, some of whom have become veritable entrepreneurs, both in West Germany after 1948 and now in the former GDR. German society is made up of a variety of professional estates. The main distinguishing element amongst them is not so much birth, income, residence, or manual versus non-manual work, but educational background and cultural orientation. The whole hugely expensive set-up of publicly funded culture mainly serves the interests of the professional and educated middle classes. Efforts to attract the working class, especially in the Ruhr area (Ruhr festivals at Recklinghausen), have met with only moderate success.

The GDR, on the other hand, offers a different picture. There, a much higher percentage of all ranks of society, including the working class, patronized theatres, concerts, museums, and the like. Operas were not exclusively middle-class institutions, with dressed-up ladies showing off their jewellery during the intervals. Tickets were affordable for everyone, and no one needed to feel out of place. Participating in the enjoyment of high culture was a matter of social distinction on one side of the Wall, and evidence of social equality on the other. In the tradition of the nineteenth-century *Arbeiterbildungsvereine* (associations for the education of workers), the SED tried to raise the level of education and interest in the arts among the working class. Attempts in the 1960s to go one step further and involve ordinary people in the creative process were, however, but a short intermezzo.[10] In the West it was the new leisure culture which attracted the working man and released him from the old proletarian milieu, though without his being absorbed into the middle class. As far as the self-employed in trade and industry are concerned, their number has shrunk considerably, but their businesses have become more cost-effective than ever. They tend to work longer hours than others, with precious little time for cultural events. Often their sons and daughters rise into the professional middle class and share the latter's cultural tastes.

Nowhere is the division of Germany into professional estates more obvious than in the upper echelons of German society. There is not just one establishment, but a variety of functional elites.[11] Since the term *Elite* is not politically correct, reference is generally made to 'leading social groups'. Those who hold leading positions, such as politicians, civil servants, industrialists, bankers, bishops, and so forth, and who exercise social power, have climbed to the top of their career ladder, tend to be in their late fifties, and are almost exclusively male. There is precious little interchange between these groups of leaders in terms of social contact, intermarriage, or exchange of personnel. It is most unusual to switch from one career to another. There is usually a marked difference in political preference between the economic and cultural elites, who may dominate the media. While there is not much horizontal mobility, social mobility is all the more marked. In the mid-1970s, 80 per cent of the top echelons derived from the lower and middle strata of society, two-thirds grew up in former Prussia, few were Catholics (25 per cent), and only 60 per cent had a university education, half of them with a degree in law. In other words, German leaders are conditioned by their career achievements rather than by birth or education. In the West there was no drastic purge of elites, apart from those who rose from the ranks of the Nazi Party and did not manage to switch over to the civil service. However, in East Germany, virtually all leading personnel of the Nazi era were replaced by new cadres, chosen for their political loyalty, not for their professional competence. The growing diversity of social and industrial functions, however, made it necessary to train reserve cadres who were both faithful to the SED and professionally qualified within the system. Conscious efforts to recruit cadres from the working class appeared to be the best way of achieving this dual aim. There was never any doubt that overall power remained firmly in the hands of a carefully groomed political elite. This was certainly never the case in West Germany. There was no plan deliberately to create a universal elite that could be trusted to run the country's affairs, because this was regarded as potentially either undemocratic or economically counter-productive. No nostalgia is felt for the Prussian aristocratic elite, with its authoritarian outlook and agrarian interests. Like the federal system itself, the plurality of elites has greatly contributed to the diffusion of political power. It is only since unification and the prospect of greater international responsibility that some commentators like Jochen Thies have been wondering whether Germany would not be better served by a more unified, well-groomed political class.[12] Others expect Berlin, the new capital, to generate, over time, both a metropolitan culture and a new cosmopolitan elite.

While in the GDR most people kept their views to themselves, West Germany developed what has been called a *Streitkultur*, a culture of public debate. The intellectual elite, though generally proud of being above politics, is given to controversies which are political, if not Manichaean, in character and reminiscent of theological disputes of earlier times. This phenomenon may be best exemplified by the so-called Fischer Controversy of the 1960s, the *Historikerstreit* of the 1980s, and the *Literaturstreit* after unification, each dispute being connected with one period of German history.

The Hamburg historian Fritz Fischer proved by meticulous research that the imperial German government fuelled the July Crisis of 1914 until it got out of control and that it therefore had a somewhat greater share of responsibility for the outbreak of the war than the other major powers.[13] Today this point of view is fully accepted. But at the time Fischer's book was first published in 1961 it caused an outcry, mainly among his own generation of historians, many of whom had advanced their careers by disproving Germany's war-guilt as laid down in the Versailles Treaty. Before Fischer took a fresh look, the question seemed to have been settled on the basis that all the powers were equally responsible and had supposedly stumbled into the war. The wider issue was whether the image of the Bismarck Reich, still held in high esteem amongst the older generation, could be saved for posterity, or whether there was too much of an unsalutary continuity between the Second and the Third Reich.

The *Historikerstreit*[14] was, strangely enough, not launched by a professional historian, but by Jürgen Habermas, a social philosopher of the Frankfurt School, which had helped to prepare the ground for the student revolution by detecting fault lines in the political system of the Federal Republic. Habermas picked on the historian Ernst Nolte, who explained the Nazi horrors as a reaction to Bolshevism in the shape of Stalin's brutal dictatorship. Nolte, a disciple of Heidegger, and more a philosopher of history than a historian proper, carried his phenomenological approach one step too far and questioned the 'uniqueness' of the Holocaust. In societies not conditioned by religious division and dogmatism, the reaction would probably have been that anyone who makes excuses for the Holocaust, however speculative, has taken leave of his senses, regardless of whether he is a professor or not. However, Habermas lumped the indefensible Nolte together with other professional historians of unblemished but conservative reputation, by conjuring up a semi-official conspiracy to whitewash German history. In no time the whole guild of historians had split into two camps, vilifying each other by insinuation and innuendo. The 'uniqueness' of the Holocaust in relation to other twentieth-century horrors such as Stalin's and Pol Pot's crimes was the central issue. Common sense would suggest that in history everything and nothing is unique. Not so when self-righteous German academics fight for *Definitions-macht* and *Deutungsprimat* (the power to define and interpret) with the same fervour with which their forebears fought for Germany on the battlefield. One of the few sensible voices was that of the political scientist Karl Dietrich Bracher, who pointed out that whatever comparisons were possible between the dictatorships of Stalin and Hitler, totalitarian in nature and therefore capable of the utmost atrocities, had been made decades ago. Yet for some time the term 'totalitarian' had been rejected by the German intelligentsia as anti-Communist and therefore politically incorrect. Foreign historians of the older generation who still remember their German colleagues' desperate struggle after the war against the charge of collective guilt must wonder what to make of the younger generation, who seem to cling tenaciously to the exclusiveness of German depravity almost as a sign of distinction. No one can take away the shame, but shame it must be, not a political argument. It is well to remember John Maynard Keynes, who said: 'Nations are not authorised, by religion or natural morals, to visit on the children of their enemies the misdoings of parents and of rulers.'[15] In retrospect, this *querelle allemande* only shows that a liberal constitution is one thing and a truly liberal and tolerant society quite another. Some of the most vigilant defenders of liberalism are anything but liberal if they are confronted with the disagreeable views of their colleagues.

The controversy over the East German writer Christa Wolf, which erupted in June 1990, was the first all-German quarrel, a German family drama, as it was dubbed.[16] The facts, and their repercussions, were miles apart. In the early summer of 1990 Christa Wolf, the most famous East German writer, formerly fêted on both sides of the Wall, had published a short novel called *Was bleibt?* (What's Left?), in which she describes one day in 1979 when her house was supposed to have been the object of Stasi surveillance all day long. She claimed to have written this piece of literature at that time, only to have revised it ten years later. On 1 June two journalists opened a debate in *Die Zeit* about the merits of this new *œuvre*. A day later Frank Schirrmacher, literary editor of the *Frankfurter Allgemeine Zeitung*, followed with a thoroughly critical review, calling the author's moral credibility as a writer into question. He reminded his readers that Christa Wolf had always urged her fellow countrymen to remain loyal to socialist Germany, from her first novel *Der geteilte Himmel* (1963) to her last passionate plea on 8 November 1989. Of course she was concerned about certain unpleasant aspects of the regime, but never questioned its authority as such. The critic suggested that Wolf understood the society in which she lived as a larger version of the *petit bourgeois* and authoritarian family to which one belongs regardless. The new novel, it was argued, gave the impression that now Wolf wished to pose as the victim of a regime which had once showered her with many honours and privileges.

The reaction to these two book reviews was unprecedented, as though a public sacrilege had been committed: they were seen as demolishing the statue of a priestess. East and West German authors rushed to her defence, crying 'character assassination', 'witch-hunt', 'denunciation', 'inquisition', and so forth. There was almost no limit to the moral indignation caused by just two allegedly arrogant 'Wessies', with no knowledge whatsoever of life in the GDR. How is this to be explained? First of all, many Germans regarded Christa Wolf as the only moral institution left intact after reunification. As one of her advocates put it: 'Anyone who knocks down Christa Wolf dismantles the self-confidence of the citizens of the other German republic at the same time.'[17] Wolf's life was one of accommodation, under difficult circumstances, covering the whole spectrum from collaboration when it helped her career to resistance when it enhanced her reputation. It came as a shock to her admirers when, three years later, she herself revealed that at one time she, too, had worked for the Stasi. However, even this news did not totally discredit Christa Wolf in the eyes of East Germans, just as the popularity of Manfred Stolpe, Minister-President of Brandenburg and one-time spokesman of the GDR's Church Council, remained undiminished by revelations about his secret contacts with the Stasi.

The more important and long-lasting impact of the Christa Wolf affair concerns the self-perception and *raison d'être* of German writers once their utopian hopes for a better world, situated somewhere between the two existing Germanies, had been dashed. West German writers envied their colleagues in the East for being feared by their government and revered by the people as the conscience of the nation. This is what Christa Wolf meant when she said that harassment, working under an authoritarian regime, inspired her creativity.[18] East German conditions seemed to deliver a more realistic scenario for the kind of delayed anti-Nazi resistance that many West German authors saw as their mission. East German writers wished to be published and read in the West, and West Germans were hoping for the same treatment in the GDR. Authors like Christa Wolf could be sure of success in the West if they were marketed as dissidents, while Böll, Grass, and others had a better chance of finding favour with the SED if they were critical of their own society. These were the unspoken assumptions, which did not, however, necessarily explain the motives of each and every individual author. The writer as the guardian of public morality was the common ground of literature in both parts of Germany, and this ground caved in with the political earthquake of the summer of 1990. That literature is something other than conviction politics in writing is a new and, for many, irritating discovery. A hint of what literature could be is given by Patrick Süskind's novel *The Perfume*, which is totally divorced from German concerns and even from morality in a narrower sense, but highly enjoyable on purely aesthetic grounds. That the novel was on the bestseller list for a long time is no indication that the author's moral integrity is flawed. Up to that point the premisses of German literature were characterized by what Ulrich Greiner, literary editor of *Die Zeit,* called *Gesinnungsästhetik* (moral aestheticism).[19] Writers in both halves of Germany, he maintains, were commissioned to fight against restoration, fascism, clericalism, Stalinism, etc., and those who commissioned them had different names like conscience, party, politics, morale, and the past, which together led in the Federal Republic to the term *engagierte Literatur.* Famous authors like Böll, Grass, Lenz, Walser, Enzensberger, Weiss, Kipphardt, Andersch, and others of the 'Gruppe 47' belonged to this category and shaped the literature of the Federal Republic.

What unites the plurality of leading groups in the Federal Republic, as well as the deposed political elite of the former GDR, is a common cultural identity mainly based on German language and literature and the great works of art. The historical achievements of German culture up to 1933 and the aberrations afterwards are no longer in dispute. The problem is how to evaluate the last forty years. Today, six years after unification, East and West Germans do not know what to think of each other's contemporary culture and the way it has influenced them. Prejudice is still rampant. Was cultural policy for the benefit of the working class and in the manner of Socialist Realism really as worthless as Nazi art exhibited in the Munich *Haus der Kunst*? Has West German culture really degenerated into American pop culture?

The so-called Americanization[20] of West Germany is a very superficial description, which does not stand up to scrutiny. It is based on the immediate impact of the US forces: the import of chewing-gum, instant coffee, Coca-Cola, Lucky Strike cigarettes, and American movies, and, for a minority of fans, jazz and gospel songs. Very few Germans had a chance to see for themselves what the United States was really like. The reaction to the American way of life, notably among the older generation, was fuelled by the resentment of defeat, of denazification, and of re-education. This picture was then distorted still further by Communist propaganda in the East, which railed against American cultural imperialism in the hope of winning proselytes among West German nationalists. Ever since there has been a curious alliance of right- and left-wing critics against the so-called 'Coca-Cola' or 'McDonalds' culture. The rejection of foreign cultural imports is not a new phenomenon, but has been a constituent element of German national consciousness since the eighteenth century. A closer look at what really happened after 1945 reveals a more complex landscape. Of course, the impact of Anglo-Saxon culture cannot be denied, because it was identified with modernization in every respect. But as soon as German self-esteem had recovered after 1948, the American model lost much of its appeal. After 1945 American cigarettes and coffee rose to the status of a reserve currency, whole communities were fed on US rations from PX stores, and American motor cars were greatly admired. Less than a decade later German food manfacturers like

Dr Oetker and car companies such as Volkswagen had discovered the American market and had won the export battle in manufactured goods. The cars produced by Ford in Cologne and General Motors in Rüsselsheim, though streamlined as was the fashion, retained European dimensions.

High culture remained firmly rooted in German traditions and was never seriously challenged by America. As far as classical music, ballet, and so forth are concerned, it was almost one-way traffic from Germany to the States. American influence was, and still is, undeniable in the field of popular culture, in particular Hollywood movies, which flooded the German market after 1946. Now the rest of the population was allowed to watch the great epic film *Gone with the Wind* (the novel by Margaret Mitchell), previously only enjoyed by Goebbels and his entourage. As early as December 1944 Harry M. Warner had urged Roosevelt 'to flood Germany with American films . . . for there can be no better antidote for the poison of Nazism than the true American motion picture entertainment.'[21] More important still was the impact of rock and beat music, first received through the American Forces Network (AFN). Even though the majority still preferred classical melodies (operettas), folk-songs and contemporary hits (*Schlager*), the arrival of the rock culture signalled, to the dismay of parents and educators, the end of the German youth movement which had begun before the First World War with a strong anti-urban and anti-modern impetus. In the 1960s the new youth culture, epitomized by jeans and rock, suffused Germany like other Western countries. It grew so strong and irresistible that it even penetrated the Wall. Much though it was initially opposed by the East German 'guardians of culture', who tried to keep Western decadence at bay, in the end the authorities gave in and decided to control the new wave that seemed to be engulfing all those between the ages of ten and twenty-five, more than a quarter of the population (3.3 million).[22] Pop music was to be mixed with 'agitprop', all bands had to be licensed, 60 per cent of their music had to be home-made, with radio being the main producer of rock music. The idea of having rock music bureaucratically controlled and ideologically supervised is, of course, a contradiction in itself. Musicians were constantly tempted to trespass over the political boundaries, and that was part of their appeal to the young generation. The *cause célèbre* is linked with the name of Wolf Biermann, the modern folk-singer who could not be muzzled and was expelled to the West in 1976. Many artistes dared to register their protest and were subsequently deprived of their citizenship.

An essential ingredient of post-war re-education was the fight against racism, which had expressed itself in the unthinking use of national stereotypes. Allied and German efforts to eradicate such tendencies reinforced each other, since it was now the Germans themselves, the 'brazen horde' as Vansittart called them,[23] who were the victims of vilification. As a result, most Germans were so thoroughly re-educated, at least in this respect, that they even denied their own identity, i.e. that they, as other nations too, constitute a recognizably different social group, conditioned by its own history. That is why so many German intellectuals claim to have transcended the atavistic concept of 'nationhood', to have moved on to a higher plane. Even here they are donning an old hat, once worn by Goethe and Schiller, who were proud of their cosmopolitan outlook. When it comes to the fine arts, there is no denying that artists work in a very specific historical and cultural environment. No doubt, certain phenomena are common to all artists, but in Germany some are particularly relevant: clubbing together in schools (Gruppe 47 in literature, ZERO in painting, etc.), often at loggerheads with each other, a penchant for making strong statements, an obsession with the past and the corruption of power, and all in all a preference for forceful expressionist style. The idea that the history of German fine art in the twentieth century could be summarized under the heading 'Romanticism'[24] stretches the imagination well beyond any meaningful concept of this notion. In fact, all the political and social cataclysms of this century were translated into imagery of one kind or another.

The uninitiated observer of German visual art might well come to the conclusion that pleasing the eye is the cardinal sin, while conveying a message by striking, even bombarding, the mind meets the general expectation. Perhaps this is least true of the abstract and colourful paintings of Willi Baumeister and Ernst-Wilhelm Nay, who were banned by the Nazis and enjoyed a real comeback after the war. Baumeister was, at the same time, the great herald of abstract art, against critics like Hans Sedlmayr (*Verlust der Mitte*) who resented aesthetic pluralism and depicted the whole course of modern art as the progressive decomposition of a once coherent world-view.[25] More a symptom of post-war religious revivalism than a reflection of contemporary aesthetics, Sedlmayr's views were very influential among the conservative bourgeoisie, with its nostalgia for the pre-ordained world as God's creation. In fact, just because of Hitler's condemnation of modern, specifically abstract art, the pendulum swung all the more in that direction. It was some time before the conflict between Objectivity and Abstraction was resolved: both had their place and justification.

After the war, museums, eager to make amends, repurchased and exhibited pictures which only a few years before had been disposed of as 'degenerate art'. The younger generation was attracted to the new mode of abstract painting, whereas older people, notably in the Soviet Zone, hoped to reconnect their work with the pre-1933 period. Wieland Schmied observes that young German artists regarded the language of abstraction as 'a moral force which was internationally binding'. Post-war Germany 'yearned to be accepted once again into the fold of nations and to be recognised as an equal partner'.[26] The breakthrough to recognition of avant-garde works at home came with the 'Documenta' exhibition in Kassel in 1955, the first of many.

Quite a few painters like Georg Baselitz, Siegmar Polke, Gerhard Richter, and others came from East Germany, either by crossing from East to West Berlin, or by migrating to Düsseldorf, the other centre of modern German art.[27] Some of these painters, who had turned their backs on Socialist Realism as officially imposed in the East, had retained a preference for figurative, non-abstract art in the great tradition of German expressionism. The same even applied, to some extent, to many artists who stayed behind, like Bernhard Heisig, Willi Sitte, Werner Tüpke, and others, and who focused on topics, though not necessarily on a style, which found favour with their political masters.[28] Their workers did not look as happy and contented as they were supposed to be. For instance, a triptych by Tüpke on German workers parading before three sour-looking leaders with clenched fists and stern faces, in the manner of historical realism, strikes one as a perfect satire.[29] Painters cannot be dismissed just because of their official recognition by the East German authorities. Even if freedom of expression was constantly curtailed, there was still more leeway than during the Nazi period. At least conflict was possible and led to a growing extension of artistic freedom. After all, one of the rebels, Willi Sitte, became chairman of the artists' association. Scope for new experiments may account for the decision to stage an exhibition on *Auftragskunst* (commissioned art) in the GDR five years after its demise,[30] whereas Nazi art is still a taboo and all works once exhibited in the Munich *Haus der Kunst* are locked away in vaults. Of course, there are striking similarities between the two dictatorships as well. Not only were the visual arts meant to demonstrate the ideological goals of both regimes, the organizational frameworks in which artists were allowed to work also bore a remarkable resemblance to each other. No artist in East Germany could make a living unless he was a member of the guild, one of exactly six thousand of the *Verband Bildender Künstler* (VBK),[31] which counted in its ranks, amongst others, 1,511 painters and designers, 400 sculptors, 550 art historians, and so forth. The 90 cartoonists who also had to be members must have been tempted to transgress on a more or less daily basis. Members of the guild enjoyed certain privileges, such as a much lower tax rate, lucrative commissions, and the much-coveted visas for travelling to the West. However, there was also an underground of dissident artists who were more or less tolerated, and have only now come into the open.[32]

An artist's reputation in the GDR was twofold: recognition by the authorities of craftsmanship and loyalty, by way of prizes, exhibitions, commissions, etc., and appreciation by the public, both in the East and the West, for subtle and hidden criticism of the regime. Today this peculiar environment in which East German writers and painters worked and flourished has passed into history. It is too early to tell whether posterity will remember GDR art for historical reasons alone, or for aesthetic ones too. No doubt the famous names of Berthold Brecht and Wolf Biermann, both hailed and censored at the same time, will form an integral part of German cultural history. However, if one includes those artists who received their schooling in the East and then left for the West, their main contribution may eventually be seen as their reconnection of post-war German art with the earlier tradition of figurative expressionism. One day, some as-yet-unknown East German sculptor might outshine such West German luminaries as Joseph Beuys who thrived on scandal if nothing else. Here, as in so many other respects, the

East Germans proved to be the standard-bearers of an unmistakably German disposition. A break with Tachism and with abstract art in general occurred in the early 1960s under the impact of painters from the East like Baselitz and others. Far from being shunned because of their 'German connection', this was the very reason why they received international recognition, while those who had yearned for it in the post-war years were, with a few exceptions, hardly noticed outside Germany. Expressionist forcefulness, so Doris Schmidt says, is considered by the world to be typically German.[33] Nowadays German museums, rather than private collectors, are the chief purchasers and arbiters of modern art. As an example of modern art in themselves, incidentally, the many new museum buildings have, in some way, replaced church architecture, which flourished in the 1950s.

Late in the day came the international breakthrough of the modern German film.[34] For a long time the West German film industry, though commercially quite successful at home before the arrival of television, had no chance of competing with foreign-made films, especially those from Hollywood. Germany exported everything except film and television productions. The 'new German film' began with an angry protest by young film directors in Oberhausen in the early 1960s, who urged the government to sponsor film as an art-form, not just as a consumer commodity. In 1964 the Committee for the New German Film was established in order to promote and subsidize new ventures. Without public support the German film miracle would not have been possible. Since then directors like Alexander Kluge, Werner Herzog, Volker Schlöndorff, Rainer–Werner Fassbinder, Wim Wenders, Hans-Jürgen Syberberg, and Edgar Reiz have been able to produce highly esteemed films, even though they are not all commercially viable. In Germany these films are often watched by a small elite of cineasts in studios supported by local government.

As a general conclusion one could say that Germany, including the former GDR, spends huge sums of money on the performing arts, to the envy of other countries, though without producing a comparable number of creative artists of international standing. Of contemporary German writers, only Heinrich Böll, Günter Grass, and Bert Brecht are well known, though not necessarily read, outside the confines of German language departments. Nowhere will a young

German learn how to write a good short story, nor is drama as well established in German schools as it is in Britain. The impetus of German education is towards high performance, academic and professional achievement, at the expense of genuine creativity. Schiller's reference to life being serious while art is cheerful seems to have been lost on the Germans, whose life experiences since those days of cultural blossoming have been too serious to leave much room for cheerfulness. Two periods of inflation this century mean that there are few people with independent means who could afford to pursue a life of cultured leisure. Now that private fortunes are being passed down to the next generation for the first time, this may prepare the ground for a more relaxed and confident society, giving greater scope to the gentlemen of leisure.

8 German Unification

The rapid transition towards unification in 1989–90, colloquially called *die Wende*, no doubt constitutes the climax of the Federal Republic's history since 1949. Does it also mark the end of the Bonn republic and what it stood for? Only time will tell. But it is a fair assumption that the lessons learned from this experience are likely to have no less an impact on the political culture of the country than the political events surrounding the first unification. At that time, the failure of the Frankfurt Parliament of 1848 and the proclamation of the German Empire on the battlefields in 1871 persuaded many Germans that Bismarck was right in saying that blood and iron mattered more than fine words and resolutions.[1] From then on, power politics appeared to be the most decisive agent in history. Unconditional surrender in 1945 and the breach of the Wall in 1989 entailed very different lessons: war did not pay, while peaceful and patient perseverance did indeed reward Germany with a second chance. The politics of 'small steps' led to a great leap forward which nobody had expected. And this is another significant implication of *die Wende*, which is bound to reverberate: history is still a force to be reckoned with. The cataclysm of 1989–90 developed a momentum of its own, which could hardly be controlled by politicians. German unification was more the result of crisis management than of rational predetermination. It is only in retrospect that the causes and effects can be more clearly discerned.

The Berlin Wall became the most telling symbol of the GDR's failure to achieve legitimacy. If it had not been for the closing of this last escape route to the West, and a more ruthless Soviet leadership, the East German regime would certainly have collapsed in 1961,[2] in circumstances similar to those of 1989. Now we can see that it had been living, ever since, on borrowed time. If it was unable to retain its own citizens without repression, it was doomed in the long run. The GDR's congenital defect was that right from its conception it was neither German nor democratic. Throughout its existence East Germany depended on protection from the occupying power against its own population, as had become manifest

in the uprising of 17 June 1953. By comparison, the security which
NATO provided for West Germany was always directed against an
outside aggressor. The dilemma which the SED leadership faced after
its new lease of life in 1961 was almost impossible to overcome:
it had to instil a separate identity based not on German national
feeling but on socialism, which was the *raison d'être* for another,
supposedly 'better' Germany, and at the same time to satisfy the
economic aspirations of its citizens. Yet the command economy could
never successfully compete with the free market economy in the
West. The party looked east and congratulated itself on its economic performance in comparison with other Comecon countries,
while ordinary people watched West German television every night,
news and consumer advertisements, and saw no reason to be self-
satisfied. Leadership and people never looked into the same mir-
ror. Consequently a make-believe presentation of reality and an
intense surveillance system by the Stasi kept the regime in power.
But in the course of time both these means, propaganda and repression, began to wear thin and in the end failed to intimidate the
population any longer.

However, in the last resort the system was held together by outside constraints, an allegedly revanchist enemy in the West which
fuelled the propaganda machine, and the big brother in Moscow
who could be relied upon never to surrender his western bulwark.
When these two props gave way as détente intensified, the whole
fabric of the GDR began to crumble. From the memoirs of Schabowski[3] we now know that the precarious political and economic
situation of the GDR was never openly discussed in the Politbüro.
The latter's decision-making was conditioned by wishful thinking
over a long period. All the signals from the West, notably West
Germany, could be interpreted as evidence of a definite recognition of the GDR's sovereignty. Communist spying activities in
Bonn, in which the GDR excelled, particularly Markus Wolf,[4] showed
that to all intents and purposes there was no sinister plot in the
making to destabilize the regime in East Berlin. As has now been
revealed,[5] this did not deflect the GDR 'National Defence Council'
from preparing in quite ludicrous detail its own aggressive plans
vis-à-vis West Germany. A growing self-confidence thus provided
by the Federal Republic, together with material aid, served to stave
off necessary reforms demanded by both the new Soviet leader,

Gorbachev, and the internal opposition movement. The constant improvement in intra-German relations and the growing tensions between East Berlin and Moscow were among the most important long-term causes of the demise of the GDR. It is therefore worth while looking at them in more detail.

By the time Helmut Kohl had taken over as Chancellor from Schmidt in 1982 it had become clear that the Federal Republic, not just the government in power, had an overriding interest in maintaining détente for the sake of better relations with the GDR, or rather further improvements in human contacts between the two Germanies. The new Chancellor had accepted the foreign policy premisses of the previous government, in spite of growing tensions between the United States and the Soviet Union over Afghanistan, the Polish crisis, and NATO's dual-track policy. Foreign Minister Hans-Dietrich Genscher, who had switched sides to stay in power, was the outward manifestation of the fact that the SPD's *Ostpolitik* would be continued. There was only a slight change in the political rhetoric, more insistence on human rights and legal positions, but that was all. In security matters, or to be more precise, the installation of a new missile system, Kohl's loyalty to Washington remained unshaken. At the same time he pursued his own agenda in relations with Honecker, who badly needed economic assistance to avert total bankruptcy and was therefore open to deals. As Peter Bender, one of the most perceptive observers of developments over the years, put it succinctly: 'Whoever is chancellor in Bonn, he will have his supporting leg in the West and his playing leg in the East.'[6] German unification was more an article of faith for the new government than an operative policy which governed day-to-day business with East Germany. In the meantime priority was given to a policy of demanding freedom and self-determination rather than national unity within one state. It was up to the East Germans to decide in a free vote whether they wished to be united with the Federal Republic. This also meant that a united 'fatherland', if and when it came about, could only materialize under the terms of Western democracy and a common European roof.

For the time being all that seemed to matter to the government was to 'keep the German question open,' as the saying went. Time and again Honecker was assured by West German visitors that the issue of German unification was not on the political agenda: it would neither be forced nor abandoned, but left to the decision of future generations. The new *modus vivendi* was couched in euphemistic terms, which, at times, irritated Anglo-Saxon commentators. They referred to *Genscherismus*, a new kind of appeasement. A joint declaration by the Bundestag on 9 February 1984 referred to both Germanies linked by a 'common responsibility for peace and security in Europe' (*Verantwortungsgemeinschaft*).[7] Never again should Germany be the cause of war (*Von deutschem Boden darf niemals wieder Krieg ausgehen*). Bonn subsequently granted credit facilities in return for an extension of visa arrangements for East Germans below retirement age. Pensioners had been the first category allowed to travel west, because they were nothing but a burden on the strained East German economy. The cynicism of this and similar decisions was not lost on the citizens who deeply resented travel restrictions. The increase in the number of visitors to West Germany between 1984 and 1987 was considerable: the number of old-age pensioners rose from 1.5 million to 3.8 million and that of relatives (for urgent family matters) from 61,000 to 1.2 million. Agreements regulating cultural exchanges and town twinnings were to follow. Chancellor Kohl felt strongly that the German nation was 'not at the disposition of governments' and that a common culture was the strongest bond which kept it together. It was therefore a worthy investment for the future.[8] It is doubtful whether he fully realized at the time that this was also a shrewd exercise in *Realpolitik*. Many of those who had seen what West Germany was like would, in the autumn of 1989, be among the demonstrators in Leipzig and elsewhere, who brought the SED to its knees. At the time it looked like a bargain for East Berlin, which was heavily in debt to foreign banks, notably the Japanese, and was unable to raise further foreign loans. Credits from Bonn helped to restore the creditworthiness of the GDR. The memoirs of Günther Mittag, the long-standing supremo of the GDR's economy, reveal how desperate the situation was by 1983–4. They also show how the East German leaders hoped to buy time by manipulating West German politicians like Franz-Josef Strauß into believing that economic disaster would spell the end of détente and 'a renewed lowering of the Iron Curtain'.[9] In other words, economic assistance by the capitalist West was interpreted as a far-sighted contribution to peace and stability in Europe. In the second half of the 1980s there was a steady stream of West German VIPs to East Germany, keen to talk to Honecker and his entourage. We do not yet know exactly what was discussed at such meetings. But it is symptomatic of the tacit agreement between the political leadership in East and West Germany that Helmut Schmidt should express this view on 19 September 1989: 'An eruption in the GDR would jeopardize the reform process in Eastern Europe.'[10] Was it not also Bonn's responsibility to prevent civil unrest and bloody repression by helping East Germany to sustain a reasonable standard of living? Such scenarios would go a long way to explain why the Bonn government had been most reluctant to exploit the situation in the autumn of 1989. No doubt this restraint was conducive to the successful outcome of the revolution. Slogans like *Verantwortungsgemeinschaft* or *Sicherheitspartnerschaft* ('partnership in security'—SPD vocabulary) are open to interpretation: while officially they referred to security and stability in Europe in general, they also covered the avoidance of grassroots unrest in the GDR. Bonn hoped for an evolutionary process towards confederation, leading to an eventual federation some time in the distant future.

Erich Honecker's visit to West Germany in 1987, including his native Saarland, was the climax of his political career and of intra-German *rapprochement*.[11] The visit had been postponed several times before Moscow gave its final blessing. Questions of protocol were of the utmost importance, because they appeared to signal that the GDR was now on an equal footing with the Federal Republic. Honecker basked in the glory of his new international standing. Invitations by the Belgian and Spanish royal families and the French Prime Minister followed, and were gladly accepted. Efforts to gain invitations from the United States and Britain, two of the four main Allies, were eagerly pursued. Domestic affairs, the area where his fate would be decided in less than two years, were left in the hands of his acolytes as a matter of routine. From his confidential talks James McAdams gained the impression that even the most loyal members of the SED could admit, in those two years, 'that their party's leader and those around him had become infected with an almost unfathomable sense of complacency about their achievements'.[12] Not only is it power that corrupts, as Lord Acton concluded, but also unearned recognition.

According to the East German Party paper *Neues Deutschland*, but also according to opinion polls in West Germany, the visit consolidated the division of Germany. As it turned out, it was the beginning of the end for the GDR, which experienced increasing destabilization as a result of disappointed expectations among the population. After the triumphant reception of the Party leader in West Germany, the regime felt sufficiently confident to crack down on dissidents and disregard demands for fundamental reform. Not surprisingly, the groundswell of protest grew stronger by the day. Now the image of a hostile Federal Republic could no longer be conjured up to justify repression. While the Federal government remained aloof, West Germany's media coverage of all dissident activities tended to encourage the opposition to press on with their demands for more basic rights. However, the regime would not budge, confident that West Germany would refrain from interfering and that Soviet troops would be on stand-by if the situation got out of hand. It was just inconceivable that the Soviet government would not come to the rescue of the ruling East German Party, which had been its loyal agent for so long.

The *Ostpolitik* of the SED is still shrouded in secrecy. All we know is that East Berlin's relations with the Soviet leadership were no less crucial than those with Bonn. That the key to the German question lay in Moscow, one of the standard phrases of German politics, proved to be correct, except that one side hoped to open the lock, while the other wanted it to remain firmly closed. Ever since Gorbachev had embarked upon his policy of *perestroika* and *glasnost*, Honecker and his old guard in Pankow had felt increasingly uneasy about the uncharted course of Soviet reforms.[13] To someone like Gorbachev the SED Politbüro looked like a geriatric ward, with eight members over seventy years old, among them Günther Mittag and Erich Mielke, the security chief, who was a particularly sinister figure. Up to the autumn unrest of 1989 Honecker remained firmly in command and was not in any way disposed to be lectured to by the much younger Gorbachev, who still had to prove that his reforms were paying off and benefiting the economy. Honecker could also point out that his people were heavily exposed to West German television and that any loosening of the Party's grip was so much more fraught with dangers. Even though it is less than fair to describe the GDR in the late 1980s as the last outpost of Stalinism, Egon Krenz, heir apparent to the General Secretary, is probably right to conclude that Honecker was never able 'to free himself from the fateful legacy of Stalin, in a political and personal sense'.[14] We shall never know whether earlier reforms could have preserved the GDR's integrity or would have precipitated the regime's demise. What matters here is that timely change, both of leadership and policies, was with hindsight the only alternative. The growing divergence between Moscow and East Berlin in domestic affairs was to some extent offset and also camouflaged by the latter's unequivocal support for Gorbachev's initiatives in the area of arms reduction. Not surprisingly, this twin-track approach was also pursued by Bonn in its dealings with Washington. In security matters, both German governments remained firmly anchored in their respective camps. Intra-German relations were played down as frontier trading which would benefit both sides.

The rift between the Soviet and East German leadership, simmering for some time, burst into the open when in 1988 the SED banned the November issue of the Soviet magazine *Sputnik*, which had attacked the German Communists' shameful approval of the Hitler-Stalin Pact in 1939.[15] The determination to keep Soviet reform impulses at bay could be interpreted as an expression of greater independence in the same way as closer relations with Bonn served to enhance East Berlin's diplomatic position. However, the GDR's foreign policy always had domestic repercussions, which were most difficult to assess and to control. For the forces of opposition the wind of change blowing through Poland, Hungary, and above all the Soviet Union was an exhilarating sign that the embattled SED Politbüro would sooner or later have to yield to pressure for reform. Though surrounded by advocates of controlled liberalization from the East and from within, the regime saw no grounds for immediate action. The Stasi seemed to be fully in control. Nor was the silhouette of unification to be seen anywhere on the horizon. The Protestant dissidents did not look forward to being embraced by the capitalist Federal Republic. In no uncertain terms, Gorbachev had told the West German Chancellor on the occasion of the latter's visit to Moscow in October 1988 that the division of Germany was 'the result of history', and that any attempt to change the situation would be 'unpredictable and even dangerous'.[16] This was, incidentally, also the general view of quite a few German historians who had long since written off the German nation state as an alternative that was neither attainable nor desirable.[17] Kohl, himself a historian by training, and more aware of the significance of the *Kulturnation* than most, was more guarded in his statements. He did not wish to be seen to be pushing for a solution to the German problem which, in December 1988, he thought was no nearer. Any operative policy in that direction was regarded as counter-productive. No secret plans had been drawn up in Bonn for 'Day X plus one', which explains why the government was so unprepared in 1990 for the colossal task ahead. It is no exaggeration to say that all four Allies responsible for Germany as a whole were psychologically more disposed to anticipate and to accept the inevitable outcome of any major turmoil in East Germany, such as the events surrounding the fall of the Wall, than was the Federal government. Hans-Dietrich Genscher, one of the chief architects of the softly-softly approach, still treated unification as a taboo, while the American ambassador to Bonn referred to it as a foregone conclusion. After 9 November 1989 Vernon Walters was no longer able to stand this holier-than-thou attitude of the German foreign minister.[18] Genscher's restraint reminds one of Clemenceau's advice *vis-à-vis* Alsace-Lorraine before 1914: always on your mind but never on your tongue. No doubt the West German and Soviet policy of non-interference was among the most crucial elements in the revolutionary process which brought down not only the Honecker regime, but subsequently the GDR itself. The German Communists, installed by a foreign power in 1945–6, were left to their own devices in the final hour of their destiny. They could not blame the crisis on West Germany or expect succour from their Soviet ally.

By April 1989, the ingredients for a chain reaction were all in place. It was in Hungary that the fuse was eventually ignited, if not accidentally, then certainly without any clear notion of what was to happen. When Gorbachev visited Budapest in April 1989 he quietly dropped the Brezhnev Doctrine[19], which had legitimized Soviet intervention in Eastern Europe, notably the crushing of the Prague Spring in 1968. In view of his previous handling of the Polish crisis, which attracted much international attention, this was no spectacular turning-point in the Soviet leader's policy towards Warsaw Pact countries. But it did encourage the Hungarian government to start dismantling the barbed-wire fences along the Austrian frontier on 2 May 1989, at the beginning of the holiday season. Even before that, the less-fortified Hungarian–Austrian border had been a favourite escape route for East Germans who were irresistibly drawn to the promised land of the Federal Republic. If we look upon the Berlin Wall as a gigantic dam holding back a flood of potential refugees, this was the first leak.

Refusal to grant free elections had been the most serious and constant charge against the GDR. The fraudulent manipulation of the local government elections of 7 May 1989 was the last incident in a long history of self-deception, except that people were no longer prepared to stay silent. They openly questioned the results and thus challenged the regime's authority.[20] The various opposition groups who had found a safe haven in the Church could no longer be subdued. The number of East Germans who voted with their feet by escaping to the West via Hungary exposed the election results as yet another blatant lie. In the course of the ensuing summer months hundreds and thousands of East Germans, skilled professionals badly needed at home like doctors, nurses, and engineers, turned their backs on 'socialism in the colours of the GDR' (Honecker), and took advantage of the new opening through Hungary. Others sought refuge in West German embassies in Prague, Warsaw, and elsewhere, thus forcing Bonn to facilitate their emigration. By the end of September 1989 more than 30,000 East German citizens had, in one way or another, reached the safe shores of the West and applied for West German passports, to which they were entitled. There was no end to this mass exodus in sight. The television coverage of these events, for instance Genscher's emotional appeal to the thousands camping on the grounds of the Prague embassy,[21] exposed the fundamental weakness of the GDR to both its own people and the outside world. East Germans wondered whether to follow suit and leave, and foreign journalists began to ask themselves where all this was to end.

Neither East nor West German leaders were prepared for the upheaval which was unfolding before their eyes. Both were at a loss to know how to adapt their policies to a situation which they had been trying hard to avert all along: the unwelcome fact that the East German people were taking their fate into their own hands. Hitherto the addressees of West German overtures had always been GDR officials. Even the Social Democrats largely ignored the dissidents, except for church leaders, in order not to jeopardize their established relations with the SED. East German citizens were never thought to be anything but the mute subjects of a Party dictatorship who did not figure as a political constituency like the West German electorate. Their basic rights and human desires, such as the lifting of travel restrictions, were a matter for negotiations between their would-be masters in the East and their would-be counsellors in the West. All of a sudden they began to mass together, raise their voices, and shout 'We are the people.'[22] For over forty years the regime had worked hard at domesticating the 'people', folding them into orchestrated mass organizations. The East German decision-making system was, not unlike the Führer-state, incapable of adjusting to new challenges if the leader saw no need for change. Honecker sent Egon Krenz, his designated successor, on holiday when he became nervous and dared to make suggestions. Then Honecker himself was taken out of action due to a gallbladder operation between 21 August and the end of September 1989, with no one left in overall control during the most crucial weeks of the GDR's entire history. However, it is most unlikely that Honecker would have acted in any other way than his deputy, Günther Mittag, who resorted to intimidating rhetoric.[23] On his return, Honecker totally miscalculated the mood. He denounced the refugees: no tears should be shed for those deserting socialism.

There is general agreement among experts that the crucial date for the unstoppable demise of the GDR was not 9 November, with the spectacular fall of the Wall, but Monday, 9 October, when the regime mustered all its moral and military armour for a final show of strength against the demonstrators in Leipzig. It was the potential scene for a Tiananmen Square repeat, an event which had been given East Berlin's official blessing by Krenz during his visit to Beijing. Only two days before, the GDR had celebrated its fortieth anniversary in the presence of Gorbachev in a staged flight from reality: a display of tanks, missiles, and rhetorical self-assurances. It was on this occasion that Gorbachev dropped the famous sentence: 'When we fall behind, life punishes us immediately.'[24] In his official speech he made it clear that questions concerning the GDR would henceforth not be decided in Moscow but in Berlin. This could be interpreted as his backing for reform, if need be by the removal of Honecker, which was being plotted behind the scenes by Krenz, the heir apparent, and Günther Schabowski, the Berlin Party Secretary.[25] Gorbachev was hardly airborne before the great bluff was called. By now the Monday demonstrations in Leipzig had proved to be an even greater embarrassment to the regime than the flight of individual citizens. Therefore something had to be done to stop these demonstrations of defiance once and for all.

Nevertheless, people would not be deterred and turned out in even larger numbers than the week before (when 20,000 had taken to the streets). These 70,000 citizens, not the hundreds of thousands in Berlin at a later stage, brought down the regime, above all by their personal courage and the utter peacefulness of the occasion: no banners, no provocation whatsoever, just a huge impenetrable wall of people defying the authorities.[26] Several theories have been put forward as to why the security forces did not intervene: the crowd was too large to disperse without risking a bloodbath; possible warnings by the Russians, who would not have intervened if violence had flared up; the realization that those who were demonstrating did not wish to leave but to reform their country. Instead of 'Wir wollen raus' (We want to get out), the majority of demonstrators were now shouting 'Wir bleiben hier' (We shall stay). Whether the leadership had given the order to move in and was disobeyed by local commanders has never been ascertained. There were two local Party Secretaries among the signatories to an appeal for calmness as a precondition for a dialogue with the government. From that day on, the spell was broken and the SED was forced to open its clenched fist.

The Monday demonstrations in Leipzig were preceded by prayers for peace in the Nicolaikirche (Church of St Nicholas) and the chant *Dona nobis pacem*. Undeniably, the Protestant Church in East Germany had acquired a political significance well beyond its spiritual appeal by providing a safe haven and moral support for the civil rights movement. Theirs was a fine balancing act between adaptation and resistance. Peaceful co-existence with the prevailing social order was expressed in the judicious formula 'Kirche im Sozialismus', which was open to interpretation.[27] There was also an uncanny division of responsibility: the hierarchy was inclined to collaborate with the authorities in order to safeguard the *modus vivendi* with an atheist regime, while individual pastors often cooperated in their parishes with the civil rights movement. Bishops

and Church officials like Manfred Stolpe often appeared to be acting in concert with the state by containing and depoliticizing, as it
were, grassroots opposition. In actual fact the logistic support for
the dissidents and the freedom of speech prevailing in the Protestant synods, the only platforms for practising democracy, greatly
helped to foster the process of political fermentation. Both Church
and state persuaded each other that in spite of the ideological antagonism they cared for their 'country' and the moral well-being of
its citizens *vis-à-vis* the capitalist West. Both had adopted a patronizing attitude towards their flock, who should not be led astray.
In 1989 this meant that the exodus to the moral wilderness of the
West should be stopped by introducing domestic reforms and thus
changing the face of socialism. As late as mid-November, a week
after the Wall had come down, Heino Falcke, one of the spiritual
leaders, demanded a viable alternative to capitalism: 'We must not
simply be swallowed up by the West. We need an alternative to
capitalism.'[28] He pointed to the destructiveness of capitalism in the
Third World, while the rest of the population was deeply impressed
by the ostensibly constructive effects of the free market in West
Germany. Many East German theologians now hoped that the time
had come to realize their dreams of an ideal socialist state which
would prove to be morally superior to the Federal Republic. No doubt
from a theological point of view social justice had a far higher priority than political freedom for the individual. Not surprisingly,
the Church's influence was soon eclipsed since people who were
just being released into the real world would not be fobbed off
with a new set of exhortations.

The revolutionary dynamics triggered off by the events of 9
October produced two interacting chain reactions: the rapid transformation of the regime, and simultaneously the emergence and
mushrooming of civil rights groups.[29] The first and most important movement was *Neues Forum*, which had published its manifesto in early September 1989 and called for a reconstruction of
society on the basis of justice, democracy, peace, and protection of
the environment. Freedom from fear and the rule of law rather
than that of the guardian state and the secret police were the most
pressing demands. The agenda was moderate: recognition by and
dialogue with the party bosses. Nor was there any talk of abandoning socialism. The so-called *Ellenbogengesellschaft* of the West

(literally, 'elbow society')—a term soon to become a cliché—was explicitly rejected. Whereas *Neues Forum* wished to remain a citizens' movement, other associations, such as *Demokratischer Aufbruch* and *Demokratie Jetzt*, adopted a more party-political line and contested the monopoly of the SED. The most serious challenge to the latter was the re-emergence of an independent Social Democratic Party (SDP). Even though the Church hierarchy remained in the background, individual pastors and theologians were among the leading spokesmen of these movements. Their messages were very similar: socialism with a human face and no annexation by the Federal Republic. Their concern for a better world, not just a better quality of life, imprinted itself on the autumn declarations. The unworldliness of their language limited their appeal among ordinary folk who had no church affiliation and were fed up with the unfulfilled promises of socialism. This is one of the reasons why the vanguard of the revolution was soon left behind.

The East German revolution can be encapsulated in the two slogans 'We are *the* people' and, a couple of months later, 'We are *one* people.' It was indeed the gathering momentum of the mass protests which led to the collapse of the repressive SED regime and, finally, the GDR itself. The irony is that the very masses which left-wing revolutionaries always wished to rouse emerged in strength without a conspicuous leader, only to bring down 'the real existing socialism'. There were two fronts on which the battle for self-determination was fought: the exodus to the West, which exploded still further, and regular mass demonstrations in all major cities, notably Leipzig and Berlin, which kept up the pressure for change with their dramatically swelling numbers of participants and anti-government messages on ready-made posters and placards. In Leipzig alone an average of 150,000 people turned out every Monday night. Since Hungary (11 September) and Czechoslovakia (3 November) had opened their borders to refugees, the number rose steeply from 33,000 in September to 133,000 in November (and 343,854 altogether for the whole of 1989).[30]

In vain did the SED now try to retain credibility and power by yielding to popular demands. People were in no mood to be appeased by half-measures. On 18 October Honecker and his old guard were forced out, to make way for Egon Krenz as the new Party boss and head of state. By 24 October the SED was prepared to enter into a dialogue with the opposition, only to be told that the time for a one-party system was over. The so-called bloc parties distanced themselves from the SED and demanded a free and secret ballot. The CDU shrewdly elected a new chairman, the hitherto unknown lawyer Lothar de Maizière, who was to become the last Prime Minister of the GDR. The agenda for change was dictated by the people in the streets. Naturally, one of the first demands was for the lifting of travel restrictions. Hitherto visas for the West had been among the most coveted privileges of the GDR: tourism outside the confines of Comecon countries was out of the question. One of the more popular placards in Leipzig's Monday rallies read *Visafrei bis Hawaii*.[31] In early November the government extended travel privileges to thirty days per year, but only after bureaucratic approval and without making foreign currency available. The East Berlin parliament (*Volkskammer*) rejected these proposals as too timid. First the Cabinet resigned, then, a day later, the entire Politbüro of the SED. A reconstituted Party leadership under Egon Krenz and Günter Schabowski and a government led by the new Prime Minister Hans Modrow, a known reformer, now tried to catch up with the bandwagon in order to slow it down and reassert political authority. The new Council of Ministers came up with travel regulations which would appease the ever more excited public. Party press spokesman Günter Schabowski had no idea of the immediate and historical impact of his haphazard announcement at a press conference on 9 November regarding the forthcoming Party conference: 'Private trips to foreign countries can be applied for without preconditions.'[32] Local police stations were to be instructed to issue visas for permanent exit without delay. Asked by journalists when this would come into force and whether it would also apply to Berlin, Schabowski rummaged in his papers and said: 'Yes, at once.' What happened is well known. The media blasted out this news without referring to proper procedures and a few hours later thousands of people had gathered near the Wall and forced their way into West Berlin on the same night.

The fall of the Wall sparked off the second phase of the revolution, which only came to a halt with unification less than twelve months later. The relentless pressure from mass rallies and mass migration to the West was the most potent force at work. The East German media embraced the opportunity for uncensured reporting

and exposed the utterly corrupt nature of the SED regime, in particular the privileges of the *nomenklatura* in the Wandlitz district of
East Berlin, the true state of public finances and the economy, and
the damage done to the environment over forty years. However,
no revelation was more damaging to the SED than that of the widespread activities of the Stasi, who had spied on the entire population, including the top brass of the ruling party.[33]

The contrast to the Federal Republic now came into focus more
sharply than ever before, as millions, probably two-thirds of the
population within the space of two or three months, crossed the
border on day trips to see what it was like. The TV image of West
Germany was no distortion of reality. What met the eye as regards
the infrastructure, public services and utilities, showed that the
GDR lagged so far behind that ordinary people could not imagine
how a reformed but still socialist government could ever catch up
with the West. The statement 'We are one people' was essentially
a cry for help addressed to their West German fellow countrymen
who looked on in amazement.[34] What was now on offer was another utopia or the West German model. It was not pan-German
nationalism, as some West and East German intellectuals would
have it, but the hitherto suppressed common sense of the people
which was making itself felt. A similar development took place in
the Western zones of occupation after 1948 when, after years of
shortage, people had had enough of a planned economy and opted
for the free market against the advice of the many well-meaning
politicians and bureaucrats on the left.

After 9 November the public discourse was marked by the new
leaders of the civil rights movement, who pleaded for the preservation of a separate East German identity, against the popular demand
for *Deutschland einig Vaterland* (the suppressed verse of the East
German national anthem). It became increasingly evident that
the call for free elections could not be ignored much longer and
that this would inevitably turn into a plebiscite for or against unification. There was, though, a sizeable minority of demonstrators
warning against the alleged dangers of capitalism in the guise of
nationalism and fascism, with slogans like: 'Even after Honecker
and Krenz, never Daimler-Benz!' or 'Never again: Germany awake!'
or 'No Fourth Reich!' etc.[35] What is most remarkable is that citizens holding the placards for and against a united Germany stood

in close proximity without any violence flaring up. The rallies were peaceful throughout. Indeed, this revolution did not produce one single casualty, let alone one violent death, on the streets or elsewhere. The GDR referred to itself as the 'workers' and peasants' state'. However, it was the skilled workers and master craftsmen among the demonstrators, especially those of the older generation, who now opted for unification without delay, whereas students defended the SED and a separate socialist state.[36] They had the most to lose since they had just embarked upon safe and not too strenuous office careers, without yet having experienced the frustrations of the 'real existing socialism'. *Neues Forum* also misread the mood of the people when its leaders protested against the opening of the Wall. They lost their popular appeal at the very moment they were about to be included in the decision-making process, when the first Round Table was set up in Berlin in early December 1989.

On 26 November East German intellectuals, among them Stefan Heym, Christa Wolf, and Volker Braun, published a manifesto (*Für unser Land*—For our Country) which called for a 'socialist alternative to the Federal Republic'.[37] They felt strongly that East Germans should not sell out their 'material and moral values' and should reflect on their original 'anti-fascist and humanist ideals'. Later they were to refer to the GDR's history as a 'failed experiment', as though it had been a voluntary effort by the people and not a foreign imposition all along. It now turned out that many East German intellectuals had cherished their position as a kind of grace-and-favour opposition to the regime and had serious problems with democracy when it ceased to be a distant goal and emerged as a new reality. Not surprisingly, the East German left was soon left behind. In a perceptive study of Germany's road to unification, Elizabeth Pond points out that for the first time since 1848 their was no contradiction between German unity and individual freedom: 'Forty years of decaying apartments, bans on holidays in the Alps, constant nagging by the state and a standard of living only half that of West Germany had totally discredited the illiberal political option. It was not chauvinism that drove the Leipzigers to display pan-German flags. It was the utilitarian reckoning which swiftly became a consensus that unification would be the fastest way to acquire the economic and political perquisite that West Germans took for granted.'[38]

Politicians on either side of the crumbling Wall could no longer turn a blind eye to what was happening. With the chorus in the streets of Leipzig, Berlin, and Dresden swelling hourly, and the exodus to the West unrelenting (though down to 50,000 in December from 133,000 in November), the eventual merger of the two German states was only a matter of how and when. Hans Modrow and Helmut Kohl tried to steady the course of events in an attempt to gain time to find a sensible solution. In his first government declaration Modrow went further than any of his predecessors and called for a 'contractual community', knowing that without massive economic assistance the GDR was doomed. Would this assistance be forthcoming to shore up a government and a state that were in deep trouble? Ten days later, on 28 November, Chancellor Kohl came up with his own agenda, the so-called 'Ten-Point Declaration'[39] accepting Modrow's idea of a contractual community and pledging Bonn's help in exchange for fundamental political and economic reforms, such as no one-party rule, free elections, and private enterprise. Most importantly, the Chancellor indicated how unification, the ultimate goal of the Federal Government, might eventually be brought about within the future architecture of Europe: confederal structures between the two states, equally legitimized in democratic terms, with the aim of creating a federal order. Though the scenario for unification was vague and without a timeframe, the impact of Kohl's speech was still a political bombshell. The Chancellor had not briefed his allies, or even Genscher, but had been encouraged to put unification on the international agenda for the first time by his personal adviser. Horst Teltschik had, in turn, been steered on to this course by Portugalev, acting at the behest of Valentin Falin, head of the Central Committee's International Relations Department, and former Soviet Ambassador to Bonn. The object was to create a new framework for co-operation between the two states, in order to safeguard the GDR's existence. Kohl, however, employed the same structure to opposite ends, which he revealed in the last of his ten points.[40] He had now staked out his claim and the international community could not ignore the crucial issue, which hitherto had only been a battle-cry in the streets of East Germany.

Within a few weeks Bonn had reversed its assessment of the political process. By mid-November there was still agreement that German unification must not endanger the stability of Europe. Three

weeks later Bonn and Washington had both come to the conclusion that it was the impediments to unification which were bound
to create the most serious problems for Europe. The constant
encouragement and diplomatic support received from US President Bush and Foreign Secretary Baker proved to be Bonn's most
important asset during the next eight months. The United States,
for which self-determination was a gospel truth, did not feel threatened by a larger Germany that would still only be the size of Mon-
tana. At the NATO council in Brussels Bush reminded the other
Allies that they had, after all, been pledged to support unification
for four decades.[41] US Ambassador Vernon Walters was one of the
first diplomats to anticipate the force and direction of political developments. In his telegrams to Moscow the last Soviet ambassador
to Bonn, Julij Kwizinskij, was no less forthright in his gloomy forecast of the survival chances of the GDR after the fall of the Wall,
with the difference that he was reproached for dramatizing the situation.[42] That the two superpowers were, from an early stage, prepared,
reluctantly or not, to think the unthinkable helped to make the
impossible possible within a short period of time. After all, the Cold
War was over anyway and there was no need for a garrison state
in the middle of Europe.

Gorbachev's consent to unification—*das Ja-Wort im Kreml*—on
10 February 1990, on the occasion of a visit by Kohl and Genscher,
was the first breakthrough.[43] Kohl had been briefed by President
Bush to insist on NATO membership for a united Germany. Shortly
before then Hans Modrow had visited Moscow and had painted a
gloomy picture of a fast-disintegrating GDR. Soon afterwards, on
his return to Berlin, he presented his own plan for a reconstituted
Germany outside NATO which was in line with what most East
Germans favoured at the time. From now on NATO membership
looked like a roadblock which seemed to be impossible to remove.
Was not a neutral Germany what even Stalin had had in mind?
The question was how to come to a solution which would take
account of Soviet security interests. Genscher hoped to satisfy Moscow by not extending NATO structures to the Oder–Neiße border.

To synchronize the internal and external process was an enormous diplomatic challenge. In February 1990 it was by no means clear
that the two strands would indeed come together in the autumn.
Not only Moscow, but also Britain and France were most reluctant

to relinquish their special rights in Berlin. Policy was in a constant state of flux; no position could be maintained for very long. At first it looked as if EC foreign ministers, including Genscher, were inclined towards a CSCE approach, which would have complicated matters considerably—in the same way as a merger of the two Germanies would have raised more problems than the eventual take-over solution. According to two Washington National Security Council aides, Philip Zelikow and Condoleezza Rice, who have written the most comprehensive account of the diplomatic process of German unification so far, the successful outcome was due in no small measure to the close co-operation between President Bush and Chancellor Kohl, and their determination to restrict negotiations to the Four Powers, in conjunction with the two Germanies.[44] Of course, the United States was most concerned—without making these concerns public—about another Rapallo, a German–Russian understanding, at the expense of NATO. Their plan was helped by the fact that a former German defence minister, Manfred Wörner, happened to be NATO's general secretary at this crucial moment in history. Had the first free elections in East Germany turned out differently, the FDP might well have been persuaded to join forces with the SPD once more in order to make NATO obsolete and thereby realize unification.

The mechanism by which the foreign policy and security aspects of German unification would be dealt with was decided on 13 February 1990, at a joint conference of NATO and Warsaw Pact states in Ottawa. Bonn had ruled out a peace conference à la Versailles, which would bring up, amongst other things, the issue of reparations. Nor was a Four Power conference to the exclusion of Germany any longer appropriate. The acceptable formula was the 'two plus four' arrangement, because after all the two Germanies were the chief protagonists. The British Foreign Secretary Douglas Hurd was reported as preferring a 'zero plus four' formula. From Bonn's point of view the most important issues were: the equal status of all participants, sovereignty for Germany, i.e. rescinding of the Four Power rights, withdrawal of Soviet troops, recognition of Germany's eastern border, and last but not least a united Germany's membership of NATO.[45]

Soviet diplomats found the fact hard to swallow that their troops would have to leave East Germany while Western troops were to remain stationed west of the Elbe for the foreseeable future. And they argued that, naturally enough, the Germans would want to get rid of all foreign troops at the same time. One of Gorbachev's most influential advisers, Valentin Falin, who was later to accuse him of lacking an overall concept, hoped that at least the equivalent of France's status could be achieved for Germany: political, but not military inclusion in the structure of NATO.[46]

The arguments put forward by the Western Allies for keeping Germany firmly locked within NATO may well have had the unintended effect of fostering a tacit understanding between Bonn and Moscow. Certainly they revealed strong reservations about an unfettered Germany in the centre of Europe. Bonn's position, strongly supported by the American President, was that national sovereignty implied free choice of alliance system. Once this principle was firmly established Washington had no qualms about rapid unification. Julij Kwizinskij points out in his memoirs that the division of Germany suited many in the West, provided responsibility for it could be laid at the Soviets' door.[47] This made it possible for the Western powers to pose as Germany's friends, supporting her right to self-determination, leaving Moscow to bear the brunt of German national grievances. Now the tables had been turned.

Looking back, it is hardly conceivable that all these problems should have been solved satisfactorily within one year. The multitude of international agreements and treaties to this end bear witness to one of the greatest triumphs of diplomacy in the twentieth century. Apart from the goodwill of all participants, this was also due to what President Bush called the 'window of opportunity'. One year later Gorbachev might not have had the clout to rid his country of the liabilities of the Cold War. Kohl used another image in conversation with Douglas Hurd: 'Foreign policy was like mowing grass or hay. You had to gather what you had cut in case of a thunderstorm.'[48] The collapse of the SED regime with no alternative but merger with the Federal Republic in sight appeared to be the most forceful argument. Earlier than other Soviet leaders, Gorbachev and his Foreign Secretary Eduard Shevardnadze realized that it was counter-productive and, in the end, futile to try to turn the tide. Apparently, Gorbachev made reference to being afraid that 'the train had already departed,' according to Falin's memoirs.[49] But at least he succeeded in conveying the impression that he was the stationmaster who had given the signal. In view of his fast-disintegrating bargaining position he sold his approval at the best terms available: financial compensation, future economic assistance, and above all the gratitude of the German people, which is bound to have a lasting impact on German–Russian relations. The author remembers a speech by the late Franz-Josef Strauß in Murnau in the mid-1980s where he referred to his grandfather's and father's attitude towards France, the 'hereditary enemy' (*Erbfeind*), which was now a thing of the past, only to conclude that one day the Germans would experience the same mental metamorphosis *vis-à-vis* Russia.

From the memoirs of Horst Teltschik, close confidant of the German Chancellor, we know that Soviet acquiescence was given all the more readily because of German financial credits granted at a crucial juncture between the first 'two plus four' negotiations in Bonn and the currency union.[50] The Soviet Union was facing a crisis of confidence on the international financial markets because she was unable to meet her obligations. No further credits could be raised to finance the reform programme and the whole of *perestroika* seemed to be at stake. Teltschik and two leading German bankers flew to Moscow on a most secret mission and were met by all the top Russian leaders, including Gorbachev. The Federal Republic was Moscow's chief creditor, to the tune of 6 billion DM, followed by Japan (5.2 billion DM) and Italy (4.3 billion DM); Britain was only in sixth place with 1.5 billion DM. Kohl saw his chance and agreed to short-term credit of 5 billion DM guaranteed by the government, provided Gorbachev did not let him down in the 'two plus four' negotiations. The chancellor also pledged to back long-term credit of 15–20 billion DM, to be raised on the international markets. The combination of German financial support and the prospect of a comprehensive treaty between the united Germany and the Soviet Union is what won the Russians over.

The shift in the balance of power as a result of German unification was, of course, more marked in Europe than on a global level. Both superpowers could afford to take a more detached view than Britain and France, the other two powers with special rights as regards Germany as a whole accruing from the post-war settlement. Officially, both Paris and London had been committed to supporting German unification since the 1950s. Nor was there any serious intention to go back on this promise now. The prospect of Germany returning to its former status understandably caused a certain unease. The British Prime Minister was most outspoken in her warnings and hoped either to 'check the German juggernaut' or at least to retain some vestiges of special rights in Berlin.[51] Margaret Thatcher posed as Gorbachev's Western defence council, arguing that a rush towards unification would endanger his position and subsequently European stability. On the other hand, Genscher and his officials got on very well with the Foreign Office, which proved to be more professional in its assessment of the situation. Douglas Hurd expressed his conviction that 'at the end of an orderly transition German unity and a new stable architecture in Europe could be completed together.'[52] Historians should be more honest and give credit to government officials for certain decisions, not only to their 'political masters', whose utterances are often quite irrelevant. It is as well to remember that during the war most Foreign Office experts rejected enforced dismemberment of Germany, whereas politicians, notably the 'Big Three', tended to be in favour of such a policy.[53]

François Mitterrand was more far-sighted than the lady in Downing Street. At the end of November he confided to Genscher that German unification was 'a historical compulsion' and would be supported by France.[54] Some irritation was caused, however, when he paid a state visit to the GDR as late as 20 December, as if he wished to envigorate a dying body. After all, it was the first state visit by one of the three Western Allies since the war. Clearly, he too envisaged a much longer transition period and he was upset that the German Chancellor had not briefed him in advance about his own plans for an initial confederation. Throughout 1990 the French government pursued two objectives: first, to support the Poles in their efforts to gain definite recognition of their western borders and second, to use the opportunity to extract from Bonn a commitment to further European integration, in particular to monetary union. The German government was suspected of being lukewarm about these objectives. For France restraining Germany within the European Community by strengthening its institutional framework was almost as important as Germany's unquestioned adherence to NATO, which was given priority by the Anglo-Saxon powers. In fact, the French concern was more in line with German thinking than the idea, favoured by Britain, of a more open

European arena allowing for the full play of conventional diplomacy. Whatever reminds the Germans of their traumatic past makes them cringe. After all, the 'Concert of Europe' was eventually blown apart by the guns of August 1914.

Polish anxieties were soon appeased by two resolutions of the Bundestag and the Volkskammer to the effect that a united Germany would once more recognize the inviolability of the Oder–Neiße border. This pledge was then incorporated into the crucial treaty of 12 September 1990, which regulated the international framework of unification. The final accord was reached on 14 November with a treaty confirming the validity of previous agreements made by the Federal Republic (1970) and the GDR (1951) and solemnly recognizing the political sovereignty and territorial integrity of both countries.[55] Even though all this was never in dispute amongst the great majority of West and East Germans, Kohl apparently had the greatest difficulties in persuading the right wing of his party, and the CSU, to toe the line. In the spring of 1990 the coalition was at breaking point over this issue, i.e. the definitive loss of a quarter of the former Reich, and the Chancellor was seriously contemplating resignation.[56]

We must now return to the course of events in East Germany, which gave the impression of a downhill train out of control. Measures were constantly taken to calm down the public mood, which in fact accelerated the disintegration of the GDR. The SED party congress was brought forward from spring 1990 to December, after the resignation of all the ruling bodies of the party. However, the cosmetic changes, a new name (Party of Democratic Socialism: PDS) and a new leadership (Gregor Gysi, Hans Modrow), failed to secure public confidence. In order to retain some credibility and a minimum of authority Modrow, the new Prime Minister, took a more positive line towards unification than his party and agreed, though reluctantly, to co-operate with the Round Table, which was launched by the Protestant Church and was meant to fill the power vacuum created by the collapse of the old state party. However, this new institution did not have, according to Glässner, 'the vision, personnel or organisation to assume power'.[57] Nevertheless, the opposition made sure that the old powers, notably the Stasi, would not reassert themselves in a new guise. Perhaps this was all the

Round Table, re-created on all levels of government further down, could be expected to achieve. One of the most grotesque scenes of the revolution took place in the Volkskammer when Erich Mielke, the hitherto-feared head of the Stasi, exclaimed: 'But I love you, all of you.' His words, though received with uninhibited laughter, should, however, be taken more seriously: they were the genuine expression of an authoritarian mind-set, the suffocating love of an all-embracing, well-meaning *Vater Staat* who disciplines those he cares for.[58]

Step by step the Round Table was transformed from a 'veto organ into an instrument of government'.[59] With the crisis of confidence deepening, Modrow invited representatives of the Round Table to join the government and agreed to bring forward to 18 March the date of the first free elections to the Volkskammer. Some of the most outspoken critics of the old SED now tried to hold on to a distinct GDR identity on behalf of a reformed socialism. However, the continued exodus of young people to the West and public pressure in the streets were clear indications that the forthcoming election would be a referendum for or against unification; more than that, for or against 'merger tomorrow'. If it had not been for this issue dominating all others, the newly founded SDP, which soon adopted the old label 'SPD' (the 'D' for Germany), might have scored much better considering the party-political geography before 1933. Nor did it help that Oskar Lafontaine, the SPD's challenger to Kohl, kept stressing the social, financial, and economic problems of unification. The strongest vote-puller proved to be the 'Alliance for Germany', formed on 5 February with strong support from Kohl and consisting of the CDU, the German Social Union (DSU, sister party of the Bavarian CSU), and Democratic Awakening (*Demokratischer Aufbruch*). The governmental party in the West was credited with greater economic competence and a higher international standing. The Chancellor in particular seemed to exude more optimism than all his rivals on the left. In retrospect the election results of 18 March are perhaps less surprising than appeared at the time.[60] The 'Alliance for Germany' emerged victorious, with 48.1 per cent (192 out of 400 seats), the SPD 21.9 per cent (87 seats), the Liberals 5.3 per cent (21 seats), a majority for those parties clearly in favour of unification. They would form a transitional coalition government under Lothar de Maizière, leader of the reformed CDU, by far the strongest party (163 seats). Yet there were distinct differences concerning the approach to unification which were reflected in the election results: the Alliance had promised a fast-track solution, while the Liberals pleaded for 'moderate speed'. The PDS, which had ruled the country for forty years under the name of the Socialist Unity Party (SED), was reduced to 16.4 per cent (66 seats). In the south the Alliance gained up to 60 per cent of the vote, whereas in East Berlin, residence of the SED *nomenklatura*, the CDU's share dropped to half the average. The great majority of the working class voted for the CDU, not the SPD as in the West. Conversely, the PDS had some of its worst results in working-class districts. Leading members of the citizens' movement joined the whole spectrum of parties (except for the PDS), with a clear preference for the SPD. The one party which was the most genuine expression of the spirit of '89 (*Bündnis 90*) only received 2.9 per cent of the vote (12 seats).

The grand coalition, which had a clear mandate for unification, agreed to accede to the Federal Republic under the terms of Article 23 of the Basic Law. This was the constitutional procedure which provided for the accession of individual *Länder*, such as the Saarland in 1957. Now the whole of the GDR would be incorporated following the resurrection of the five *Länder* which had been abolished in 1952 in favour of fourteen districts. Not only was this the most popular approach, because it promised a quick transition, it was also recommended by constitutional lawyers who were attracted by its simplicity. Since this form of accession gave rise to the charge that the GDR was the victim of a West German takeover bid, it is important to stress that the decision was arrived at quite democratically. After a long and exciting session, the Volkskammer approved the accession under the terms of Article 23, and thereby the definitive demise of the GDR, on 23 August at 2.47 a.m.

How was it possible to liquidate a European state like an insolvent company in less than six months? Some dissidents turned ministers would have preferred to enjoy the trappings of power for a little longer and Bonn officials would have liked more time to ponder the implications of certain regulations. With thousands leaving for the West every week, and further revelations about the state of public finances, the GDR's economic situation was fast approaching total bankruptcy. Facilities in the Federal Republic for absorbing such large numbers of refugees were also reaching crisis point. The introduction of the West German Mark at an early stage seemed to be the best stopgap measure. Crisis management was the dictate of the hour. On 18 May 1990 Walter Romberg, the GDR Finance Minister, signed the treaty establishing a Monetary, Economic and Social Union, to come into force on 1 July. It would bring the East Germans the cherished Deutschmark and was the clearest indication yet that the unification process was 'irreversible'. The preamble to the treaty stated as the aim of the contracting parties 'to achieve in freedom as soon as possible the unity of Germany within a European peace order'.[61] The evident crisis in the GDR and the emphasis on the peaceful and internationally sanctioned approach to unification reconciled the Four Powers to the unprecedented speed of the development. Then and later it was the domestic, not the international, dimension which proved to be fraught with difficulties. Purely for political reasons and against the clear advice of the Bundesbank, Bonn had agreed to an exchange rate of one Deutschmark to one Ostmark. It was, as de Maizière put it, a 'generous political gesture. But no one should forget what the Ostmark would really be worth today on a free market.'[62] The short-term benefits for the East Germans were there for all to see and appreciate, while the long-term effects on the East German economy could only be assessed by a few hard-headed experts. Chancellor Kohl, aware that he would soon be facing the first all-German election, wished to buy the goodwill of the East Germans, who should not be made to feel like second-class citizens. At the time it seemed as if everything else could be put on the back boiler. The East German economy was not at all prepared for the sudden exposure to market forces. There had been no precedent for the fusion of two economies based on diametrically opposed principles. In the East all previous terms of trade, such as subsidized prices for products on the Western market, vanished overnight. Instead, the place was flooded with Western consumer goods. As a result the West German economy experienced an unprecedented, though short-lived, boom, while industry in the East suffered a dramatic slump. The economy took a nosedive.

The currency union had all the hallmarks of a West German takeover. Ordinary people did not mind, but the GDR's new political class resented it deeply. After all, in international law the GDR was still an independent and, for the first time, truly democratic state. To avoid the impression that the country was about to be swallowed up by the Federal Republic, another state treaty, freely negotiated, on all outstanding matters was required. This was the so-called Unification Treaty of 31 August 1990, a document of 900 typescript pages covering the most diverse issues from public administration, welfare, and education to the use of dachas on allotments. Considering the shortage of time, the achievement by the two negotiators, Wolfgang Schäuble (Bonn's Interior Minister) and East German Secretary of State Günther Krause, was quite remarkable.[63] However, the treaty did not pay sufficient attention to the state of the administrative machinery, which was soon to hamper recovery. Nor were the costs of unification in any way anticipated. Again, because of the forthcoming election Bonn tended to play down this unwelcome aspect and gave the impression that it was possible to raise the necessary funds on the financial markets. This optimism proved to be totally misplaced and the national debt soon began to spiral out of control. Within a few years the united Germany had borrowed more than West Germany had done in the previous forty years. The new *Länder* could not survive without constant transfusions of huge sums to keep the administration and the welfare system going. Their own revenue was not remotely adequate. In February 1991 a revision of the Unification Treaty became necessary to avoid lasting damage and safeguard the economic future of the new *Länder*.

To synchronize the foreign and security aspects of unification with internal development, now hurtling towards early merger, was one of the greatest challenges to German diplomacy. At the first 'two plus four' meeting in Bonn on 5 May Soviet Foreign Minister, Eduard Shevardnadze, suggested that the rights of the Four Powers could remain in force for some time after German unification, i.e. the international and national problems did not necessarily have to be resolved at the same time.[64] Nor was the Soviet government yet prepared to accept a united Germany as a member of NATO. The Soviet Foreign Minister hinted at the enormous pressure from hard-liners at home who were urging the leadership not to surrender too much to the West. The stability of the Soviet Union seemed to be at risk if her justified security interests were not met. The Foreign Secretaries of the West did not dismiss these anxieties as groundless, and this allowed a climate of mutual understanding to develop.

In the course of further 'two plus four' conferences it emerged that the Soviet government, rather than trying to hold on to obsolete rights, was genuinely concerned about a sudden collapse of the GDR and a hasty retreat by their forces from German soil. It was due to the intimate co-operation between German and US diplomats and their joint efforts *vis-à-vis* Moscow that these negotiations were crowned with success: Washington addressed the wider NATO issue and Bonn worked out a satisfactory arrangement for the transitional period. According to a close confidant of Genscher, Frank Elbe, who ran his office between 1987 and 1992, Bonn tried to convey to Moscow a number of messages: German unity would overcome the division of Europe; this would not end at Poland's eastern border; the Soviet Union would benefit from a new and closer relationship with the European Union, under the common roof of the CSCE.[65] Genscher's maxim was 'to include, not to exclude'. German unification offered the chance of establishing a new security framework, which would allow NATO to abandon its confrontational stance and to press on with disarmament. An example would be set by reducing the new German army to below the strength of the Federal forces. A united Germany would be a much more attractive business partner than the former two Germanies and was bound to further the policy of *perestroika* and the implementation of the reforms necessary in the Soviet Union. These were not empty promises, but genuine strategic goals based on German national interest.

The Western powers, notably France and Britain, employed different arguments in their efforts to keep Germany within NATO: a neutral Germany would insist on an adequate defence force and would be more difficult to control than if it were integrated into an alliance structure. At one stage Gorbachev suggested that Germany should be a member of both NATO and the Warsaw Pact. 'One anchor is good, but two are better,' he told President Bush.[66] During the second 'two plus four' meeting (22 June, in Berlin) Shevardnadze submitted another proposal, equally unacceptable to the Western powers: five years after unification all foreign troops, not only the Red Army, should have left Germany. Bonn might have consented if this had been the final offer. By now it was clear that Britain and France were more worried about a totally unfettered Germany than about any threat from the Warsaw Pact. And this they must have impressed upon Soviet diplomats whenever there was half a chance.

Gorbachev's position at home was greatly strengthened by the so-called 'message of Turnberry' (8 June). By that time Washington had realized that an adjustment of NATO to the new realities in Eastern Europe was overdue. At the meeting of NATO foreign ministers in Turnberry, Scotland, Baker urged his colleagues to revise their relationship with the former enemy radically. According to the final communiqué, NATO would stretch out its hand in friendship to the Warsaw Pact states. More important still, according to Zelikow and Rice, was the NATO summit in London on 5 July, where the Americans, against serious reservations from Margaret Thatcher and President Mitterrand, pushed through NATO's new strategy. This declared nuclear forces to be 'truly weapons of last resort', consigning 'forward defence' and 'flexible response' to the past.[67] The conference also adopted the proposal for a joint NATO–Warsaw Pact declaration, pointing out that the two were 'no longer adversaries'.

The ground had been carefully prepared for the sensational tête-à-tête between Gorbachev and Kohl in the Caucasus which brought about the final breakthrough. All of the points which were raised had been discussed before but were now settled at one go, to the great astonishment of the world.[68] Agreement was reached on the following matters: unification meant the joining together of the Federal Republic, the GDR, and the whole of Berlin. The rights and responsibilities of the Four Powers would cease and Germany would be a fully sovereign and independent state. As laid down by the Helsinki Accord (CSCE), Germany would be free to decide which alliance she wanted to join. The withdrawal of Soviet troops within three to four years was to be arranged by a special treaty between Germany and the Soviet Union. For that period NATO command structures would not be extended to East Germany, even though non-integrated German forces could be stationed there. Afterwards, German NATO units could move in, provided no nuclear weapons were installed. Germany would never either produce or acquire ABC weapons and would continue to adhere to the Non-Proliferation Treaty. For the transitional period military contingents of the three

Western powers would remain stationed in Berlin on the basis of a new agreement. Within three to four years German armed forces would be reduced to 370,000 troops. All this was to be incorporated into the final 'two plus four' treaty, which was signed in Moscow on 12 September[69] and gave the green light to the merger of the two German states on 3 October.

However, there was a last-minute hiccup when the British government insisted on a new provision which would allow NATO manœuvres in East Germany. Genscher was so desperate that he woke Baker up in the middle of the night before the signing ceremony and asked him to put pressure on the British to see sense.[70] At the last moment a formula was agreed upon which would leave this matter to the discretion of the German government. The incident seemed to show that the West European powers were by now more anxious about their diminished position than the Russians, who had made such substantial concessions. Gorbachev had far more serious problems to worry about at home. Moscow needed German financial and economic assistance to cope with the aftermath of these agreements and with the implementation of its reform programme. Following unification further bilateral treaties had to be signed concerning the presence, maintenance, and eventual withdrawal of Soviet troops. Gorbachev and Kohl were determined to put relations between their two countries on a completely new footing. It was for this reason that a treaty on 'neighbourly relations, partnership, and co-operation' was signed in Bonn on 9 November 1990, which may have far-reaching consequences if taken seriously.[71] Among the Western powers Germany is henceforth likely to be the most committed advocate of legitimate Russian interests vis-à-vis Europe. As the strongest trading nation on the Continent Germany has a natural interest in developing the Russian market now that it is opening up. However, expectations in the East by far exceed German financial resources. Not only did the two governments confirm previous non-aggression understandings, but agreed, furthermore, that should one of the two contracting parties be the object of aggression, the other would lend no support whatsoever to the aggressor. The Americans had no problems with this stipulation. NATO is, after all, a defensive alliance. It can be safely assumed that this was one of the crucial preconditions for Gorbachev's consent to German membership of NATO.

The undeniable success in bringing about German unification with the consent of all powers concerned was not matched by the internal arrangements, which were more haphazard. Of course, there was not much time for sober reflection on all the domestic aspects once the foundations of the GDR had been swept away. Bonn had been caught totally unprepared for dealing with questions such as property ownership, the judiciary, and the like. More serious is the charge against the government that it underestimated the financial requirements. One of the most persistent misconceptions was the Bonn government's belief that monetary union would produce a kick-start for the East German economy in the same way as the currency reform and the transition to a free market economy in 1948, which had contributed to West Germany's 'economic miracle'. Historical analogies are always a dubious intellectual game because the similarities are so much more obvious than discrepancies in the underlying conditions. These conditions were totally different in 1948: for one thing the new Deutschmark was then in much better, more competitive shape. If the Chancellor had made a serious appeal to his fellow countrymen to share the burden in the summer of 1990, even the West German consumer society would have risen to this challenge by making substantial sacrifices. Yet while Kohl promised 'blossoming landscapes' in the East, he was reluctant to lose any voters in the West in what was, unfortunately, an election year. Never before in the history of the Federal Republic had there been a better case for forming a grand coalition in order to tackle the momentous tasks ahead. Prime Minister de Maizière had shown the way. But the government was not to be diverted. Regaining power was all they had in mind. It was also short-sighted to trust market forces and not to realize that the economic development of East Germany required state intervention on a large scale, if only for a transitional period. It is fair to say, though, that individual *Länder*, as well as cities in the West, did lend a helping hand in the East. But there was no concerted effort to steady the transition of the East German economy, which was simply left to the receiver in the shape of the controversial *Treuhand*.[72] The result was mass unemployment and further migration to the West.

A short history of the *Treuhand*, which has meanwhile been wound down, provides the most revealing evidence of the daunting task of transforming a command economy into a free market economy. A research team close to the citizens' movement persuaded the Modrow government and the Round Table in the spring of 1990 that now was the time to opt for a 'third way' between GDR socialism and West German capitalism. A holding company (*Treuhand*) was to be set up to protect the people's assets from the greedy fingers of both the old guard and 'evil' Western capitalists. Experts from both East and West produced estimates like rabbits out of a hat and came up with figures as high as 1,600 billion DM, or 100,000 DM per person, to be offered as citizens' shares. Privatization as practised later was not yet on the cards. With forty years of self-deception and camouflaged statistics, nobody had a clue what the 8,000 'People's Own Companies' (VEB) were really worth on the open market. After the first free elections of 18 March the SPD insisted that these 'Alice in Wonderland' projections should form an integral part of the coalition agreement. However, in the course of negotiations about the currency union these ideas had to be abandoned as a *quid pro quo* for a generous exchange rate. Now it was the Bonn government which indulged in wishful thinking and believed that by selling East German assets lock, stock, and barrel they might net at least some 500 billion DM, which would go a long way to financing the transitional costs arising from monetary union. Claus Köhler, a board member both of the Bundesbank and the *Treuhand*, later admitted: '*Wir hatten überhaupt kein Schimmer*' (We did not have the faintest idea).[73]

After 1 July many East German plants became insolvent overnight and the Treuhand had to come to their rescue with global cover to enable them to raise credit on the financial markets. Rather than making a fortune from selling, the Treuhand was forced to pump large amounts of money into companies in order to attract buyers. Exposure to the market proved to be the moment of truth. Within less than one year estimates had to be revised downwards from a huge imagined gain to a loss of around 250–300 billion DM. Initially officials of the *Treuhand* believed that the East German economy would continue to supply whatever was needed in Eastern Europe, thus creating a breathing space for its industry in which to transform itself into a competitive player on the Western markets. However, when the Soviet Union and the Eastern markets collapsed, this period of grace for the unreconstructed industries of the GDR vanished as well. In the majority of cases, putting businesses on a sound footing amounted, in financial terms, to a complete reconstruction of existing plant. It was certainly no help that West German trade unions pressed for a speedy equalization of wages and salaries with arguments which appeared all too persuasive. In this way they deprived the East of its only advantageous prospect, that of lower labour costs. The result was a steep rise in unemployment. The question is therefore justified as to whether this was an act of working-class solidarity or a ploy to safeguard West German jobs.[74]

Naturally, after forty years of anti-capitalist propaganda East Germans were more suspicious of entrepreneurs and their penchant for exploitation than of the first free unions. Rumours spread of a sell-out, of West German firms moving in with the intention of pocketing subsidies and cheap credit, of asset-stripping, of smothering potential competitors, and so forth.[75] The new authorities appeared to be powerless in the face of widespread corruption which seemed to confirm the worst suspicions about the nature of capitalism. East Germans had not been exposed to a free press since 1933. All of a sudden they had to try to make sense of deeply disturbing information. Considering the gigantic undertaking of the Treuhand it is not surprising that fraudulent activities did go on. Since these were the target of investigative journalism, Easterners were easily tempted to draw general conclusions. Who would want to admit that forty years of hard work, bolstered by official propaganda, had not been enough to pay for his miserable life? It was as though pin-striped experts from the West had told people that they had sweated for nothing and that their wages and salaries were just government handouts or concealed sinecures. The psychological wreckage left by socialism is perhaps more difficult to assess and to salvage than the material loss.

With gloom spreading, some predict that the East might become Germany's Mezzogiorno. Statistics are indeed depressing. East German GDP shrank by 40 per cent between 1989 and 1994, industrial production by 70 per cent up to 1992, and employment by 40 per cent up to 1993.[76] By 1994 the East German economy, once the pride of Comecon, contributed only 7.9 per cent of German GDP. Fears of de-industrialization became widespread, reminiscent of the Morgenthau Plan. It is certainly true to say that unity has only been achieved in a political sense, while the social division of the country is more evident than ever. East Germans cannot help feeling that they are, through no fault of their own, the poor relations of a united family. The wounds inflicted by forty-five years of separation will not heal overnight.

9 The Search for Identity

Post-natal depression is perhaps the best way to describe the mood in Germany six years after the event: an almost traumatic realization that, with new family responsibilities encroaching from all directions, the free and easy life-style of the old Federal Republic cannot be maintained any longer. Now that one of the chief aims of the constitution, national self-determination for all Germans, has been achieved, what else is there to strive for? Other nations might have taken a more relaxed attitude, quietly enjoying their enhanced power status and influence in the world. Not, however, the Germans of the enlarged Federal Republic, who felt as if they had inherited a huge estate that was proving to be more of a liability than an asset. After the rebirth of their nation state they embarked on a search for a new corporate identity, which would shelter them from their anxieties and worries. There is no shortage of pundits (historians in particular are in the forefront)[1] who feel called upon to give advice on how to overcome the loss of direction. Though soul-searching has always been a favourite German occupation, there can be no doubt that it is now recognized as more justified than ever.

Among the many bewildering symptoms which have caused this crisis of confidence four should be singled out.

First, the burden of unifying the two estranged parts of Germany. It is generally acknowledged that this is not just a matter of economic but also of cultural and psychological assimilation. Now that Germany is united to all intents and purposes, the separate identities of West and East Germany are exposed for the first time. Many left-wing intellectuals in both parts are suddenly revealing a certain nostalgia for their own state, with which they were at odds in the past: the 'non-national Federal Republic' and the 'paternalistic guardian state of the SED'. Two societies still exist within one state. As the historian Jürgen Kocka observes: 'Even in united Berlin, the circles of intensive communication and collegiality, friendship, and marriage continue to be divided between East and West.'[2]

Jens Reich, one of the leaders of the civil rights movement, has coined the term *Trotzidentität* (identity of defiance) for the East German feeling.[3]

Secondly, the re-emergence of the nation state as a viable entity in both Germany and Eastern Europe, together with the reawakening of nationalism and xenophobia at home and abroad. In Germany confusion between national identity, taken for granted elsewhere, and nationalism is widespread, even among academics who ought to know the difference. A perceptive French observer, Anne-Marie Le Gloannec, believes that for most German intellectuals the 'nation is to be understood solely as a prepolitical phenomenon, not a democratic one'.[4] Hence the aversion to such categories as nation, national identity, and national unity. For too long well-meaning historians and journalists have distanced themselves from the nation state of the past, whose follies and vices they were eager to expose. Quite a few of them had dismissed the 'silly dream' of German unification in the name of peace and reconciliation. All of a sudden, East Germans were claiming to be members of a common fatherland, thus exhibiting sentiments which had long been outdated in the West. The term 'brothers and sisters', commonly used in the 1950s and early 1960s for the have-nots in the East, had lost all true meaning by the time burden-sharing was called for in earnest. The melting of the Cold War ice had opened up a mental crevasse between the two Germanies.

Thirdly, the economic recession, which hit Germany when the country, engaged in a monumental salvage operation, was least prepared for it. It was, above all, the superior economic and social system of the Federal Republic that had triggered the westward stampede by East Germans and subsequently contributed to the demise of the GDR. Now experts were calling into question the blessings of the West, such as high wages and salaries, coupled with the shortest working hours and the longest holidays in any industrial society, at the very moment when they were being transferred to the new Federal *Länder*, along with a host of rules and regulations which were no recipe for fast growth. The West Germans were told that they too might soon be left behind in a more competitive world without any big brother there to rescue them. The public debate centred around Germany's future as a viable industrial base (*Standort Deutschland*)[5] now that production costs were much cheaper in the developing economies of Eastern Europe and elsewhere in the world. As one expert put it in 1994: 'In the last ten years of the former Federal Republic potential growth in productivity was sacrificed in favour of an increase in the standard of living.'[6] While German investment abroad tripled during this time-span, direct foreign investment declined from 10 per cent annually in the boom years to 1.5 per cent. The result is an unemployment rate of 8.3 per cent in the West and 13.9 per cent in the East, though at last the number of new jobs now seems to exceed the number of people made redundant. In East Germany unemployment on this scale, never experienced before, is perceived as the single most traumatic effect of unification. The traditional Protestant work ethic, hitherto enhanced by propaganda if not in reality, has received a serious blow at a time when it should be invigorated. To be told now that the 'workers' state' was not all that productive in real terms, due to lack of incentives, adds insult to injury. The monetary aspect of a modern economy never seemed to matter as much as in the West. Work almost transcended its financial evaluation, becoming a value in itself. When the idea of a new constitution briefly surfaced it was suggested that the 'right to work' should be incorporated into the catalogue of human rights. This is indicative of the discrepancy between the real world that the East Germans were now entering and the make-believe one they were leaving behind.

Fourthly, expectations that the united Germany would assume a leadership role, due to its elevated power status and its geopolitical position in Central Europe after the demise of the Soviet empire. Bonn felt both flattered and embarrassed by the United States President's offer to make Germany a 'partner in leadership'.[7] Though always the most loyal of American allies, the Federal Republic is acutely aware of the limitations imposed by Germany's hegemonic aspirations of the past. Nor are ordinary citizens, who are not nagged by foreign statesmen and leader writers, any too keen to see Germany assuming a greater share of responsibility for the world's trouble spots. They are not jealous of the superpower status of the United States and would prefer to model themselves on Switzerland, if only they could. After the demonstrable success of the 'ethics of restraint'[8] (the opposite of power politics) there is little enthusiasm for unlearning the lessons of re-education, the Bundeswehr being the best example. The Federal Forces, more like the Post Office at arms than the reincarnation of the Wehrmacht, were only trained for an all-out war against the Red Army, which was never to happen. The 'citizens in uniform' concept has worked well in the past, but does not foster a fighting force ready for action. Significantly, the Federal Defence Ministry will not be moving to Berlin or Potsdam, the old Prussian garrison town, but will remain in Bonn. Today's Bundeswehr, with 370,000 servicemen, is smaller than the armed forces of the old Federal Republic (490,000). But even these reduced ranks, the product of much haggling behind closed doors in 1990, are difficult to fill, since there are almost as many conscientious objectors as conscripts.[9] With the end of the Cold War many youngsters feel they are doing a more worthwhile job by looking after the elderly and the sick than polishing military hardware. The so-called *Zivildienst* (community service instead of conscription) has lost all of its former stigma. Even though in terms of financial transfers to Eastern Europe and the Third World, as well as shelter for asylum seekers, Germany's record is rather better than that of her European allies, there is still a marked discrepancy between what the world expects of a united Germany and what its citizens feel they can truthfully accomplish. Some foreign commentators think that this is yet another symptom of the German neurosis. In fact, the reluctance to fly the flag can also be interpreted as a sign of growing self-confidence.

Germany's comparatively short history as a nation state since 1871 is the master key to understanding the Federal Republic's political culture, from which a new identity must be distilled. The horrors of the once-popular Hitler regime and the division of the former Reich after 1945 were not conducive to producing a new national identity. Now the united Germany has to come to terms with the legacy of two dictatorships, with the Holocaust and the Stasi state.[10] East Germans are as reluctant as the Germans in the Western zones were after 1945 to face up to their past. They are fully preoccupied with the change-over from their sheltered but miserable lives under socialism to a democratic but competitive society. The psychological conditions for re-education are less propitious than after the war, because the East Germans have to cope with their fellow countrymen who pose as know-alls, not in the

wake of unconditional surrender, but following the successful over-
throw of a hated regime.

Moreover, the East Germans had no chance to learn the true
and untempered lessons of the Hitler period. Their new leaders
had been persecuted by the Nazis and returned from exile or prison
camps in order to forge a 'better', i.e. anti-fascist, Germany. Legitimized by military government, not by popular vote, they has-
tened to absolve the citizens from all responsibility for the crimes
of the Hitler regime. They maintained that its evil spirit, fascism and
militarism, lived on in the Federal Republic, which claimed to be
its successor state, while the GDR owed its existence to the resistance against Hitler's Germany: 'Anti-fascism became the congenital
myth of the GDR.'[11] The ideological antagonism between National
Socialism and Communism served to hide the similarities of the
systems at work, and their impact on the mental disposition of
their subjects. Whether or not one accepts the theory of totalitari-
anism, there is no denying that the Germans east of the Elbe lived
under conditions that had more in common with the previous
regime—notwithstanding substantial ethical differences—than with
the democratic structure of the Federal Republic: a one-party system coupled with ruthless repression of political dissidents, no
independent judiciary, no freedom of the press and other media,
mobilization and indoctrination of the people in mass organizations, and above all, a totally ideological and propagandist interpretation of politics. Even though the Communist regime was resolved
to form a new society and, by implication, reformed human beings,
the 'socialist personality', it is now recognized that the mentality
of East Germans had changed less than that of their cousins in
the West under the impact of liberal democracy and the market
economy. Whether the transformation of West Germany has been
for the better in all respects is another matter.

Since 1933 East Germans have not experienced free and liberal
public opinion. Through no fault of their own their frame of mind
has been shaped into what Adorno and others diagnosed as the
'authoritarian personality'.[12] According to Joachim Maaz, a leading psychiatrist in East Germany, GDR society was characterized
by repression in all walks of life and constant pressure to conform
to standards which were defined by those in authority. This disposition, he argues, facilitated the imposition of West Germany's

way of life, but at a price: growing frustration and social neurosis.[13] The views Maaz entertains about West German society, probably shared by many of his fellow countrymen, are very one-sided: only money matters, achievement through competition at the expense of human relations, growth without regard for the environment, democracy as the rule of the manipulated majority, which equals suppression of minorities, and so forth. It shows that forty years of propaganda and indoctrination have left their mark even amongst the most self-critical and enlightened of East German intellectuals. Again, it cannot be held against East Germans that they have not learned how parliamentary systems or market economies work in practice, and that they therefore resort to easy generalizations. After the war the Germans in the Western zones were no wiser. It is precisely because the West Germans are confronted with their own shortcomings of not so long ago that they now appear so impatient with their compatriots in the East. Not surprisingly, the latter refer to them as *Besserwessies* (know-alls).[14] In turn, the East Germans are labelled as *Jammerossies* (whingeing Easterners), because they are said to be constantly complaining about and lamenting their lot, even if individually many are much better off than before. It is just as well to be reminded that in August 1945 British Intelligence officers observed among the Germans 'a sense of impotence . . . mixed with a feeling of self-pity characteristic of many Germans when in distress.'[15]

Unification may be described as an unexpected marriage of two populations from totally different backgrounds, which started with a short honeymoon, only to be followed by a long period of recriminations. Westerners are said to expect gratitude, Easterners a sense of charity and sharing: both are unrealistic propositions. Easterners are being told to pull themselves up by their own bootstraps 'as we in the West did after 1945'; Westerners are accused of arrogance and coldness. The assumed superiority of one side and the alleged helplessness of the other are both rooted in a common history, which has not lent itself to instilling a sense of quiet confidence.

East Germany has rightly been described as an 'authoritarian kindergarten' (Timothy Garton Ash), which sheltered its charges from life's real and sometimes painful experiences. West Germany saw fit to provide only financial and technical assistance. Moral support and spiritual guidance, on the other hand, have not been forthcoming. But in any case, in order to be convincing, this has to come from their own leaders, from those with an open mind and common sense like the Berlin theologian Richard Schröder, who knows how to act as an honest broker between East and West. According to recent opinion polls, 97 per cent of East Germans agreed to the proposition that 'Only people who lived in the GDR are entitled to talk about life there.'[16] As a matter of fact, most 'respectable' books about the former GDR are now being written by West German academics who have made it their business to observe the other German state all along. It should be added here that these West German experts now have to make up for their totally inadequate analysis of the former GDR, describing the façade in every detail on the basis of official documents without telling us what went on behind the scenes, and certainly having no idea about the state of the economy or the mood of the people. When it comes to understanding life in the old GDR, West Germans are almost as ignorant as British officers were after 1945 about the mechanics of everyday life under the suspicious eyes of a Nazi *Blockwart* (spy in a block of flats).[17]

Historians and political scientists agree that the new *Länder* have no option but to be fully integrated into the old Federal Republic in more than a purely institutional sense. Konrad Jarausch observes that by confirming the loss of the Eastern provinces reunification created the most 'Western' Germany in history. He also refers approvingly to Hans-Peter Schwarz's suggestion that as the most successful German state the Federal Republic has a right to shape the character of the new Berlin Republic.[18] However, this is exactly what the majority of East German opinion leaders dispute. They reject the one-sided process of unification and employ terms like 'colonization', 'annexation', 'violation', or 'merciless expansion of the Western life-style', conveniently forgetting that this is what a clear majority of their own people voted for. The most common and least loaded expression for what has happened is *Abwicklung*, i.e. the unwinding of the old structures. To some extent this is the voice of frustrated former dissidents who feel that their early warnings, unheeded in 1990, have been confirmed by events. The question is whether this is just a transitory malaise or a serious historical interpretation which will carry weight with the electorate in the long run. For many former East German citizens the scale of redundancies and the total submission to a new political and economic system are traumatic experiences from which they have not yet recovered. According to a popular phrase, they are now 'foreigners in their own country'. They are made to feel that their life and honest work of forty years have been completely devalued. They know that they need all the help they can get from the West, but that the West does not need them. Their willingness to contribute to a united Germany has been rubbished by the West and dismissed as immaterial: nothing achieved by the old GDR seemed suitable for adaptation by the West. No concessions were made to the feelings of the other half: no new name for the reconstituted whole; no new flag or national anthem; above all, no new constitution. Nor are East Germans adequately represented on the governing boards of the Federal Republic or in any other prominent positions. Their pride has been deeply wounded. Therefore a certain nostalgia for old times, or rather for a normal life under difficult conditions, has recently resurfaced. Nevertheless, hardly anyone, even among the most outspoken critics of the present situation, would wish to return to the *status quo ante*: the old SED regime is totally discredited. East Germans tend to make a sharp distinction between the Communist state, which was held in low esteem, and their own struggle to manage their lives, of which they are proud.

The majority of East Germans would favour a different, more caring, and less achievement-oriented Federal Republic. Elisabeth Noelle-Neumann, the grand old lady of German opinion polls, suggests from the evidence she has gathered that Germany is facing a shift to the left, because left values such as security, equality, and solidarity are in the ascendant.[19] She feels that the two value systems may be finely balanced. According to surveys by EMNID, one of Germany's two major public opinion polls, all the East Germans' nostalgic thoughts and feelings could be summarized in one single word: *Sicherheit*, i.e. security of tenure in both work and housing. According to a tacit *contrat social* of the GDR, Schröder suggests, the regime offered *Wohlergehen* (in the sense of the state providing the basic necessities of life) in exchange for *Wohlverhalten* (good behaviour). More than three-quarters of former GDR citizens, asked what they thought of the old regime, still believed that socialism was a good idea, badly carried out.[20] This means that the dream of a 'third way' has not been abandoned altogether. One may draw some comfort from the uncomfortable reminder that post-war West Germans felt equally ambivalent about National Socialism.[21] After all, a majority of Germans in the Western zones remained attached to the idea of economic planning, only to embrace the market economy when it had proved its worth after 1949. It took some time to flush out the last vestiges of Nazi propaganda, more than most observers could bear. In view of forty years of Communist indoctrination an even higher dose of patience seems to be called for. If Noelle-Neumann's forecast should prove correct, then it would not bode well for a flourishing economy, which was the most convincing means of attracting post-war Germans to a liberal democracy. The other argument, fear of Soviet expansion, is no longer relevant. It is a reflection on human nature that fear of a common enemy and hope for a better life have so far proved to be the most effective bonding mechanisms.

In the long run, the East German disposition is bound to have an impact on the new German identity, which is still in the making. It has been pointed out that Germany is about to become again a more 'Protestant' and more 'German' country. What does this mean? There is more consensus on what it does not mean than on what it really amounts to. Formal affiliation to the Protestant Church has dramatically declined in the former GDR and is now less than one-third of that in the old *Länder*.[22] The Protestant Church is unlikely to regain its previous influence, either in statistical terms (as before 1945) or in political terms (as before 1989). The former initiation rite of the *Jugendweihe*, a substitute for confirmation, though now with humanist rather than socialist phraseology, is as popular as before. However, the influence of Luther's teaching on the subconscious of the people over centuries will not vanish in a few decades. How it will manifest itself in the future is another matter. Two dictatorships have thoroughly discredited the concept of divine authority.[23] Nor is nationalism in the name of German Protestantism likely to re-emerge. And what is so Prussian about the East Germans? The reference to 'red Prussia', so common before the *Wende*, is misleading, as Peter Bender has observed,

because the GDR did not live by its 'essence' (*Sein*), but by its pre-
tence (*Schein*). 'It was not Prussian poverty that characterized the
country,' he writes, 'but Communist decay. It was not sobriety that
determined the actions of the rulers, but lack of imagination. It
was not duty-bound civil servants who managed the GDR, but
the subservient functionary.'[24] Moreover, only two of the five new
Länder, Brandenburg and Sachsen-Anhalt, once formed part of Prussia.
Nevertheless, the East Germans are, and more importantly feel, more
German than their fellow countrymen in the West. Under the
cloak of socialism, the lack of openness in economic activity, the
country and its people remained more intact, more true to themselves than in the booming society of the West. Faced with a repressive government and a shortage of everything, people tended
to withdraw into their respective niches (*Nischengesellschaft*).[25] Time
moved more slowly because it did not equal money. Friendships
were important for personal as well as economic reasons. The environment was rotting away, but in a strange way, human beings
were more sheltered and protected. Being spied on by state security did not prevent them from developing close friendships and
neighbourhood communities. For all these reasons people preserved
traits and features, some very appealing, some less so, which were
more prevalent among their ancestors than among their West German relatives. More often than not, the latter mistook this enforced
go-slow as backwardness. In their turn East German intellectuals
and clergymen were inclined to make a virtue out of necessity.
Material inferiority was all too easily equated with moral superiority. However, the revelations about the many Stasi informers—as
a matter of fact, 95,000 officials and 173,000 informal collaborators[26]—who spied on their fellow countrymen, sometimes even
friends and relatives, has put an end to this line of thinking. The
idea of a people united in solidarity against their oppressors turned
out to be just another myth.

One other aspect must be mentioned because it also explains
the somewhat acrimonious relationship between the two parts
of Germany. A levelling of GDR society in all its facets did take
place. To some extent the regime succeeded in its avowed aim of
creating a proletarian way of life, due partly to the exodus of the
bourgeois elements before 1961 and the policy of positive as well
as negative discrimination. The educational chances of the old

Bildungsbürgertum, referred to as *Intelligenz*, were certainly systematically curtailed. What was meant to be the dictatorship of the
proletariat turned out to be the *Spießerstaat*, i.e. the *diktat* of petit-
bourgeois values and life-styles.

In spite of the desperate attempts by their rulers to instil a separate corporate identity, the former citizens of the GDR also feel
a certain pride in being German. Perhaps this is the most striking
and long-lasting outcome of forty years of repression. The Federal
Republic's attitude was contradictory, in as much as it claimed to
speak for all Germans while at the same time questioning the concept of national identity. It would have been inconceivable for West
Germans, who have embraced all sorts of issues in the course of
forty years, to go into the streets in their hundreds of thousands
and demand self-determination for the Germans beyond the Wall.
Growing identification with the Federal Republic went hand in hand
with diminishing national solidarity. The phrase 'typically German' is almost an insult in West Germany, but not in East Germany. Friedrich Schorlemmer writes: ' "A German, how proud that
sounds"—this is what we humiliated, betrayed GDR Germans would
like to say.'[27] This is certainly not what the West German youngsters interviewed by Alan Watson said. They feel proud about a
whole range of things, but not really about being German, even
though they now recognize what has been achieved since 1945.[28]
Accepting oneself does not, of course, necessarily imply being proud
of one's nation. What it does mean is accepting one's background,
warts and all.

By virtue of the Basic Law all East Germans were automatically citizens of the Federal Republic and entitled to its passport.
Of all the promises held out by Bonn, this was perhaps the most
substantial in the eyes of East Germans. If they escaped from the
narrow confines of the GDR, they would be recognized at once as
Germans, citizens of a larger, more liberal, and more prosperous
community of the same stock. In other words, as long as the Wall
stood in the way of a collective merger, they could always hope
to achieve union with the 'fatherland' as inividuals. Freedom, unity,
and the 'Greater Germany' of the Federal Republic constituted one
comprehensive option for a better future. Since this could not be
realized for most people it took on the character of an unfulfilled
dream which, once the Wall had come down, was bound to clash

with reality. To some extent, then, the widespread disappointment after 1990 was psychologically predetermined. The Germans in the West, so it seemed, did not live up to the challenge of a united 'fatherland', but remained fairly unemotional and went about their business as usual.

The attitudes towards foreigners inside and outside Germany must also be taken into account. After 1945 West Germans wanted to be part of the West in every respect and saw no reason to cultivate a separate German identity. In matters of politics, economics, and culture they were intent on catching up and being recognized as an equal partner. Not so the East Germans, whose relations with their political allies were much more ambivalent. Officially Warsaw Pact countries, in particular the Soviet Union, were referred to as 'our friends', but everybody regarded the Red Army as an occupation force, ready to back up the government against its own people if ever there was trouble, as happened on 17 June 1953. The Soviet Union possessed the superior firepower, while the GDR enjoyed a higher standard of living. Nor was there any feeling of cultural inferiority. The most telling evidence for the dichotomy between ideological and popular corporate identity is the reluctant but irresistible recognition of German, in particular Prussian history by the regime. Selective though the approach was, it nevertheless focused on the positive or 'progressive' aspects of German history, rather than, as in the West, on reassessing the whole in a critical spirit. History too, at any rate purified by socialism, could make one feel proud to be German.[29]

In the eyes of the world, the aftermath of German unification was linked with news about increased violence and xenophobia. Can any causal connections be made? Neo-Nazism seemed to be rearing its ugly head again, manifested in groups of marauding skinheads. It should be pointed out that the influx of asylum seekers after 1990 had nothing to do with German unification, while ensuing attempts to settle foreigners, if only temporarily, did, of course, strain already tight resources. The overall number of asylum seekers went up from 129,318 (1989) to 438,191 (1992). During that period the number of refugees from Yugoslavia rose from 19,423 to 122,666, and the number from Romania from 2,634 (1988) to 103,787 (1992). The number from Africa grew tenfold within four years, to 67,408 (1992). All this happened at a time of unprecedented migration from East to West Germany, which did not completely stop after unification, though it was no longer officially recorded. Regardless of the situation on the spot, foreigners were settled in the old, as well as the new *Länder*, whose 'face-to-face' experiences with foreigners were virtually non-existent.

Most of the 160,000 foreigners in the GDR (approximately 1 per cent of the population as against 10 per cent in the FRG) lived in separate boarding houses. Contacts between Germans and foreigners were not encouraged. Nor were foreigners recognized as minorities with special needs. Everyone was expected to conform to the norms as laid down by the SED. The official attitude towards minorities is best summarized by the title of a book, *Anders sein gab es nicht* (Being Different was Not On).[30] The largest groups of foreign labourers came from North Vietnam (53,000), Mozambique (14,000), and Cuba (10,000). By the time of the currency union the number of foreigners with a resident's permit had dwindled to under 50,000. How is this to be explained? Most of the unskilled workers were sent home when their unproductive plants closed down. Mozambicans were often sent straight into the civil-war armies. Others, like the Vietnamese, were ordered back by their governments, or stayed behind and ended up controlling the vegetable trade or dabbling in the black market in the East. After the fall of the Wall, most foreigners experienced a climatic change of a paradoxical nature: more open hostility and discrimination at work, coupled with a greater awareness on the part of the authorities of their special needs, often in response to acts of violence by German youngsters, which were now openly reported in the press. Solidarity with foreigners had been a matter of ideological correctness in the name of anti-fascism, never a practical necessity backed up by public opinion. Foreigners became the weakest link in a chain under tension. Faced with large-scale redundancies and the influx of asylum seekers, otherwise peaceful people vented their frustrations against foreigners, who were looked after by the authorities and were perceived as unwelcome rivals on the labour market. It was this atmosphere of simmering xenophobia, rather than ideological fanaticism, that encouraged neo-Nazi skinheads to commit atrocious acts of violence in Rostock and Hoyerswerda, which made headlines all over the world. The most shocking aspects were the seemingly approving attitude of onlookers, and the sheer incompetence of the police force. Soon afterwards, similar atrocities were committed in West Germany, though without any evidence that the 'silent majority' was condoning them. Public anxieties were greatly eased when the government, with the reluctant consent of the opposition, revised the exceptionally liberal asylum law of the constitution, on 1 July 1993. The founding fathers of the Federal Republic had opted for a generous asylum law as an act of atonement for the many refugees from Nazi Germany who had sought and found a safe haven abroad. Therefore many liberal-minded Germans opposed any change, not realizing that the law had become counter-productive. The new legislation excludes economic migrants, but still protects, as is customary elsewhere, those who have been persecuted on political grounds. As a consequence, foreigners who enter Germany from countries with a good record on human rights may no longer invoke the right of asylum.[31]

To what extent the political culture and national identity of the old Federal Republic will be changed by the East German input is difficult to assess. The general assumption is that the citizens of the new *Länder* have no option but to conform to the majority. This is indeed the most likely end result. The track was laid down by the refugees from the Eastern territories after the Second World War. Within ten years, so the argument runs, 12 million refugees were absorbed into the Federal Republic (the same percentage of the total population as now). Comparisons with post-war development, however, are too suggestive always to be reliable. The argument could also be turned around. Expellees, driven from their homes by the Red Army, proved to be the stalwart supporters of successive conservative governments. Their contribution to both the political culture and the economic prosperity of the Federal Republic should not be underestimated. It has been suggested above that a preference for a more caring, less competitive society is not necessarily at odds with a pronounced national consciousness. The latter does not imply a more assertive foreign policy or leadership ambitions, but rather a claim to more national solidarity. The East German people are saddened and demoralized because the sensational departure towards peaceful self-determination experienced in 1989–90 could not be sustained. However, the limits of this trend are clearly marked: to the far left, by the utter failure of socialism, or rather 'the real existing socialism', as experienced over the years, and to the far right by the disaster of National Socialism. The Federal elections, the second all-German elections, on 16 October 1994 were very reassuring in one crucial respect. In spite of the widespread malaise in the East, and the so-called *Parteienverdrossenheit* in the West, the result was not at all shattering or indicative of any major tectonic shift. In fact, the turnout went up slightly (from 78.8 per cent to 79.1 per cent), generally the most important barometer for political awareness. The governing party lost two dozen seats (244 as opposed to 268 in 1990) as expected, the CSU won 50 instead of 51, the Liberal coalition partners lost 32 seats (47 instead of 79), the Greens returned to the Bundestag and were rumoured to be likely replacements for the Liberals in the long run. Predictably, the protest vote of the PDS, the former Socialist Unity Party, rose from 17 to 30 seats. It is probably safe to say that the frustrations experienced in the wake of unification were not translated into serious protest when it came to the ballot box, but continued to rumble on as a sort of emotional undercurrent.

So far, reunification has meant the institutional enlargement of the old Federal Republic. Many frustrated Easterners and quite a few well-meaning West Germans do not think that this will do if the division is to be truly overcome. But they cannot put their finger on any viable alternative because they know in their heart of hearts that there is none. There are insufficient grievances against the Basic Law to justify convening a Constituent Assembly to work out a new, all-German constitution. Nor do Germany's neighbours, who have learned to live with the old democratically respectable republic, wish to accommodate a new, potentially unstable Germany. What seems to be missing is a more sympathetic approach to the many problems of transition. The East Germans do not really feel welcome in the new state, and regard themselves as second-class citizens. They have been fed on a propagandist perception of politics for nearly sixty years, only to be left, now, to their own devices without any moral encouragement from their leaders. For decades, to give but one example, the Free German Youth (FDJ) looked after the younger generation, who, while increasingly indifferent towards political indoctrination, were still attracted to the Boy Scout and Girl Guide organization and the many facilities on offer. Now, unemployed youngsters are demoralized and seek new allegiances in dubious youth gangs.[32] One is reminded of the lack of pomp and circumstance in the Weimar Republic following the sudden collapse of centuries-old dynasties in a matter of days in 1918. This problem has not been addressed by German leaders because it is outside their terms of reference, their technocratic, managerial understanding of politics. In material terms, 'sharing' with the East has so far been confined to the so-called 'solidarity contribution' of 7.5 per cent levied on income tax, roughly the equivalent of the church tax. It has not hurt many in the West.

A new awareness of a common history and culture would go a long way towards overcoming the division of present-day Germany, which is still all too glaring. This would enhance the East Germans' claim to equality of status and rekindle a sense of community and solidarity amongst the West Germans. However, the latter feel most uneasy about the meaning of *Gemeinschaft*, or worse, *Volksgemeinschaft*, an idea which reminds them of how their idealism was abused in two world wars. To many, 'nation' and 'war' are almost synonymous and linked by the same objectionable atavism, as though the term 'nation' is only defined by its exclusiveness and enmity towards others. This is not how the French or British see themselves. Britishness, for instance, encompasses not only Scotsmen and Welshmen, but also ethnic minorities from the 'new commonwealth'. Germans have not been granted a deeper insight into human nature because of their twentieth-century record of inhumanity. The writer Günter Grass is not the only intellectual high priest seriously to believe that because of Auschwitz the Germans have somehow forfeited the right to national self-determination. This self-denying ordinance is, more often than not, coupled with a moral superiority *vis-à-vis* other European nations, who apparently have not yet overcome their despicable tribal instincts. As so often, morality and arrogance are closely related. German national identity amounts to no more than what is self-evident to other nations: first, acceptance of the nation state as a matter of fact, whatever its future role in Europe may be, and second, a consensus about Germany's national interests now that the chief aim, national unity, has been achieved. Straightforward as this agenda might seem to others, in Germany it has caused endless recriminations. For some time to come, the country will be preoccupied with itself, with its coming of age as a modern nation. Goethe and Schiller, Germany's greatest poets, were very dismissive: 'You hope of shaping a nation, Germans, in vain!'[33] They should strive, instead, to become 'freer human beings'—a line of thought not unfamiliar to modern German intellectuals. These are unlikely to succeed where Goethe and Schiller failed to convince if they do not realize that the modern nation state is not at all incompatible with parliamentary democracy. For the Germans this would be a new lesson, not one implied by their history since 1871.

Most Germans of today wish to be, and above all to be accepted as, a *normal nation*, one amongst others with no special claims. Even though this may seem to be quite a legitimate desire, the term *Normalnation* has gained such wide currency that it has alarmed the guardians of the past, lest it imply any mitigation of Germany's exceptionally bad historical record.[34] Germans are less prepared than others to accept that strictly speaking no one is 'normal' ('No one is perfect' is usually quoted in English), or that no one should be particularly proud of being 'normal'. They do not have much time for eccentricity. The yearning for 'normality' after forty years of division and barbed wire can be explained in such simple terms without resorting to the intricacies of German historiography. In a sense, even the idea that German history since 1871 has deviated from a pre-ordained Western paradigm of democratization and modernization—the so-called *Sonderweg* thesis—is based on a concept of normality which is debatable. But German historians, being first and foremost German in their mental disposition, cannot do without 'norms' or 'paradigms' of historical development.

The intelligentsia, or those who influence public opinion, will only be reconciled to a new sense of national identity as a means of welding the two societies together if German nationality and, by implication, citizenship are redefined to include foreigners, notably those born and brought up in Germany. Some far-sighted intellectuals, like the East German Richard Schröder and the West German historian August Heinrich Winkler, have raised this issue. They have not, however, met with much response from the political establishment, which does not wish to cause an uproar amongst all 'right-minded' Germans. But this issue will not go away and will have to be tackled if the Germans are serious about becoming a 'normal nation'. As Winkler put it: 'The new formation of the German nation can only succeed if it coincides with a Westernization of the German understanding of nation.'[35] The common sense of this view is not undermined, but perhaps explained, by the fact that Winkler was one of those historians who defended the 'historical logic' of the 'two states' up to and beyond the appearance of evidence to the contrary. Afterwards he hurried to make amends and embraced the nation as a valid concept. The East German Richard Schröder, though fully in agreement with Winkler, pleads for more national solidarity and a new community spirit, encapsulated in 'us and we', and wholly suspect to many West German intellectuals: 'Otherwise the East Germans will never shed their embarrassing role as the unloved and uncomfortable petitioner with the East German congenital defect.'[36]

The Federal Republic still holds on to the ethnocentric nationality legislation of 1913, based on descent (*ius sanguinis*) rather than place of birth (*ius soli*). One important reason for doing so after 1949, of course, was that it provided the justification for not recognizing separate East German citizenship and made it possible to accommodate the refugees from the Eastern territories, by then under Polish administration. Both these reasons are obsolete, now that the country has been unified and the refugees long since assimilated. In spite of all the talk of a 'post-national society', so fashionable before 1989, in legal terms the German nation is defined as a community of common stock. One of the Nazi district commissioners told Alsatian recruits, drafted into the Wehrmacht, that they were Germans whether they liked, knew, or believed it, just as the Chinese were Chinese.[37] These young men from Alsace were still French because, in most cases, German citizenship had not been conferred upon them and because they wished to remain French. This example illustrates two aspects of the modern concept of nationality, which will please neither the 'silent majority' nor the vociferous intelligentsia: first, nationality can be acquired by naturalization, not only by birth; secondly, if it rests upon the will of the individual, it presupposes a readiness on the part of the newcomer to embrace a new identity, be it only by learning to speak German. Maybe East Germans can help to reintroduce a more common-sense approach since they are less affected by the pernicious ideology of political correctness. Richard Schröder, who has no problems with Islamic or black Germans, is right to query the superficial presumption of a multi-cultural society. It would be fatal, he writes, if the programme of a multi-cultural society were allowed to produce, in the name of humanity, an uncontrollable potential for conflict.[38] Moreover, and this will be even more controversial, the right to choose works both ways: society also has a right to impose conditions on those whom it is prepared to adopt. In view of its fast-declining birth rate, sooner or later the Federal Republic will have to introduce an immigration law.

To some extent national identity is defined by national interests. The fact that German unification was never abandoned as a constitutional objective suggests that there were still remnants of a national identity even without a nation state. The same can now be said about Germany's continued adherence to the idea of European integration, which has been depicted as a mere ersatz solution to the missing national dimension. Now that the nation state has been reinstated it turns out that Europe is, and has always been, Germany's second most important national interest. More than that, there is general agreement that the new nation state can only be securely anchored as an integral part of a European Union that transcends interstate co-operation. The preamble to the Basic Law has been purged of the sentence calling upon the entire German people 'to achieve in free self-determination, the unity and the freedom of Germany.' However, it still contains 'the resolve to serve world peace as an equal partner in a united Europe.' This pledge still awaits fulfilment. Chancellor Kohl frequently reiterates the phrase that German and European unity are 'two sides of the same coin'. And he means it: he is not prepared to abandon the Deutschmark without real progress towards political union. German politicians are not pleased to be constantly told that their country is the biggest and most powerful member of the European Union. Another 'concert of Europe', with changing alliances and alignments, is no longer acceptable. It should be a community of equal partners, with no room for old-style diplomatic manœuvring.[39] For the united Germany 'security' in a wider sense is as essential as it is for the East Germans in the domestic sphere. In every respect Germany is now one of the 'haves', whereas before, notably between 1890 and 1939, it was perceived as and behaved like one of the most dangerous 'have nots'. While before 1989 West Germany's identity was, at least to some extent, derived from its position as the bulwark of the Western world, Germans are now told that they have more neighbours than any other European state.

The implication is that in view of the extensive communications network good neighbourly relations require a much firmer set of rules and regulations than allowed for by traditional diplomacy. This is why Germany has not called for a moratorium on Europe with a view to consolidating its new power status.

The second most powerful argument in favour of Europe is the direction of the German economy. In statistical terms, the country may be the world's foremost trading nation. As mentioned above, however, more than 70 per cent of exports are directed to Europe, including Germany's eastern neighbours—for instance, as much to Sweden as to the whole of Africa. German prosperity rests on a European market which is to conform with the domestic market as far as is politically feasible. It should not be forgotten that Germany's own market was not properly developed until the mid-nineteenth century, and that this was the crucial precondition for the country's spectacular industrial take-off. Clashes over regulation and overregulation, given the German disposition to the rule of law, are bound to arise from time to time and need to be settled according to the rules of the European club.

The third justification for further European integration has only come to the fore since the transformation of Eastern Europe. The political and economic development of that part of the world is perceived as a challenge and at the same time as a threat. Both can only be met by a united effort on the part of the European Union. The expectations of assistance emanating from Russia alone are well beyond Germany's capacities. Pushing the frontiers of civilization further east has taken on a very different meaning from what it used to imply for German empire-builders in the past: not enforced Christianization or colonization, not even economic penetration, but aiding the process of modernization in order to achieve a certain degree of stability, or, one might say, a kind of *terrain sanitaire*. It is no exaggeration to say that individual Germans today are more afraid of the Russian mafia and mass migration from the East than the political establishment ever was of the Soviet menace. Given its penchant for order, and faced with a world of encroaching chaos, the Federal Republic feels extremely vulnerable without the back-up of Western Europe and the United States.

Over the years the Germans have learned to be more flexible in the pursuit of their European interests. They no longer parade their own federal constitution as a blueprint for Europe. Nor are they pressing for a fixed timetable. Because of the unique character of Europe as a continent of long-established nation states, the 'ever closer union' cannot be defined in advance. Whether there will eventually be a binding and written constitution is an open question.

German goverments are usually most concerned about how to enhance the European Union's capacity for action (*Handlungsfähigkeit*), mainly in the fields of foreign and defence policy and public order. However, Germany's partners are increasingly irritated by her double standards: asking for joint decision-making without providing the means for executing the common policy thus arrived at. Responsibility for the deployment of troops outside NATO has been endlessly debated, only for the final ruling to be left to the Constitutional Court, which has now given its blessing. There is some justification for complaints from journalists and intellectuals close to the government that their fellow countrymen do not live up to their new responsibilities and tend to hide behind the constraints imposed by the past and their constitution.[40]

While most of these voices are pleading for greater German involvement in international peacekeeping, there are those on the New Right who are reinventing the importance of geopolitics and emphasizing Germany's *Mittellage* (central position in Europe). They begin by questioning the Federal Republic's *Westbindung*[41] (integration into the West), as though Germany were once again in a position to choose between East and West. The Angry Right brigade has rallied behind the old Right with their clarion call for a new, positive, and more traditional self-perception. Postwar 're-education' is not the last word, they say, and Europe is not to replace the nation state as the final arbiter.

It is good to know that these 'Eurosceptics' do not in any way represent the 'official mind'. However, a 'renationalization of politics' is bound to gain strength if the momentum towards an ever-closer European Union inherent in the European integration process is lost. No doubt younger Germans, as well as most East Germans, are less inspired by the vision of a united Europe than the generation to which Chancellor Kohl belongs. For as long as it takes to fuse the two halves together Germany is unlikely to take on the additional responsiblities accruing from a leadership role. At the end of this process the European Union, in its turn, may well have made further progress towards integration, so that none of its member states will be able to pursue an independent foreign policy. It is important for the Germans to realize that by recognizing their own identity—accepting themselves, as it were—they will make it easier for others to embrace a European future. None of the other nations wish to part with their corporate identity as a result of the transfer of certain powers to Brussels. Prussia's 'mission' to unite the German states and to mould them in her image is perhaps the most conspicuous warning of how not to proceed. The result was a disaster for both Germany and Europe. This is what German speechmakers may have in mind, all too often it seems, when they quote Thomas Mann, who wished for a European Germany, not a German Europe. But even that is not called for. If Germany is serious about becoming a *Normalnation* it is time to give up all pretensions to being more advanced than others. The Germans are not, after all, the first 'post-national' nation.

The whole debate about Germany's 'national interests' or supposed role in world affairs is redundant. Is it really appropriate to define the maintenance of peace and prosperity, respect for human rights, the fight against organized crime, etc. as 'national interests' when such aims are in the interests of mankind in general and best pursued in co-operation with others? The notion has clearly been discredited by its misguided application in the past. More often than not 'national interests' are distilled from totally illusory perceptions of status and 'manifest' destiny. All classifications such as 'super-', 'world', 'great', or 'European' power are ultimately meaningless. The most fantastic claims have been made for the 'Reich', from the Holy Roman (neither holy nor Roman) to the Thousand-Year (in fact twelve-year) Empire. To be suspicious of 'national interests' is one of the most fundamental lessons of German history which—and of this one can be sure—has been taken on board. No one has been able to persuade the Germans in the past forty years that they ought to have their own nuclear *force de frappe* in order to be on a par with other league members, as was the case a hundred years ago when great-power status was associated with the possession of colonies. It is unlikely that the Germans will now be talked into adopting a whole new array of 'national interests' beyond their slightly expanded borders. Christoph Bertram is right to stress that his country has become a fully fledged democracy 'in its domestic as well as in its international behaviour' and that therefore its leaders 'will not be adventurous but cautious. Their instinct will be not to promote German power but to assure German living standards and to avoid being out of touch with domestic public opinion'.[42] Of course, the Germans cannot shirk their fair share of international responsibilities. But this surely does not require a concerted effort of 're-re-education'. When the pundits keep outlining the new concerns of the post-Cold War era, it is important to be reminded of those concerns which have not changed. In foreign policy the Federal Republic always doggedly pursued two aims which were clearly marked out for all its neighbours to see: with German unification now achieved, only European integration is left on the agenda. And if this goal should also be reached in one way or another there is, on the national plane, nothing else worth striving for but cultural self-preservation within a larger English-speaking Union.

10 Conclusion

In retrospect, the period between 1949 and 1989–90 appears more and more as a self-contained epoch of German history, to be summarized in future textbooks as 'Germany Divided' or 'The Time of Division'. It has already become quite common in the West to refer to the 'old Federal Republic', no less nostalgically, incidentally, than some East Germans recall their GDR past with all its hardship. The 'Bonn Republic' was, after all, the provisional state as conceived by the founding fathers, not the definitive outcome of German history as a later generation came to believe. However transitory it may have been, the Bonn Republic was, and is increasingly perceived as, the most successful and stable state ever created on German soil. As such, it has changed German political culture for good. There is a discrepancy in perception which is at the root of many misunderstandings between the Germans and their neighbours. The latter still think that the turbulent first half of the twentieth century is more significant than the peaceful second half, and that with reunification Germany has, so to speak, 'come home' again. This is pure fantasy and makes no allowance for the simple truth that everything in history is subject to change. For the purpose of surveying the last fifty years it makes more sense to stress the formative influences which moulded today's Germany, rather than discussing the various caesuras brought about by the political shifts from Adenauer (1949–63) to Brandt/Schmidt (1969–82) and back to the CDU/CSU government under Kohl (1982–), or the 'Wall' (1961) as a second chance for the GDR.

The new Germany was not born in 1949, when it was officially christened, but in 1945. Utter defeat, unconditional surrender, and total occupation proved to be the most drastic and successful shock therapy ever administered to a nation. It provided the impetus for a new departure and, in the long run, for a psychological metamorphosis. Neither the past nor the present offered any comfort; only the hope for a better and saner future held out any promise. The energy generated by this state of affairs and state of mind was unique and quite extraordinary.

It is generally assumed that with the passage of time a more understanding interpretation of the past will emerge, in the sense of *tout comprendre, c'est tout pardonner*. However, this has not happened in Germany, not least because of the horrors of the Holocaust, which cannot be explained away. That chapter of contemporary German history cannot ever be considered as closed. Each new generation is more perplexed than the last by the mentality of their ancestors, as though these had not lived in the same century, but at a time as long ago as the Crusades. Nevertheless, the Holocaust is likely to become an integral part of German national identity. The idea that this identity needs to be nurtured on pride alone is in any case outdated. There is much to be said for the argument put forward be Count Krockow that after 1945 West Germany returned to the liberal tradition of the nineteenth-century *Bürgertum*.[1] At that time western Germany was already more developed, both in economic and constitutional terms, than the eastern territories from which Prussia drew its military strength. Perhaps the so-called *preußische Geschichtslegende* should now be put the other way round. In this light 1871 marks the onset of a historical aberration, rather than the culmination of German history. In any case, 'fears of a fundamental re-orientation of German policy, away from its Western-dominated position', are *not* justified.[2] The impact of the intellectual debate, ranging from one end of the political spectrum to the other, does not really affect the overall historic transformation that has occurred.

The second traumatic experience which shaped German post-war consciousness is, no doubt, the threat of Communism as perceived in the West, and as experienced firsthand by the East Germans. The anxiety in the West was probably more acute than the real danger emanating from the Red Army. This was due to a variety of reasons: the impact of Nazi anti-Bolshevist propaganda, the horror stories told by the refugees from the Eastern territories, and not least the deprivations suffered by relations in the Soviet Zone of occupation. Thus the post-war misery was tempered by the feeling of having had a lucky escape, mixed with constant fear. There was no substantial German contribution to the defence of the West during the Stalin phase of the Cold War (1945–53). The West Germans were totally dependent for their protection on their former enemies. Could these be trusted? Altogether the post-war period exacerbated a deep sense of insecurity which had been instilled through centuries of relative weakness in the heart of a troubled Continent. After a short interval of seventy-five years of national hubris, Germany seemed once again to be at the mercy of foreign powers, though with one crucial difference. For once, these were truly protecting powers (*Schutzmächte*). Total occupation after 1945 proved to be a much more wholesome experience than partial occupation as in the period after 1918.

Today a growing number of neo-conservative thinkers such as Hans-Peter Schwarz, Christian Hacke, Michael Stürmer, and Gregor Schöllgen, to name but a few, maintain that Germany has become too accustomed to the security provided by others.[3] The notion of power, it is argued, once sanctified by the Prussian school of history, is now vilified by sanctimonious and ineffectual politicians and intellectuals. The First World War reference by Werner Sombart to *Helden* (heroes, the Germans) versus *Händler* (shopkeepers, the British) has been turned upside down: the Germans are now the traders who prefer to pay tribute (as in the Gulf War, which accounted for almost one-third of the entire defence budget) rather than risk the deployment of their own troops. It is time, so the argument runs, to pay back the debt and contribute to safeguarding the freedom and security of others. These neo-conservative thinkers are desperate to invent a new role for the enlarged Germany in helping to police the world, admittedly only as the deputy sheriff of the United States. Germany is called upon to act as a European *Ordnungsmacht* with world-wide responsibilities. In this context a German proverb is most appropriate: *Schuster, bleib bei deinen Leisten* (Cobbler, stick to your last). The expectations raised by unification are as misplaced as the early apprehensions swelling up in 1990. The new Germany has enough on its plate as it is, above all assimilating the two unequal parts of the country. Dabbling in world affairs should be left to others who have shown themselves to be more experienced in the past. Does Germany really need a seat on the Security Council of the United Nations in order to prove her worth, if she is already one of the major financial contributors? The easy answer to this follows the dubious wisdom of an all-too-popular German saying: *Wer zahlt, schafft an*—'He who pays the piper calls the tune.' But being on the board is surely not the only way of bearing responsibility. The plea for a more active and coherent foreign policy,[4] based on a redefinition of Germany's 'national interests', is meant to further collective identity and self-confidence. However, 'national interests' are not as self-evident as they are made to appear. Nor is national identity something which can be cultivated like an allotment plot. It is devoutly to be hoped that once this cherished identity is in place, there will be no need to exhibit it. In the last resort it cannot amount to anything but self-acceptance and *tranquilitas animi*.

For some time to come, the political debate in Germany will be characterized by the striking contrast between the bad lessons of the pre-1945 period and the success story of the old Federal Republic. One important lesson is the realization that Germany can never hope to be once again a truly independent power, whose influence rests on non-alignment. The United States remains Germany's most important ally. All German Chancellors and Foreign Ministers have repeatedly and almost ritualistically pledged their unwavering support for NATO. For the first time Germany has experienced lasting security and prosperity within a strong, truly defensive alliance. The temptation to go it alone has all but vanished from the political agenda. To remain a trusted ally within the North Atlantic community clearly is in the national interest and is no longer disputed by any of the major parties. It is for this reason that Bonn feels it cannot permanently retreat from commitments 'out of area', but the government prefers, and for good reason, to supply economic rather than military assistance wherever possible.

It was a novel experience for Germany that membership of NATO and a certain degree of independent political action were perfectly compatible and even complementary. First this was successfully tried within the overall Western Alliance by the close and lasting rapport with France. More important still was the venture of *Ostpolitik*. Within a few years the Federal Republic changed from the last Western bastion of the Cold War into the most persistent advocate of détente, thereby softening up the icy territories of Eastern Europe. The politics of peace seem to have replaced power politics. In order to be ethical and effective, the two should, of course, go hand in hand. *Ostpolitik* has not come to an end with unification. It is likely to be continued on the same premisses as before: a firm anchorage in the Western Alliance. However, the driving force is not any grandiose political concept of *Mittellage* or

Mitteleuropa, but sheer anxiety about once again coming close to the abyss. Being themselves almost obsessed with order, what the Germans see in the East is encroaching chaos, growing disorder, the scourge of nationalism, reminiscent of the breakdown of empires at the end of the First World War. Even more than at the height of the Cold War, Germans perceive themselves as inhabiting the eastern marches of Western civilization, i.e. parliamentary democracy and economic prosperity. They feel that they need all the backing they can get from a united Europe to cope with an uncertain future looming in the East. The problem is that they are tempted to impose their concept of order, in particular in fiscal and ecological terms, on a reluctant continent, only to be flabbergasted if accused of wishing to dominate Europe. There is still a lesson to be learned, namely to be content with a world that is less than perfect.

For most of their history Germans have conceived of power purely, or certainly mainly, in military terms: soldiers and battles and the relationship between the two. Naïve as it may seem, the idea that economic influence should also amount to power is still something fairly new for the German political mind. Most Germans are rather embarrassed to learn that they are the biggest and most powerful member of the European Union. In actual fact, Germany has now undergone a complete metamorphosis from a *Militärmacht* to a *Handelsstaat*. The credo is not so much 'to make the world safe for democracy' (US President Wilson) as 'to turn the world into a gigantic marketplace for German goods and services'. However, a small but vociferous group of Germans would give priority to making the globe an ecologically sound habitat. German nationalism has always been devoid of any message to the world transcending the interests of the nation state. Will concern for the environment perhaps one day be seen as the German contribution to a better world, on a par with the fanfares of the American and French revolutions in the eighteenth century? David Marsh[5] has suggested that the ecological movement in Germany has given new meaning to Geibel's naïve belief that the world might still be saved by emulating German thoroughness (*Und es mag am deutschen Wesen einmal noch die Welt genesen*[6]).

The undeniable achievements of the social market economy, founded on industrial co-operation and co-determination at the workplace, go a long way to explaining why Germany has established a stable democracy. Clearly in today's world Germany belongs to the 'haves', determined to hold on to its newly acquired property, to what in trade union parlance is called *Besitzstand*. However, the Federal Republic's economic boom, most marked between 1950 and 1975, and mainly export-driven, can hardly be sustained for ever. Like the GDR, which was always threatened from within, not from without, despite all propaganda to the contrary, Germany's prosperity is now most endangered from within, by its very success. German workers enjoy the highest wages and most generous social benefits. These facts are now being interpreted in a different way: Germany has the highest unit labour costs in the world, not least because of the massive social insurance contributions. In order to remain competitive, German industry is investing abroad, often just a few kilometres beyond the German border, mostly in the East, where German private enterprise is now welcome and labour considerably cheaper. Whether rising unemployment and diminishing growth will lead to a major economic crisis in the future, no one can tell. So far, German industry has responded to the challenge—though not fast enough for some experts—by rationalizing and streamlining production, and introducing flexible working hours in return for preserving jobs (with Volkswagen in the vanguard). Until 1994 the East German economy appeared to be Europe's primary growth area, thanks, no doubt, to massive capital transfers from West Germany (525 billion DM between 1 July 1990 and 1995), and a new infrastructure that is one of the most advanced in the Western world, especially in the telecommunications sector.[7] To a large extent the take-off effect has been achieved by an unprecedented building boom, fuelled by tax incentive. Since then economic development has slowed down considerably. It is true that within four years the average gross income level has reached 74 per cent of the West German average (79 per cent of the basic West German pensions). However, this is mainly due to continued life support from the West, by way of subsidized labour (*Arbeitsbeschaffungsmaßnahmen*: ABM)—now seriously questioned—rather than to a corresponding rise in productivity. With a population of approximately one-fifth of the total, the new *Bundesländer* contribute no more than 6–7 per cent of Germany's overall production. Among the top one hundred German companies, there is not one from the East. Industrial reconstruction will take considerably longer than anticipated, and the government understands that this is a vital task in the years to come. Transferring the German capital from Bonn to Berlin (greatly resented by the civil service) was intended to demonstrate this resolve and will be a further boost to the economy in the East. After all, the struggle for democracy was finally won in the West on the economic battlefield. It therefore makes sense to assume that the East Germans will also wish to benefit from the political as well as the economic advantages of Western democracy. The problem is that, as with the currency union in July 1990, political and economic priorities are at loggerheads. For this reason the Germans are only too aware that the same syndrome applies to political and monetary union in Europe. In the end, political priorities are of overriding importance if the economic costs are at all bearable.

Some say that German democracy, which failed for the first time during the Great Depression, has not yet had to weather a real slump and has therefore not stood the acid test. However, local democracy worked fairly well before the onset of the economic boom and in the meantime the political culture has changed too. And now there is a national and international co-ordinating machinery in place which is more likely to prevent a major crisis than in the early 1930s. The Federal Republic's 'Magna Carta', the *Grundgesetz*, safeguarding democracy and human rights, is more firmly implanted than any previous constitution. While determining the political system, the Basic Law is non-committal as far as the economic order is concerned. As a matter of fact, Article 15 gives the government the right, if need be, to nationalize by law property, national resources, and means of production, provided the owners are properly compensated. By now there have been more than forty alterations to the Basic Law, none of which affects Article 15. In any serious crisis, no German government, whatever its political composition, would refrain from taking charge of the economy. The market economy has served the country very well indeed, but it is a means to an end, not a political dogma. The concept of German democracy is primarily based on the rule of law and respect for human rights, not on economic liberalism. The *Grundgesetz* and the *Länder* constitutions were in place before the economic order of the Federal Republic was decided by ballot. The state will always be expected to come to the rescue of society if dire need should arise.

The feeling is widespread that whatever Germany does in Europe it will always be in the wrong and will be accused of dominating the continent, either consciously or by default. With Germany's first unification in 1871 Europe, so the much-quoted saying goes, exchanged a mistress (France) for a master. It is precisely this prospect of Germany turning into a 'hated schoolmaster' which worries perceptive intellectuals like Arnulf Baring when they consider the effects of monetary union and the likely German urge to interfere in other nations' domestic affairs for the sake of fiscal rectitude. The wagging finger is one of the most widespread expressions in German body-language. In the end it is a matter of political leadership and common resolve whether Europe will become an ever closer union or an ever larger free-market area. If the obstacles on the road to political union should prove insurmountable, then neo-conservative thinkers and politicians are likely to succeed in reinventing German national interests separate from and outside the European Union. They feel encouraged by the growing disenchantment with Europe, both amongst the German people, who are loath to lose their cherished currency, and on the part of foreign governments who have been expressing reservations. Rejection of Europe would clearly be a step back into the past. In actual fact, the majority of issues have a global dimension and concern Europe as a whole as much as any single state. But there is one difference: the Germans tend to worry more than others—they are *the* 'worrier nation'—and this is the real reason why they always seem so pushy. 'The German capacity', says one economist, 'to make a drama out of a crisis, may well be the partial source of the recoveries staged in 1967, 1974 and 1981.'[8]

Indeed, Germans are more easily given than others to periodic panic attacks, which may either precipitate necessary reforms and adjustments or lead to a more fundamental shift of opinion (like the ecology movement). It is an expression of the existential German *Angst*: *Angst* about forfeiting God's grace (Martin Luther); *Angst* about being wiped out as in the Thirty Years' War (1618–47: more than one-third of the population perished); about being encircled, partitioned, economically ruined; and, more recently, about being poisoned by a deadly environment. This German *Angst* can only be put to rest in a united Europe. The strongest argument for a united Europe is not monetary union but perpetual security, and the hope of perpetual peace.

The Reich is gone for ever, the First, the Second, and the Third, each of which, in its own way, claimed a leadership role in Europe. The most recent and comprehensive account of German foreign policy between 1871 and 1945, by Klaus Hildebrand, is aptly called *Das vergangene Reich*,[9] which stresses the definitive demise of the Reich and all it stood for. If there is one lingering dream loosely connected with former ambitions, it is the hope that by ceaseless effort and sacrifice Germany will make a substantial, perhaps even the most decisive, contribution to the political unification of Europe, and might thereby redeem its past. Here, too, the Federal Republic's post-war lesson, that patience pays, the 'policy of small steps', should prove to be a valuable asset.

Notes

Introduction (pages 1–3)

1. For photographic details of the extent of the destruction at the end of the war see Charles Whiting, *Norddeutschland Stunde Null: April–September 1945* (Düsseldorf, 1980). Eberhard Schmidt's thesis (*Die verhinderte Neuordnung*, Frankfurt am Main, 1970) has remained controversial. See Rolf Steininger, *Deutsche Geschichte seit 1945: Darstellung und Dokumente in 4 Bänden*, vol. ii (Frankfurt am Main, 1996), 53–84.
2. Ralf Dahrendorf, *Gesellschaft und Demokratie in Deutschland* (Munich, 1966), 432; David Schoenbaum, *Hitler's Social Revolution: Class and Status in Nazi Germany 1933–1939* (London, 1967). For Hitler's self-perception, see Rainer Zitelmann, *Hitler: Selbstverständnis eines Revolutionärs*, 2nd edn. (Stuttgart, 1989).
3. By decree of the Control Council (Official Gazette No. 14, Mar. 1947, p. 262).

Chapter 1 (pages 5–36)

1. 'German Reaction to Defeat', 10 Jan. 1945, Public Record Office (PRO): WP (45)18, FO 371/46791/C150.
2. W. Averell Harriman and Elie Abel, *Special Envoy to Churchill and Stalin 1941–1946* (London, 1971), 484.
3. Sir Orme Sargent, 4 May 1945, FO 371/46720/C1644.
4. Statistics in Alfred M. De Zayas, *Nemesis at Potsdam: The Anglo-Americans and the Expulsion of the Germans* (London, 1977).
5. See Lothar Kettenacker, *Krieg zur Friedenssicherung: Die Deutschlandplanung der britischen Regierung während des Zweiten Weltkrieges* (Göttingen, 1989).
6. Reply to Eden's enquiry of 10 Sept. 1941, FO 371/26543/C0855. For the frustrated attempts by the German Resistance to contact the Allies see Klemens von Klemperer, *German Resistance against Hitler: The Search for Allies Abroad 1938–1945* (Oxford, 1992).
7. Apart from Wolfgang Leonhard's memoirs (*Child of Revolution*, Chicago, 1958) the most thoroughly researched study of Soviet policy *vis-à-vis* Germany is Alexander Fischer, *Sowjetische Deutschlandpolitik im Zweiten Weltkrieg 1941–1945* (Stuttgart, 1975).
8. See Keith Eubank, *Summit at Teheran* (New York, 1985).
9. See Winston S. Churchill, *The Second World War*, vol. vi (London, 1954), 386–98.
10. Lord Strang, *Home and Abroad* (London, 1956), 213.
11. Minute by John G. Ward, 5 May 1945, FO 371/50762/U3598.

12. Field Marshal Montgomery to Eden, 6 June 1945, FO 371/50766/U4391.

13. Dwight D. Eisenhower, *Crusade in Europe* (London, 1948), 471.

14. Eden to Churchill, 9 Sept. 1944, FO 371/40663/U7366.

15. Eisenhower, *Crusade in Europe*, 475.

16. Speech in House of Commons, 21 Sept. 1943; text in Charles Eade (ed.), *The War Speeches of the Rt. Hon. Winston S. Churchill*, vol. iii (London, 1962), 18.

17. Charles L. Mee, *Meeting at Potsdam* (London, 1975), app. ii, pp. 321–2.

18. F. S. V. Donnison, *Civil Affairs and Military Government: Central Organisation and Planning* (London, 1966), 105.

19. Lord Strang, *Home and Abroad*, 218.

20. See note 17. The most authoritative study on the question is now Elisabeth Kraus, *Ministerien für das ganze Deutschland? Der Alliierte Kontrollrat und die Frage gesamtdeutscher Zentralverwaltungen* (Munich, 1990).

21. Quoted in Mee, *Meeting at Potsdam*, 188–9.

22. See note 17.

23. Harriman and Abel, *Special Envoy*, 484.

24. Alec Cairncross, *The Price of War: British Policy on German Reparations 1941–1949* (Oxford, 1986), 194–218.

25. See the massive documentation on German prisoners of war in Erich Mascke (ed.), *Zur Geschichte der deutschen Kriegsgefangenen des Zweiten Weltkrieges*, 15 vols. (Bielefeld, 1962–74).

26. Discussed in Cabinet on 10 Nov. 1943, WM 152 (43) 7, CAB 65/36.

27. Churchill, *The Second World War*, v. 330.

28. Churchill to Roosevelt, 22 Oct. 1944; Warren Kimball (ed.), *Churchill and Roosevelt: The Complete Correspondence*, vol. iii (Princeton, 1984), C-801, p. 364.

29. For details see Bradley F. Smith, *Reaching Judgement at Nuremberg* (London, 1977).

30. John Gimbel, *The American Occupation of Germany* (Stanford, Calif., 1968), 16–38. After visiting Buchenwald concentration camp Eisenhower had experienced the shock of his life and had urged London and Washington 'to send instantly to Germany a random group of newspaper editors'.

31. Lutz Niethammer, *Die Mitläuferfabrik: Die Entnazifizierung am Beispiel Bayerns* (Berlin and Bonn, 1982). See also the study by Norbert Frei, *Vergangenheitspolitik: Die Anfänge der Bundesrepublik und die NS-Vergangenheit* (Munich, 1986), which could not be considered fully here. The emphasis is on the pressure from society at large in the early 1950s to 'put an end to the unpleasant matter'.

32. Text in Christoph Kleßmann, *Die doppelte Staatsgründung: Deutsche Geschichte 1945–1955* (Göttingen, 1982), 378. See also Gerhard Besier and Gerhard Sauter, *Wie Christen ihre Schuld bekennen* (Göttingen, 1985).

33. Anna J. Merritt and Richard L. Merritt, *Public Opinion in Occupied Germany: The OMGUS-Surveys 1945–1949* (Urbana, Ill., 1970), 32.

34. See Alexander Mitscherlich and Margarete Mitscherlich, *Die Unfähigkeit zu trauern: Grundlagen kollektiven Verhaltens* (Munich, 1968).

35. Leonhard, *Child of Revolution*, 303.

36. See note 17.

37. FO 371/39080/C12599.

38. Comprehensive documentation by Rolf Steininger (ed.), *Die Ruhrfrage 1945/46 und die Entstehung des Landes Nordrhein-Westfalen: Britische, französische und amerikanische Akten* (Düsseldorf, 1988).

39. Declaration of 11 June 1945; text in Kleßmann, *Die doppelte Staatsgründung*, 411–14.

40. Paraphrased in his memoirs: James F. Byrnes, *Frankly Speaking* (London, 1947), 187–94.

41. Quoted by Wolfgang Benz in Theodor Eschenburg, *Geschichte der Bundesrepublik Deutschland*, vol. i: *Jahre der Besatzung 1945–1949* (Wiesbaden, 1985), 410–11.

42. Quoted by Benz, *ibid.* 430.

43. Quoted by Anthony J. Nicholls, *Freedom with Responsibility: The Social Market Economy in Germany 1918–1963* (Oxford, 1994), 217.

44. Quoted by Benz in Eschenburg, *Geschichte der Bundesrepublik Deutschland*, i. 452.

45. Ibid.

46. Jean Edward Smith (ed.), *The Papers of Lucius D. Clay: Germany 1945–1952*, vol. ii (Bloomington, Ind., 1974), 623.

47. Quoted in Rolf Steininger, *Deutsche Geschichte 1945–1961*, vol. i (Frankfurt am Main, 1983), 232. See also the new biography of Schumacher by Peter Merseburger, *Der schwierige Deutsche: Kurt Schumacher, eine Biographie* (Stuttgart, 1995).

48. Hoover Report, *New York Times*, 24 Mar. 1947.

49. Victor Gollancz, *In Darkest Germany* (London, 1947).

50. See the memoirs of one of the biggest East Elbian landowners: Alexander Fürst zu Dohna Schlobitten, *Erinnerungen eines alten Ostpreußen* (Berlin, 1992), 342–4.

51. See Wolfgang Jacobmeyer, *Vom Zwangsarbeiter zum heimatlosen Ausländer: Die Displaced Persons in Westdeutschland 1945–1951* (Göttingen, 1985).

Chapter 2 (pages 37–52)

1. Carlo Schmid, *Erinnerungen* (Munich, 1980), 328–9.

2. *Tagesspiegel*, 15 July 1948.

3. *Foreign Relations of the United States* (FRUS), 3 (1948), 82–4. See also John H. Backer, *Winds of Change: The German Years of Lucius Du Bignon Clay* (New York, 1983).

4. Ernst Reuter, in Eschenburg, *Geschichte der Bundesrepublik Deutschland*, i. 469.

5. Apart from his memoirs, Konrad Adenauer, *Erinnerungen*, 4 vols. (Frankfurt am Main, 1965–8), see the most authoritative biography of the first

Chancellor by Hans-Peter Schwarz, *Konrad Adenauer: A German Politician and Statesman in a Period of War, Revolution and Reconstruction* (Providence, RI and Oxford, 1995). Schwarz also contributed the two volumes on the Adenauer era in the prestigious *Geschichte der Bundesrepublik*: vol. ii (covering 1949–57) and vol. iii (covering 1957–63) (Wiesbaden, 1981 and 1985).

6. Schmid, *Erinnerungen*, 358.
7. Eschenburg, *Geschichte der Bundesrepublik Deutschland*, i. 506.
8. Adenauer, *Erinnerungen*, i. 176.
9. Merseburger, *Der schwierige Deutsche*, 434–6.
10. Quoted by Benz in Eschenburg, *Geschichte der Bundesrepublik Deutschland*, i. 533.
11. See Horst Moeller, *Theodor Heuß, Staatsmann und Schriftsteller* (Bonn, 1990).
12. See now Wilfried Loth, *Stalins ungeliebtes Kind: Warum Moskau die DDR nicht wollte* (Berlin, 1994).
13. Kleßmann, *Die doppelte Staatsgründung*, 206.
14. *Neues Deutschland*, 14 Oct. 1949.
15. Herman Weber, *DDR: Grundriß der Geschichte 1945–1990* (Hanover, 1991), 52.
16. Arnulf Baring, *Der 17. Juni 1953*, new edn. (Stuttgart, 1983); Axel Bust-Bartels, 'Der Arbeiteraufstand am 17. Juni 1953', *Aus Politik und Zeitgeschichte*, 25 (1980), 24–54.
17. Quoted by Bust-Bartels, 'Der Arbeiteraufstand', 45.
18. Armin Mitter and Stefan Wolle, *Untergang auf Raten: Unbekannte Kapitel der DDR-Geschichte* (Munich, 1993), 27–162. See also the impressive documentation (unpublished documents, interviews, and photos) by the West German labour historian Gerhard Beier, *Wir wollen freie Menschen sein* (Frankfurt am Main, 1993).

Chapter 3 (pages 53–79)

1. Letter to the Lord Mayor of Duisburg, 5 Oct. 1945, see Adenauer, *Erinnerungen*, i. 35.
2. Sebastian Haffner, *Im Schatten der Geschichte* (Stuttgart, 1985), 291. See also Kurt Sontheimer, *Die Adenauer-Ära: Grundlegung der Bundesrepublik* (Munich, 1991), 16–19.
3. 20 Sept. 1949; text in Werner Bührer (ed.), *Die Adenauer-Ära* (Munich, 1993), 37–44.
4. See Adolf M. Birke, *Nation ohne Haus: Deutschland 1945–1961* (Berlin, 1989), 268.
5. Quoted by Steininger, *Deutsche Geschichte 1945–1961*, ii. 361.
6. Adenauer, *Erinnerungen*, i. 257. See also Dennis L. Bark and David R. Gress, *A History of West Germany*, 2 vols. (Oxford, 1993), i. 265.
7. Quoted by Steininger, *Deutsche Geschichte 1945–1961*, ii. 363.
8. Anselm Doering-Manteuffel, *Die Bundesrepublik Deutschland in der Ära Adenauer* (Darmstadt, 1983), 61–2. Text in Steininger, *Deutsche Geschichte 1945–1961*, ii. 403–4. The controversial transference clause (7(3)), which

could have been binding on a reunited Germany, was dropped when the treaty was revised after the failure of the EDC.

9. One of the most forceful critics of Adenauer's handling of the affair is Rolf Steininger; see *The German Question: The Stalin Note of 1952 and the Problem of Reunification* (New York, 1990).

10. John Wheeler-Bennett and Anthony Nicholls, *The Semblance of Peace: The Political Settlement after the Second World War* (London, 1972), 595. The authors elaborate more than others on Eden's initiative.

11. The most recent and comprehensive treatment is Rainer Hudemann and Raymond Poidevin (eds.), *Die Saar 1945–1955: Ein Problem der europäischen Geschichte* (Munich, 1992).

12. Text of letters by Ollenhauer (23 Jan. 1955) and Adenauer (25 Jan. 1955) in Steininger, *Deutsche Geschichte 1945–1961*, ii. 484–9.

13. See the most recent defence of the controversial Hallstein Doctrine (named after the Secretary of State in the Foreign Ministry and later first President of the European Commission) by Rüdiger M. Booz, '*Hallsteinzeit': Deutsche Außenpolitik 1955–1972* (Bonn, 1995).

14. Hans Buchheim, *Deutschlandpolitik 1949–1972* (Stuttgart, 1974), 99–100. See also Adenauer, *Erinnerungen*, iii. 369–80.

15. Quoted by Curtis Cate, *The Ides of August: The Berlin Wall Crisis 1961* (London, 1978), 140.

16. Apart from Cate, the most comprehensive account in English, see now the chapter in Mitter and Wolle, *Untergang auf Raten*, on the situation in the GDR in the early 1960s, pp. 297–366; also Siegfried Prokop, *Unternehmen 'Chinese Wall': Die DDR im Zwielicht der Mauer* (Frankfurt am Main, 1993), by a 'converted' SED historian.

17. Klaus-Jürgen Müller, *Adenauer and de Gaulle—de Gaulle and Germany: A Special Relationship*, Konrad Adenauer Memorial Lecture 1992, St Antony's College, Oxford (Oxford, 1993).

18. Quoted in Boris Meißner (ed.), *Die deutsche Ostpolitik 1961–1970: Kontinuität und Wandel* (Cologne, 1970), 41. See also Paul Noack, *Die Außenpolitik der Bundesrepublik Deutschland* (Stuttgart, 1981), 92–102.

19. Buchheim, *Deutschlandpolitik 1949–1972*, 100–4.

20. William E. Griffith, *The Ostpolitik of the Federal Republic of Germany* (Cambridge, Mass., 1978), 181.

21. Ibid. 166.

22. *Documentation Relating to the Federal Government's Policy of Détente*, publ. by the Press and Information Office (Bonn, 1978), 18.

23. Ibid. 20. From the German point of view this later formed an integral part of the treaty.

24. Apparently Soviet ambassador Abrassimov rather than his superiors in Moscow was the driving force for a change of leadership. See Julij A. Kwizinskij, *Vor dem Sturm: Erinnerungen eines Diplomaten* (Berlin, 1993), 255–8; also now Gerhard Neumann and Eckhard Trümpler, *Von Ulbricht zu Honecker* (Berlin, 1990).

25. Text of the 'Quadripartite Agreement on Berlin and Agreement between Competent German Authorities' in *Documentation*, 87–152.

26. Text of the treaties with Warsaw and Prague in *Documentation*, 28–82.

27. Theo Sommer, in Frank Grube and Gerhard Richter (eds.), *Der SPD-Staat* (Munich, 1977), 309.

28. Quoted by Bark and Gress, *A History of West Germany*, ii. 178.

29. Friedrich Meinecke, *Weltbürgertum und Nationalstaat* (1907), in *Werke* (Munich, 1969), 9–26.

30. Willy Brandt, *People and Politics: The Years 1960–1975* (Boston, 1975), 372.

31. Benno Zündorf, *Die Ostverträge* (Munich, 1979), 214.

32. Text of the Basic Treaty and Other Agreements with the German Democratic Republic in *Documentation*, 153–293.

33. Quoted by Bark and Gress, *A History of West Germany*, ii. 303–4.

34. See now his somewhat uninspiring memoirs: Hans-Dietrich Genscher, *Erinnerungen* (Berlin, 1995).

35. Schmidt about himself at a meeting of newspaper publishers, 10 Nov. 1981, quoted by Bark and Gress, *A History of West Germany*, ii. 334. See also Helmut Schmidt's Henry L. Stimson Lecture, *A Grand Victory for the West* (New Haven, 1985).

36. See now Mary Fulbrook, *Anatomy of a Dictatorship: Inside the GDR 1949–1989* (Oxford, 1995), 203–36.

37. Annual Address on the State of the Nation, 23 June 1983, quoted by Bark and Gress, *A History of West Germany*, ii. 411. See also Matthias Zimmer, *Nationales Interesse und Staatsraison: Zur Deutschlandpolitik der Regierung Kohl 1982–1989* (Paderborn, 1992), 112–36.

38. See Avril Pittman, *From Ostpolitik to Reunification: West German–Soviet Political Relations since 1974* (Cambridge, 1992).

39. Josef Joffe, in *Süddeutsche Zeitung*, 25–6 Dec. 1988.

40. Bark and Gress, *A History of West Germany*, ii. 546–7, referring to the *San Francisco Chronicle*, 25 Jan. 1989.

Chapter 4 (pages 80–105)

1. See Ben Pimlott (ed.), *The Second World War Diaries of Hugh Dalton (1940–1945)* (London, 1986), 275.

2. John Maynard Keynes, *The Collected Writings*, ed. Donald Moggeridge, vol. xxvi (London, 1979), 337–41.

3. Ernest F. Penrose, *Economic Planning for Peace* (Princeton, NJ, 1953), 63–86.

4. Quoted by Llewellyn Woodward, *British Foreign Policy in the Second World War*, vol. v (London, 1976), 225.

5. Telegram to Octagon, 14 Sept. 1944, quoted by Kettenacker, *Krieg zur Friedenssicherung*, 425.

6. See Cairncross, *The Price of War*.

7. See note 5.

8. The most authoritative account is Rolf Steininger, *Ein neues Land an Rhein und Ruhr* (Cologne, 1990).

9. See especially Werner Abelshauser, *Wirtschaftsgeschichte der Bundesrepublik Deutschland 1945–1980* (Frankfurt am Main, 1983); also Alan Kramer, *The West German Economy, 1945–1955* (Oxford, 1991).

10. Herbert C. Mayer, *German Recovery and the Marshall Plan 1948–1952* (New York, 1969), 100. For allocations to various countries see table on p. 73.

11. See Volker Berghahn, *Unternehmer und Politik in der Bundesrepublik* (Frankfurt am Main, 1985).

12. Nicholls, *Freedom with Responsibility*, 114. See also Dieter Grosser *et al.*, *Soziale Marktwirtschaft: Geschichte, Konzept, Leistung* (Stuttgart, 1988).

13. David McIsaac (ed.), *The United States Strategic Bombing Survey*, vol. i (New York and London, 1976), 230.

14. See Mark Roseman, 'The Uncontrolled Economy: Ruhr Coal Production 1945–58', in Ian Turner (ed.), *Reconstruction in Post-War Germany: British Occupation Policies and the Western Zones* (Oxford, 1989), 93–124.

15. Kramer, *The West German Economy, 1945–1955*, 86.

16. Quoted by Nicholls, *Freedom with Responsibility*, 221.

17. Ibid. 222.

18. Text in *Vierteljahreshefte für Zeitgeschichte*, 30 (1982), 734–8.

19. Nicholls, *Freedom with Responsibility*, 290.

20. See Christoph Buchheim, *Die Wiedereingliederung Westdeutschlands in die Weltwirtschaft, 1945–1958* (Munich, 1990), 171–81.

21. Kramer, *The West German Economy, 1945–1955*, 182.

22. See Hans-Peter Schwarz, *Die gezähmten Deutschen Deutschen: Von der Machtbesessenheit zur Machtvergessenheit* (Stuttgart, 1985).

23. Günther Gillessen, *Konrad Adenauer and Israel*, Konrad Adenauer Memorial Lecture 1986, St Antony's College, Oxford (Oxford, 1986). See also Lily Gardner Feldman, *The Special Relationship between West Germany and Israel* (London, 1984).

24. See the officially sponsored *Facts about Germany* (Frankfurt am Main, 1995), 292.

25. For the following statistics see chiefly Heinrich Lützel, 'Entwicklung des Sozialprodukts 1950–1984', *Wirtschaft und Statistik*, 6 (1985), 433–44.

26. See Ch. 6.

27. For these and similar data see *Facts about Germany*, 236–9 and 264–9.

28. See Peter Hubsch, 'DGB Economic Policy with Particular Reference to the British Zone, 1945–9', in Turner, *Reconstruction in Post-War Germany*, 271–300.

29. Berghahn, *Unternehmer und Politik*, esp. 180–228.

30. Quoted in Nicholls, *Freedom with Responsibility*, 333.

31. Eugon Kogon deplored the relative decline of the professions on German boards; see his *Die Stunde der Ingenieure: Technologische Intelligenz und Politik* (Düsseldorf, 1976).

32. David Marsh, *The Bundesbank: The Bank that Rules Europe* (London, 1992). He asserts, though, about EMU: 'European Monetary Union is not an attempt to expand Germany's dominance. Rather it is an effort, led by France and Italy, to clip Germany's wings' (261).

33. See now the most comprehensive history of the Deutsche Bank, one of the Big Three, along with the Dresdner Bank and the Commerzbank: Lothar Gall *et al.* (eds.), *The Deutsche Bank 1870–1995* (London, 1995).

34. Data from Karl Hardach, *Wirtschaftsgeschichte Deutschlands im 20. Jahrhundert* (Göttingen, 1976), 211, who points out that, significantly, there are no official statistics about the distribution of wealth in the Federal Republic.

35. See the unsurpassed work by Hans-Günther Hockerts, *Sozialpolitische Entscheidungen im Nachkriegsdeutschland: Alliierte und deutsche Sozialpolitik 1945 bis 1957* (Stuttgart, 1980). A useful summary is Detlev Zöllner, 'Sozialpolitik', in Wolfgang Benz (ed.), *Die Geschichte der Bundesrepublik*, vol. ii (Frankfurt am Main, 1989), 362–92.

36. See the memoirs of the chief negotiatior: Ludwig Geißel, *Unterhändler der Menschlichkeit* (Stuttgart, 1991).

37. Helge Heidemeyer, *Flucht und Zuwanderung aus der SBZ/DDR, 1945–1961: Die Flüchtlingspolitik der Bundesrepublik Deutschland bis zum Bau der Berliner Mauer* (Düsseldorf, 1994).

38. Dietrich Staritz, *Geschichte der DDR 1949–1985* (Frankfurt am Main, 1985).

39. *Facts about Germany*, 240–5.

40. See Günter Mittag, *Um jeden Preis: Im Spannungsfeld zweier Systeme* (Berlin, 1991), 128–31.

41. *Berliner Morgenpost*, 11 Feb. 1994, repr. in Andreas Grünberg, *Der eingemauerte Staat: Die DDR vor der 'Wende'* (Stuttgart, 1995), 80.

Chapter 5 (pages 106–124)

1. See Manfred Hanisch, *Für Fürst und Vaterland: Legitimationsstiftung in Bayern zwischen Revolution und deutscher Einheit* (Munich, 1991).

2. See Werner Rutz, Konrad Scherl, and Wilfried Strenz, *Die fünf neuen Bundesländer* (Darmstadt, 1993).

3. Otto von Bismarck, *Gedanken und Erinnerungen* (Goldmann Paperback edn., Munich, n.d.), 222, based on the Friedrichsruher edition, vol. xiii (1932).

4. Cf. Ch. 6.

5. See Kraus, *Ministerien für das ganze Deutschland?*, 102–19.

6. See Frank R. Pfetsch, *Ursprünge der Zweiten Republik: Prozesse der Verfassungsgebung in den Westzonen und in der Bundesrepublik* (Opladen, 1990).

7. *Facts about Germany*, 150.

8. See, more recently, Peter Alter (ed.), *Im Banne der Metropolen: Berlin und London in den Zwanziger Jahren* (Göttingen, 1993).

9. See *Berlin–Bonn, Die Debatte: Alle Bundestagsreden vom 20.6.1991*, ed. Deutscher Bundestag (Cologne, 1991); also Ekkehard Kohrs, *Kontroverse ohne Ende: Der Hauptstadt-Streit* (Weinheim, 1991).

10. Raymond Ebsworth, *Restoring Germany: The British Contribution* (London, 1960), 81.

11. See Wolfgang Rudzio, *Die Neuordnung des Kommunalwesens in der Britischen Zone* (Stuttgart, 1968).

12. See Statistical Appendix, Graph 3.

13. Georg Picht, *Die deutsche Bildungskatastrophe* (Olten and Freiburg, 1964), 17. See also Hansgert Peisert and Gerhild Framhein, *Das Hochschulsystem der Bundesrepublik Deutschland* (Stuttgart, 1979).

14. Michael Mertes, 'Germany's Social and Political Culture: Change through Consensus', *Daedalus* (Winter 1994), 12.

15. Numbers are difficult to obtain, but expenses speak for themselves: a rise from 8,686m DM in 1951 to 276,530m DM in 1991 (see Statistical Appendix, Graph 7).

16. See Klaus Schrode, *Beamtenabgeordnete in Landtagen der Bundesrepublik Deutschland* (Heidelberg, 1977), 273.

17. Comprehensively surveyed by Ulrich Reusch, 'Beamtentum und Beamtenrecht in der Besatzungsära: Die Reformpläne und Reformversuchen der Alliierten für den öffentlichen Dienst in Westdeutschland 1945–1950 (1952)', in Carl August Lückerath (ed.), *Berufsbeamtentum und Beamtenorganisationen* (Cologne, 1987), 53–77.

18. The term, now generally attributed to the social philosopher Jürgen Habermas, was in fact first introduced by the Heidelberg political scientist Dolf Sternberger; see his *Schriften*, vol. x (Frankfurt am Main, 1990), esp. 13–31.

19. As a useful introduction in English see Wolfgang Heyde, *Justice and the Law in the Federal Republic of Germany* (Heidelberg, 1994).

20. Dahrendorf, *Gesellschaft und Demokratie in Deutschland*, 260–76.

21. Quoted in Irmgard Wilharm (ed.), *Deutsche Geschichte 1962–1983*, vol. ii (Frankfurt am Main, 1985), 145.

Chapter 6 (pages 125–158)

1. Max Domerus (ed.), *Hitler: Reden und Proklamationen 1932–1945*, vol. i (Munich, 1965), 116.

2. e.g. Heinrich Triepel. See the useful textbook by Günter Olzog and Arthur Herzig, *Die politischen Parteien in der Bundesrepublik Deutschland* (Munich, 1977), 8.

3. *Grundgesetz der Bundesrepublik Deutschland* (15 Nov. 1994), ed. Deutscher Bundestag (Bonn, 1994), 22. For the problematic nature of modern parties, see Christian Graf von Krockow and Peter Lösche (eds.), *Parteien in der Krise: Das Parteiensystem der Bundesrepublik und der Aufstand des Bürgerwillens* (Munich, 1986).

4. Quoted by Olzog and Herzig, *Die politischen Parteien*, 34.

5. Nevil Johnson, 'Parties and the Conditions of Political Leadership', in Herbert Döring and Gordon Smith (eds.), *Party Government and Political Culture in West Germany* (London, 1982), 154–73.

6. See the excellent study by Karl Rohe, *Wahlen und Wählertraditionen in*

Deutschland (Frankfurt am Main, 1992), 164–91; see also in English Karl Rohe (ed.), *Elections, Parties and Political Traditions: Social Foundations of German Parties and Party Systems, 1967–1987* (Oxford, 1990).

7. See Helga Grebing, 'Die Parteien', in Wolfgang Benz (ed.), *Die Geschichte der Bundesrepublik Deutschland*, vol. i (Frankfurt am Main, 1989), 71–150.

8. See Günter Buchstab and Klaus Gotto, *Die Gründung der Union: Tradition, Entstehung und Repräsentanten* (Munich, 1981); also Wulf Schönbohm, *CDU: Porträt einer Partei* (Munich, 1979), and in English Geoffrey Pridham, *Christian Democracy in Western Germany: The CDU/CSU in Government and Opposition 1945–1976* (London, 1977).

9. The expert on the history of the CSU is Alf Mintzel; see his *Geschichte der CSU: Ein Überblick* (Opladen, 1977).

10. The most authoritative and independent account of its post-war history is Kurt Klotzbach, *Der Weg zur Staatspartei: Programmatik, praktische Politik und Organisation der deutschen Sozialdemokratie 1945 bis 1965* (Bonn, 1982).

11. Schumacher was indeed, as Peter Merseburger suggests in the title of his biography, a 'difficult German'.

12. See Jürgen Dittberner, *FDP—Partei der zweiten Wahl: Ein Beitrag zur Geschichte der liberalen Partei und ihrer Funktion im Parteiensystem der Bundesrepublik* (Opladen, 1987).

13. 'Summary of Principal Peace Feelers, September 1939–March 1941', FO 371/26542/C4216, repr. in Lothar Kettenacker (ed.), *The 'Other Germany' in the Second World War: Emigration and Resistance in International Perspective* (Stuttgart, 1977), 173.

14. For details and political repercussions see Bark and Gress, *A History of West Germany*, i. 498–509.

15. The formative 1950s have now come into their own as a topic of research. The most comprehensive study is now Axel Schildt and Arnold Sywottek, *Modernisierung im Wiederaufbau: Die westdeutsche Gesellschaft der 50er Jahre* (Bonn, 1993); also Werner Abelshauser, *Die Langen Fünfziger Jahre: Wirtschaft und Gesellschaft der Bundesrepublik Deutschland 1949–1966* (Düsseldorf, 1987).

16. See in particular Hermann Korte, *Eine Gesellschaft im Aufbruch: Die Bundesrepublik in den sechziger Jahren* (Frankfurt am Main, 1987).

17. See Elisabeth Nolle-Neumann and Renate Köcher, *Die verletzte Nation: Über den Versuch der Deutschen, ihren Charakter zu ändern* (Stuttgart, 1987), 297 and 341; also Josef Schmid, *Bevölkerungsveränderungen in der Bundesrepublik Deutschland: Eine Revolution auf leisen Sohlen* (Stuttgart, 1984), 93–102.

18. There are, however, exceptions: according to Noelle-Neumann and Köcher (*Die verletzte Nation*, 346), in 1981–2 61% (against 18%) of West Germans, but only 40% (against 42%) of Britons, felt that there ought to be moral rules for sexual behaviour.

19. Klaus Hildebrand, *Geschichte der Bundesrepublik Deutschland*, vol. iv: *Von Erhard zur Großen Koalition (1963–1969)* (Wiesbaden, 1984), 369–71.

20. Apart from Hildebrand's sober assessment see also the intimate account by two of Kiesinger's private secretaries: Reinhard Schmoeckel and Bruno Kaiser, *Die vergessene Regierung: Die große Koalition und ihre langfristigen Wirkungen* (Bonn, 1991).

21. Jeremy Leaman, *The Political Economy of West Germany, 1945–85,* vol. ii (London, 1988), 82–9.

22. See the short but useful survey of the protest movement, including bibliography and chronology, by Dieter Rucht, 'Protestbewegungen', in Benz, *Die Geschichte der Bundesrepublik Deutschland*, iii. 311–44. The British public was misinformed by one-sided English translations such as Sebastian Cobler, *Law, Order and Protest in West Germany* (Harmondsworth, 1978) —'West Germany is on the way to becoming a Big Brother police state' etc., p. 143. A good survey in English is Bob Brown and Wilfried van der Will, *Protest and Democracy in West Germany* (London, 1988).

23. See Schmoeckel and Kaiser, *Die vergessene Regierung*, 233–53; Hildebrand, *Geschichte der Bundesrepublik Deutschland*, iv. 218–40.

24. See Lutz Niethammer, *Angepaßter Faschismus: Politische Praxis der NPD* (Frankfurt am Main, 1969). See also the recent biography of Rudi Dutschke by his wife, Gretchen Dutschke, *Wir hatten ein barbarisches, schönes Leben: Rudi Dutschke—eine Biographie* (Cologne, 1996).

25. The classic on this change-over is Arnulf Baring, *Machtwechsel: Die Ära Brandt-Scheel* (Stuttgart, 1982); see also in English Barbara Marshall, *Willy Brandt* (London, 1990).

26. Quoted by Bark and Gress, *A History of West Germany*, ii. 224.

27. Summary of reform legislation in Peter Borowsky, *Deutschland 1969–1982* (Hanover, 1987), 55–100.

28. Bark and Gress, *A History of West Germany*, ii. 242.

29. See Schmid, *Bevölkerungsveränderungen in der Bundesrepublik Deutschland*, 16–26; also Hermann Korte, 'Bevölkerungsstruktur und -entwicklung', in Benz, *Die Geschichte der Bundesrepublik Deutschland*, iii. 11–34.

30. For his first reaction see Willy Brandt, *Über den Tag hinaus* (Hamburg, 1974), 181.

31. For his motives, see Brandt, *People and Politics*, 399. 54% of those between the ages of 30 and 60 rejected the gesture (Marshall, *Willy Brandt*, 78). See also Willy Brandt, *Erinnerungen* (Frankfurt am Main, 1990), 211–24.

32. See references to Schmidt in Stephen Padgett (ed.), *Adenauer to Kohl: The Development of the German Chancellorship* (London, 1994).

33. See Borowsky, *Deutschland 1969–1982*, 122–8, who lists the most relevant literature.

34. Karl Wilhelm Fricke, *MfS intern: Macht, Strukturen, Auflösung der DDR Staatssicherheit* (Cologne, 1991), 57–60; also Butz Peters, *Terrorismus in Deutschland* (Stuttgart, 1991), 324–34.

35. See Dieter Rebentisch, 'Gipfeldiplomatie und Weltökonomie: Weltwirt-

schaftliches Krisenmanagement während der Kanzlerschaft Helmut Schmidts (1974–1982)', *Archiv für Sozialgeschichte*, 28 (1988), 307–32.

36. For details see Wolfgang Jäger and Werner Link, *Republik im Wandel 1974–1982: Die Ära Schmidt* (Mannheim, 1987), 234–51. See now also Genscher, *Erinnerungen*, 457–64, who emphasizes that the FDP did not wish to desert the coalition government, as Schmidt insinuated.

37. Vernon A. Walters, *Die Vereinigung war voraussehbar: Hinter den Kulissen eines entscheidenden Jahres. Die Aufzeichnungen des amerikanischen Botschafters* (Berlin, 1994), 39.

38. See the two excellent articles by Kenneth Dyson and Nevil Johnson in Döring and Smith, *Party Government and Political Culture in Western Germany*, esp. p. 159.

39. See E. Gene Frankland and Donald Schoonmaker, *Between Protest and Power: The Green Party in Germany* (Boulder, Colo., 1992); also Brown and van der Will, *Protest and Democracy in West Germany*, chs. 5 and 7. For the background, see Karl-Werner Brand *et al.* (eds.), *Aufbruch in eine andere Gesellschaft: Neue soziale Bewegungen in der Bundesrepublik* (Frankfurt am Main, 1983).

40. Kurt Biedenkopf, quoted in ibid. 188.

41. Joschka Fischer, *Risiko Deutschland: Krise und Zukunft der deutschen Politik* (Cologne, 1994), 185–233.

42. See Claus Leggewie, *Die Republikaner: Ein Phantom nimmt Gestalt an* (Berlin, 1990).

43. Quoted in Hans-Joachim Veen *et al.*, *The Republikaner Party in Germany: Right-Wing Menace or Protest Catchall?* (Westport, Conn., 1993), 16–21.

44. Jürgen Falter, *Wer wählt rechts? Die Wähler und Anhänger rechtsextremer Parteien im vereinigten Deutschland* (Munich, 1994), 106.

45. See Klaus von Beyme, 'Der Parteienstaat und die Vertrauenskrise der Politik', in Siegfried Unseld (ed.), *Politik ohne Projekt? Nachdenken über Deutschland* (Frankfurt am Main, 1993), 25.

46. Hans Herbert von Arnim, 'Der Staat—Beute der Parteien?', ibid. 12. Von Beyme, who has exposed party corruption on many occasions, gives a critical response to von Arnim (p. 44).

47. Erwin K. Scheuch and Ute Scheuch, *Cliquen, Klüngel und Karrieren: Über den Verfall der politischen Parteien—eine Studie* (Reinbek, 1992).

48. Gunter Hofmann and Werner A. Perger (eds.), *Die Kontroverse: Weizsäckers Parteienkritik in der Diskussion* (Frankfurt am Main, 1992).

49. See Noelle-Neumann and Köcher, *Die verletzte Nation*, 290.

Chapter 7 (pages 159–178)

1. See Henning Rischbieter, 'Theater', in Benz, *Die Geschichte der Bundesrepublik Deutschland*, iv. 86.

2. Birley was to become Educational Advisor to the British Military Governor in Germany from 1947 to 1949. See Arthur Hearnden (ed.), *The British in Germany: Educational Reconstruction after 1945* (London, 1978).

3. See in particular Jost Hermand, *Kultur im Wiederaufbau: Die Bundesrepublik Deutschland 1945–1965* (Frankfurt am Main and Berlin, 1989).

4. M. Rainer Lepsius, 'Die Bundesrepublik in der Kontinuität und Diskontinuität historischer Entwicklungen: Einige methodische Überlegungen', in Werner Conze and M. Rainer Lepsius (eds.), *Sozialgeschichte der Bundesrepublik Deutschland* (Stuttgart, 1983), pp. 11–19.

5. According to the 1995 edition of *Facts about Germany*, p. 471, the 587 public and 176 private theatres receive over 3 billion DM in subsidies every season.

6. See Jürgen Rostock, 'Risse im Beton', in Gabriele Mutscher and Rüdiger Thomas (eds.), *Jenseits der Staatskultur: Traditionen autonomer Kunst in der DDR* (Munich, 1992), 217–34; also Karl-Heinz Hüter, 'Das Bauhaus in der DDR—Schwierigkeiten einer Rezeption', in Eckhart Gillen and Rainer Haarmann (eds.), *Kunst in der DDR* (Cologne, 1990), 434–9.

7. Kant's much-acclaimed law of ethics and duty is usually quoted in English as follows: 'Act only according to that maxim by which you can at the same time will that it should become a universal law.' Supposedly Martin Bormann, for whom the Führer's will was law, also referred to this Kantian imperative. See interview with his son, *Frankfurter Rundschau*, 3 June 1996.

8. Apart from his incomplete memoirs (*Erinnerungen*, Berlin, 1989) see now the short biography by Wolfgang Krieger, *Franz Josef Strauß: Der barocke Demokrat aus Bayern* (Göttingen, 1995).

9. See the contributions by Josef Mooser about the working class and Jürgen Kocka and Michael Prinz on employees in Conze and Lepsius, *Sozialgeschichte der Bundesrepublik Deutschland*, 143–86 and 210–55.

10. A principle first enunciated by the conference at Bitterfeld on 24 Apr. 1959 postulating that art and literature had to celebrate 'heroism at work'. The motto was: 'Grab a pen, mate, the socialist national literature needs you!'

11. Friedrich Fürstenberg, *Die Sozialstruktur der Bundesrepublik* (Opladen, 1976), 118–31.

12. Jochen Thies, foreign editor of *Die Welt*, has expressed this view more than once; see, for example, 'Observations on the Political Class in Germany', *Daedalus*, 123 (1994), 263–76; also 'Perspektiven deutscher Außenpolitik', in Rainer Zitelmann *et al.* (eds.), *Westbindung: Risiken und Chancen für Deutschland* (Berlin, 1993), 532–3.

13. See John A. Moses, *The Politics of Illusion: The Fischer Controversy in German Historiography* (London, 1975).

14. Richard J. Evans, *In Hitler's Shadow: West German Historians and the Attempt to Escape from the Nazi Past* (London and New York, 1989). Evans takes sides with Hans-Ulrich Wehler, *Entsorgung der deutschen Vergangenheit?* (Munich, 1988). More balanced is Christian Meier, *Vierzig Jahre nach Auschwitz* (Munich, 1987).

15. John Maynard Keynes, *The Economic Consequences of the Peace* (London, 1924), 210.

16. See the two publications by Luchterhand Publishers: Karl Deiritz and Hannes Kraus (eds.), *Der deutsch-deutsche Literaturstreit* (Hamburg, 1991) and Hermann Vinke (ed.), *Akteneinsicht Christa Wolf* (Hamburg, 1993).

17. Fritz-Jochen Kopka, 'Who's Afraid of Christa Wolf?', *Sonntag*, 22 July 1990, in Deiritz and Kraus, *Der deutsch-deutsche Literaturstreit*, 156.

18. Vinke, *Akteneinsicht Christa Wolf*, 148. However, in Jan. 1993 she did not regard herself as a 'victim' of the regime which had both fêted and observed her (*ibid.* 165).

19. *Die Zeit*, 2 Nov. 1990, in Deiritz and Kraus, *Der deutsch-deutsche Literaturstreit*, 139–45.

20. For a sober assessment see Michael Ermath (ed.), *America and the Shaping of German Society 1945–1955* (Providence, RI and Oxford, 1993), especially Arnold Sywottek on everyday life, pp. 132–52. See also Rainer Pommerin (ed.), *The American Impact on Postwar Germany* (Providence, RI and Oxford, 1995), esp. 83–124.

21. Quoted in Kettenacker, *Krieg zur Friedenssicherung*, 378.

22. See the article on 'Rockkultur' in Wolfgang R. Langenbucher *et al.* (eds.), *Kulturpolitisches Wörterbuch: Bundesrepublik/DDR im Vergleich* (Stuttgart, 1983), 614–19; also more recently Christoph Tannert, 'Rock aus dem Unterholz', in Mutscher and Thomas, *Jenseits der Staatskultur*, 155–78.

23. Robert Vansittart, *Black Record* (London, 1941).

24. See the catalogue to the exhibition *The Romantic Spirit in German Art 1790–1990* (London, Edinburgh, and Stuttgart, 1994), first staged by the Royal Scottish Academy and the Fruitmarket Gallery in Edinburgh in 1994.

25. On Sedlmayr's impact see Hermand, *Kultur im Wiederaufbau*, 211–13.

26. Christos Joachimides *et al.* (eds.), *German Art in the 20th Century: Painting and Sculpture 1905–1985*, exhibition catalogue (Munich, 1985), 56.

27. Ibid. 64.

28. See Ullrich Kuhirt (ed.), *Kunst der DDR 1945–1980* (Leipzig, 1982–3).

29. Eckhart Gillen and Rainer Haarmann, *Kunst in der DDR* (Cologne, 1990), 377.

30. See the exhibition catalogue, *Auftrag: Kunst 1949–1990. Bildende Künstler in der DDR zwischen Ästhetik und Politik*, ed. Monika Flacke (Munich and Berlin, 1995). The climax of commissioned art was Werner Tübke's gigantic panorama of the Peasants' War near Bad Frankenhausen (ibid. 369–82).

31. For details see Günter Freist, 'Künstlergilde VBK', in Gillen and Haarmann, *Kunst in der DDR*, 49–54.

32. See *Eigenart und Eigensinn: Alternative Kunstszenen in der DDR (1980–1990)*, ed. Forschungsstelle Osteuropa (Bremen, 1993); see also Mutscher and Thomas, *Jenseits der Staatskultur*.

33. Doris Schmidt, 'Bildende Kunst', in Benz, *Die Geschichte der Bundesrepublik*, iv. 265.
34. See the excellent article by Friedrich P. Kahlenberg, president of the Federal Archives, ibid. iv. 464–512.

Chapter 8 (pages 179–212)

1. No famous quotation demonstrates more clearly the change in Germany's political culture than Bismarck's words in the Prussian Diet on 30 Sept. 1862: *'Nicht durch Reden und Majoritätsbeschlüsse werden die Großen Fragen der Zeit entschieden—das ist der Fehler von 1848 und 1849 gewesen—, sondern durch Eisen und Blut'* The great questions of our time are not resolved by speeches and majority decisions—that was the mistake of 1848–9—but by iron and blood: (Georg Büchmann (ed.), *Geflügelte Worte* (Berlin, 1918), 546).
2. See p. 63.
3. Günter Schabowski, *Das Politbüro: Ende eines Mythos* (Hamburg, 1990).
4. Markus Wolf, *In eigenem Auftrag* (Munich, 1991).
5. See also Otto Wenzel, *Kriegsbereitschaft: Der Nationale Verteidigungsrat der DDR 1960 bis 1989* (Cologne, 1995).
6. Peter Bender, *Deutsche Parallelen: Anmerkungen zu einer gemeinsamen Geschichte zweier getrennter Staaten* (Berlin, 1989), 134–5.
7. Text in Bundesministerium für innerdeutsche Beziehungen (ed.), *Texte zur Deutschlandpolitik*, Ser. III, vol. ii (Bonn, 1985), 45–7.
8. See his impressive State of the Nation Address on 23 June 1983, quoted extensively in Bark and Gress, *A History of West Germany*, ii. 411–12; also Zimmer, *Nationales Interesse und Staatsräson*.
9. Mittag, *Um jeden Preis*, 83.
10. Konrad H. Jarausch and Volker Gransow (eds.), *Uniting Germany: Documents and Debates 1944–1993* (Providence, RI, 1994), 25–7; *Die Zeit*, 22 Sept. 1989.
11. See above all A. James MacAdams, *Germany Divided: From the Wall to Unification* (Princeton, NJ, 1993), 173–9.
12. Ibid. 179.
13. On the Honecker–Gorbachev relationship in the context of Eastern Europe, see Elizabeth Pond, *Beyond the Wall: Germany's Road to Unification* (Washington, DC, 1993), 69–84.
14. Ernest Plock, *East German–West German Relations and the Fall of the GDR* (Boulder, Colo., 1993), 144.
15. See Konrad H. Jarausch, *The Rush to German Unity* (Oxford, 1994), 58.
16. *Izvestia*, 16 Oct. 1988, quoted by Philip Zelikow and Condoleezza Rice, *Germany Unified and Europe Transformed* (Cambridge, Mass. and London, 1996), 33.
17. Hans-Peter Schwarz, 'Mit gestopften Trompeten: Die Wiedervereinigung Deutschlands aus der Sicht westdeutscher Historiker', *Geschichte in Wissenschaft und Unterricht*, 44 (1993), 683–704.

18. Walters, *Die Vereinigung war voraussehbar*, 36 and 90–1. See also Genscher, *Erinnerungen*, 670–2.

19. Officially the Brezhnev Doctrine was repudiated when Gorbachev addressed the Council of Europe in Strasburg in July 1989. See Zimmer, *Nationales Interesse und Staatsräson*, 206.

20. See Gert-Joachim Glässner, *The Unification Process in Germany: From Dictatorship to Democracy* (London, 1992).

21. The best description of the exodus is by Genscher's *chef de cabinet* Frank Elbe (and Richard Kiessler), *A Round Table with Sharp Corners: The Diplomatic Path to German Unity* (Baden-Baden, 1996), 32–42.

22. For a visual impression see Wolfgang Schneider (ed.), *Leipziger Demontagebuch* (Leipzig and Weimar, 1990).

23. See his self-justification in Mittag, *Um jeden Preis*, 179–80.

24. See Pond, *Beyond the Wall*, 106.

25. See Schabowski, *Das Politbüro* and Egon Krenz, *Wenn Mauern fallen: Die friedliche Revolution: Vorgeschichte, Ablauf, Auswirkungen* (Vienna, 1990).

26. See Ekkehard Kuhn, *Der Tag der Entscheidung: Leipzig, 9. Oktober 1989* (Berlin, 1992).

27. The most pertinent of which is Richard Schröder, *Vom Gebrauch der Freiheit: Gedanken über Deutschland nach der Vereinigung* (Stuttgart, 1996), 162–7; also, in English, Robert F. Goeckel, *The Lutheran Church and the East German State* (London and Ithaca, NY, 1990), and Wolf Jürgen Grabner *et al.* (eds.), *Leipzig im Oktober. Kirchen und alternativen Gruppen im Umbruch der DDR: Analysen zur Wende* (Berlin, 1990) and Günter Hanisch *et al.* (eds.), *Dona nobis pacem: Fürbitten und Friedensgebete Herbst '89 in Leipzig* (Berlin, 1990). See also the articles by Heino Falcke and Edelbert Richter in Günther Heydemann and Lothar Kettenacker (eds.), *Kirchen in der Diktatur: Drittes Reich und SED-Staat* (Göttingen, 1993), pp. 259–81 and 313–20 respectively. See also Fulbrook, *Anatomy of a Dictatorship*, 87–125.

28. Heino Falcke, 'Die Kirchen sind jetz die Politik nicht los', in Gerhard Rein (ed.), *Die Opposition in der DDR: Entwürfe für einen anderen Sozialismus* (Berlin, 1989), 228.

29. See documentation, in English, of the citizens' movement in Glässner, *The Unification Process in Germany*, 137–54, also Jarausch and Gransow, *Uniting Germany*, 30–63.

30. See graph in Andreas Grünberg, *'Wir sind das Volk': Der Weg der DDR zur deutschen Einheit* (Stuttgart, 1990), 59. See also Timothy Garton Ash, *We are the People* (London, 1990), 61–77.

31. See Schneider, *Leipziger Demontagebuch*.

32. See the report by the *Süddeutsche Zeitung*, quoted extensively by Bark and Gress, *A History of West Germany*, 649–50. For general background to this see Ralf Georg Reuth and Andreas Bönte, *Das Komplott: Wie es wirklich zur deutschen Einheit kam* (Munich, 1993).

33. The most thorough investigation among many books on the Stasi is David Gill and Ulrich Schröter, *Das Ministerium für Staatssicherheit: Anatomie des Mielke-Imperiums* (Berlin, 1991).

34. This is how Schröder sees it (*Vom Gebrauch der Freiheit*, 16).

35. See Schneider, *Leipziger Demontagebuch passim* (translation of slogans mine). In West German publications these posters were generally suppressed.

36. See Günter Rarki and Peter Förster, 'Leipziger Demoskopie', ibid. 173–6.

37. Text in Jarausch and Gransow, *Uniting Germany*, 85.

38. Pond, *Beyond the Wall*, 137.

39. Text in Jarausch and Gransow, *Uniting Germany*, 86–9. For its diplomatic repercussions, see Elbe and Kiessler, *A Round Table with Sharp Corners*, 48–54.

40. See Helmut Kohl, *Ich wollte Deutschlands Einheit* (Berlin, 1996), 159; Horst Teltschik, *329 Tage: Innenansichten der Einigung* (Berlin, 1991), 42–5.

41. See ibid. 55; also Pond, *Beyond the Wall*, 161–9 ('The American Yes'). For an inside account of US policy towards Germany see Zelikow and Rice, *Germany Unified*.

42. Kwizinskij, *Vor dem Sturm*, 11–16.

43. Elbe and Kiessler, *A Round Table with Sharp Corners*, 94–5. '*Ja-Wort*' is taken from the German original because it refers to the acceptance of a marriage proposal. See also Teltschik, *329 Tage*.

44. Zelikow and Rice, *Germany Unified*.

45. Elbe and Kiessler, *A Round Table with Sharp Corners*, 84, 102.

46. Valentin Falin, *Politische Erinnerungen* (Munich, 1993), 480–92.

47. Kwizinskij, *Vor dem Sturm*, 18.

48. Zelikow and Rice, *Germany Unified*, 255.

49. See Falin, *Politische Erinnerungen*, 492.

50. See Teltschik, *329 Tage*, 230–5.

51. Margaret Thatcher, *The Downing Street Years* (London, 1993), 769 and 797. She saw 'at once' that the revolution for freedom sweeping Eastern Europe had 'profound implications for the balance of power in Europe, where a reunified Germany would be dominant'.

52. Quoted by Elbe and Kiessler, *A Round Table with Sharp Corners*, 64. See also Karl Kaiser, *Deutschlands Vereinigung: Die Internationalen Aspekte* (Bergisch Gladbach, 1991), 64–8, as well as Julian Bullard, 'Die britische Haltung zur deutschen Wiedervereinigung', in Josef Becker (ed.), *Wiedervereinigung in Mitteleuropa* (Munich, 1992), 27–42.

53. See Kettenacker, *Krieg zur Friedenssicherung*, 479–502.

54. See Elbe and Kiessler, *A Round Table with Sharp Corners*, 59; Kaiser, *Deutschlands Vereinigung*, 65.

55. Text ibid. 358–60.

56. According to Elbe and Kiessler, *A Round Table with Sharp Corners*, 112; also Jarausch, *The Rush to German Unity*, 164–5.

57. Glässner, *The Unification Process in Germany*, 59.

58. See Helmut Herles and Ewald Rose (eds.), *Parlaments-Szenen einer deutschen Revolution: Bundestag und Volkskammer im November 1989* (Bonn, 1989), 193. See also the last attempt to stem the flood in Armin Mitter and Stefan Wolle (eds.), *Ich liebe euch doch alle! Befehle und Lageberichte des MfS. Januar–November 1989* (Berlin, 1990); and Fulbrook, *Anatomy of a Dictatorship*, 45–56.

59. Uwe Thaysen, *Der Runde Tisch oder: Wo bleibt das Volk? Der Weg der DDR in die Demokratie* (Opladen, 1990), 76.

60. Detailed results in Weber, *DDR*, 230–2; for voting behaviour see Glässner, *The Unification Process in Germany*, 86–90.

61. Text ibid. 176–95.

62. Statement on 18 May 1990, ibid. 201. More controversial was his claim that 'No one will be worse off than he has been. Quite the contrary!' (ibid. 98).

63. Shortened English version in Jarausch and Gransow, *Uniting Germany*, 188–99. See also Wolfgang Schäuble, *Der Vertrag: Wie ich über die deutsche Einheit verhandelte* (Munich, 1993).

64. Elbe and Kiessler, *A Round Table with Sharp Corners*, 119.

65. See ibid. 132–6.

66. Ibid. 143.

67. Zelikow and Rice, *Germany Unified*, 323.

68. The most detailed account is by a government press spokesman, Hans Klein: *Es begann im Kauskasus: Der entscheidende Schritt in die Einheit Deutschlands* (Berlin, 1991); also Teltschik, *329 Tage*, 313–45.

69. Text in Kaiser, *Deutschlands Vereinigung*, 260–8; Elbe and Kiessler, *A Round Table with Sharp Corners*, 193–200.

70. Ibid. 198. Britain's last-minute intervention only served to strengthen the new German-Russian entente: Kwizinskij, *Vor dem Sturm*, 60–3.

71. Text in Kaiser, *Deutschlands Vereinigung*, 346–60.

72. The Treuhand, staffed by many officials of the old regime, had been set up by the Volkskammer on 17 June 1990. For its charter see Jarausch and Gransow, *Uniting Germany*, 164–6.

73. Marc Kemmler, *Die Entstehung der Treuhand: Von der Wahrung zur Privatisierung des DDR-Volkseigentums* (Frankfurt am Main, 1994), 354; see also A. Ghanie Ghaussey and Wolf Schäfer (eds.), *The Economics of German Unification* (London and New York, 1993).

74. See the *Spiegel* interview with the economist Hans-Werner Sinn, 17 June 1996. This is disputed by Rudolf Hickel and Jan Priewe (*Nach dem Fehlstart: Ökonomische Perspektiven der deutschen Einigung*, Frankfurt am Main, 1994, 39–45), who argue that it would not have stemmed the flood of migration from East to West.

75. For a first sober assessment of privatization see Christopher Freese, *Die Privatisierungstätigkeit der Treuhandanstalt: Strategien und Verfahren der*

Privatisierung in der Systemtransformation (Frankfurt am Main, 1995); also Hickel and Priewe, *Nach dem Fehlstart*, 47–82.

76. See ibid. 21. See also Gaussy and Schäfer, *The Economics of German Unification*.

Chapter 9 (pages 213–235)

1. See, for example, Udo Wengst (ed.), *Historiker betrachten Deutschland: Beiträge zum Vereinigungsprozeß und zur Hauptstadtdiskussion* (Bonn, 1992). See also the perceptive review of other titles of this sort by Peter Pulzer, 'Nation-State and National Sovereignty', *Bulletin of the German Historical Institute, London*, 17:3 (1995), 5–14.

2. See Jürgen Kocka, 'Crisis of Unification: How Germany Changes', *Daedalus*, 123 (1994), 186; also Wolfgang Hardtwig and Heinrich August Winkler (eds.), *Deutsche Entfremdung: Zum Befinden in Ost und West* (Munich, 1994).

3. Quoted in *Spiegel*, 17 Aug. 1992.

4. Anne-Marie Le Gloannec, 'On German Identity', *Daedalus*, 123 (1994), 133.

5. There is now a law in place called *'Standortsicherungsgesetz'* (Law for the Assurance of Germany as a Productive Site). The campaign against the overindulgent welfare state has been conducted most vigorously by the *Frankfurter Allgemeine Zeitung* and *Der Spiegel* (e.g. 13 May 1996: 'Schlaraffenland ist abgebrannt: Die Pleite des Sozialstaates').

6. Kurt J. Land, 'Germany at the Crossroads: On the Efficiency of the German Economy', *Daedalus*, 123 (1994), 78.

7. English text of his speech in Mainz (May 1989) in *Jahresbericht des Koordinators für die deutsch-amerikanische zwischengesellschaftliche, kultur- und informationspolitische Zusammenarbeit* (Bonn [Auswärtiges Amt], 1990).

8. See Jochen Thies, 'Germany: Europe's Reluctant Great Power', *The World Today* (Royal Institute of International Affairs), 51:10 (Oct. 1995), 189.

9. According to *Der Spiegel* (3 June 1996, p. 24), there were 160,000 applications for 1995 even though alternative service is 15 months, five months longer than ordinary military service. 51% of West Germans and 38% of East Germans approved of those opting for *Zivildienst*. For an account by the West German general charged with winding up the NVA and incorporating the remnants into the Bundeswehr see Jörg Schönbohm, *Two Armies and One Fatherland: The End of the Nationale Volksarmee* (Oxford, 1996).

10. See Klaus Sühl (ed.), *Vergangenheitsbewältigung 1945 und 1989: Ein unmöglicher Vergleich?* (Berlin, 1994).

11. Schröder, *Gebrauch der Freiheit*, 26 and 94. See also Lothar Mertens, 'Die SED und die NS-Vergangenheit', in Werner Bergmann *et al.* (eds.), *Schwieriges Erbe* (Frankfurt am Main, 1995), 194–211.

12. Theodor W. Adorno *et al.*, *The Authoritarian Personality* (New York, 1950).
13. Hans-Joachim Maaz, *Der Gefühlstau: Ein Psychoprogramm der DDR* (Berlin, 1991), esp. 135–83; see also his *Die Entrüstung* (Berlin, 1992), 75, and Michael Schmitz, *Wendestress: Die psychologischen Kosten der deutschen Einheit* (Berlin, 1995).
14. See Maaz, *Die Entrüstung*, 39–48.
15. PID-Report, 24 Aug. 1945, Public Record Office: FO 1049/264.
16. *Der Spiegel*, 3 July 1995, p. 49.
17. For the equivalent practice in the GDR see Chronology, German Democratic Republic, entry for 6 Nov. 1952.
18. Jarausch, *The Rush to German Unity*, 182 and 199.
19. Social justice is marginally more important than freedom for 40% of West Germans (Aug. 1995) and 63% of East Germans. For East Germans personal freedom counted for more in Mar. 1990 (46%) than in Aug. 1995 (36%). See Elisabeth Noelle-Neumann, 'Die linken und rechten Werte: Ein Ringen um das Meinungsklima', in Karl Graf Ballestrem and Henning Ottmann (eds.), *Theorie und Praxis: Festschrift für Nikolas Lobkowitz* (Berlin, 1996), 243–67; see also Noelle-Neumann's article 'Die Dritte Partei', *Frankfurter Allgemeine Zeitung*, 12 July 1985.
20. *Der Spiegel*, 3 July 1995, pp. 43 and 46; Schröder, *Gebrauch der Freiheit*, 36.
21. The percentage of positive answers on the nature of National Socialism ('a good thing, badly carried out') never dropped below 42% between Nov. 1945 and Jan. 1948. See Michael Balfour, 'In Retrospect: Britain's Policy of Re-education', in Nicholas Pronay and Keith Wilson (eds.), *The Political Re-education of Germany and her Allies* (London, 1985), 148.
22. One indication is church tax. The revenue of all the new *Länder* for 1994 is considerably less than that of the Protestant diocese of Nordelbien (Hamburg and Schleswig-Holstein); see Statistical Appendix, Graph 12.
23. See Ulrich Kühn, 'Die theologische Rechtfertigung der "Obrigkeit" ', in Heydemann and Kettenacker, *Kirchen in der Diktatur*, 238–58.
24. Peter Bender, *Unsere Erbschaft: Was war die DDR—was bleibt von ihr?* (Hamburg, 1992), 155.
25. See the very perceptive chapter 'Patterns of Popular Compliance and Complaint', in Fulbrook, *Anatomy of a Dictatorship*, 129–50.
26. Latest figures in *Der Spiegel*, 23 Oct. 1995. See also on the expansion of the 'service' Joachim Gauck, *Die Stasi-Akten: Das unheimliche Erbe der DDR* (Reinbek, 1992), 61–8.
27. Friedrich Schorlemmer, *Zu seinem Wort stehen* (Munich, 1994), 38.
28. Alan Watson, *The Germans: Who Are They Now?* (London, 1994), 310–20.
29. See Alexander Fischer and Günther Heydemann (eds.), *Geschichtswissenschaft in der DDR*, 2 vols. (Berlin, 1988–90).
30. Marianne Krüger-Potratz, *Anderssein gab es nicht: Ausländer und Minderheiten in der DDR* (Münster, 1991).

31. See now the badly phrased paragraph 16a of the Basic Law, which is one detailed qualification of the first sentence: *Politisch Verfolgte genießen Asylrecht* (Victims of political persecution are entitled to asylum). See also Jürgen Fijalkowski, 'Aggressive Nationalism, Immigration Pressure, and Asylum Policy Disputes in Contemporary Germany', Occasional Paper No. 9, German Historical Institute Washington (Washington, DC, 1993).

32. Karl-Heinz Heinemann and Wilfried Schubarth (ed.), *Der antifaschistische Staat entläßt seine Kinder: Jugend und Rechtsextremismus in Ostdeutschland* (Cologne, 1992).

33. Xenien, 'Gifts to Departing Guests' (satirical verses by Goethe and Schiller, published in *Musenalmanach*, 1797). See Peter Alter, *Nationalism*, 2nd edn. (London, 1994), 60.

34. See for example the collection of essays by Peter Glotz, *Die falsche Normalisierung* (Frankfurt am Main, 1994).

35. Heinrich August Winkler, 'Rebuilding a Nation: The Germans before and after Unification', *Daedalus*, 123 (1994), 123. See also his 'Auf dem Weg zur neuen Nation', *Berliner Morgenpost*, 9 Apr. 1995.

36. Schröder, *Vom Gebrauch der Freiheit*, 47.

37. Lothar Kettenacker, *Nationalsozialistische Volkstumspolitik in Elsaß* (Stuttgart, 1973), 175.

38. Richard Schröder, *Deutschland schwierig Vaterland: Für eine neue politische Kultur* (Freiburg, 1993), 25.

39. See Wolfgang Schäuble's speech: 'The Future of Europe in an Era of Transition'. Konrad Adenauer Memorial Lecture 1995, St Antony's College, Oxford (Oxford, 1995).

40. See in particular Hans-Peter Schwarz, *Die Zentralmacht Europas: Deutschlands Rückkehr auf die Weltbühne* (Berlin, 1994) and Gregor Schöllgen, *Angst vor der Macht: Die Deutschen und ihre Außenpolitik* (Berlin, 1993). See also Arnulf Baring (ed.), *Germany's New Position in Europe: Problems and Perspectives* (Oxford, 1994), and the collection of papers given at St Antony's College, Oxford and edited by Hans-Peter Schwarz and Gregor Schöllgen.

41. Rainer Zitelmann *et al.* (eds.), *Westbindung: Risiken und Chancen für Deutschland* (Berlin, 1993). See note 1.

42. Christoph Bertram, 'The Power and the Past: Germany's New International Loneliness', in Baring, *Germany's New Position in Europe*, 104.

Chapter 10 (pages 236–244)

1. Christian Graf von Krockow, *Die Deutschen in ihrem Jahrhundert 1880–1990* (Reinbek, 1990), 290.

2. Expressed by Hans-Joachim Hahn, *German Thought and Culture: From the Holy Roman Empire to the Present Day* (Manchester, 1995), 224. Hahn, like many re-educated and well-meaning Germans, is confused about national identity and nationalism.

3. Representative of the other names mentioned, but intellectually more forceful, is Schwarz, *Die Zentralmacht Europas*.

4. See Christian Hacke, *Weltmacht wider Willen: Die Außenpolitik der Bundesrepublik Deutschland*, new edn. (Frankfurt am Main and Berlin, 1993), 584–93.

5. David Marsh, *The New Germany at the Crossroads* (London, 1989), 288.

6. From the poem by Emanuel Geibel, 'Deutschlands Beruf' (1861).

7. For statistical details see *Five Years On: Drawing the Balance*, ed. the German Embassy (London, 1995).

8. Eric Owen Smith, *The German Economy* (London and New York, 1994), 540.

9. Klaus Hildebrand, *Das vergangene Reich* (Stuttgart, 1994).

Statistical Appendix

Statistical Appendix

1. Population by Age Groups (millions)

	Total Population	under 1	1–5	6–13	14	15–17	18–20	21–39	40–59	60–64	65 and over
1951	51.4	0.76	3.6	6.6	0.86	2.5	2.0	13.2	14.5	2.4	4.9
1956	53.3	0.82	3.8	5.60	0.75	2.9	2.7	13.7	14.8	2.7	5.5
1961	56.6	0.98	4.4	6.2	0.71	2.0	2.5	15.6	14.5	3.3	6.3
1966	59.8	1.0	5.1	6.8	0.78	2.4	2.2	16.2	14.3	3.6	7.4
1971	61.5	0.76	4.6	7.8	0.87	2.5	2.4	16.5	14.0	3.7	8.3
1976	61.4	0.59	3.3	7.8	1.0	2.9	2.7	16.5	14.5	3.1	9.1
1981	61.7	0.62	3.0.	6.0	1.0	3.2	3.2	16.2	16.3	2.7	9.4
1986	61.1	0.63	3.0	4.7	0.69	2.5	3.1	17.8	16.2	3.3	9.3
1991*	80.3	0.83	4.5	6.9	0.82	2.4	2.8	24.3	21.2	4.4	12.0

* 1991 figures for unified Germany
Source: Statistisches Bundesamt, Wiesbaden

2. Population and Foreigners: Selected Nationalities (millions)

	Total Population[a]	Total Number of Foreigners[b]	Total Number of Italians[b]	Total Number of Yugoslavs[b]	Total Number of Spaniards[b]	Total Number of Turks[b]
1951	51.4	0.5	0.02	0.02	0.001	0.001
1956[c]	53.3					
1961	56.6	0.7	0.2	0.02	0.04	0.007
1966[c]	59.8					
1971	61.5	3.4	0.59	0.59	0.28	0.65
1976	61.4	3.9	0.57	0.64	0.22	1.1
1981	61.7	4.6	0.62	0.64	0.18	1.5
1986	61.1	4.5	0.54	0.59	0.15	1.4
1991	80.3*	5.9	0.56	0.78	0.14	1.8
1992	81	6.5	0.56	Table 2a	0.13	1.9
1993	81.3	6.9	0.56	Table 2a	0.13	1.9
1994	81.5	7.0	0.57	Table 2a	0.13	2.0
1995	81.8[1]	7.1	0.59	Table 2a	0.13	2.0

* Figures from 1991 are for unified Germany.
a 1995 census dated 31 Dec.
b 1951 census dated 1 Oct.; 1961, 6 June; 1971, 31 Dec.; 1976 and 1981, 30 Sept.; 1986 to 1995, 31 Dec.
c No figures for 1956 and 1966 available.
Source: Statistisches Bundesamt, Wiesbaden.

2a. Foreigners from the new independent states of the former Yugoslavia, 1992 onward (millions)

	Total Population[a]	Total Number of Foreigners[b]	Bosnia-Herzogovina[b]	Croatia[b]	Yugoslavia[b]	Macedonia[b]	Slovenia[b]
1992	81.0	6.5	0.02	0.08	0.92	0.0	0.0
1993	81.3	6.9	0.14	0.15	0.93	0.003	0.01
1994	81.5	7.0	0.25	0.18	0.83	0.02	0.02
1995	81.8 [1]	7.2	0.32	0.19	0.80	0.03	0.02

a 1995 census dated 31 Dec.
b 1992 to 1995 censuses dated 31 Dec.
Source: Statistisches Bundesamt, Wiesbaden

3. Students (Winter Semester)
(in thousands)

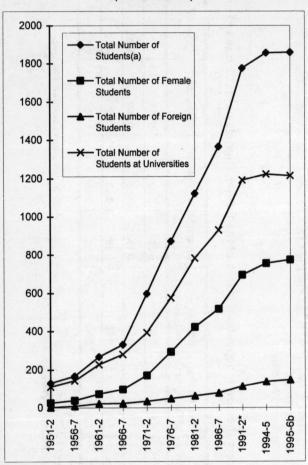

* Unified Germany from 1991

(a) Includes all higher education establishments

(b) Provisional

Source: Statistisches Bundesamt, Wiesbaden

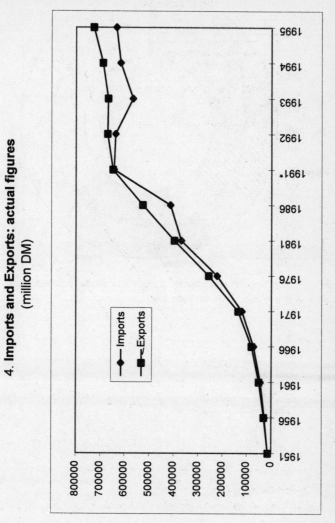

4. Imports and Exports: actual figures
(million DM)

* Figures from 1991 are for unified Germany.

Source: Statistisches Bundesamt, Wiesbaden

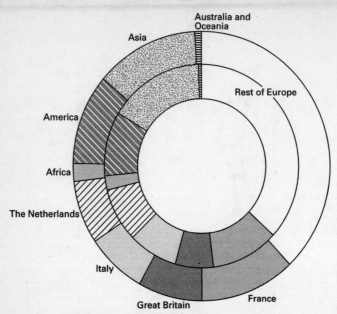

Graph 5. German Imports and Exports: Europe as a whole, Selected Countries, Rest of the World; 1994 (million DM)

6. Gross Domestic Product
(million DM)

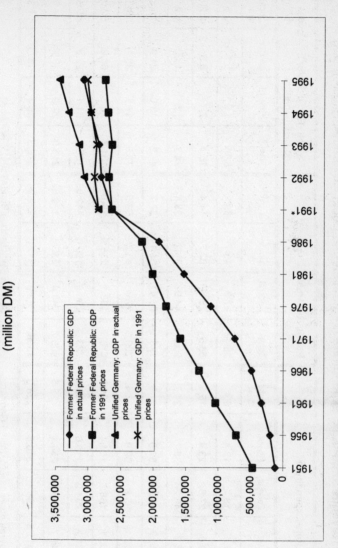

Legend:
- Former Federal Republic: GDP in actual prices
- Former Federal Republic: GDP in 1991 prices
- Unified Germany: GDP in actual prices
- Unified Germany: GDP in 1991 prices

Years: 1951, 1956, 1961, 1966, 1971, 1976, 1981, 1986, 1991*, 1992, 1993, 1994, 1995

Values: 0, 500,000, 1,000,000, 1,500,000, 2,000,000, 2,500,000, 3,000,000, 3,500,000

* Figures from 1991 are for unified Germany.
Source: Statistisches Bundesamt, Wiesbaden

7. Public Revenue and Public Expenditure (Federal/*Länder*/Local Government) (billion DM)

	Public Expenditure				Public Revenue				Payroll (Public Sector Employees and Civil Servants)			
	Total	Federal	*Länder*	Local Govt.	Total	Federal	*Länder*	Local Govt.	Total	Federal	*Länder*	Local Govt.
1951	37.4	18.7	13.4	8.4	36.1	17.3	13.7	8.4	8.7	1.0	5.1	2.6
1956	60.0	27.8	23.4	15.5	58.6	28.3	22.7	14.4	15.4	2.7	8.5	4.2
1961	95.3	46.2	36.7	24.2	95.6	44.9	39.2	23.4	24.7	5.5	13.0	6.2
1966	146.7	68.5	57.9	41.0	138.1	66.4	54.1	37.7	41.3	10.0	21.0	10.3
1971	225.1	98.8	89.0	67.4	209.8	97.6	83.5	58.5	73.5	17.1	38.1	18.3
1976	560.1	166.7	154.4	104.3	513.3	138.1	138.9	100.4	131.3	26.3	66.2	32.0
1981	791.2	234.9	216.6	152.1	723.6	196.9	190.6	142.0	182.1	34.1	92.8	45.6
1986	941.7	263.7	254.1	172.5	905.7	240.4	236.4	170.8	213.0	37.9	108.1	54.5
1991*	1411.8	406.1	330.8	228.9	1306	352.9	312.5	222.9	276.5	48.7	137.6	71.6

* Federal figures apply only to unified Germany

Source: Statistisches Bundesamt, Wiesbaden

8. Public Debt: Banks and Private Sector
(billion DM)

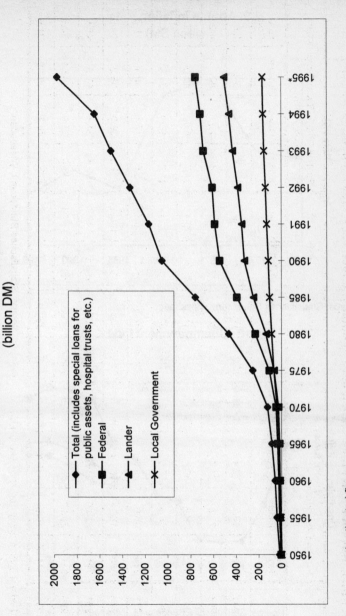

◆ Total (includes special loans for public assets, hospital trusts, etc.)

■ Federal

◀ Lander

✕ Local Government

* estimated figures

Source: Statistisches Bundesamt, Wiesbaden

9. Annual Inflation Rate
(million DM)

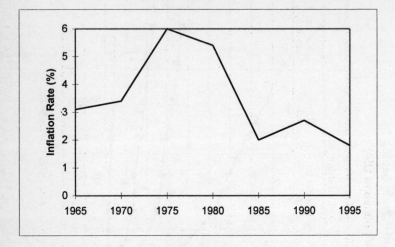

Source: Statistisches Bundesamt, Wiesbaden

10. Unemployment Index

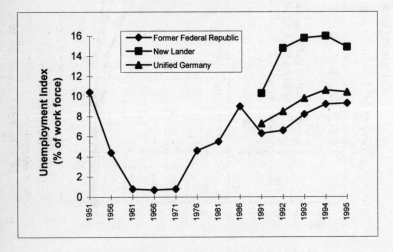

Source: Statistisches Bundesamt, Wiesbaden

11. Average Wages and Salaries per Employee (thousand DM)

	Former Federal Republic			Unified Germany		
	Annual Gross Income[a]	Annual Gross Salary/Wages	Annual Net Salary/Wages	Annual Gross Income[a]	Annual Gross Salary/Wages	Annual Net Salary/Wages
1960	7.1	6.1	5.2			
1965	10.5	9.3	7.7			
1970	16.2	13.8	10.7			
1975	27.3	22.4	16.3			
1980	36.2	29.7	21.2			
1985	44.5	35.8	24.1			
1990	51.7	42.0	29.2			
1991*	54.9	44.5	30.1	48.6	39.6	27.1
1992	58.1	47.1	31.3	53.6	43.7	29.3
1993	60.0	48.4	32.2	56.1	45.5	30.6
1994	61.6	49.3	32.2	57.9	46.7	30.7

* Figures are provisional from 1991. [a] Includes all employer's contributions.

Source: Statistisches Bundesamt, Wiesbaden

12. Church Taxes[1] (net, billion DM)

	Total	Protestant	Catholic
1975	6.4	3.5	2.9
1980	9.3	4.9	4.5
1985	11.1	5.6	5.5
1990	13.1	6.5	6.6
1991*	15.2	7.6	7.6
1992	16.9	8.4	8.5
1993	16.8	8.4	8.4
1994	16.5	8.2	8.2
1995	16.8	8.4	8.4

[1] Church tax is an additional tax, calculated as a percentage of income tax (8–10%)

Division of Church Taxes between Former Federal Republic and New *Länder*

		Former Federal Republic		New *Länder*	
	Total	Protestant	Catholic	Protestant	Catholic
1991*	15.2	7.5	7.6	0.14	0.02
1992	16.9	8.1	8.4	0.34	0.07
1993	16.8	8.0	8.3	0.43	0.09
1994	16.5	7.7	8.1	0.52	0.11
1995	16.7	7.9	8.3	0.49	0.11

* up to 1991 former Federal Republic, thereafter unified Germany

Sources: Evangelische Kirche in Deutschland, Hanover
Steuerkommission des Verbandes der Diözesen Deutschlands, Münster

Chronology

6 Sept.	Speech by US Foreign Secretary Byrnes in Stuttgart: signals new departure of US policy for Germany
19 Sept.	Speech by Churchill in Zurich: calls for 'United States of Europe'
20 Oct.	Elections for Greater Berlin, under Allied supervision

1947

1 Jan.	British and American zones fused into Bizone. Joint Economic Council established
25 Feb.	State of Prussia officially dissolved by Control Council
10 Mar.–	Conference of Foreign Ministers: agrees on release of all
24 Apr.	German prisoners of war by 31 December 1948
4 June	SMAD sets up Deutsche Wirtschaftskommission (DWK)
5 June	Marshall announces European Recovery Programme (Marshall Plan)
5–7 June	Conference of all *Länder* Minister-Presidents in Munich fails to hold Germany together
25 Nov.–	Fifth Conference of Foreign Ministers in London: definite
15 Dec.	breakup of wartime alliance and intensification of Cold War
6–7 Dec.	SED calls for a German People's Congress (Deutscher Volkskongreß)

1948

9 Feb.	Frankfurt Wirtschaftsrat (Economic Council) takes on character of West German parliament (104 members)
12 Feb.	DWK of Soviet Zone empowered to exercise governmental functions
23 Feb.–	London Six Power Conference (three Western Allies and
6 Mar.	Benelux states): recommends federal system for West Germany as precondition for unification
17 Mar.	Brussels Pact signed
17–18 Mar.	Second Deutscher Volkskongreß in East Berlin elects Volksrat as preliminary parliament for united Germany
20 Mar.	Marshal Sokolovski leaves Control Council. End of joint Four Power administration
16 Apr.	Marshall Plan to be administered by Organisation for European Economic Co-operation (OEEC); includes West Germany
20 Apr.–	Six Power Conference in London: Minister-Presidents of
2 June	West Germany urged to convene constitutional assembly
16 June	Soviet Union abandons inter-Allied administration of Berlin. Western Allies establish their own command (21 December)

20 June	Currency reform in Western zones
24–8 June	Currency reform in Soviet Zone. Extension of new currency to West Berlin rejected by Allied Commanders. West German Deutschmark introduced there
24 June	Total blockade of West Berlin. All land communications and utilities cut off
26 June	Lucius D. Clay provides supplies for besieged city by air. Royal Air Force joins airlift two days later
8–10 July	Minister-Presidents of Western zones meet in Koblenz. Parliamentary representation of new *Länder* to be set up in lieu of constitutional assembly
29 July	SED to adopt Stalinist model of Soviet Communist Party
26 Aug.	Disruption of Berlin City Council by Communist agitators. Western councillors move to town hall in Schöneberg, West Berlin
5 Sept.	Parlamentarischer Rat (Parliamentary Council) meets in Bonn to debate draft constitution
14 Nov.	Volksrat of Soviet Zone passes draft constitution for German Democratic Republic
30 Nov.	Separate city administrations for East and West Berlin
11–12 Dec.	Liberal Party (FDP) founded for all three Western zones: Theodor Heuss elected chairman
28 Dec.	London Six Power Conference: treaty for International Ruhr Authority signed

1949

25 Jan.	Council for Mutual Economic Aid founded in Warsaw (Comecon)
28 Jan.	First SED Party Conference sets up Politburo
4 Apr.	North Atlantic Treaty Organisation (NATO) founded
5 May	Council of Europe set up in London
12 May	Soviet Union lifts Berlin blockade
23 May–20 June	Conference of Foreign Ministers in Paris: no solution to German question

German Democratic Republic

1949

30 May	Third People's Congress in Berlin: constitution of German Democratic Republic (GDR) confirmed
7 Oct.	Provisional People's Chamber (Volkskammer) puts constitution into force: GDR founded
8 Oct.	Intra-German trade agreement (Interzonenabkommen)
10 Oct.	SMAD replaced by a Soviet Control Commission. GDR government assumes all administrative functions
12 Oct.	Volkskammer confirms provisional government under Grotewohl

1950

8 Feb.	Ministry for State Security (Staatssicherheit) set up
23 June	GDR and Czechoslovakia mutually renounce all territorial claims: expulsion of Sudeten Germans declared 'unalterable' and 'just'
6 July	Görlitz agreement with Poland: GDR recognizes the Oder–Neiße line as a 'peace and friendship border'
20–4 July	SED Party Congress: party perceives itself as avant-garde of German working class. Walter Ulbricht elected General Secretary of Central Committee (ZK)
24 Aug.	Prominent functionaries expelled from SED
7 Sept.	Hohenzollern Palace in Berlin pulled down
8 Sept.	GDR joins Comecon
15 Oct.	Elections to the Volkskammer and other parliaments

1951

1 Feb.	Marxism-Leninism made an obligatory subject for all university students
15–17 Mar.	ZK starts campaign against formalism in art
27 Sept.	Long-term trade agreement between GDR and Soviet Union
1 Dec.	First Five-Year Plan: 100 per cent increase in industrial production, 60 per cent in productivity, emphasis on expansion of heavy industry

1952

26 May	GDR begins to block border with Federal Republic of Germany (FRG). Five-kilometre-wide prohibited zone

Federal Republic (FRG) and International Affairs

1949

23 May	FRG Basic Law promulgated
14 Aug.	First Bundestag elections
12 Sept.	Theodor Heuss first President of FRG
15 Sept.	Konrad Adenauer first Chancellor: coalition government
22 Sept.	Occupation statute takes effect in three Western zones
12–14 Oct.	Deutscher Gewerkschaftsbund founded. Hans Böckler first chairman
31 Oct.	FRG joins OEEC
22 Nov.	Petersberg Treaty signed: FRG accedes to International Ruhr Authority

1950

16 Mar.	Churchill advocates German rearmament: offer taken up by Adenauer after outbreak of Korean War
31 Mar.	End of rationing in FRG
9 May	Robert Schuman proposes Western European authority to administer coal and steel production (Montan-Union)
25 June	Outbreak of Korean War
9 Aug.	West Berlin adopts FRG constitution (Allied rights reserved)
24 Oct.	René Pleven proposes European army to integrate West German defence contribution
26 Oct.	Adenauer appoints Theodor Blank as commissioner for security matters (origins of German Defence Ministry)

1951

15 Mar.	Auswärtiges Amt re-established: Adenauer first Foreign Minister
16 Mar.	Federal Border Guard (Bundesgrenzschutz) set up
15 Apr.	European Coal and Steel Community (Montan-Union) supersedes Ruhr statute
9 July	Britain officially ends state of war with Germany (France: 13 July, USA: 24 October)
27 Sept.	Federal government proposes free all-German elections under UN control
20 Dec.	UN to send delegations to both parts of Germany to examine conditions for all-German elections. Entry refused by GDR spring 1952

1952

8 Feb.	Bundestag votes in favour of European Defence Community (EDC): opposition from SPD

9–12 July	Second SED Party Congress: collective farming to be introduced
23 July	GDR *Länder* dissolved, replaced by fourteen districts. East Berlin becomes fifteenth after Wall built
7 Aug.	Gesellschaft für Sport und Technik set up to organize paramilitary training for younger generation
6 Nov.	All blocks of flats have to run so-called 'house books' (*Hausbücher*)
19 Dec.	Government announces three-stage plan for establishment of agricultural productive co-operatives (*Landwirtschaftliche Produktionsgenossenschaften*)

1953

28 May	Government decrees increase in productivity levels of at least 10 per cent
9 June	SED Politbüro adopts Moscow's post-Stalinist line
16 June	Government refuses to rescind increase in productivity levels: East Berlin building workers go on strike
17 June	Strike quickly develops into general uprising
21 June	SED condemns rebellion as 'counter-revolutionary fascist *putsch*' incited by West, but decreed increase in productivity levels abandoned

1954

1 Jan.	Soviet Union renounces further reparations from GDR, returns last dispossessed companies (SAG) in Soviet hands
23 July	Wilhelm Zaisser and Rudolf Herrnstadt expelled from Party

1955

25 Jan.	Soviet Union officially declares end of war with Germany
27 Mar.	First *Jugendweihen* (SED initiation rites) in East Berlin
1 May	Workers' brigades (*Betriebskampfgruppen*) established, prepared to 'defend their country'
14 May	Warsaw Pact set up, including GDR
20 Sept.	Friendship treaty between Soviet Union and GDR
1 Dec.	GDR border police take over border patrols with FRG and West Berlin from Soviet troops. Borders called 'state boundaries' for first time

10 Mar.	Exchange of notes between Stalin and Western powers
24 Apr.	Adenauer stresses provisional character of FRG's treaties. 'Unity in freedom' remains supreme objective
26 May	*Deutschland-Vertrag* signed
27 May	EDC Treaty signed in Paris
2 Aug.	FRG joins International Monetary Fund (IMF)
23 Oct.	Right-wing Sozialistische Reichspartei banned by Constitutional Court

1953

5 Mar.	Stalin dies, succeeded by Khrushchev (13 September)
27 July	End of Korean War
4 Aug.	Bundestag declares 17 June 'Day of German Unity'
6 Sept.	Federal elections: Adenauer coalition continues

1954

25 Jan.–18 Feb.	Four Power Conference in Berlin: no agreement on agenda for German unification
26 Feb.	Amendment to Basic Law (opposed by SPD) allows buildup of German armed forces
3 July	FRG wins World Cup
31 Aug.	EDC fails to win majority in French Assemblée nationale
19–23 Oct.	Nine Power Conference in Paris: Brussels Treaty becomes West European Union including Germany and Italy, Germany to join NATO, German sovereignty to be restored

1955

5 May	Paris Treaties in force. FRG becomes sovereign state
9 May	FRG joins NATO
15 May	State treaty signed with Austria: Four Powers guarantee sovereignty and neutrality (withdrawal of Allied occupation forces)
6 June	FRG Ministry of Defence set up
9–13 Sept.	Adenauer visits Moscow: negotiates resumption of diplomatic relations and return of 10,000 German prisoners of war

1956

18 Jan.   Kasernierte Volkspolizei transformed into Nationale
               Volksarmee, initially 110,000 men

24–30 Mar.   Third SED Party Congress: Ulbricht prevents open debate
               on de-Stalinization

1957

25 Apr.   Freie Deutsche Jugend declared official socialist youth
               organization

27 July   GDR proposes confederation between GDR and FRG based
               on parity

1958

9 Jan.   Second Five-Year Plan provides for 50 per cent increase in
               industrial production and productivity

3 Feb.   Another ZK purge: Schirdewan, Wollweber, and others
               accused of advocating national Communist positions

28 May   Ration cards for meat, sugar, and other items abandoned

6–10 July   Fifth SED Party Congress: Ulbricht vows to reach and
               surpass FRG per capita consumption in all important
               consumer goods by 1961

1959

24 Apr.   First conference of artists and writers in Bitterfeld

1 Oct.   Second Five-Year Plan abandoned. Volkskammer passes law
               on new Seven-Year Plan (1959–65), also abandoned
               prematurely

22 Sept.	Hallstein Doctrine announced
23 Oct.	Population of Saar region rejects Saar statute (part of Paris Treaties). New treaty and final accession of Saar to FRG on 1 January 1957
27 Oct.– 16 Nov.	Geneva foreign ministers conference: Molotov rejects all-German elections, advocates two separate states

1956

14–25 Feb.	Khrushchev condemns Stalinism in secret speech at Twentieth Party Congress in Moscow
28 June	Working-class unrest in Posna (Poland) suppressed by military
21 July	Military service introduced in FRG, with right to conscientious objection
17 Aug.	West German Communist Party (KPD) banned by Constitutional Court
23 Oct.	General uprising in Hungary brutally suppressed by Red Army

1957

25 Mar.	Treaty of Rome signed
19 Sept.	FRG severs diplomatic relations with Yugoslavia, which has recognized GDR (Hallstein Doctrine)
3 Oct.	Polish foreign minister Rapacki submits plan for a nuclear-free zone in Europe

1958

| 1 Jan. | EEC treaty takes effect. Walter Hallstein first President of Commission |
| 27 Nov. | Khrushchev triggers international crisis: wants Berlin to be demilitarized 'free city' (end of Four Power status). Rejected by Western powers 31 December |

1959

5 Jan.	Federal government rejects Soviet proposals for 'free city of West Berlin', recognition of GDR, and confederation of two German states. Submits Globke Plan for procedure towards unification
18 Mar.	SPD advocates demilitarized nuclear-free zone in central Europe
19 Mar.	Khrushchev recognizes rights of three Western powers in Berlin and asks for peace conference

1960

16 Aug.   Intra-German trade agreement complemented by 'swing'
            (interest-free credit)
12 Sept.   President Pieck dies. Walter Ulbricht chairman of new State
            Council

1961

11 Jan.   All-German Protestant Church Congress in East Berlin
            prohibited
12 Apr.   Volkskammer passes *Weißes Gesetzbuch* (work-permit law)
16 July   At press conference in East Berlin Ulbricht says: *'Niemand
            hat die Absicht, eine Mauer zu bauen'* (No one intends to
            build a wall)
13 Aug.   Border between Berlin's Eastern and Western sectors sealed
            by Wall and barbed wire
16 Aug.   Border between GDR and FRG closed to all GDR citizens

1962

24 Jan.   Volkskammer introduces military service for all men
            between 18 and 50 (no right to conscientious objection)
22 Aug.   Soviet *Kommandatura* in East Berlin dissolved. Western
            powers protest

1963

25 June   Council of Ministers introduces 'new economic system'
17 Dec.   First transit agreement between West Berlin Senate and
            GDR government

11 May–	Four Power foreign ministers conference in Geneva (both
15 Aug.	German states attend with advisory status)
8 Sept.	Brandt stresses core principles of his Berlin policy: adherence to FRG, self-determination, Four Power responsibility, free access
13–15 Nov.	Extraordinary SPD Party Congress approves Godesberg programme and abandons Marxism

1960

16–17 May	Khruschev storms out of Paris Four Power summit conference
13 June	Herbert Wehner announces new departure in SPD foreign policy: support for European and Atlantic alliance system
14 Dec.	OEEC becomes Organisation for Economic Cooperation and Development (OECD)

1961

5 May	Soviet government refuses to include West Berlin in negotiations with FRG on cultural exchanges
25 July	Kennedy stresses US resolve to defend Allied rights in Berlin
12 Aug.	40,000 escape from GDR through West Berlin, last remaining exit to West
13 Aug.	West Berlin sealed off from GDR by concrete wall. Final blow to hopes for unification

1962

6 June	Adenauer approaches Soviet ambassador: proposes truce for ten years to relieve tensions
4–9 Sept.	De Gaulle visits FRG, welcomed enthusiastically by population
17 Sept.	USA rejects unilateral Soviet declaration on suspension of Berlin's Four Power status
26 Oct.	*Spiegel* crisis. Franz Josef Strauß forced to resign (9 November)

1963

22 Jan.	Adenauer and de Gaulle sign Elysée Treaty
23–6 June	Kennedy visits FRG. *'Ich bin ein Berliner'* speech in West Berlin
15 July	Egon Bahr (SPD) announces new concept of *Ostpolitik*: change through *rapprochement*
18 Sept.	FRG sets up commercial representation in Warsaw
14 Oct.	Adenauer resigns, succeeded by Erhard

1964

13 Mar.   Robert Havemann suspended from chair at Humboldt University for criticizing regime

7 Sept.   Unarmed military service now possible (*Baueinheiten*) after pressure from Protestant Church

9 Sept.   GDR pensioners allowed to visit relations in FRG and West Berlin once a year

24 Sept.   Willi Stoph becomes chairman of Council of Ministers after Grotewohl's death

1 Dec.   Minimum exchange introduced for all visitors to the GDR from non-socialist countries

1965

24 Feb.   President Nasser of Egypt receives Ulbricht as head of state

3 Dec.   Erich Apel, initiator of economic reform, commits suicide

1966

29 June   GDR cancels exchange of speakers arranged between SPD and SED

1967

15 Mar.   GDR and Poland conclude friendship treaty

10 May   First exchange of diplomatic notes between the two Germanies

1968

8 Apr.   New constitution defines GDR as a 'socialist state of German nationality'

13 Apr.   GDR refuses transit of Federal ministers and civil servants to West Berlin

11 June   Passport and visa requirements for travelling and transit between FRG and West Berlin

21 Aug.   Nationale Volksarmee participates in military occupation of Czechoslovakia by Warsaw Pact states

1964

16 Feb.	Brandt new SPD chairman
10–24 Oct.	Last all-German team at Olympic Games (Tokyo)
14 Oct.	Khruschev falls from power, succeeded by Brezhnev as General Secretary, and Kosygin as Prime Minister
28 Nov.	Right-wing National-Demokratische Partei Deutschlands (NDP) founded

1965

19 Aug.	Life sentences for six former SS members at Frankfurt Auschwitz trial
19 Sept.	Federal elections: conservative coalition continues
1 Oct.	Protestant Church advocates new *Ostpolitik* and recognition of Oder–Neiße border. Catholic bishops favour reconciliation with Poland (5 December)

1966

25 Mar.	Bonn offers non-aggression treaties to all Eastern European countries (except GDR): welcomed by Western powers but rejected by Soviet Union and all other Eastern European governments (17 May)
13 Dec.	Policy statement by new Kiesinger government (Grand Coalition): no official recognition of GDR, but offer of closer human, economic, and cultural relations

1967

19 Apr.	Adenauer dies

1968

11 Apr.	Rudi Dutschke attacked and severely wounded in Berlin. Demonstrations all over Germany
30 May	Bundestag passes emergency laws against popular protest in streets
1 July	EEC becomes customs union, all internal tariffs lifted
21 Aug.	Prague Spring movement crushed by Warsaw Pact troops
22 Sept.	German Communist Party legalized in FRG

1969

10 June   GDR Evangelical Churches form separate Bund der
            Evangelischen Kirchen in der DDR

1970

19 Mar.   Brandt and Stoph meet in Erfurt. Brandt cordially received
            by local population

9–11 Dec.   ZK criticizes 'new economic system': shortages of food,
            textiles, and fuel have not been overcome

1971

3 May   Ulbricht forced to resign as head of Party, but remains
            chairman of State Council: succeeded by Honecker

15–19 June   Eighth SED Party Congress: pledges to raise citizens' living
            standard

18 Nov.   Price freeze on consumer goods and services until 1975.
            Beginning of massive subsidization ('welfare socialism')

1972

Feb.   SED decides to nationalize all remaining private enterprises

1973

9 Feb.   Britain and France take up diplomatic relations with GDR

5–7 Mar.   West German television correspondents and journalists
            accredited by GDR

1 Aug.   Ulbricht dies

3 Oct.   Stoph elected to succeed Ulbricht as chairman of State
            Council. Sindermann succeeds Stoph as chairman of
            Council of Ministers

1969

5 Mar.	Gustav Heinemann (SPD) new FRG President
28 Sept.	Federal elections: SPD-FDP coalition
21 Oct.	Brandt elected Federal Chancellor
28 Oct.	Brandt's official policy statement: two states and one nation
28 Nov.	FRG signs Non-Proliferation Treaty

1970

21 May	Stoph visits Brandt in Kassel
11–13 Aug.	Brandt visits Moscow, signs treaty on normalization of relations between FRG and Soviet Union
7 Dec.	German-Polish treaty signed in Warsaw, recognizes Oder–Neiße line as Polish western border

1971

3 Sept.	Four Power Agreement on Berlin: confirms their rights and traditional links between FRG and West Berlin
16–18 Sept.	Brandt meets Brezhnev in Crimea
20 Oct.	Brandt receives Nobel Peace Prize
17 Dec.	First official treaty between FRG and GDR (transit to West Berlin)

1972

28 Jan.	Brandt and *Länder* Minister-Presidents agree that 'extremists' should not be employed as civil servants
27 Apr.	Constructive vote of no confidence in Brandt government fails in Bundestag (two votes short of absolute majority)
17 May	Federal parliament approves treaties with Moscow and Warsaw, most CDU/CSU members abstain
1 June	Leading members of Baader–Meinhof gang arrested, Ulrike Meinhof herself soon afterwards
19 Oct.	Heinrich Böll receives Nobel Prize for Literature
19 Nov.	Federal elections: SPD strongest party for first time, Lib-Lab coalition continues, Brandt as Chancellor
21 Dec.	*Grundlagenvertrag* between FRG and GDR signed in East Berlin

1973

18 Sept.	FRG and GDR join United Nations
19 Nov.	FRG prohibits use of cars on Sundays, in accordance with new energy-saving law
11 Dec.	Prague Treaty between FRG and Czechoslovakia signed. Munich Treaty of 1938 declared null and void
19 Dec.	Unemployment figure reaches 1 million for first time

1974

1 Jan.	GDR vehicles now carry 'DDR' plates instead of 'D' plates
4 Sept.	USA takes up diplomatic relations with GDR
7 Oct.	Amendment to 1968 constitution: alliance with Soviet Union becomes constitutional, reference to Germany and German nation eliminated from text

1975

7 Oct.	New friendship treaty between Soviet Union and GDR. So-called Brezhnev Doctrine incorporated into treaty

1976

1 Jan.	German *bürgerliches Gesetzbuch* replaced by GDR civil code
23 Apr.	'Palace of the Republic' inaugurated, on the site of the old Hohenzollern city palace
18 Aug.	Oskar Prüsewitz immolates himself in public in protest against government's repressive policy towards churches
29 Oct.	Honecker becomes head of state and chairman of National Defence Council. Sindermann becomes President of People's Chamber and Stoph Prime Minister
16 Nov.	Wolf Biermann expatriated while on tour in FRG
15 Dec.	Five-Year Plan for 1976–80 emphasizes building programme and further integration into Comecon. Key role for micro-electronics

1977

26 Sept.	Honecker defends Inter-Shops as providers of foreign currency and announces the expansion of Exquisit-Shops

1978

6 Mar.	Honecker meets leaders of East German Protestant Church
1 Sept.	Paramilitary training and education new subject at polytechnic high schools. Protestant and Catholic bishops object

1974

14 Mar.	Protocol on 'permanent representations of the two German states' signed, to function as embassies in both capitals
24 April.	Günther Guillaume arrested as GDR spy
6 May	Brandt resigns as Chancellor, remains SPD chairman
15 May	Walter Scheel elected Federal President
16 May	Helmut Schmidt new Chancellor
5 Sept.	Treaty with Soviet Union on delivery of gas until the year 2000

1975

18 Feb.	Opponents of nuclear power occupy site of proposed power plant in Wyhl. Ecology movement gathers momentum
7 July	Constitutional Court approached by Bavarian government: Court rules that Eastern Treaties do not violate Basic Law, do not determine territorial status of Germany as a whole
1 Aug.	Conference on security and co-operation in Europe reaches successful conclusion in Helsinki

1976

9 May	Ulrike Meinhof commits suicide in prison
18 Aug.	Formation of terrorist organizations declared new criminal activity
3 Oct.	Federal elections: CDU/CSU strongest party but Lib-Lab government continues

1977

7 Apr.	Siegfried Bubak murdered by terrorists
5 May	Erhard dies
30 July	Jürgen Ponto murdered by terrorists
5 Sept.	Hanns-Martin Schleyer kidnapped and murdered by Red Army Faction
18 Oct.	Special unit of federal border guards frees hostages on Lufthansa plane in Mogadishu. Andreas Baader and others commit suicide in prison

1978

4–7 May	Brezhnev state visit to FRG: long-term agreement on economic co-operation signed
6 Nov.	Strauß becomes Minister-President of Bavaria

1979

19 Feb.   Friendship treaty between GDR and Angola. Similar to follow with Mozambique, Ethiopia, People's Republic of Yemen, Cambodia and Cuba

14 Apr.   Western journalists have to apply for interviews in advance, also for travel outside East Berlin

1980

13 Oct.   Honecker issues *Geraer Forderungen* (conditions for normalizing FRG–GDR relations): rejected by FRG government

1981

11–13 Dec. Honecker and Schmidt meet at Werbellinsee: pledge to continue neighbourly relations

1982

14 Feb.   5,000 youngsters take part in peace forum at Dresden Kreuzkirche. Widespread response to appeal by Berlin youth vicar Rainer Eppelmann

19 Dec.   Transit motorway Berlin–Hamburg opened

1983

5 Oct.   Honecker announces dismantling of *Selbstschußanlagen* (automatic shooting devices) along the inner-German border

1979

22 Jan.	*Holocaust* shown on West German TV: unexpected emotional impact
13 Mar.	European Monetary System in force
3 July	Bundestag decree: no statute of limitations for genocide
14 Dec.	NATO council resolution: medium-range nuclear missiles to be stationed in Europe, response to new-category Soviet SS-20 missiles
27 Dec.	Soviet invasion of Afghanistan

1980

12–13 Jan.	Founding congress of Green Party in Karlsruhe
8 May	Soviet invasion of Afghanistan leads to Moscow Olympics boycott
1 July	Disarmament negotiations between Schmidt and Brezhnev in Moscow
5 Oct.	Federal elections: CDU/CSU remains strongest party, but Lib-Lab coalition increases majority

1981

10 Oct.	Peace movement demonstration in Bonn against NATO dual-track decision

1982

17 Sept.	Schmidt dissolves Lib-Lab coalition. Liberals negotiate with CDU/CSU
1 Oct.	Kohl elected Chancellor
10 Nov.	Brezhnev dies
17 Dec.	Kohl deliberately loses vote of confidence, forces new elections
31 Dec.	Unemployment figure reaches 2 million for first time since 1955

1983

6 Mar.	Federal elections: CDU/CSU just misses overall majority. Coalition with FDP continues. Greens represented for first time
29 Mar.	Kohl re-elected as Chancellor, Genscher confirmed as Vice-Chancellor and Foreign Minister
29 June	First large bank loan to GDR guaranteed by federal government
22 Nov.	Bundestag approves installation of new US medium-range missiles: large peace demonstrations

1984

8 Mar.	Delegation of SPD Deputies visits Volkskammer
1 Aug.	Further easing of travel restrictions for East German pensioners
Nov.	International group of banks grants GDR 400 million dollars credit
12 Nov.	Delivery agreements between Volkswagen and GDR government
end of year	GDR has granted 34,900 exit visas to the West (1983: 7,500)

1985

6 July	International group of banks, including Americans and Japanese, grants GDR 600 million dollars credit
3 Nov.	Removal of mines along inner-German border

1986

19–22 Feb.	Sindermann visits SPD Bundestag party
6 May	Cultural agreement between FRG and GDR

1987

8 Apr.	Kurt Hager, member of the Politbüro, distances himself from Gorbachev's reform policy
7 June	East German youths gather near Wall, shout *'Die Mauer muß weg'* (The Wall must go). Same in Unter den Linden two days later with appeals to Gorbachev
17 July	Death penalty abolished
5 Nov.	State Security confiscates material belonging to the 'Environmental Library' of East Berlin Protestant parish

1984

23 May	Weizsäcker elected FRG President
25 July	Second large loan awarded to GDR, guaranteed by federal government, easing of travel restrictions between FRG and GDR, GDR reduces obligatory daily exchange rate for visitors

1985

7 Feb.	Unemployment figure reaches 2.6 million, highest since 1949
11 Mar.	Gorbachev becomes General Secretary of Soviet Communist Party
5 July	'Swing' (interest-free credit for GDR) brought up to old level of 800 million currency units (DM)

1986

6 June	Ernst Nolte's article in *Frankfurter Allgemeine Zeitung* triggers off so-called *Historikerstreit*
6 July	Federal Ministry for Environment set up, after nuclear disaster at Chernobyl
6 Oct.	First East-West town twinning: Saarlouis and Eisenhüttenstadt
31 Dec.	Economic upswing in FRG: volume of exports surpasses USA for first time

1987

5 Jan.	Federal elections: CDU/CSU-FDP coalition continues
23 Mar.	Brandt resigns as SPD chairman, replaced by Hans-Jochen Vogel
12 June	Reagan visits West Berlin, asks Gorbachev to pull down Wall
1 July	Single European Act in force
27 Aug.	SPD and SED publish joint paper on 'peaceful competition between the two social systems'
7–11 Sept.	Honecker state visit to FRG
19 Oct.	Black Monday stock exchange crash wipes one-third off value of all German shares
5 Dec.	Third Washington summit: Reagan and Gorbachev agree to dismantle and destroy all US and Soviet medium-range missiles in Europe within three years

1988

15 Jan.	Demonstration commemorating murder of Karl Liebknecht and Rosa Luxemburg: members of peace, ecology, and human rights groups arrested
19 Mar.	Western journalists forbidden to record or film synod of the Saxon Protestant Church
15 Aug.	GDR and EEC take up official relations
20 Nov.	Soviet magazine *Sputnik* prohibited in GDR. Some Soviet films also banned
14 Dec.	Further lifting of travel restrictions

1989

7 May	Massive fraud in local government elections, exposed for first time by human rights groups
7 July	Warsaw Pact revokes Brezhnev Doctrine
Aug.	Exodus of East German citizens via Poland, Czechoslovakia, and Hungary takes on dramatic dimensions
10 Sept.	Bärbel Bohley and Jens Reich found Neues Forum, first opposition movement independent of Church
11 Sept.	Hungarian government opens borders to all GDR citizens. Within three days 5,000 East Germans flee to FRG; 50,000 by end of October
16 Sept.	Demokratie Jetzt formed
7 Oct.	Gorbachev attends GDR fortieth anniversary celebrations: spontaneous demonstrations against SED erupt; GDR Social Democratic Party founded in secrecy
9 Oct.	Seventy thousand demonstrate peacefully in Leipzig against SED regime. Demonstrations continue every Monday
18 Oct.	Honecker dismissed, succeeded by Egon Krenz
4 Nov.	Huge demonstrations in East Berlin: demands for free elections and democracy
8 Nov.	Entire SED Politbüro resigns
9 Nov.	Wall opened: thousands cross to West Berlin, followed by millions over next weeks
13 Nov.	Modrow becomes Prime Minister
28 Nov.	Artists and writers sign 'For our country', advocating democratic GDR
1 Dec	Volkskammer eliminates SED's leading role from constitution
4 Dec.	Honecker and other leaders expelled from party. Entire ZK and Politbüro resign
7 Dec.	'Round Table' agrees with SED and bloc parties to hold free elections on 6 May 1990
8 Dec.	Honecker arrested, charged with corruption
10 Dec.	Special SED Party Congress elects Gregor Gysi (lawyer) as

1988

15 May	Soviet army begins withdrawal from Afghanistan
25 June	EC and Comecon agree on official diplomatic relations
24–7 Oct.	Kohl visits Soviet Union

1989

20 Jan.	Bush becomes US President
2 May	Hungarian border guards begin to dismantle barbed wire along frontier with Austria
25 May	Gorbachev elected State President of Soviet Union
12–15 June	Gorbachev visits FRG
17 July	Dismantling of border fortifications along Austrian–Hungarian frontier
9 Nov.	Kohl visits Poland: confirms Germany has no territorial claims
28 Nov.	Kohl's ten-point programme for solution to German question envisages confederation for transitional period
30 Nov.	Alfred Herrnhausen murdered by terrorists
12 Dec.	Gorbachev declares to Central Committee that Soviet Union will not interfere in internal development of Warsaw Pact states
19 Dec.	Shevardnadze visits NATO headquarters in Brussels for first time: declares Cold War over for good

chairman. He names party 'Party of Democratic Socialism' (PDS)

16 Dec.   Eastern CDU Special Party Congress: Lothar de Maizière, as chairman, opts for social market economy and German unity

19 Dec.   Kohl and Modrow meet in Dresden

22 Dec.   Wall opened at Brandenburg Gate

1990

19 Jan.   Former State Security offices in East Berlin stormed

5 Feb.   New ministers without portfolio from opposition groups taken into Modrow government

13–14 Feb. Modrow visits Bonn: rejects currency union and asks in vain for immediate aid

18 Mar.   First free elections in GDR: victory for 'conservative alliance' and speedy unification

12 Apr.   Volkskammer elects de Maizière as Prime Minister and confirms grand coalition including SPD. Government to strive for unification in accordance with Basic Law Article 23

1 July   Currency, economic, and social union between FRG and GDR in force

23 Aug.   Volkskammer decides GDR to join FRG on 3 October

31 Aug.   Schäuble (FRG) and Krause (GDR) sign Unification Treaty

20 Sept.   Volkskammer approves Unification Treaty: opposition from PDS and sections of Bündnis '90

3 Oct.   Unification according to Basic Law Article 23

1990

25 Feb.	Bush assures Kohl of full US support for unification: united Germany should remain member of NATO
1 July	Currency, economic, and social union between FRG and GDR in force
15–16 July	Gorbachev and Kohl meet in Caucasus: agree terms for unification
31 Aug.	*Einigungsvertrag* signed between FRG and GDR
12 Sept.	Final 'two plus four treaty' signed in Moscow: sorts out international aspects of German unification
3 Oct.	GDR joins FRG in accordance with Basic Law Article 23. 3 October declared official public holiday (*Tag der Deutschen Einheit*)

Further Reading

I. Federal Republic of Germany

The history of Germany after 1945 is mainly, if not exclusively, identified with that of the Federal Republic. This was the habitat of the majority, it was free and democratic, and ultimately it survived while the GDR did not. The most useful history in English is the updated, two-volume *History of West Germany* by Dennis L. Bark and David R. Gress. As regards other general interpretations of German history in the twentieth century, attention should be drawn to the works by Michael Balfour, Volker Berghahn, Mary Fulbrook, and Anthony Glees, which all have a textbook character. The most popular presentations of present-day Germany are those by David Marsh (first edition entitled *Rich, Bothered and Divided*) and Alan Watson. The most authoritative account in German is the Brockhaus *Geschichte der Bundesrepublik Deutschland*, each volume by one or more authors. However, this series is also expensive and somewhat unwieldy. This does not apply to most of the other general histories mentioned in section (a). Highly recommended are the four volumes *Die Geschichte der Bundesrepublik Deutschland*, edited by Wolfgang Benz and published in paperback by S. Fischer (Frankfurt am Main). These volumes will be listed separately according to their contents. The Innsbruck historian Rolf Steininger has published a history of Germany from 1945 to 1961 concentrating on politics and the division of Germany and including documentary evidence (some of it from the Public Record Office). His paperback edition has now been revised and, with two volumes now out, is being extended to 1990. A similar approach (story and documents) has been chosen by Christoph Kleßmann, probably the most detailed paperback on the first ten years (1945–55). Adolf M. Birke has covered the period 1949–61 in the Siedler series *Die Deutschen und ihre Nation*. Robert Hettlage has edited what he calls a 'historical balance sheet' pertaining to all aspects of West German society since 1945.

(a) General History

BALFOUR, MICHAEL, *West Germany: A Contemporary History* (London, 1982).

BARK, DENNIS L., and GRESS, DAVID R., *A History of West Germany. Vol. 1: From Shadow to Substance 1945–1963. Vol. 2: Democracy and its Discontents 1963–1991.* 2nd edn. (Oxford, 1993).

BERGHAHN, VOLKER R., *Modern Germany: Society, Economy and Politics in the Twentieth Century* (Cambridge, 1982).

BIRKE, ADOLF M., *Nation ohne Haus: Deutschland 1945–1961* (Berlin, 1989).

BOROWSKY, PETER, *Deutschland 1969–1982* (Hanover, 1982).

BRACHER, KARL-DIETRICH et al., *Republik im Wandel (1969–1974): Die Ära Brandt* [*Geschichte der Bundesrepublik Deutschland*, vol. v/1] (Stuttgart and Mannheim, 1986).

BUCHHEIM, HANS, *Deutschlandpolitik 1949–1972: Der politisch-diplomatische Prozeß* (Stuttgart, 1984).

BÜHRER, WERNER (ed.), *Die Adenauer-Ära: Die Bundesrepublik Deutschland 1949–1963* [Piper Dokumentation] (Munich, 1993).

DOERING-MANTEUFFEL, ANSELM, *Die Bundesrepublik Deutschland in der Ära Adenauer* (Darmstadt, 1983).

ESCHENBERG, THEODOR, *Jahre der Besatzung (1945–1949)* [*Geschichte der Bundesrepublik Deutschland*, vol. i] (Stuttgart and Wiesbaden, 1983).

FULBROOK, MARY, *Germany 1918–1990: The Divided Nation* (London, 1991).

GLEES, ANTHONY, *Reinventing Germany: German Political Development since 1945* (Oxford, 1996).

GRAML, HERMANN, *Die Alliierten und die Teilung Deutschlands: Konflikte und Entscheidungen 1941–1948* (Frankfurt am Main, 1985).

GRIFFITH, WILLIAM E., *The Ostpolitik of the Federal Republic of Germany* (Cambridge, Mass., 1978).

GROSSER, ALFRED, *Deutschland: Geschichte Deutschlands seit 1945* (Munich, 1980).

HETTLAGE, ROBERT, *Die Bundesrepublik: Eine historische Bilanz* (Munich, 1990).

HILDEBRAND, KLAUS, *Von Erhard zur Großen Koalition (1963–1969)* [*Geschichte der Bundesrepublik Deutschland*, vol. iv] (Stuttgart and Wiesbaden, 1984).

JÄGER, WOLFGANG, and LINK, WERNER, *Republik im Wandel (1974–1982): Die Ära Schmidt* [*Geschichte der Bundesrepublik Deutschland*, vol. v/2] (Stuttgart and Mannheim, 1987).

KAPPLER, ARNO, and GREVEL, ADRIANE (eds.), *Facts about Germany*, official pubn. (Frankfurt am Main, 1995).

KLESSMANN, CHRISTOPH, *Die doppelte Staatsgründung: Deutsche Geschichte 1945–1955* (Göttingen, 1982).

MARSH, DAVID, *The New Germany: At the Crossroads* (London, 1991).

MARSHALL, BARBARA, *The Origins of Post-War German Politics* (London, 1988).

PULZER, PETER, *German Politics 1945–1995* (Oxford, 1995).

SCHWARZ, HANS-PETER, *Die Ära Adenauer: Gründerjahre der Republik (1949–1957)* [*Geschichte der Bundesrepublik Deutschland*, vol. ii] (Stuttgart and Wiesbaden, 1981).

—— *Die Ära Adenauer: Epochenwechsel (1957–1963)* [*Geschichte der Bundesrepublik Deutschland*, vol. iii] (Stuttgart and Wiesbaden, 1983).

SONTHEIMER, KURT, *Die Adenauer-Ära: Grundlegung der Republik* (Munich, 1991).

STEININGER, ROLF, *Deutsche Geschichte seit 1945: Darstellung und Dokumente*, 4 vols. projected, vols. i and ii (Frankfurt am Main, 1996).

THRÄNHARDT, DIETRICH, *Geschichte der Bundesrepublik Deutschland* (Frankfurt am Main, 1986).

TURNER, HENRY ASHBY, *The Two Germanies Since 1945* (New Haven, 1987).

308 **Further Reading**

(b) Politics and Society

ABELSHAUSER, WERNER, *Die Langen Fünfziger Jahre: Wirtschaft und Gesellschaft der Bundesrepublik Deutschland 1949–1966* (Düsseldorf, 1987).

BARING, ARNULF, *Machtwechsel: Die Ära Brandt-Scheel* (Stuttgart, 1982).

BENZ, WOLFGANG (ed.), *Die Geschichte der Bundesrepublik*, vol. i: *Politik* (Frankfurt am Main, 1989).

—— (ed.), *Die Geschichte der Bundesrepublik*, vol. iii: *Gesellschaft* (Frankfurt am Main, 1989).

BEYME, KLAUS VON, *The Political System of the Federal Republic of Germany* (Aldershot, 1986).

BRAND, KARL-WERNER et al., *Aufbruch in eine neue Gesellschaft: Neue soziale Bewegungen in der Bundesrepublik* (Frankfurt am Main, 1983).

BURNS, ROB, and VAN DER WILL, WILFRIED, *Protest and Democracy in West Germany: Extra-Parliamentary Opposition and the Democratic Agenda* (London, 1988).

CHILDS, DAVID, and JOHNSON, JEFFREY, *West Germany: Politics and Society* (London, 1982).

CONZE, WERNER, and LEPSIUS, M. RAINER (eds.), *Sozialgeschichte der Bundesrepublik Deutschland: Beiträge zum Kontinuitätsproblem* (Stuttgart, 1983).

DAHRENDORF, RALF, *Gesellschaft und Demokratie in Deutschland* (Munich, 1966).

DUTSCHKE, GRETCHEN, *Wir hatten ein barbarisches, schönes Leben: Rudi Dutschke —eine Biographie* (Cologne, 1996).

ERMARTH, MICHAEL (ed.), *America and the Shaping of German Society 1945– 1955* (Oxford, 1993).

FREI, NORBERT, *Vergangenheitspolitik: Die Anfänge der Bundesrepublik und die NS-Vergangenheit* (Munich, 1996).

FÜRSTENBERG, FRIEDRICH, *Die Sozialstruktur der Bundesrepublik Deutschland* (Opladen, 1976).

GENSCHER, HANS-DIETRICH, *Erinnerungen* (Berlin, 1995).

GREIFFENHAGEN, MARTIN, and GREIFFENHAGEN, SYLVIA, *Ein schwieriges Vaterland: Zur politischen Kultur Deutschlands* (Munich, 1979).

HACKE, CHRISTIAN, *Weltmacht wider Willen: Die Außenpolitik der Bundesrepublik Deutschland* (Berlin, 1993).

JEFFREY, CHARLIE, and SAVIGEAR, PETER, *German Federalism Today* (Leicester, 1991).

KORTE, HERMANN, *Eine Gesellschaft im Aufbruch: Die Bundesrepublik Deutschland in den sechziger Jahren* (Frankfurt am Main, 1987).

KRIEGER, WOLFGANG, *Franz Josef Strauß: Der barocke Demokrat aus Bayern* (Göttingen, 1995).

MARSHALL, BARBARA, *Willy Brandt* (London, 1990).

NOACK, PAUL, *Die Außenpolitik der Bundesrepublik Deutschland* (Stuttgart, 1981).

NOELLE-NEUMANN, ELISABETH, *Die verletzte Nation: Über den Versuch der Deutschen, ihren Charakter zu ändern* (Stuttgart, 1987).

OLZOG, GÜNTER, and HERZIG, ARTHUR, *Die politischen Parteien in der Bundesrepublik Deutschland* (Munich, 1977).

PADGETT, STEPHEN (ed.), *Adenauer to Kohl: The Development of the German Chancellorship* (London, 1994).

PFETSCH, FRANK R., *Die Außenpolitik der Bundesrepublik 1949–1992* (Munich, 1993).

—— *Ursprünge der Zweiten Republik: Prozesse der Verfassungsgebung* (Opladen, 1990).

Press and Information Office of the Government of the Federal Republic of Germany, *Documentation Relating to the Federal Government's Policy of Détente* (Bonn, 1978).

RITTER, GERHARD A., and NIEHUSS, MERITH, *Wahlen in Deutschland (1946–1991): Ein Handbuch* (Munich, 1991).

ROHE, KARL (ed.), *Elections, Parties and Political Traditions: Social Foundations of German Parties and Party Systems, 1867–1987* (Oxford, 1990).

SCHMID, JOSEF, *Bevölkerungsveränderungen in der Bundesrepublik Deutschland: Eine Revolution auf leisen Sohlen* (Stuttgart, 1984).

SCHMOECKEL, REINHARD, and KAISER, BRUNO, *Die vergessene Regierung: Die große Koalition 1966–1969 und ihre langfristigen Wirkungen* (Bonn, 1991).

SCHWARZ, HANS-PETER, *Adenauer*, 2 vols. (Stuttgart, 1986–91).

TURNER, IAN D. (ed.), *Reconstruction in Post-War Germany: British Occupation Policy in the Western Zones* (Oxford, 1989).

WEIDENFELD, WERNER (ed.), *Politische Kultur und deutsche Frage: Materialien zum Staats- und Nationalbewußtsein in der Bundesrepublik Deutschland* (Cologne, 1989).

ZIMMER, MATTHIAS, *Nationales Interesse und Staatsräson: Zur Deutschlandpolitik der Regierung Kohl 1982–1989* (Paderborn, 1992).

(c) Economics

ABELSHAUSER, WERNER, *Wirtschaftsgeschichte der Bundesrepublik Deutschland 1945–1980* (Frankfurt am Main, 1983).

BENZ, WOLFGANG (ed.), *Die Geschichte der Bundesrepublik Deutschland*, vol. ii: *Wirtschaft* (Frankfurt am Main, 1989).

BERGHAHN, VOLKER, *Unternehmer und Politik in der Bundesrepublik* (Frankfurt am Main, 1985).

BRACKMANN, MICHAEL, *Vom totalen Krieg zum Wirtschaftswunder: Die Vorgeschichte der westdeutschen Währungsreform* (Essen, 1993).

BUCHHEIM, CHRISTOPH, *Die Wiedereingliederung Westdeutschlands in die Weltwirtschaft 1945–1959* (Munich, 1990).

FARQUHARSON, JOHN E., *The Western Allies and the Politics of Food: Agrarian Management in Postwar Germany* (Oxford, 1985).

GLASTETTER, WERNER, et al., *Die wirtschaftliche Entwicklung in der Bundesrepublik Deutschland 1950–1989* (Frankfurt am Main, 1991).

GROSSER, DIETER, et al., *Soziale Marktwirtschaft: Geschichte, Konzept, Leistung* (Stuttgart, 1988).

HARDACH, KARL, *Wirtschaftsgeschichte Deutschlands im 20. Jahrhundert* (Göttingen, 1976).

JÄGER, HANS, *Geschichte der Wirtschaftsordnung in Deutschland* (Frankfurt am Main, 1988).

JERCHOW, FRIEDRICH, *Deutschland in der Weltwirtschaft: Alliierte Deutschland- und Reparationspolitik und die Anfänge der westdeutschen Außenwirtschaft* (Düsseldorf, 1978).

KRAMER, ALAN, *The West German Economy 1945–1955* (Oxford, 1991).

LEAMAN, JEREMY, *The Political Economy of West Germany, 1945–85* (London, 1988).

MARSH, DAVID, *The Bundesbank: The Bank that Rules Europe* (London, 1992).

NICHOLLS, ANTHONY J., *Freedom with Responsibility: The Social Market Economy in Germany 1918–1963* (Oxford, 1994).

SMITH, ERIC OWEN, *The German Economy* (London, 1994).

(d) Culture

BAUMERT, JÜRGEN, *et al.*, *Bildung in der Bundesrepublik Deutschland* [Max-Planck-Institut für Bildungsforschung], 2 vols. (Reinbeck, 1980).

BENZ, WOLFGANG (ed.), *Die Geschichte der Bundesrepublik Deutschland*, vol. iv: *Kultur* (Frankfurt am Main, 1989).

GLASER, HERMANN, *Kulturgeschichte der Bundesrepublik Deutschland*, vol. i: *Zwischen Kapitulation und Währungsreform 1945–1948* (Munich, 1985).

HERMAND, JOST, *Kultur im Wiederaufbau: Die Bundesrepublik Deutschland 1945–1965* (Berlin, 1989).

INTER NATIONES, *Cultural Life in the Federal Republic of Germany* (Munich, 1989).

KNOLL, JOACHIM H., *Bildung und Wissenschaft in der Bundesrepublik Deutschland* (Munich, 1977).

PEISERT, HANSGERT, and FRAMHEIN, GERHILD, *Das Hochschulsystem der Bundesrepublik Deutschland* (Stuttgart, 1979).

SCHALLÜCK, PAUL, *Germany: Cultural Developments Since 1945* (Munich, 1971).

II German Democratic Republic and the Unification Process

By definition history is the story told at the end of a never-ending day. Therefore the history of the GDR is inexorably linked with its demise. The latter marks the climax of both the regime's unsuccessful struggle for legitimacy and of the people's successful revolution. Most histories of the unification process contain some kind of synopsis of the GDR's history—if not of the whole period, then at least the last few years of its existence. This is true of the major narrative histories in English by Glässner, Jarausch, McAdams, and Pond. Mary Fulbrook's is the first valid attempt in English to grapple with the complex story of accommodation, repression, and dissent in East Germany.

Before the *Wende*, the turn of events in 1989–90, a whole academic industry of research on the GDR had sprung up over the years but gave no indication of the true state of affairs. Most of these studies, all based on published documentary evidence, can be safely ignored now that archival material is available. Despite all their efforts at self-justification, what should not be ignored are the memoirs of former GDR functionaries, which do provide revealing insights into the regime's decision-making processes (especially Honecker, Krenz, Mittag, and Schabowski). Helmut Kohl's memoirs were not available to the author until this book was in proof. They seem to confirm the detailed account of the diplomatic process given by Zelikow and Rice, in particular the crucial role played by the US President Bush. The driving force for change came from ordinary East Germans (refugees, demonstrators, voters). Kohl, more than any other, was their spokesman, insisting on their right to self-determination, to which nobody could object.

ANDERT, REINHOLD, and HERZBERG, WOLFGANG, *Der Sturz: Erich Honecker im Kreuzverhör* (Berlin, 1991).

BADE, KLAUS J., *et al.*, 'Germany in Transition', *Daedalus*, 123 (1994).

BARING, ARNULF (ed.), *Germany's New Position in Europe: Problems and Perspectives* (Providence, RI, 1994).

BENDER, PETER, *Unsere Erbschaft: Was war die DDR—was bleibt von ihr?* (Hamburg, 1993).

BESIER, GERHARD, *Der SED-Staat und die Kirche: Der Weg in die Anpassung* (Munich, 1993).

CHILDS, DAVID, *The GDR: Moscow's German Ally* (London, 1985).

ELBE, FRANK, and KIESSLER, RICHARD, *A Round Table with Sharp Corners: The Diplomatic Path to German Unity* (Baden-Baden, 1996).

EPPELMANN, RAINER, *Fremd im eigenen Haus: Mein Leben im anderen Deutschland* (Cologne, 1993).

FALIN, VALENTIN, *Politische Erinnerungen* (Munich, 1993).

FISCHER, ALEXANDER, and HEYDEMANN, GÜNTHER (eds.), *Geschichtswissenschaft in der DDR*, 2 vols. (Berlin, 1988–90).

FRICKE, KARL WILHELM, *MfS Intern: Macht, Strukturen, Auflösung der DDR-Staatssicherhheit* (Cologne, 1991).

FREESE, CHRISTOPHER, *Die Privatisierungstätigkeit der Treuhandanstalt* (Frankfurt am Main, 1995).

FULBROOK, MARY, *Anatomy of a Dictatorship: Inside the GDR 1949–1989* (Oxford, 1995).

GARTON ASH, TIMOTHY, *In Europe's Name: Germany and the Divided Continent* (London, 1993).

GAUSSY, A. GHANIE, and SCHÄFER, WOLF (eds.), *The Economics of German Unification* (London, 1993).

GILL, DAVID, and SCHRÖTER, ULRICH, *Das Ministerium für Staatssicherheit: Anatomie des Mielke-Imperiums* (Berlin, 1991).

GLÄSSNER, GERT-JOACHIM, *The Unification Process in Germany: From Dictatorship to Democracy* (London, 1992).

GLATZER, WOLFGANG, and NOLL HEINZ-HERBERT, (eds.), *Getrennt Vereint: Lebensverhältnisse in Deutschland seit der Wiedervereinigung* (Frankfurt am Main, 1995).

GRABNER, WOLF-JÜRGEN, *et al.* (eds.), *Leipzig im Oktober: Kirchen und alternativen Gruppen im Umbruch der DDR* (Berlin, 1990).

GRÜNBERG, ANDREAS, *'Wir sind das Volk': Der Weg der DDR zur deutschen Einheit* [Quellen zur Geschichte und Politik/Sekundarstufe II] (Stuttgart, 1990).

—— *Die DDR vor der 'Wende'* [Quellen zur Geschichte und Politik/Sekundarstufe II] (Stuttgart, 1995).

HANCOCK, M. DONALD, and WELSH, HELGA A. (eds.), *German Unification: Process and Outcomes* (Boulder, Colo., 1994).

HARDTWIG, WOLFGANG, and WINKLER, HEINRICH-AUGUST (eds.), *Deutsche Entfremdung: Zum Befinden in Ost und West* (Munich, 1994).

HENKYS, REINHARD (ed.), *Die Evangelischen Kirchen in der DDR* (Munich, 1982).

HICKEL, RUDOLF, and PRIEWE, JAN, *Nach dem Fehlstart: Ökonomische Perspektiven der deutschen Einigung* (Frankfurt am Main, 1994).

JAMES, HAROLD, and STONE, MARLA (eds.), *When the Wall Came Down: Reactions to German Unification* (London, 1992).

JARAUSCH, KONRAD H., *The Rush to German Unity* (Oxford, 1994).

—— and GRANSOW, VOLKER (eds.), *Uniting Germany: Documents and Debates, 1944–1993* (Providence, RI, 1994).

JEFFRIES, IAN, and MELZER, MANFRED (eds.), *The East German Economy* (London, 1987).

JESSE, ECKHARD, and MITTER, ARMIN (eds.), *Die Gestaltung der deutschen Einheit* (Bonn, 1992).

KAELBLE, HARTMUT, *et al.* (eds.), *Sozialgeschichte der DDR* (Stuttgart, 1994).

KAISER, KARL, *Deutschlands Vereinigung: Die internationalen Aspekte* (Bergisch-Gladbach, 1991).

KEMMLER, MARC, *Die Entstehung der Treuhandanstalt: Von der Währung zur Privatisierung des DDR-Volkseigentums* (Frankfurt am Main, 1994).

KOCKA, JÜRGEN, and SABROW, MARTIN (eds.), *Die DDR als Geschichte: Fragen, Hypothesen, Perspektiven* (Berlin, 1994).

KOHL, HELMUT, *Ich wollte Deutschlands Einheit* (Berlin, 1996).

KRENZ, EGON, *Wenn Mauern fallen: Die friedliche Revolution* (Vienna, 1990).

KUHN, EKKEHARD, *Der Tag der Entscheidung: Leipzig, 9. Oktober 1989* (Berlin, 1992).

KWIZINSKIJ, JULIJ A., *Vor dem Sturm: Erinnerungen eines Diplomaten* (Berlin, 1993).

LANGENBUCHER, WOLFGANG R., *et al.* (eds.), *Kulturpolitisches Wörterbuch: Bundesrepublik Deutschland/DDR im Vergleich* (Stuttgart, 1983).

LANGGUTH, GERD, *In Search of Security: A Socio-Psychological Portrait of Today's Germany* (Westport, Conn., 1995).

LEWIS, DEREK, and MCKENZIE, JOHN R. P., *The New Germany: Social, Political and Cultural Challenges of Unification* (Exeter, 1995).

LOTH, WILFRIED, *Stalins ungeliebtes Kind: Warum Moskau die DDR nicht wollte* (Berlin, 1994).

MAAZ, HANS-JOACHIM, *Der Gefühlstau: Ein Psychoprogramm der DDR* (Berlin, 1991).

McADAMS, A. JAMES, *Germany Divided: From the Wall to Reunification* (Princeton, NJ, 1993).

McCAULEY, MARTIN, *Marxism-Leninism in the GDR: The Socialist Unity Party* (London, 1979).

McELVOY, ANNE, *The Saddled Cow: East Germany's Life and Legacy* (London, 1992).

MAIER, GERHART, *Die Wende in der DDR* [Bundeszentrale für politische Bildung] (Bonn, 1990).

MARSH, DAVID, *Germany and Europe: The Crisis of Unity* (London, 1994).

MITTAG, GÜNTER, *Um jeden Preis: Im Spannungsfeld zweier Systeme* (Berlin, 1991).

MITTER, ARMIN, and WOLLE, STEFAN, *Untergang auf Raten: Unbekannte Kapitel der DDR-Geschichte* (Munich, 1993).

—— —— (eds.), *Ich liebe Euch doch alle! Befehle und Lageberichte des MfS (Januar–November 1989)* (Berlin, 1990).

NOELLE–NEUMANN, ELISABETH, *Demoskopische Geschichtsstunde: Vom Wartesaal der Geschichte zur deutschen Einheit* (Zurich, 1991).

OPP, KARL-DIETER, and VOSS, PETER, *Die volkseigene Revolution* (Stuttgart, 1993).

PHILIPSEN, DIRK, *We Were the People: Voices from East Germany's Revolutionary Autumn of 1989* (Durham, NC, 1993).

POND, ELIZABETH, *Beyond the Wall: Germany's Road to Unification* (Washington, DC, 1993).

PRZYBYLSKI, PETER, *Tatort Politbüro: Die Akte Honecker* (Berlin, 1991).

RADICE, GILES, *The New Germans* (London, 1995).

REIN, GERHARD (ed.), *Die Opposition in der DDR: Entwürfe für einen anderen Sozialismus* (Berlin, 1989).

RUTZ, WERNER, *et al.*, *Die Fünf Neuen Bundesländer: Historisch begründet, politisch gewollt und künftig vernünftig* (Darmstadt, 1993).

SCHMITZ, MICHAEL, *Wendestress: Die psychosozialen Kosten der deutschen Einheit* (Berlin, 1995).

SCHÖNBOHM, JÖRG, *Two Armies and One Fatherland: The End of the Nationale Volksarmee* (Providence, RI, 1996).

SCHRÖDER, RICHARD, *Deutschland schwierig Vaterland: Für eine neue politische Kultur* (Freiburg, 1993).

—— *Vom Gebrauch der Freiheit: Gedanken über Deutschland nach der Vereinigung* (Stuttgart, 1996).

SCHWARZ, HANS-PETER, *Die Zentralmacht Europas: Deutschlands Rückkehr auf die Weltbühne* (Berlin, 1994).

STARITZ, DIETRICH, *Geschichte der DDR 1949–1985* (Frankfurt am Main, 1985).

TELTSCHIK, HORST, *329 Tage* (Berlin, 1991).

WATSON, ALAN, *The Germans: Who Are They Now?*, rev. edn. (London, 1995).

WEBER, HERMANN, *DDR: Grundriß der Geschichte 1945–1990* (Hanover, 1991).

WEIDENFELD, WERNER, and KORTE, KARL-RUDOLF (eds.), *Handbuch der deutschen Einheit* [Bundeszentrale für politische Bildung] (Bonn, 1993).

ZELIKOW, PHILIP, and RICE, CONDOLEEZZA, *Germany Unified and Europe Transformed* (Cambridge, Mass. and London, 1996).

ZWAHR, HARTMUT, *Ende einer Selbstzerstörung: Leipzig und die Revolution in der DDR* (Göttingen, 1993).

Index

Note: The index does not include entries from the notes, statistical appendix, and chronology.

OXFORD

MORE OXFORD PAPERBACKS

This book is just one of nearly 1000 Oxford Paperbacks currently in print. If you would like details of other Oxford Paperbacks, including titles in the World's Classics, Oxford Reference, Oxford Books, OPUS, Past Masters, Oxford Authors, and Oxford Shakespeare series, please write to:

UK and Europe: Oxford Paperbacks Publicity Manager, Arts and Reference Publicity Department, Oxford University Press, Walton Street, Oxford OX2 6DP.

Customers in UK and Europe will find Oxford Paperbacks available in all good bookshops. But in case of difficulty please send orders to the Cash-with-Order Department, Oxford University Press Distribution Services, Saxon Way West, Corby, Northants NN18 9ES. Tel: 01536 741519; Fax: 01536 746337. Please send a cheque for the total cost of the books, plus £1.75 postage and packing for orders under £20; £2.75 for orders over £20. Customers outside the UK should add 10% of the cost of the books for postage and packing.

USA: Oxford Paperbacks Marketing Manager, Oxford University Press, Inc., 200 Madison Avenue, New York, N.Y. 10016.

Canada: Trade Department, Oxford University Press, 70 Wynford Drive, Don Mills, Ontario M3C 1J9.

Australia: Trade Marketing Manager, Oxford University Press, G.P.O. Box 2784Y, Melbourne 3001, Victoria.

South Africa: Oxford University Press, P.O. Box 1141, Cape Town 8000.

PAST MASTERS

A wide range of unique, short, clear introductions to the lives and work of the world's most influential thinkers. Written by experts, they cover the history of ideas from Aristotle to Wittgenstein. Readers need no previous knowledge of the subject, so they are ideal for students and general readers alike.

Each book takes as its main focus the thought and work of its subject. There is a short section on the life and a final chapter on the legacy and influence of the thinker. A section of further reading helps in further research.

The series continues to grow, and future Past Masters will include **Owen Gingerich** on *Copernicus*, **R G Frey** on *Joseph Butler*, **Bhiku Parekh** on *Gandhi*, **Christopher Taylor** on *Socrates*, **Michael Inwood** on *Heidegger*, and **Peter Ghosh** on *Weber*.

**Oxford
Paperback
Reference**

OXFORD PAPERBACK REFERENCE

From *Art and Artists* to *Zoology*, the Oxford Paperback Reference series offers the very best subject reference books at the most affordable prices.

Authoritative, accessible, and up to date, the series features dictionaries in key student areas, as well as a range of fascinating books for a general readership. Included are such well-established titles as Fowler's *Modern English Usage*, Margaret Drabble's *Concise Companion to English Literature*, and the bestselling science and medical dictionaries.

The series has now been relaunched in handsome new covers. Highlights include new editions of some of the most popular titles, as well as brand new paperback reference books on *Politics*, *Philosophy*, and *Twentieth-Century Poetry*.

With new titles being constantly added, and existing titles regularly updated, Oxford Paperback Reference is unrivalled in its breadth of coverage and expansive publishing programme. New dictionaries of *Film*, *Economics*, *Linguistics*, *Architecture*, *Archaeology*, *Astronomy*, and *The Bible* are just a few of those coming in the future.

HISTORY IN OXFORD PAPERBACKS

THE STRUGGLE FOR
THE MASTERY OF EUROPE 1848–1918

A. J. P. Taylor

The fall of Metternich in the revolutions of 1848 heralded an era of unprecedented nationalism in Europe, culminating in the collapse of the Hapsburg, Romanov, and Hohenzollern dynasties at the end of the First World War. In the intervening seventy years the boundaries of Europe changed dramatically from those established at Vienna in 1815. Cavour championed the cause of *Risorgimento* in Italy; Bismarck's three wars brought about the unification of Germany; Serbia and Bulgaria gained their independence courtesy of the decline of Turkey—'the sick man of Europe'; while the great powers scrambled for places in the sun in Africa. However, with America's entry into the war and President Wilson's adherence to idealistic internationalist principles, Europe ceased to be the centre of the world, although its problems, still primarily revolving around nationalist aspirations, were to smash the Treaty of Versailles and plunge the world into war once more.

A. J. P. Taylor has drawn the material for his account of this turbulent period from the many volumes of diplomatic documents which have been published in the five major European languages. By using vivid language and forceful characterization, he has produced a book that is as much a work of literature as a contribution to scientific history.

'One of the glories of twentieth-century writing.'
Observer

OPUS

TWENTIETH-CENTURY FRENCH PHILOSOPHY

Eric Matthews

This book gives a chronological survey of the works of the major French philosophers of the twentieth century.

Eric Matthews offers various explanations for the enduring importance of philosophy in French intellectual life and traces the developments which French philosophy has taken in the twentieth century from its roots in the thought of Descartes, with examinations of key figures such as Bergson, Sartre, Marcel, Merleau-Ponty, Foucault, and Derrida, and the recent French Feminists.

'*Twentieth-Century French Philosophy* is a clear, yet critical introduction to contemporary French Philosophy. . . . The undergraduate or other reader who comes to the area for the first time will gain a definite sense of an intellectual movement with its own questions and answers and its own rigour . . . not least of the book's virtues is its clarity.'
Garrett Barden
Author of *After Principles*

POLITICS

Kenneth Minogue

Since politics is both complex and controversial it is easy to miss the wood for the trees. In this Very Short Introduction Kenneth Minogue has brought the many dimensions of politics into a single focus: he discusses both the everyday grind of democracy and the attraction of grand ideals such as freedom and justice.

'Kenneth Minogue is a very lively stylist who does not distort difficult ideas.'
Maurice Cranston

'a dazzling but unpretentious display of great scholarship and humane reflection'
Professor Neil O'Sullivan, University of Hull

'Minogue is an admirable choice for showing us the nuts and bolts of the subject.'
Nicholas Lezard, *Guardian*

'This is a fascinating book which sketches, in a very short space, one view of the nature of politics . . . the reader is challenged, provoked and stimulated by Minogue's trenchant views.'
Talking Politics